Best wishes—
enjoy reading this
enjoyed living it!

Steve Darby

September 2012

ALL CHANGE FOR
UPTON PARK

Steve Derby

Steve Derby and Associates
Smiths Lane
Ditcheat
Somerset
BA4 6PR
Telephone 01749 860571

www.stevederby.co.uk

British Library Cataloguing in Publication Data

A Catalogue record for this book is available from the British Library

Every effort has been made to fulfil requirements with regard to reproducing copyright material. The author and publisher will be glad to rectify any omissions at the earliest opportunity

"Goin Back" words and music by Gerry Goffin and Carole King © 1966. Reproduced by permission of GEMS-EMI Music Ltd, London W8 5SW

ISBN 978-0-9572227-0-0

ALL CHANGE FOR UPTON PARK

An affectionate, reflective, and humorous rummage through memories of a childhood spent in Upton Park, East London between 1943 and 1959

By

Steve Derby

To my wife Ann, our children and grandchildren, who have had to put up with these stories for their lifetime – they can now read them!

Also, everyone mentioned in this book – thank you for being there.

And Fletch for finding me again!!!

First published by Steve Derby and Associates 2012
Typesetting and origination by Mercury Print and Packaging Ltd

Printed in Great Britain

CONTENTS

PART ONE

PART TWO

The challenge of recording reflections over a period of time is trying to fit everything into where it should be. Some things that happen to us early in life don't bear profound fruit until much later on. It is only then that they can they be jerked into public view.

What I have written so far really embraces education - social, spiritual, and secular – a structure of life common to most of us. But in the tapestry of every structure are those threads, weaves, and patterns that add extra colour and meaning, the picture painted on the canvas of our being. I shall be greatly surprised if anyone who grew up in the 1940s and 1950s has failed to recognise themselves and their own life experiences in amongst the preceding pages. Here are some more to add to them.

CHAPTER SEVEN   UNCLE HARRY'S LEGACY   204

For every boy who ever spent just a little of his 1950s life standing on the platform of a railway station, book and pencil in hand, logging the numbers of steam engines as they hurtled, strolled, or shuffled past. All hail, the trainspotter!

CHAPTER EIGHT   THAT'S ENTERTAINMENT   238

Long before Sky television, there was radio. Long before Michael McIntyre, there was Max Miller. Long before DVDs, there was Saturday morning pictures. Long before Robbie Williams, there was Lonnie Donegan.

Heartland

"I think I'm going back to the things I
learned so well in my youth;
I think I'm returning to those days when
I was young enough to know the truth.

Now there are no games to only pass the time;
No more electric trains, no more trees to climb.
Thinking young and growing older is no sin;
And I can play the game of life to win.

Let everyone debate the true reality,
I'd rather see the world the way it used to be.
A little bit of freedom's all we lack;
So catch me if you can, I'm going back."

(Gerry Goffin, Carole King)

It is Monday, mid-morning, mid-week, and mid-February at the station in Upton Park, East London. Early morning rush hour has long passed. Two hours earlier, the platform serving trains heading west would have been teeming with City-bound staff, male and female, young and old, and all stations in between. The newsagent would have taken a fair few pounds, selling papers and periodicals reflecting the varied range of political bias and taste still found in this neck of the woods. But by the time that the sleek District Line train that has brought me here hums and glides into Upton Park station for its intermediate stop *en route* from Ealing to Upminster, an air of calm and tranquillity has been restored.

Since Mile End, there have been plenty of seats available on the train. Yet, ever since it emerged from under ground at Bow Road to moan and groan up the embankment into daylight, I've been content to stand by the pneumatic door, looking out on changes in landscapes once so familiar during the years of my childhood.

7

Buildings and infrastructures that I had no reason to believe would not be there for eternity, have disappeared or changed beyond recognition. Bow locomotive works once snuggled in a confined corner just west of Bromley-by-Bow station. Where is it now? Gone, replaced by flats where the track of the Docklands Light Railway running close by provides the only clue to any railway connection. Alongside Bromley station itself, St. Andrew's hospital has not only long since ceased to ply its trade – it has disappeared entirely, the site now sporting housing development.

Beyond Bromley, the River Lea continues to thread its way through what was always a scruffy industrial area. But now, unattractive buildings erected with no apparent regard for quality or empathy with those close to them are set in expanses of wasteland, hemmed in by graffiti-adorned walls. Perhaps the 2012 Olympics will create something new, inspiring, and exciting for future generations, but no one is holding their breath. I do not anticipate seeing a sadder sight on this my return to East London.

Before sneaking under the bridge that carries the Northern Outfall Sewer over the line, my train passes the ground and clubhouse of the East London Rugby Club. On this very spot, from 1911, the London, Tilbury and Southend Railway Company stored and serviced their locomotives. Smokey and smutty "goings-on" were the order of many a subsequent day, until the whole operation was deemed surplus to requirements by the Beeching Report of 1963, and the show was shut down.

When my train whispers to a halt in Upton Park station, I am, at last, once again amongst my roots, my heartland, the place where I grew up. The automatic door slides open and half a dozen of us alight and make for the stairs that lead to the ticket barrier. Permitting myself a smile, I remember Ted, the porter, a miserable, scruffy old boy who had once prowled these platforms. When we were boarding for a trip to the City, he would insist that all unaccompanied kids sat down before he would allow the train to depart. For a quiet life, we did as we were told until the train began to move. Then, we'd be up again like demented monkeys, laughing and pointing, to leave poor old Ted cussing and war-dancing on the platform. This little drama was enacted every time my mates and I travelled from Upton Park. He knew what was coming, but fell for it every time. At the barrier, I feed my Oyster Card into some piece of gadgetry. Ticket collectors have long since left the stage at to be replaced by impersonal yet efficient technology. Cost saving has caused the demise of the like of good-natured and long since departed Bill Stevenson.

A cursory glance at my *A-Z Street Map* suggests that very little has changed in Upton Park. Yet it takes me no more than one step from the concourse into the hustle, bustle, and general untidiness that is modern-day Green Street for the truth to be there for me to see - *everything* has changed for Upton Park. The ice cream vendor's shop on the corner of Park Road that once delighted us all, has succumbed to a car rental business. Chambers' toyshop, once much favoured by me when choosing Christmas and birthday presents, has been succeeded by a none-too-attractive *bureau de change*. Quality grocer David Greig some time ago sold out and premises that once smelt of a range of fresh cheeses are now a branch of Habibsons Bank.

Mr. Rosewall's dental surgery, formerly situated across the road and responsible for pulling all my Dad's teeth out, and plugging the gaps with the false variety, has gone. I recall how he performed much the same trick with Mum during a time of dental unenlightenment when, if teeth were a problem, the dentist took the pliers and yanked the lot of 'em out....problem solved! Mum and Dad were only in their early 40s when they underwent this process and the very thought of it makes my Denplan investment look one of the smartest I have ever made.

To my right, Queens Road market still sits alongside the station and, perhaps, will exist to eternity. But I've said things like that before and been wrong. Between 1920 and 1960, Queens Road itself had been a centre for the local Jewish quarter. The narrow street had stalls crammed and jammed up against the kerbs where you could buy practically anything and everything. My paternal grandmother – a very competent dressmaker – was one of many regular customers who came to Queens Road to obtain her stock-in-

9

trade. There was always excitement created by the shouting of traders, busily insisting that – cross their hearts – they lost money on everything that they sold. The air was a rich compound of oranges, bruised cabbage, and the uninviting public urinal, which stood on the stepped island at the head of the market. A stale smell emanated from the bowels of this unhygienic bastion (perhaps, even, from some of the regular users) which was always more than enough to persuade me that it was worth holding on until I reached home.

And, oh, the market was always a hub for gossip. Tales would be passed around and when, on Sundays, my mum and dad visited my dress-making grandmother, we were brought up to speed with who had done what, why, when, where, and with whom. Sometimes, when the subject was, shall we say, a little sensitive, Grandma would drop her voice to a whisper. If it were *really* sensitive, she would mouth the words inaudibly. It seemed that she almost expected the maligned subject to burst into the privacy of her living room and call her a lying old cow! Well, you couldn't have that, could you? Not in your own living room.

Since those days, the market has come of age, evolving into a covered arcade. Perhaps, for some, it remains a way of life, but the colour of past days has faded and I mourn for those larger-than-life traders who once used to be ten-a-penny. Where, I ask, is Mr. Robins, or his successor, with his fruit, veg, and greens? Nowhere to be seen. The community has changed beyond all recognition, evidence constantly before me as I continue my exploration. The vast majority of the modern Upton Park population are from Asian, Middle Eastern, West Indian stock. That is how society in this part of the metropolis has developed. Opportunities were seen and seized by this new community, and good luck to them. Many of the population that I grew up with have moved out far and wide. It's not wrong – it's just how it is. Societies evolve.

I turn right for a walk toward Barking Road, which takes me past Tudor Road where, on the corner, is the building which was once the nerve centre of Maycocks Laundry. Even after all these years, above the doorway – and in full working order - is the clock bearing the slogan, "Don't kill your wife – let us do it!" around the face. In my days of childish innocence, I wondered how the writer could have missed the ambiguity. Now, armed with fifty years of experience, I recognise it for what it was – an advanced marketing ploy. Although long since under the new ownership of Blossom and Browne, it continues to provide a laundry service, so perhaps that marketeer had something going for him after all.

Opposite Tudor Road is a row of scruffy, terraced houses, crying out for a bit of T.L.C. I recall how, in the days of my childhood, this very same block was ….a row of scruffy, terraced houses, crying out for a bit of T.L.C. In the mid-late 1950's, one enterprising entrepreneur converted his personal share of this dross into a record shop. Painted vertically on the pillars framing the bay window was the legend "Orpheus" and I pause to pay my respects. Here it was that I bought my very first plastic 45-rpm records – Duane Eddy's "Cannonball" and "The Chipmunk Song" by, surprise, surprise, the Chipmunks. The Chipmunks?! What on earth was I thinking about? One lunchtime in 1958, on my way home from school, I looked in the "Orpheus" window to see a new Buddy Holly record on display. "Rave On" it said, and I wondered if it was any good.

Holly's records bore a distinctive black and white Coral label which became a magnet for those of us besotted by that jangly, razor-edge guitar sound. London American always seemed to have the monopoly of quality artists. RCA might be able to boast Elvis, but London American had the Drifters, The Coasters, Bobby Darin, Laverne Baker, Clyde McPhatter, and a host of others. Great as they were, even Elvis and Buddy couldn't make up the shortfall when measured against London American's embarrassment of riches. But the sight of a Coral label always screamed, "Over here folks….Buddy Holly and the Crickets" and a few days after my first sighting of "Rave On," the record was mine. Was it any good? You bet! It still is.

Okay, deep breath. Just another couple of hundred yards brings me to the somewhat imposing – or is it pretentious – Boleyn Ground, the home of West Ham United. You can't miss it, although 'twas not always thus. Up until the 1960s, the walls of the old

Boleyn Castle had prevented an unencumbered view of the ground itself. We kids were taught that Anne Boleyn had been shacked up there (in the castle, that is, not the football ground) whilst randy old King Henry Vlll tried to have his wicked way. The theory doesn't have unanimous historical approval, although no one is in doubt that Henry ultimately got a result. I suppose Anne did too until, not for the first or last time, the old boy's wandering eyes wandered and poor old Anne departed this world due to lack of bonce.

When the remains of the castle walls were demolished, the site was subjected to a series of facelifts, resulting in something quite beyond recognition for those who recall its origin. The modern Boleyn Ground – and not Upton Park, as the misinformed would have you believe – is far removed from the ramshackle edifice of pre-1960. In deference to the site's history, the entrance to the ground is marked by two yellow mock castle towers that, frankly, look naff. Once inside the ramparts, you will find an acceptable quality hotel, restaurant, bar, and museum, together with a merchandise store full of (dependent upon your age) "must have" or "don't want" West Ham United related product. It has been described by some, as *Disney World* and, in fairness, there have been some pretty pantomimes and fiascos played out by the occupants over the years. It's all a far cry from the times when, in exchange for a few bob, you could go to watch a game of football and have a good laugh. Football in the 21st Century is no longer working man's theatre.

The game itself has evolved into a lucrative industry and profession for those who play, manage, or administer in the Premiership. Following the Hillsborough disaster of 1989, when ninety-five people lost their lives in a crush of awesome proportions, "all-seater" stadiums became legal requirement for senior clubs across the land. Famous old grounds like Sunderland's Roker Park, Bolton's Burnden Park, Manchester City's Maine Road, and even Arsenal's palatial Highbury came under scrutiny, were found wanting, and abandoned to developers. Grounds are, undoubtedly, safer places, but the price of individuality has been demanded and paid. Once was a time when fans could recognise the distinctive architecture of most major grounds throughout the country Nowadays, they all seem to be sanitised, sporting versions of MacDonalds, lacking in soul.

West Ham, as a team, has clambered regularly from the Championship, only to fall from the grace of the Premiership as a matter of course. A cursory study of their record reveals that, at regular distant intervals, entertainment would be provided by eleven blokes producing a passable standard of football – but even that has always been a moveable feast. The dizzy heights climbed by the team during the '60s, with the holy trinity of Bobby Moore, Geoff Hurst, and Martin Peters, or even the comparative dignity of the '80s may or may not be repeated. Money is king and as far as the earth is from the stars, so is the distance between West Ham and Manchester United, Chelsea, and - Lord save us all – Manchester City. Not all that long ago, the Hammers consistently turned the lot of them over. Nowadays, too many results are known before the fixtures are announced and the game at large is the poorer for it.

As a perpetual reminder of paradise lost, at the junction where Green Street meets Barking Road, is a tasteful bronze sculpture of the aforesaid Bobby, Geoff, and Martin. It serves to celebrate and remind current and forthcoming generations that the club spawned three of England's World Cup winners of 1966. Others feel that it conveys a foreboding that, never again, will England reach such dizzy heights. With that salutary thought in mind, I retrace my steps to the station.

Green Street. In the 1950s, Marks and Spencer, Boots the Chemist, Woolworths, British Home Stores, and John Lewis were all in prominent residence, but no longer – particularly Woolworths. To paraphrase Captain Kirk, of the *Starship Enterprise,* "It's Green Street, Steve, but not as you knew it." This commercial artery of Upton Park now plays host to pint pot shops trying to cope with the proverbial quart of merchandise and humanity. The social changes of the past fifty years means that the market is, by and large, responding to a very different demand. Colourful sari stores and Halal meat shops interfuse with fast food suppliers and small commercial concerns run, more often than not, by a new community of enterprising businessmen and women.

But it is not the commercial side of Upton Park that really draws me. It's okay, of course, but my Upton Park, the area I love best – my true heartland - is to be found in the residential quarters, short streets close to, yet apart from, Green Street. Opposite the station, Park Road runs parallel to the railway line for an hundred yards or so, before an obtuse left-hand bend takes me toward Plashet Grove. On that very bend, once had stood a small, prefabricated building, serving as the Elim church. In fact, prefabrication was the name of the immediate post-war game in Park Road. In the wake of World War ll bombing, "prefabs" provided convenient and economical housing until such times as something more substantial could be built. And there is the footbridge where once I regularly stood to watch trains with my friends. Back then, it was primarily a wooden structure. The current version is a safer, yet less attractive, concrete and metal version.

The short walk to Plashet Grove takes me to the edge of my sacred ground. I negotiate the zebra crossing to the opposite side of the Grove where, on my right, on the corner of Whitfield Road, the Full Gospel Hall stands defiant against Mammon. External evidence suggests that it continues to thrive and I'm mightily glad about that, for this is where, between 1950 and 1957, I – and plenty more like me - received my inaugural Christian education. In my wallet, I have a photograph of something like eighty kids, lining the terraced steps at the front of the church. The year is 1956. I can't resist trotting up those same steps to stand on the exact spot where I had been photographed all those years ago. I take a little time to meditate on all that this place has meant to me. In doing so, I come to the conclusion that, were I to be issued with an invoice for services rendered by the people who worshipped, preached, and taught me there, I would file immediately for bankruptcy.

Beyond the truncated Whitaker Road is Wyndham Road. My Dad had two brothers, Jack and Len. Uncle Jack was the eldest and, like me, loved reading and music, although our tastes might have differed just a tad. He had a wonderful way with words and could reduce me to laughter not so much by what he said, but rather the caustic and laid-back way he delivered his lines. In his middle years, he recorded many events from his early life and I fondly recall laughing when I first read his account of a séance. He just sat there quietly, proud as Punch that he was the cause of my mirth. So I am grateful for his recollection of an incident in the early 1920s, which occurred in this very same Wyndham Road.

"The second brush with the law was when Nashy nipped into Mr. Howard's provision shop in Plashet Grove, with the intention of grabbing a handful of broken biscuits from the tea chest that always stood just inside the shop door. The chest was nearly empty, and Nashy couldn't reach the biscuits without falling in. Mr. Howard always had a great round of Cheddar cheese on his counter, which he sliced up with a sharp length of wire. Poor old Nashy must have been very hungry, for he whipped up the large wedge of Cheddar that Mr. Howard had just cut off, and was away.

As he rushed out, pursued by Mr. Howard, Nashy almost bowled over a big copper, complete with paunch and walrus moustache. With the law hard on his heels, Nashy cut along and into Wyndham Road. I ran after them, with some mad idea that I might be able to help Nashy. Halfway down Wyndham Road, with the copper reaching down at his collar, Nashy suddenly dropped to the ground, and the copper went tumbling over him, coming down with a crash that laid him out, completely winded. We both went in fear for a while, especially whenever we saw a distant police helmet but, strangely, never saw that particular policeman again."

I paused at, roughly, where that incident must have taken place and leaned against someone or other's boundary wall. The whole scenario unfolded in my imagination and as it did so, I am sure that I must have smiled as much as young Uncle Jack had done all those years ago.

The area bordered by the roads Wyndham, St. Stephens, Whitfield, and Plashet Grove had, during the war, been decimated by the Luftwaffe, and when Upton Park began to dust itself down post-war, a small nursery was developed on the site. Before Hitler and his hordes did their worst, a row of terraced houses had lined this side of St. Stephens Road and, as best I could estimate, I was stood where once No. 93 had been. This was the house where my paternal grandparents had lived with my dad, his brothers, and my great grandmother. Over the years, the nursery has expanded and been upgraded to become a school and, on the day of my visit, the site is littered with unkempt foliage and appears generally untidy and not a little chaotic. Children are at play, under the supervision of a couple of their teachers. These days, you can't smile at a kid, much less say, "Hello," without running the risk of an accusing eye. Blow the fact that I have worked with Cubs, Scouts, youth clubs, and Sunday schools all my life, and that I have four grandchildren, whom I adore to pieces. To harm a child is a total abhoration to me. Yet, all of that could count for nothing should I do anything more than smile or say a friendly word. We mustn't have that sort of stuff, must we? Kids knowing that some adults genuinely care about them.

Yet, there is hope. One of the teachers greets me politely, and I smile back at her. Sensing a need to justify my presence and innocence, I explain the importance of this spot. To my delight, she is fascinated and tells my story to the little ones who have gathered around her. I'm not sure how much they take on board but, at least, they're listening. I look at them, smile and say, "Hi. How are you?" They smile back, tell me that they are fine...we all feel good...the world hasn't stopped turning...and we all continue about our business.

Past Whitfield Road on to the next turning. High on the wall of the end terrace property, a street sign announces, "Walpole Road." It's an enamel plate under which a cemented scar testifies to where the original cast iron version had once been. Restored to its original glory, it is resides somewhere in Somerset, in the hands of a private collector. I'll leave you to work that one out. When I turn into this road, I know I have truly "come home" for, here in this very street, surrounded by relatives, friends, and a quite remarkable community, I had lived with my parents from 1944 until almost the end of 1958. It is less than a couple of hundred yards long and motorcars now take up every available parking space, where once it had been possible for kids to play several-a-side football, or cricket, and run about in the street without fear of coming to harm. The worst one might have encountered was a collision with Uncle Fred's bicycle.

The two facing end-terraced walls once had goal areas chalked on them and served as our concrete Wembley. Mr. And Mrs. Roast, the occupants of one of the houses so decorated, must have been driven barmy, what with the constant thud of a football interrupting their peace. Visions of china falling off the mantelpiece every time the ball whacked against their wall come to mind. Yet the times that they came out from their home and "invaded" the pitch to complain were remarkably few, although we still thought they were a right pair of moaners. Today, I see them in an entirely different light. They had the patience of saints and why they ever stayed there so long beats me.

On the right, Gricks's eel yard once stood between Nos. 24 and 26, producing a pong to make your stomach churn. In a former life, the yard had been home to a wholesale, removal and haulage business, run by my maternal grandfather and his brother, Uncle Harry. Now the site is taken up by a couple of two-storey flats. Architecturally, they stand out like sore thumbs, blots on the landscape, spare parts of Frankenstein's monster "bolted on" at some stage for the sake of convenience. Further down the street, the wall outside No.11 was where we kids would sit and, generally, put the world to rights. Terry and Ricky Young lived there with their mum and, just like Mr. and Mrs. Roast, Mrs. Young paid a heavy toll for the privilege. A lamp post and a high stench pipe, spaced some ten feet apart, served as goal posts, framing, as they did, Mrs. Young's bay window. The change of season would see the lamp post become our wicket, so there was an all-year round risk of a football or tennis ball flying through the window pane and, without a by your leave, landing straight in your bread and butter pud, and splashing custard all over your glasses. Directly opposite, at No. 10, dwelt the redoubtable Mrs. Finch who, in response to anyone so much as daring to trespass into her front garden to retrieve a ball, would come out roaring - and I'm not talking "Howzat!"

The Clarks, at No.5, had lived in this part of the world from time immemorial. Their families had, by and large, grown up around them and stayed put in the area. Within a space of, say a couple of hundred yards, aunts, uncles, cousins, grandparents, and grandchildren from the Clark lineage lived out their lives. I'm very glad about that because one of those Clarks happened to be my mum. No. 7, which had been my home of earliest memory until we moved away in 1958, no longer has the brown door that I remember and the porch is now enclosed by a secure door. The chute where the coalman would come and tip his wares into the bowels of the house has long been blocked and cemented over. I just wonder how it has all changed behind closed doors.

So many years have passed since those halcyon days of my childhood innocence. Outside my former home, I reflected on the good people who had lived in this area, alongside a very tiny selection of lovable rascals. Names and the antics we all got up to emerge easily from my subconscious, although I know that I am now a stranger. Surely, nobody living in Walpole Road remembers my family - or me? The streams of laughter I recall spilling merrily down the road have dried up. Familiar houses, long occupied by new people, keep their secrets about all they had witnessed. As far as my generation is concerned, the play has been performed, the audience gone home, the props put away, and the final performance over and done.

An elderly lady saunters by, lugging an over-laden shopping basket. We both smile and greet each other. I wonder what she made of a grown man with a far away look in his eyes and a couple of tears meandering down his cheeks? I knew it would come to this. Every step that I have taken through this, my heartland, has reminded me of some piece of fun, some old neighbour, a friend, a tight spot or two, and I just can't let them go. Or is it that *they* won't let *me* go? Thank God for that, say I.

CHAPTER ONE

RELATIVELY SPEAKING

I'm going to come clean and tell you that this is the autobiographical section. Despite your strong and understandable desire to skip it, I'd really like it if you would come along on this part of the journey with me. One of my proof readers told me that parts of this chapter had made her cry. I said I didn't think it was that bad.

"No," she said," you don't understand. You see – it's your Aunt Alice and Uncle Harry who were so kind to you and your mum when she took you away from London. I had an Aunt Susie who did exactly the same for my mum and me. What you wrote only made me cry because it reminded me of her kindness." There, I'm giving the plot away already.

Perhaps you are curious about just who Aunt Alice and Uncle Harry were – and how they've got themselves into this stuff? 'Course you are! So, come and meet them and a host of others. Allow them to remind you of important people in your life – and let's all be thankful that they were around.

Mum and I performed our double act at approximately 6.10 pm on 13th January 1943, venue Suntrap Hospital, Epping, Essex. Personally, I don't recall much about it, which is in direct contrast to Mum's recollection of bringing me into the world. I would prove to be an only child and occasionally wondered whether it had been a case of "tried it once, didn't like it," for Mum. Much later in life, I broached the subject with her.

"It was just that Dad and I wanted to give you everything in life that we'd never had," she explained.

And on that count, they never failed me. Their love, care, encouragement, and pride in anything and everything that I ever achieved – or tried to achieve - provided me with wealth beyond anything measurable in monetary terms. Had it been up to me, I would have rather liked an older brother or younger sister – either way, I think I would have made a pretty good job of being a brother. But it wasn't to be. Instead, I have been over-compensated with wonderful cousins and friends, all of whom I love dearly. I have no complaints.

I've never really had the urge to go trawling amongst ancient records to find out if I have connections with the nobility. So what if I found that, in 1660, one of my ancestors did a bit of clerical stuff for Samuel Pepys? I'm hardly going to get a drink out of that, am I? No, it's family members that I met and those just out of reach that give me my buzz, because they are the ones whose influence I can easily detect in my thinking and temperament. So let's start with the Derby side of the story.

My dad's family originated from Kilkenny, in Southern Ireland. As far as I have been able to ascertain, great grandfather came to England for a better and, certainly, more prosperous way of life. His wife, Mary Ann - always referred to as Granny Derby - was a devout Roman Catholic whose faith and commitment were, by all accounts, beyond reproach. A son, John Patrick O'Brien Derby, was born to the couple in 1888, and would grow up to take employment as a car man at the Southern Railway's Nine Elms goods depot, in south London. On 24th September 1911, John married Eliza Amelia Pearce (born 11th December 1886) and, between them, they produced three sons. First, another John Patrick O'Brien (always known as Jack), then my Dad, Joseph Frederick, and finally, Leonard.

Tragically, the marriage did not last. My grandfather died on 8th March 1922, aged just 34, when what was thought to be nothing more than a chill turned into chronic bronchitis and pneumonia. Whilst that might not cause too much concern for our medics nowadays, in 1922 it could be fatal and, in my grandfather's case, was so. My paternal grandmother was widowed at the age of just 34.

Uncle Jack recalls the event:-

"They brought my Dad home to die, late on a sunny March morning. Two of his workmates half-carried him down the road

from Upton Park station, all three of them still in their railway uniforms of heavy blue jackets, peaked caps and leather aprons. He hung between their shoulders and his boot caps scraped against the steps as they lifted him through the front door of our terraced house in St.Stephens Road.

In the big bedroom, I climbed onto my bed-chair as the women hurried about above me. Mum and Aunt Kitty struggled to ease my father's long white shanks into the bed and Gran came in with extra blankets and went out to put the house bricks to heat up in the scullery stove. Then Doctor Blake was in the room, rubbing at his lips, as Dad grasped for breath and moaned at the cold. Later again, Father Gahagan came, and I was ushered out. It was 1922. The combination of chronic bronchitis and pneumonia, with no drugs available to fight it, had to be fatal, even to a fit man of thirty-four. And so it proved.

They buried him in the Roman Catholic Cemetery over at Leyton. It was a big funeral for St.Stephens Road, with two carriages, in addition to the hearse, each drawn by Mr.Hurry's fine black horses, with nodding plumes. Official representatives were there from the St. John Ambulance Brigade, and from the railway depot where Dad worked.

The main body of mourners followed the cortege on foot to the top of our road, where they followed on by tramcar. Somebody minded me and my two younger brothers but I was at the reception afterwards, where everybody fussed us and gave us pennies. There were ham sandwiches and seed cake, with whiskey – or beer – for the men, and tawny port and fizzy lemonade for the ladies.

In the parlour, Dad's boss, to whom everybody was very deferential, was on his second whiskey and explaining to the ambulance superintendent what a fine fellow "John" was. I couldn't understand this, for I had been to the depot in Nine Elms with Dad, and nobody called him anything but "Jack."

" A grievous loss, sir, a grievous loss," he kept on saying.

The abiding memory of that day is of Gran, sitting erect among her weeping daughters. She stares ahead, eyes dry and expressionless, numb with grief. Dad was her youngest son and

Steve Derby

Gran lived upstairs in our house. And now she had only Patsy left of her boys, and Patsy was my uncle who held long conversations with himself and took long solitary walks, sometimes shaking his head and shouting."

My dad told me how Grandad would stand with his back to the fire and, occasionally, pass violent wind.

"A penny for the boy who catches it before it leaves the room," he would challenge.

Round the room the boys would charge like dervishes, grasping at thin air, and presenting their sweet nothings in the hope of the penny. Nobody, to the best of my knowledge, ever got it and to be frank, the terms and conditions to win a rotten penny were hardly conducive to making the effort.

On my desk, I have a photograph of Grandad, sitting with his hands clasped in his lap. In line with convention of the day, he is wearing a waistcoat, jacket, and flat cap. Slim and good-looking, he is the image of my dad and, indeed, of both my uncles. There is laughter in Grandad's eyes and I am sure that we would have got along splendidly.

Grandma's loss was, not unnaturally, extremely hard to bear. She was a resilient character, but times are never easy for a single parent and, in those particular times, they were harder than today. Shouldered with sole responsibility for three young boys, making ends meet gradually became all but beyond her. Her saving grace came through the benevolence of my grandad's employer, the Southern Railway. In Oriental Road, Woking, Surrey, the company had established the Southern Railway Servants Orphanage and, through sheer necessity, Grandma enrolled the boys. Not easy for anyone and my dad, in particular, found it very hard to cope with losing his father before reaching the age of six. Uncle Jack, being the eldest and academically inclined, made a better fist of it and went on to a successful career in railway administration. But Dad and Uncle Len were more sensitive souls, not inclined toward academia, and definitely found the parting harder to take.

22

Yet it would be very wrong to say that there were no pleasures for the boys in their new enforced environment. United by the common bond of having lost at least one parent, a tight-knit and loyal community was forged amongst the boys and girls at the orphanage. Dad's recollections of life there and the dedicated staff, gave evidence of a caring and efficient operation. The Senior Master, Mr. Dale, was constantly held up as a paragon of virtue by all three brothers and, from everything that I've learned about him, it was well deserved. His kindly generosity, fair discipline, and commitment to his charges speaks more of a calling as opposed to a job, God bless him.

By the time that he had reached his teens, Dad had developed into a very proficient – formidable, even – footballer. While Uncle Jack presented himself as a free-scoring centre forward, Dad turned out to be a brilliant goalkeeper. During one season, he had been so consistently outstanding as to be selected for a Surrey Schools trial until fate entered, stage left. On the morning of the match, a rather officious orphanage employee insisted that Dad complete some piffling chore before setting off for the game. In a fit of pique, he decided, "I'll teach 'em. I'm not going." And go he didn't. Uncle Jack was mortified. He frequently told me that Dad was a "bloody fool" and, had he put his mind to the matter, a professional career might not have been out of the question. It was a chance missed and, I suspect, often regretted.

It was during the time the boys were away that Grandma's fortunes took a decided step upward. She met Thomas George Vanner and, on 8th November 1930, married him. Although this must have come as a bit of a surprise for the three boys, it is to the everlasting credit of his stepsons that they recognised in him a dear and good man. Tell me about him, Uncle Jack.

"Uncle Tom was a shy and gentle man and if his marriage to my mother – which was to last for another thirty years – was a happy one, it was due chiefly to his innate goodness and forbearance."

Thanks – because that's exactly how I remember him.

When the time arrived for the boys to leave the orphanage and find their own way in the world, they returned home to St. Stephens Road with Grandma and Grandad Vanner (as I would always know them), along with Granny Derby. It must have been a somewhat cramped affair, but looking after your elderly kith and kin was quite commonplace in those days. Friendly relations were maintained with neighbours across back-garden fences, on front doorsteps, or sundry meetings - planned and unplanned - along the road. The concept of "you in your small corner and I in mine" was most definitely not the norm. Neighbours mixed, knew each other and, in many instances, came to the rescue of any poor souls going through hard times.

And if they lived hard, my goodness, they knew how to play hard. Regular Saturday night parties were held, where neighbours and relatives would get together for sing-songs at the piano, dancing, comic turns, and dramatic monologues. The men would put together a few shillings and buy beer, stout, and lemonade to go along with the sandwiches. These shindigs were riotous affairs and even late into my teenage years, their successors remained in evidence. By that time, of course, recorded music had rendered musicians redundant, but as far as I am able to judge, the spirit was much the same. Even if later family parties were confined to Christmas, Boxing Day, and New Year's Eve, rather than once every couple of weeks, it was not the hardest job in the world to see that party-time 1930 and party-time 1950 were very close relatives indeed.

By the time that consciousness of such matters arrived for me, Dad's two brothers had fled both the nest and area. Uncle Jack married Aunt Vera and set up home in South Benfleet, where they produced three cousins for me (well, not specifically with me in mind, you understand) – Jackie, Vanessa, and Crispin. A trip to Uncle Jack's was always a great adventure, giving my cousins and me the chance to go to Canvey Island and paddle in the Thames Estuary, masquerading as the seaside. Uncle Len and his beautiful wife, Aunt Phyllis, initially set up home in Wilson Road, off Boundary Road, before succumbing to a severe bout of wanderlust and taking up residence in various parts of south east Essex. Before they vacated the Wilson Road premises, visits to Uncle Len gave my cousin Barry and me the opportunity to torment the life out of his sister, Janet. When Uncle Len considered that hostilities had gone far enough, a warning to Barry that his bum was about to be smacked called him instantly into line. As for me, the worst that I got from my uncle was the frowning of a lifetime.

The Second World War and the Blitz saw a remarkable escape for my grandma when 93 St Stephens Road was wiped off of the map by an incendiary. Granny Derby had taken up residence in Heaven on 2nd December 1940 (aged 92), and Grandma was alone in the house when the bomb hit. Someone up there must have been looking down on her, for she was ensconced in the cellar at the time and escaped with nothing more than being a bit shaken and a great deal dusty. Going down that cellar must have been one of the best career decisions she ever made. When the War ended, she and Grandad Vanner went to live in Elm Park, just a few stops east along the District Line from Upton Park. Long before undergoing the serious development the area has undergone, a visit was tantamount to a trip into the countryside. I recall being spoiled rotten with biscuits, sweets, and lemonade virtually on tap. Quite why they foresook this idyllic scenario I never knew, but by the time that 1950 arrived, they had returned to East Ham, where they occupied a downstairs flat in a terraced property at 224 Lonsdale Avenue. Sunday afternoon visits became the norm and, in the absence of personal transport or a convenient bus service, Mum, Dad, and I would walk to Lonsdale Avenue and, somewhere around 9'o'clock, do the reverse journey, usually with me asleep on Dad's shoulders.

Throughout the remainder of their lives, I would remain close to Grandma and Grandad Vanner. It never struck me as odd that they were not "Grandma and Grandad Derby" for my cousins and I enjoyed such a loving relationship with them that it really didn't matter a fig. A rose by any other name, and all that. Grandma, in particular, was something else! In her younger days, she had been a vigorous little woman with a fierce temper and, when aroused, a ferocious flow of invective. She was rarely crossed. But

25

my earliest recollections are of a stocky little lady, always laughing or ready to laugh. Tell her a joke and her face was full of anticipation for the punch line, long before it was delivered. She would lean forward like a sprinter in the blocks as the tale unfolded, eyes sparkling through her spectacles, the broadest of grins, her mouth half open, thirsting for a reason to laugh. Any reason. Sometimes, I wasn't convinced that she always saw the joke - but she laughed anyway. She was the first adult to tell me a story containing a word that I had been told I shouldn't use. By today's standards, it was mild but in 1951, well......

"You see, there was this Jewish travelling salesman who spent a night in a particularly expensive hotel. Seeing that his employer was picking up the bill, he decided to "push the boat out" a bit. He took the best of everything going, regardless of expense.

When he came to settle the bill in the morning, he almost had a purple fit. What was his boss going to say when he saw how much he had spent? He complained long and vociferously to the poor receptionist, who could do nothing other than show his guest the signed receipts.

On and on the heated discussion went until the receptionist, tired of the fray, simply said, "I'm sorry, sir, but you have spent these sums." Waving the receipts under the traveller's nose, he added, "Look, I've got the chits."

I could see what was coming before Grandma applied the coupe de grace – and I quote.

*"You've got the "s***s" – what do you think I've got!"*

I have to confess that I laughed, although it wasn't the vulgar play on words that tickled my funnybone. It was more that Grandma had said a naughty word. More than all of my grandparents, it was Grandma Vanner who always made me laugh.

Now if that presents a gentle overview of the Derby side of my family, when we come to my mother's side, well, there were horses of an entirely different colour stabled there. Whereas I know that my paternal great grandparents originated in Ireland, quite where the Clark family sprung up from is, for me, a blank or down to assumption. My best guess is that they were Upton Park, through and through. For all but the first year of my life and through to 1958, I lived next door to them, and my recollections are sharp. There always seemed to be a sense that all was rarely well between the pair of them and older cousins, who had known them better and for longer than I, confirmed them as an unlikely couple. For sure, neither was backward when it came to coming forward.

Grandad had been down at the Duke of Edinburgh, making a personal investment in their liquid assets. Rolling home, goodness knows how late, he demanded his dinner – as you do.

Now, Nanny had been slaving over the proverbial, looking after the kids, and producing a dinner for Grandad which, on his arrival, was fit for nothing save the cat. Still, she kept her cool, which is more than can be said for Grandad.

Finding his dinner to be all but stone cold, he sought the chef's attention.

"What do ya call this? It's stone bleedin' cold Give us some sauce."

Nanny was nothing, if not quick out of the traps.

"The amount of sauce you've got slopping about in you, I should think you've got more than enough already!"

And with that, Grandad picks up the plate, dinner an' all, and chucks it up the wall.

Happy days.

My maternal grandfather had spent much of his working life in the docks, although it needn't have been that way. Many years before I was born, he ducked the opportunity to set me up for life. All the evidence I have tells me that my great grandmother Sophie Clark had set up a pretty profitable family business of wholesaling, removal, and haulage under the guise of "S. Clark and Sons," based in Green Street. In order to justify the "& Sons" element, Grandad and his brother Harry were employed by the concern. However, for reasons best known to himself, Grandad eventually opted to sell his entitlement and promptly invested much of the proceeds down at the "Duke of Edinburgh," on the corner where Green Street met Plashet Grove. The natural outcome – and you can certainly call it that - was that he pee-ed my inheritance straight up the wall. The only dividend I ever recall him receiving for his troubles was a hard time from Nanny Clark – not to be recommended.

By the time that I was old enough to form a clear image of him in my mind, the years had taken their toll, and my abiding memory is of a sick old man, battling with asthma. Throughout the late '40s and early '50s, he would spend his afternoons, sat as comfortably as he could make himself, in one of our armchairs, in No. 7. Nanny would stay next door and, in all probability, he felt safer on our side of the dividing wall than his own. Perhaps she had not yet obtained full retribution for that dinner going up the wall. The sound of his tortured breathing, and bubbling, wheezy chest, is sad enough memory. What was worse is that, in order to obtain a little extra income, he took a cardboard box of mint grown in his garden to Green Street, where he would endeavour to sell it to passers-by. Even though no more than a mere toddler, I found it distressing that this old man, who could have been running the family business, finished his days in such a way. He died on 22nd December 1951, whilst Nanny would soldier on for the better part of ten years, until 18th March 1961. They died at ages 74 and 76 respectively.

I marvelled at how this volatile pair managed to produce such a well-adjusted brood as my aunts Violet, Eileen, and Joan, Uncle Ernie, and Mum. It was entirely beyond my reasoning. Uncle Ernie died from tuberculosis on 16th June 1939, aged just 31, and it remains a major disappointment to me that I never met him. He was, by reputation, an outstanding tennis player and very much into sport generally. Mum and my aunts recalled him as a thoughtful and intelligent man and at least one said that I was very much like him. I take that as an honour.

My mum – Lilian Clark - was the fourth-born of the family, coming into the world on 27th September 1917. The story goes that she was due to be christened "Irene," after a friend or relative.

However, on the way to the grand event, Nanny Clark took umbrage over something done or said by Irene, so Mum got saddled with Lilian. She made the name shine and grew to be a stunningly beautiful lady and, if you don't believe me, I have the photographs to prove it. But she wasn't just a pretty face. Her report from Shaftesbury Senior Girls' School tells me that, in July 1931, her Form Mistress, Miss Wellow, and Head Mistress, Ethel Curtis, rated both her attendance and conduct as, "Very good," adding the general observation that she was, "Industrious, willing, and persevering in her studies." Nice one, Mum.

Leaving school comparatively early (as did most people during the recessional days of the '30s), she began work as a machinist at Marsh's, situated in Neville Road. Her sister, Eileen, had begun work at the same firm just a year or two earlier and, over the years, a deep friendship developed between the pair of them, which was to last throughout their lives. This was no poor reflection on their eldest sister, Violet, who was significantly older than the pair of them as would give space. Joan might have been something of an afterthought between Nanny and Grandad but, despite the somewhat sparky relationship between their parents, the sisters grew into a strong family unit.

My father was a good man, born Joseph Frederick Derby, on 1st May 1916. He grew to be talented in practical matters, was sensitive, loving, generous, and – as far as I was concerned - one of the world's great encouragers. As his only son, his deep, genuine desire that I should make something of myself was never in question. Throughout his life, his emotional side was often prominent and the long held tradition of the bride's mother weeping at her daughter's wedding saw me caught up in a role reversal on my own wedding day, when the father of the groom wept. I thought none the less of him for it. Given that he lived just around the corner from Walpole, his meeting with Lilian Clark could well have been one of pure chance. On the other hand, next door to the "Green Man" public house, where Plashet Grove meets Katherine Road, stood the Harmonic Hall, where youth of the day congregated. The eldest

Clark sisters would frequent the place, and it is more than likely that it is where Mum met Dad, although I have no categoric proof.

The entertainment was not the aggressive assault on the eardrums that it can be today. Music for the 1930's teenager (at that time, a term still waiting for discovery and marketing) was largely "live," and veered toward jazz, ballad, and "big band." Gatherings were orderly – decent, if you will - with waltzes, foxtrots, and quicksteps, each of which required a bit of tuition and discipline, if one was not going to make a complete fool of oneself. Learning to dance would remain something of a rite of passage right up to my teenage years when you would go along to the local dance instructor, thereby ensuring that you were capable of putting your right leg in, your right leg out, and shaking it all about. Rather than the current ill-choreographed gyrating in front of your partner, back then, hands were held, waists were clasped, and gentility was the order of the day. Thus armed, you were able to hold your head reasonably high in mixed company and stand a reasonable chance of getting a partner.

However and wherever they met, there was one thing of which I was totally sure - my Mum and Dad loved one another. Mum would, beyond doubt, have entertained suitors other than Dad, although he was far from pug-ugly. Some years ago, I found a letter he had written to her, which suggested that, during their courtship (now, *there's* a word for you to ponder), he might have overstepped some mark or other, and was running a very serious risk of losing her. The apology and tenderness in his letter was transparent and illustrates that he truly loved her beyond question. In her turn, Mum would never have made a commitment to anyone or anything without total belief, and she loved my dad dearly. Inconveniently, World War ll arrived at the very time that peace would have allowed them to marry, settle down and start their family. Yet, undeterred by the fact that Dad had been "called up" for naval military service, on 27th July 1940, in the Scottish town of Lossiemouth, they married, prior to Dad sailing off in *HMS Gorleston* to fight for King and country. Mum told me that they wanted to be married, "just in case something happened." I guess there were a lot of young couples like that and, sadly, that "something" did happen for far too many.

It's none too difficult to calculate that I must have been conceived during one of Dad's spells of welcome leave. At the time of my birth, the Second World War was in its final stages, 'though nobody was totally sure of that at the time. The Government's evacuation policy had seen herds of London kids transferred to places all around the country deemed to be safer for them than the war torn capital. Four and five year olds were sent miles away from their homes to be cared for by stand-in parents, and whilst this sometimes worked extremely well, there were occasions when it worked extremely badly and horror stories are not hard to come by. With Dad away with the Royal Navy, Mum decided that a place in the country was a far safer option for a zero-year old than chancing to luck what Adolph and his lads might care to chuck our way. She was certainly not going to hand custody of her precious infant to some stranger, and so packed her bags along with my nappies, and headed off to Wellington, in Shropshire. Why Wellington, the Good Lord only knows - we had no family connections in that part of the world. Yet maybe the Good Lord did know, for we were destined to find another situation awash with love and security, long before I was old enough to understand the commodities. I keep coming across reasons to suggest that someone up there really was looking out for me.

Wellington, in the 1940s, was a medium-sized market town, boasting insignificant development. You did not have to travel too far to find yourself in the countryside, the town sitting, as it did, in the shadow of the Wrekin, a land mass standing, then as now, proud and irregular against the horizon. So it was that one afternoon in 1944, a train from Paddington meandered its way up country, through Wolverhampton, before taking its ease alongside the Wellington arrival platform. A young woman, with a barely one-year old babe in arms, stepped off the train knowing absolutely no one, with World War II going on in the background. Mum was too sensible a woman not to have had a game plan, but I live on in ignorance. Laden with suitcase, ticket, and first-born, she made for the barrier intending to look for some suitable accommodation for the pair of us. I never tired of hearing heard Mum's account of the next moments and months.

Standing close to the ticket barrier, was a lady probably in her late thirties or early forties, hair already greying. Perhaps the wartime effort encouraged such people to look out for anyone seeking accommodation. I can't be sure. But what I am sure of is that she approached Mum and, motivated by nothing other than care and concern for a young woman and her charge, spoke in a soft Midland accent.

"Have you anywhere to go, my dear?"

The voice was kind, warm and genuine. Mum, of course, had precisely nowhere to go and said as much.

"I'm afraid I haven't. Unless, of course, I can find some "digs."

"No, no, dear. You'll not do that. Would you like to come along with me? My husband and I have a room, and it would be lovely to have you and the little one with us."

Mum was relieved.

"Oh, yes, please. Finding a room is one thing, but having people to share with is so much better. I'm ready to work. Yes, I'd really like that."

The lady smiled and stroked my cheek.

"And what is the little one's name?" she asked, taking Mum's suitcase and leading her up the station approach toward the main road.

"His name is Stephen, and he's not yet a year old. His dad is away in the Navy, and we just had to get out of London."

"Stephen. What a lovely name. I'm sure we'll get along famously. And my Harry will think the world of you both, you see if he doesn't. And what about you, dear? What's your name?

"My name is Lilian – Lilian Derby. Most people call me "Lil."

Our new friend was pensive.

"No, I think I'll call you Lilian, if that is alright with you. It's such a pretty name. Quite like you, my dear."

The three of us – or rather, two of us, given that I was carried - took the short walk that would lead to Wrekin Road. It took little more than a ten-minute walk to reach 19 Wrekin Road, an end of terrace property with a communal toilet in the garden. The house was small but cleanliness was clearly next to Godliness. When she walked into the living room, Mum's first sight of Mr. Whitney filled her with trepidation. There he was, sat in his armchair, reading the newspaper. A smart, dapper man, greying slightly with a military, waxed moustache; everything about him reflected military precision, not unlike Mr. MacKay, of "Porridge" fame.

"Harry, dear. This is Lilian – Lilian Derby and her little boy, Stephen. I met them at the station and suggested that they came and spent some time with us. Don't you think that was a good idea?"

Now, if that sounds as though he would need some persuading, it was far from the case. Harry Whitney welcomed the pair of us with such warmth that Mum later admitted that she felt a bit ashamed at having jumped to the wrong conclusion, for he was as far removed from "Mr. Mackay" as could be imagined. Mackay was a pompous, self-righteous, figure of fun whereas Harry Whitney's outwardly stern demeanour was a false front. He was a gentleman and kindness itself. It was a natural and short step to my knowing them both as Auntie Alice and Uncle Harry. With no children of their own, they both doted on me, and loved my Mum to bits. During the short time we stayed with them, we were family - and there was no one like their "Stephen."

Mind you, Uncle Harry could do the discipline bit. The austerity of war years made him totally averse to waste – particularly when it came to food. When I began to take on board a little bit of "solid", he would – gently, but firmly - admonish Mum.

"See that the boy always eats his food, Lilian. No sweets until the main course has been dealt with."

But as soon as he disappeared through the door for work and was a safe distance away, Auntie Alice would be scurrying around for some biscuit or jelly to tickle my pallet.

"His bark is far worse than his bite, Lilian," she would say of her husband. And so it was.

If I remain grateful to Uncle Harry for his loving care, how great also the debt I owe him for being responsible for one of my life-long loves. Uncle Harry earned his living as a shunter in the railway yard, just alongside Wellington station. There, in his kingdom, he held sway over fussy little locomotives with a very enhanced sense of their own importance as they coupled and un-coupled their trucks, in readiness for journeys to varying points of the compass. At the throat of the goods yard was a narrow footbridge over the main line between Wolverhampton and Shrewsbury, from which a set of steps gave access to the yard. Whenever Mum wheeled my pram across the bridge on my afternoon constitutional, Uncle Harry would be on the look out for us. Once sighted, up the steps he would come to take me in his arms, and carry me down into the world of engines and rows of wagons. Almost inevitably, some colleague or another would hoist me up onto the footplate where the warmth, aroma, and glorious sound of whistles must have caused my little eyes to glaze over. Health and Safety regulations were still but a twinkle in some job's worth's eyes.

From that point on, there was no way Mum was ever going to get past that footbridge without me creating and yelling. Each and every cunning plan she concocted to avoid the route was doomed to failure and not until she had allowed me full view of the locomotives hard at work was there any hope of peace in her time. The sound of escaping steam, rattling and clanking trucks, and the tat-tat-tat-tat of coaches negotiating the joints between the rails became magic music to accompany my infancy. Steam engines cast a never-to-be-broken spell over me, and it was all down to Uncle Harry. I can still never be in their presence without the broadest of grins breaking out across my face. Call me an "anorak" if you will but, frankly, my dears, I don't give a damn!

Auntie Alice played her own distinctive role in my education, singing various little ditties. "Chick, chick, chick, chick, chicken, lay a little egg for me," was one of her favourites, sung as an exhortation for me to eat my tea....before Uncle Harry got in from work, I suspect. There was one that remained a mystery to me until I fathomed it all out, somewhere just prior to my teenage years. The words merged into one another to made an unintelligible piece of gibberish. This is what I heard:

"Marezydotes and dozydotes and liddle lamsey-divey,
A kiddley-divey doo, wouldn't you?"

Well, of course I bloomin' well wouldn't! I didn't have a clue what Auntie Alice was on about. When light ultimately dawned, the interpretation of what was a purely logical statement went some early way to awaking my fascination with words and language. What I *should* have heard was:-

"Mares eat oats, and does eat oats, and little lambs eat ivy,
A kid'll eat ivy too, wouldn't you?"

Simple when you know how, huh?

Not without a little embarrassment, I recall the pet name that Auntie Alice dreamed up for me. These days, I look in the mirror to see the reflection of a fast – too fast - approaching seventy-year old who once was dubbed – wait for it – "Crinkspot." I can only guess at its origin and my best effort is that it was inspired by a small mole on my right hip. Anyhow, when Mum taught me to say my prayers, part of my nightly ritual would be an appeal that God would, "make Crink a good Crink." It stayed part of my little prayer life for many a year after that and - who knows? - perhaps He did.

Mum and I basked in this idyllic surround until peace and victory arrived in 1945 when families, eagerly anticipating the return of their loved ones, looked forward to getting to a point where normal service – or as near normal as possible – could resume. Alongside the families of those who were left with heartache and an empty place at the table, everyone was united in the conviction that war ain't worth it and we would never do it again. But we did, of course. Europe may have attained a reasonably stable and acceptable peace by various backdoor means, but it's the Middle East and North Korea that scare the hell out of me. If ever that explodes more than it threatens to, then we shall have a fearful time facing us. By the end of the war, then, we had learned much, although ten years into a new century, it seems we have learned nothing.

Peace was a welcome guest for a land that had come dangerously close to being overwhelmed by tyranny. But for Auntie Alice and Uncle Harry – and so many like them – the return of family servicemen was the signal that their beloved adopted family was going to have to go home. For just a year, they had cherished the "daughter" and "grandson" that nature had denied them. Only now, all these years later, have I come to understand that our departure must have been like bereavement. We had to go, and they understood that. But that was far short of providing any comfort for their pain. I thank God that we were able to stay in touch with them throughout the rest of their lives.

At the end of the 1940s, we would return with Dad for a weeks' holiday. In a quite mysterious way, given that I only knew what Mum had told me of the short time we spent with Auntie Alice and Uncle Harry, that holiday was something of a of homecoming for me. I suspect that very little had changed in Wellington during the five years I had been away, save for the fact that Hitler had been vanquished and we were moving into a different phase of life. Most people were starting to put together the shattered, scattered, and interrupted pieces of their lives and moving on to something better - certainly better than six years of war. But one thing above all others, I found, had definitely not changed.

Early on in the week, Dad took me to the footbridge, to see Uncle Harry at work in the yard. I yearned for him to trot up the steps and take me down to the engines again, but perhaps rules and regulations had been tightened during the post- war years, and the yardmaster could no longer turn a blind eye. Nevertheless, not being able to go and mingle with the engines did me no harm – it simply taught me that absence (or separation) made the heart grow fonder. I remained totally besotted and in love with steam engines – and ever more shall be so. Denied those close encounters of the third kind, Dad and I sat at the top of the footbridge steps, watching activities in the yard when, suddenly, a shrill whistle sounded from the direction of the station. Within half a minute, clouds of white steam were billowing from under the road bridge as a locomotive slowly groaned its way toward us, laden with a string of heavy goods vehicles. The bark from the chimney was deafening, and echoed off the embankment and houses. As the engine punched its way ever closer, I read the name from the cast-iron plate, arched over the middle driving wheel.

"Something Hall", I told Dad.

Well, it wasn't quite that. Certainly, it was one of the Great Western "Hall" class, but, for the life of me, I've forgotten which one it was. ""Something" will just have to do. Dad was as proud as Punch. His little lad could read! What's more, I was well on the way to being able to differentiate between a "Hall" and a "Castle."

The Whitneys effortlessly – and unsurprisingly - extended their love and kindness to Dad. Uncle Harry would take him over to "The Wrekin," a still-standing and in business public house, almost opposite No.19. A few beers, a couple of cigarettes, and the chance to watch the local ancients fiercely contest a seemingly endless round of domino competitions. Dad was highly impressed at the way these old boys played what, to my mind, was a basically simple game, largely down to luck. But, no, there was strategy and much cunning involved - and they had it in abundance.

Uncle Harry and Auntie Alice never forgot us and, without fail, each Christmas and on my birthday, I would receive a postal order, for which I would dutifully write my letter of thanks. A time would come when I returned to Wellington once more but, by then, Uncle Harry would no longer be around. He died in 1962. Even without her beloved partner, Auntie Alice faced the world with all the resolution I would have expected from this grand old trooper and, in 1964, I met her again. Toward the end of 1962, I had begun courting Ann Marsh as a serious occupation with intent. Some former Wellington neighbours had moved to Rushden, in Northamptonshire, and occasionally invited Auntie to stay with them. She would be there over the 1964 Easter holidays and as Rushden was well within striking distance from London, Mum and Dad planned a weekend visit. They suggested that Ann and I booked a Sunday coach for a reunion with the lady to whom I owed another debt beyond repayment.

On our journey, in my mind's eye, I had a very clear picture of what I expected her to look like. When we arrived, I was amazed to find that imagination and reality duplicated each other to perfection. Auntie Alice was seated as Ann and I walked in. By now, her hair was silver-grey and tied neatly in a bun. Wire-framed glasses and a face in which I was sure I could see some pain. Dressed in a sober and sensible dark blue dress, in my eyes, she seemed to have aged not at all. After all, when you are only six, someone of forty is ancient. Now I was twenty-one, and Auntie Alice was all I expected of her. Tears welled up in her eyes, as she stood and came toward me. After all, this was "Crinkspot," the little boy she had so be-friended and loved for twenty years. Nothing had changed – only the passage of time. We embraced one another for, oh, I don't know how long. Then she reached out toward Ann and I could see that she approved of my choice. There and then, we invited her to our wedding. She accepted.

Good health continued to stay with her and, true to her word, she was there when Ann and I married on 20th March 1965. Staying, as she did, at our home, I can still hear her voice of concern when, at 11.00 a.m., I hadn't washed, shaved, or bathed, despite the not irrelevant fact that the wedding wasn't due to take place until 3.00pm.

"Lilian, dear," she fretted. "He's going to be late."

Bless her heart; she would have looked after me forever.

As it happened, I wasn't late on that rain-drenched day. Grandad Vanner had died a couple of years earlier on 15th July 1963, aged 82, but Auntie Alice and Grandma Vanner teamed up splendidly on that special day. Only now, in later life, can I rejoice at just how deeply those two wonderful ladies loved me, and anyone else that I loved. Within some six months of our wedding, Grandma Vanner passed away on 28th September 1965.

But Auntie Alice stayed the course until 1970, by which time she had become very frail. The terrace block at Wrekin Road had been demolished to make way for a car park, although "The Wrekin" public house remained a landmark for what once had been. On her own, my aunt had been fortunate enough to be allocated a small warden-controlled flat and if it wasn't entirely to her liking, she never complained. In 1970, Ann and I, with our four-year old son Mark, were heading to North Wales for a camping holiday – Nicola would not arrive for another year. We would be within striking distance of Wellington and I wrote to Auntie Alice to say that we would like to call in and see her. In better health, she would have been counting the seconds but her reply hinted at a very real and concerning reluctance.

"Whilst I would love to see you both, dears, I am afraid that I am too poorly and it might be too much for me."

What could we do? Was I to go right past her doorstep, knowing that my beloved Aunt was ill - perhaps at the point of death - and make no acknowledgement? I so wanted her to see my little boy and I knew that, in her heart of hearts, that was her dear wish. Ann and I thought long and hard. The night before we had planned to call, we sat outside our little tent, holding hands and looking at the shadow traced out on the horizon by the Wrekin.

"It's up to you, Stephen," she said.

I was fighting so hard to balance what Auntie Alice had written in her letter and what I wanted – needed - so deeply. The trouble for those of us who blub easily is that tears always come with runny noses and sniffs. Gives the game away every time.

"I know, Ann. But I've got to see her just once more."

She rested her hand on mine, and spoke softly.

"Then we go."

The following day, we drove into Wellington and found the little flat that was now her home. I rang the bell to hear a gentle shuffling behind the door as she came to answer our call. When she saw us, Auntie Alice was taken back a little. She had presumed that her letter would have done the trick and we wouldn't come and, for the most fleeting of seconds, I wondered if she was going to be angry. Not a bit of it. The condition was temporary and, within moments, Ann had the kettle singing, whilst little Mark did much the same for Auntie Alice. We had explained to him who this old lady was and why she was so important. I am sure that he understood.

That time the four of us shared together was essential - written in the stars, you might say. When the time arrived for us to go, I'm sure we all knew that it would be that last time we would see each other on this earth. Yet the parting was neither tearful nor painful. It was as if this final meeting was there to allow each of us to move on. For Ann and me, that would mean bringing up our little family. For Auntie Alice, it would mean her well-deserved place in heaven – where all good aunts go – for she was truly an angel. She died just a few months after our visit.

Before leaving Wellington, I drove to the footbridge where my love of steam engines had been born. There I sat with Mark at my knee, re-enacting the same scene that Dad and I had played out in 1948. "Something" Hall had long been consigned to the scrap yards, along with all nationally owned steam traction. The yard had become a pale shadow of what it once was. But, yes, we were right to come. Now it was time to move on – and we could.

Wellington itself was beginning to be swallowed up by the burgeoning new town of Telford. The intended political message was that it was the dawning of a bright new day for the inhabitants, but it didn't feel that way to me. Many years later, when I returned for (probably) the last time, the goods yard had disappeared entirely; the walk to the bridge, once through greenery, was choked by scruffy industrial buildings; the foot bridge was smothered with graffiti of the worse kind; and the car park which had swallowed up 19 Wrekin Road had itself been devoured by a large roundabout. In short, Wellington has gone distinctly downmarket from my fond memory. 'Twas not ever thus.

I am glad that Auntie Alice and Uncle Harry never survived to see the deterioration. Somewhere in the town their graves lie, probably untended. People will pass, read the notation on their headstone, and think no more of it. Yet these people and so many others like them were giants. My memories of them both, my gratitude for the immense kindness and love they showed my mum, dad, and me will remain ever well tended in my heart. How does a little child understand that he is loved beyond reason? Simply through the fact that, where love is, there is no fear and, for just a year or so, Mum and I lived totally without fear with two of the dearest people that ever graced God's earth. Alice and Harry Whitney – and others like them - were more than giants – they were saints. As with Grandad Vanner, lack of a blood tie was outrageously compensated for by bonds of overwhelming kindness, generosity, and pure love.

So that was the family soil in which I was planted. These were the people who took the earliest responsibility for pointing me in the right direction for life. From my very earliest days of consciousness, I was never a stranger to love, care, support, and encouragement and, in that respect alone, I was well blessed. Yet it got even better for, as years passed, friendships were forged and influences brought to bear. With all these cards dealt to me, were I to take a wrong step in life, well, I would have no one else but myself to blame.

CHAPTER TWO

NEIGHBOURS

The war was over. Husbands began returning to resume interrupted careers whilst those with no careers returned to look for – and find - gainful employment. Kids came back from evacuation and things began to get back to normal.

Back to normal, did I say? What would I have known about normal? After all that had happened during the preceding six years, what was normal for those who had lived through the fearful intensity of it all? Pieces and people had been broken, removed, or moved around the board and new strategies, dreams and attitudes were inevitable. Pre-war "normality" would not – could not - return. People had been through too much. The older generation's apprehension was understandable and it would take some time for them to come to terms with the relief of an enemy vanquished and that Hitler was involved elsewhere, with weightier matters to account for.

So, as I came into consciousness of life, early recollections became my normality. With hindsight, the joy of peace, the reuniting of families, and restored communities, mixed with the aforementioned apprehension, must have spilled together in one great tidal wave. Being amongst it all made me very glad to be alive. My early life was transacted with a sense that we were living in a time of optimism, where there were opportunities for fresh starts, and excitement. The only way, for those who had survived, was up.

For six years, the country had been pleading with the Almighty to stop the awful mess of war. Ultimately, our forces, aided by our allies, won the day and the menace presented by Nazi Germany was overcome. I am deeply grateful to all those who made the ultimate sacrifice. However, the true horrors of what the British people went through cannot be imagined by my generation. Perhaps just a taste can be gleaned from witnessing the "shock and awe" tactics employed during the invasion of Iraq, which frightened the life out of me when I saw it on television from the comfort of my armchair. What it must have been like to live through is beyond comprehension and beyond what any soul should be asked to encounter.

Active service completed, Mum and Dad rented the ground floor of 7 Walpole Road from Mr. Bostock, whose offices were in Green Street, opposite Queens Road market. Each week, a representative would call round like clockwork for the dues, carefully marking off the sum paid in our rent book. Mortgages and house ownership were not yet for the like of us, the closest we ever got to that state being around the "Monopoly" board. Not everyone was able to afford the rent on an entire house, let alone contemplate buying one of the things. Hence, we occupied the downstairs section only. But I loved that house - it had a warm, friendly feel to it and was probably typical of most of the houses in Walpole Road. Beyond the front door was what seemed to me at the time, a long passageway, at the end of which, stairs led to the upstairs accommodation. On the left of the passage were two bedroom rooms, the front one for Mum and Dad; the second for me. A wooden folding door divided them. At the foot of the stairs, a sharp left turn followed by a sharp right took you into the living room, beyond which was the scullery. In this somewhat confined area, Mum cooked, washed, and dried clothes - washing machines and tumble driers patiently waiting for their time. A metal copper - looking like a forerunner of R2D2 - sat in one corner, serving to heat water for washing and Friday bath nights. A right old palaver that was!

Dad would commence the ritual by bringing in the old galvanised tin bath that hung on the fence outside the door to the garden, and setting it down in the scullery. Piping hot water was poured from the copper into the bath, whilst Mum and I - in the adjoining living room - got ready to take our turns. Pecking order was strictly observed, with Dad taking the first dip. By the time Mum had had her go and I was ready to be scrubbed up, the bath needed "topping up" with hot water from the copper. From my point of view, it needed purifying, too. Red Lifebuoy soap was *de rigueur* and whilst just about acceptable to scour body and backside, the rotten substance and second-hand water got daubed around my face and, finally, used to wash my hair. No wonder that it has steadily fallen out over the years.

The section of the house that intrigued me most was the one we occupied the least. Alongside the entry to the living room, a wooden door unlatched to reveal a flight of wooden stairs, that provided access to a below ground level cellar for storing coal. Central heating was just about the last thought on anybody's mind down Walpole in those days. Heating the home was a rather more complex exercise than turning a few dials and switching a few switches. Before going to work, Dad would get up early to gather together some newspapers and a bit of kindling wood and take them to the fireplace. There he would crumple the paper into balls, and place the kindling on top, thus creating what I can best describe as a sparse, miniature wigwam. This pyre was then topped lightly with coal before a lighted match was applied to the paper, prayers offered, when - usually - the wood would burn, the coal ignite, and Bob's yer uncle. Some householders cultivated an art involving the placing of a wire guard in front of the fire, and resting newspapers against it to create a draught – "drawing the fire," it was called. For the life of me, when I was old enough to have a go, I could never produce a blaze without at least three cracks of the whip but, once it was going, the warmth and glow was wonderful. All it took was the occasional topping up with coal and that was how we heated the house.

Uncle Ray, in Elizabeth Road, had innovatively converted his cellar into what was tantamount to a fully blown workshop. He had installed a whetstone for sharpening his knives and tools and I loved watching him at this task. What with sparks flying in all directions, it was like an indoor firework display. We were nowhere near as creative as Uncle Ray so, unimaginatively, settled down to use the cellar for what it was supposed to be for. At the far end was the storage area for our coal supply, regularly replenished by deliveries from the coalman. Don't ask me why, but coal deliveries fascinated me immensely. A horse-drawn flat cart would saunter down the street under the guidance of the coalman, encrusted from head to foot in coal dust. Deliveries went something like this. First, the round, iron cover over the round hole at the front of the house was removed. Then, humping a sack of the black stuff onto his shoulder from his cart, the coalman would make his approach and, with the accuracy of any top-notch dart player, bend forward and swing the sack to meet flush with the hole. I never saw a miss, and rarely did a stray lump of coal ever find its way onto the doorstep.

We usually had two sacks delivered and if I couldn't watch the delivery from the doorway, I would go down into the cellar itself to see and hear the nuggets crashing and tumbling onto the concrete floor. When the show was over, up I would come, with grime all over my face and clothes. Mum used to get angry at first, but she got over it. She could see my fascination, even if she didn't quite understand it. When we paid our weekly visit to Grandma and Grandad Vanner, I must have given everyone the vapours about where my future career might lead me.

"How many sacks today, Grandma?" I'd ask.

"Oh, just a couple will do fine, thank you."

And with that, I would take one of the cushions from the armchair, hoist it onto my back, and imitate my grimy hero to perfection, delivering a full cushion load of nothing into the coalscuttle, accompanied by sound effects from the back of my throat. Funny little bloke, I was.

We were blessed with a small garden and I can say without fear of contradiction, that what Dad created with that tiny patch over the next five years became the envy of virtually everyone in Walpole Road. A keen and capable gardener, he produced a pristine little showcase, with a well-manicured lawn, crazy paving path, and a few water features. The only blemish to the entire effect was the outside toilet, with its wooden door, built on to the rear of the house and shared with the Polyblank family who lived in the upstairs flat. Wind, rain, hail, or snow made trips to the lavatory perilous and it would be another thirteen years and a new home before we were able to enjoy indoor sanitation.

Steve Derby

In 1947, Dad took employment with the Central Electricity Generating Board, at Barking Power Station, in River Road. His job description read "rigger" which basically meant that he had responsibility for erecting scaffolding around the massive boilers and generators. It was the commencement of a thirty year plus career, during which he worked long and hard hours, frequently doing weekend shifts to ensure that we were all well provided for, and allow Mum to remain a full-time committed parent to little me. A pattern of setting off for work on his bicycle early in the morning and arriving home late at night became the norm for Dad. Few had motorcars so, after Dad had done his overtime, I was usually in bed by the time he arrived home. Yet it provided secure employment – a much-prized acquisition – and slowly, we were able to make some progress in our living standards which, by the way, were never "bread line."

Thursday nights were always special – Mum and Dad called it "surprise night." Well, in fact, surprise was the last thing that it was as I knew exactly what was coming. Dad would arrive home a little earlier than usual and, once he had had dinner, produced the largest block of Cadbury's whole nut chocolate you could possibly imagine. Of course, the squares were allocated to each of us on a *pro rata* basis, related to age - but who cared? Chocolate was something to be looked forward to and I loved Thursday nights.

Our family number was augmented to the power of two by a black and white cat - "Whiskey" – along with a wire-haired fox terrier, "Pat." By and large, the pair of them got on pretty well. But, if ever there was a spat, the blessed cat always came out on top. Dad always called him "a crafty sod."

Quite how hostilities commenced, I don't recall. There'd been a scuffle over something or other and now, like a pair of poseurs, cat and dog stalked around one another, neither prepared to bury the hatchet.

Pat was in the scullery, whilst Whiskey sat by the door in the living room. Good-natured cove as the dog was, after about half an hour or so, you could sense she felt the nonsense had gone on long

46

enough and was anxious for normal service to be resumed. Gingerly, she started to poke her nose round the door to seek out the antagonist. This was a serious error of judgement for, you see, no one had let Whiskey in on the fact that this was a peace initiative. On the other side of the door, the rotten cat was still steamed up and every time Pat tried to peep into the living room, her long snout gave the game away. Long before Whiskey saw the light of Pat's eyes, the dog got a smack across the nose for her troubles. Three times the dose was repeated and, for the life of her, Pat couldn't work it out..

Cat features just sat there, happy in the knowledge that he had the upper hand – or paw.

Whiskey passed on through old age but poor old Pat met a tragic end. One Sunday afternoon, during a family walk around the greenery near Snaresbrook, she was hit by a car and killed outright. Mercifully, I missed the impact and my parents fed me the line that she had, "run off into the woods and disappeared." For days, Dad maintained a charade that he had been visiting the spot, calling out Pat's name, enquiring at the police station, until sufficient time passed and the matter slipped off my agenda.

Our upstairs "neighbours" were a lovely couple, Joan and Bert Polyblank. Mum and Dad had known them both for some time and they had often taken holidays together. As with Auntie Alice and Uncle Harry, I grew up knowing them as Aunt and Uncle, for it was a distinctive sign of those times that any adult friend would be dubbed with this honorary title. Uncle Bert was tall and redheaded, with a great love of life. He had a reasonably responsible position down at the docks whilst Auntie Joan stayed at home looking after their two daughters, Joan and Cynthia, who were great fun - we all got on famously. The eldest - "Little Joan" we all called her - was just a few months older than me, and was a terrific playmate. Cynthia was a year or so younger, and not quite so ready for the high jinks of four-year olds.

Joan and I used to play in the muck around the Andersen shelter at the end of our garden. The structure was made of corrugated metal and had served as some sort of protection from the frequent air raids of war years. As soon as the air raid warning was sounded, down everyone would charge for such protection as the shelter might provide. I guess a "direct hit" would have seen all the occupants off the planet, but it was the best we could do in the circumstances. Anyhow, playing around the shelter resulted in me getting someone into trouble for the first time in my life.

As a couple of four-year olds, neither of us was at school and, one afternoon, little Joan and I had been having a fine old time making mud pies. Auntie Joan had kept a watchful eye on the pair of us from her upstairs window, insisting frequently that little Joan didn't get into "too much of a state." This I could not understand as, at the time of the first warning, she was already in such a state as to render any further warnings pointless. No matter, Auntie Joan stuck to the strategy.

I suppose matters weren't helped a great deal when I suggested that little Joan ate one of our culinary, muddy delights. Never in my wildest imaginings did I think she would go for it – but she did! For the umpteenth time, the upstairs window opened and Auntie Joan was livid to see the goings on.

"Joan, you dirty little hussy! Come up here at once!"

Leaning toward her, I added my two-penn'orth.

"Call her a cow," I whispered.

Little Joan turned her face up toward the window, mud dripping from her lips, and onto her dress.

"Cow!" she mouthed, clearly and with just the right degree of venom to make any self-respecting adult turn red, yell "WHAT!" head for the stairs, charge up the garden, and bash eight bells out of whoever they grabbed first. And that was exactly what Auntie Joan did, the unfortunate beneficiary being little Joan.

With junior kicking and screaming, the pair of them exited the scene. As for me, I crept indoors, hoping that my playmate wouldn't blow the gaff. Bless her, she never did and we stayed friends for a very long time.

When the Polyblanks took the opportunity to move to a larger house in Humberstone Road, Plaistow, fiscal matters in the Derby household were enhanced by my reaching school age, thus allowing Mum to return to fee-earning work at Marsh's. This happy state of affairs meant that we could now afford further rent so, overnight, No.7 Walpole Road became all ours, or rather, Mr. Bostock's – but you know what I mean. The additional space allowed Mum and Dad to get a bit more organised and their former downstairs bedroom was transformed into what became known as the "front room," used strictly for high days and holidays. My former bedroom became, as and when required, a playroom, a home for my train set and bicycle, and Mum's sewing materials. Some might have called it a junk room, and I wouldn't have argued.

On the first landing, the room adjoining the balcony had been the Polyblanks's main living and cooking quarters, and to be honest, was somewhat cramped for such purposes. It proved somewhat surplus to our requirements and was used mainly for storage – another junk room, if you like. A short flight of stairs to the top floor gave access to two bedrooms. Mum and Dad opted for the one at the end of the passage, overlooking the road, whilst mine was first on the right where, over the next ten years, I would reach out and claim puberty, or thereabouts, for my very own.

Our next door neighbours, in No. 9, were the quite remarkable Longhurst family. Mr. and Mrs. Longhurst – Ben and Sarah – who produced, I think, some nineteen children, sadly, not all of whom survived. But the majority did and how on earth they all managed to fit into that house was one of the wonders of the age. Nanny Clark, at her most acerbic, suggested that, "Ben only has to look at her and she's pregnant!" Mum's younger sister Joan, in later years, told me how Nanny would get exasperated when everyone was ensconced in the Andersen shelter during air raids, and Mr. Longhurst offered commentary on hostilities.

The drone of an aircraft engine could be heard in the night sky.

"No need to worry about that one, " said Mr. Longhurst. "He's one of ours."
Suddenly, there was a bloody great bang and a flash of light illuminated the sky. The ground shook. Clearly, whatever else it might have been, it was decidedly not "one of ours." Nanny took no prisoners.
"That Ben Longhurst. I'll swear he's a collaborator. Give me half a chance and I'll shave his head!"

I liked the Longhursts. They were decent and friendly neighbours, particularly one of the youngest, Albert. A couple of years my senior, he struck me as a really nice boy without a bad bone in his body. He would never pass me in the street without stopping to speak and, if I was playing in our back garden, he always gave me time. I never had quite the same rapport with his brothers and sisters, mainly due to their being that much older than me. But they'd always say "hello" if I saw them in the street, so I was never offended.

Ben Longhurst himself was employed at the bus garage at the bottom of Priory Road, which ran alongside West Ham United's ground. I never knew precisely what his duties were. This was before the advent of the cost-saving, single-manned, life-risking transportation which charges about today, and all buses would have both a driver and conductor. Doubtless, the driver got the lion's share of the pay but, for my money, it was the poor old conductor who deserved to be at the top of the food chain. Up and down the two decks he - or she - would go, issuing tickets, punched by a mysterious piece of equipment belted round their middle, which "tinged" when operated. A leather cash bag was slung over the shoulder and, at the end of a particularly long run, it must have weighed a ton. Aunt Ei's husband, Uncle Ray, would soon join that happy breed.

Dad enjoyed long conversations with Ben over the garden fence, chiefly about gardening. The majority of the Longhurst patch was given over to vegetables, whereas Dad's interest was purely horticultural. When our dog Pat produced a litter of puppies, Dad offered one to Mr. Longhurst. This seemed to me the height of folly given that the walls of No.9 must have already been creaking in their attempt to accommodate the thick end of twenty grown persons. Nevertheless, the Longhurst mind was set and, as a result, another wire-haired terrier became a neighbour. They christened the dog, "Peter," which seemed to me as daft as "Pat." At least, we could justify our choice with a bit of nursery rhyme common sense - you know, "We all pat the dog." But, Peter? You were naming a dog, for goodness sake, not your next of kin. Anyhow.

Unfortunately, Peter rarely had any regular acquaintance with the clippers and soon began to resemble an outsize floor mop, rummaging around the veg, with no visible means of support. The poor dog could hardly see or walk, much less attend to his essential private business, due to excess fur. Ultimately, a good trimming was unavoidable. When he emerged shorn of his long familiar coat, Peter presented the comic appearance of someone dragged into public view stark naked, kicking and screaming. Had he been capable, I swear he would have blushed and covered his private parts with his paws. However, within a few months, *status quo* was restored and he was woollier than ever.

In later years, Ben confided in Dad that the time might well have arrived for him to cut the umbilical cord between his family and Walpole Road to search out fresh challenges. If anyone knew a thing or nineteen about cutting umbilical cords, then Mr. Longhurst was yer man.

"Been thinking 'baht moving, Joe. You know. Getting aht of 'ere – right aht."

"Right out," Dad translated, wondering which part of the country this would-be Gulliver had in mind.

"Where you thinking of going, then, Ben?"

"Oh, you know. Right aht. Somewhere like 'Awnchurch!"

Lord save us! 'Awnchurch! Sorry – Hornchurch. A couple of stops up the District Line and dear old Ben Longhurst is waxing lyrical as if he was taking the family to the plantations. He never left, and the only time he ever went "right aht" was when they carried him from Walpole Road in his coffin. But, as I've said, I

51

liked the Longhursts for their sheer decency and good neighbourliness.

For one who was then basically very shy, I surprise myself to recall that one of my earliest friends and neighbours was another little girl. With little Joan Polyblank no longer resident, perhaps Mum thought that I needed another playmate. I just don't know. Anyway, somewhere around the age of four or five, Doreen Steele – who lived across the road from me, at No. 6 - became as regular a visitor to my home as I was to hers. She was a pleasant little girl – perhaps carrying a tad more weight than she ought to have done - a few months older than me and lived with her parents and grandparents. On the occasions that we played "at home," and when the weather allowed, our old galvanised bath was removed from the fence, placed on the lawn, and filled with water so that the pair of us could splash around to our hearts content. When I played "away," the seeds of my life-long love of music were sown.

Television had yet to take its hold and provide moving wallpaper for future generations. Back then, the best we could muster was the radio, where the "Light" and "Home" services were about as good as it got. Regularly, Doreen and I would listen to Donald Peers, from the Welsh valleys, or some such region. He wasn't a bad singer and had this theme song, "In a Shady Nook." Corny as it came, it was all about shady nooks, babbling brooks, flowers, dicky-birds, and falling in love. One evening, the pair of us were listening to Donald's radio show. As he waded up to his neck in the babbling brook, I filled my lungs and sang the melody along with him. Doreen was impressed as hell. To be honest, it caught me unawares that I could sing with confidence, and really enjoy it. Put it down as my first and last participation in Karaoke.

But the pair of us never became an item. We were just little playmates and it all ended in tears the day when, for no reason that I can recall, I pulled her hair. She blubbed enough to sink a battleship, told her mum, who told my mum, who gave me ticking off, endorsed by a good firm parental slap around the head. And that, as they say, was that as far as this little relationship was concerned.

These, then, were the people who were our most immediate neighbours. I have to go on record to say that there were characters galore within stone-throwing distance in Walpole Road. Some were quiet and refined, others were of a more colourful nature, whilst the balance group was caught somewhere in between the two extremes. Personalities emerged during the ensuing years, a pattern which, I suspect, would be common in any short street, be it in Upton Park, the 'Pool, or the Gorbals. Yet on Christmas morning, 1947, something happened that influenced my life for ever, although I was too young to understand it at the time.

Christmas Eve in the Derby household was always planned with military precision. Mum and Dad reckoned that, if they could get me to bed by around eight, I'd drop off to sleep, thus giving them the chance to get all my presents into the pillowcase hung on the end of my bed. Of course, I believed implicitly in Father Christmas - still do - and as a sign of good faith, Mum brought to my room a couple of mince pies and a small glass of sherry – not for me, you understand. No, the victuals were placed conveniently for the hairy, sooty soul to see them and fortify himself on his round.

Mum and Dad themselves would be in bed not much before eleven. But the pure adrenalin raised in anticipation of Christmas was a total guarantee that sleep would never come easily to any kid under the age of ten. Even when it did, it rarely lasted more than a precious few hours. That Christmas, Dad was due on early shift at the power station and on a short fuse, as I was no nearer to sleep at midnight than when I first lay down my sweet head. Well, of course, eventually I dozed off, but it was all too much and, somewhere just before 4.00 am, I was awake again. I lifted my head to see if Father Christmas had done his stuff. Crikey! He had – with a vengeance. My pillowcase was chock full, with an overflow of parcels on the floor, just pleading for me to unwrap them.

"Mum. Dad. Can I get up yet? Father Christmas has been."

Exactly what loving parents want to hear after little more than a few hours sleep of their own. I could hear Dad grumbling but Mum, bless her, did her best.

"Just another hour or so. Remember, Dad's got to go to work."

Another hour or so? She might as well have said several light years. Eventually, she persuaded Dad – though goodness knows how – that he ought to see the delight on his little son's face before going to work. Being the Dad that he was, he succumbed and, between us, we dragged the pillowcase and carried the excess items into his bedroom. What treasures was I about to behold? The electric train set that Dad had, during the past month, been hinting "might" arrive was there, all present and correct. With it, the "Beano" and "Dandy" annuals, which would become standard fare for future Christmases up until somewhere around age eleven. Why on earth the supply stopped then remains a mystery and disappointment to me. Books, toys, and the occasional item of knitwear from some well-meaning aunt or other – my cup truly did run over. And, just for luck, an apple and an orange.

With all parcels open, Mum and Dad put their heads down again, in the hope of grabbing just a little more rest. Pointless exercise, if you ask me. Sleep was no longer an option for Dad, and once he came to terms with this, he got up, put on his working clothes, and prepared to cycle the six miles or so to work. Mum knew she was going to get no more rest, so she got up to make them both a cup of tea, and begin cooking the day's meals. As for the architect of such early rising and attendant inconvenience, I simply lay down and dozed off until somewhere beyond eight.

When Walpole Road at large woke that Christmas morning, snow had fallen, snow on snow, and it really was something of a bleak mid-winter morning. Did I give a monkey's? Not a solitary one. With Mum busying herself downstairs, I engrossed myself in my new books and toys. For the umpteenth time, I looked at the little black tank engine and its three goods trucks, and yearned to set out the track and get the thing moving. My infant months in Wellington, filled with the sound of steam engines, allowed me to do a more than passable impression of one of the breed. Taking the locomotive from its box and setting it on the rails, I provided the sound effects and, in my imagination, visualised the little tanker chuffing along the track. Yet I was under the strictest of strict instructions that nothing more than this was to be allowed until Dad came home.

Our front room came into its' own at Christmas time. Throughout most of the year, it was out of bounds, other than on those occasions when we had special visitors. But when the festive season arrived, the room was translated into the nerve centre of our celebrations. Free to wander in and out of the room at will, I took time to look at the snow falling outside, ever deepening as it settled on the pavements and road. There I was, cocooned comfortably in my home with the fire blazing, carols on the radio, and the sweet aroma of dinner wafting through the house. Everyone down the street, just like me, was warm inside both home and heart, with family and loved ones. Except, that is.............

On the other side of the road, next to Doreen's, there was one stranger to all of this. A little boy – I didn't know his name - was pulling a toy fire engine along through the thick snow. Why wasn't he inside, playing with the rest of his toys? Surely his mum and dad couldn't be happy with him being out in the bitterly cold weather? He looked a happy little chap, totally engrossed in his toy, and perfectly content to enjoy himself in his own way. Mum interrupted my musings, coming into the room with a cup of tea and mince pie, in order to take a well-earned break from her work. I got the same fare.

"What are you looking at out there, Stephen?" she asked.

"Mum, there's a little boy over the road in the snow, playing with a fire engine. Why isn't he indoors with his mum and dad? Who is he, Mum?"

She came to the window, and I couldn't help but notice the trace of a tear in her eye.

"That's Derek. Derek Fletcher. You wouldn't know, but his dad never came back from the war. He lives with his mum, grandad and grandma, over at No.12."

I could feel myself welling up that such a little guy could be by himself on Christmas Day. Mum understood the situation and Mrs. Fletcher's loss far better than I did. I could almost see her mind at work, as she reached out for the question that I hoped she would ask.

"I wonder if Mrs. Fletcher would let Derek come over and play with you? Would you like that, Stephen?"

During my life – like most of us, I guess - I have said and done some truly daft things. I have said "yes," when I should have said "no," and vice versa. But I know, for sure, that this time I got it absolutely right, and I have never regretted my response.

"Yes, Mum. I'd really like that."

She pulled on her coat, and walked over to No.12. Mum and Mrs. Fletcher had known each other since infanthood – as had so many in Walpole. In a few minutes, for the first but not the last time, Derek crossed the threshold of No. 7. For the rest of that day, we had a fine old time. It didn't matter a jot to me that he played with all the goodies that I had been indulged with. That Christmas morning, a bond was forged that grew stronger as years passed. Long before David Jason immortalised Del Trotter; long before Ronnie Barker made Norman Stanley Fletcher a household name, both "Del" and "Fletcher" were welded inextricably into my life. He would become a considerable finger in the pie of my growing up and there would never be a time in my life when Derek Fletcher didn't mean something precious to me. We were set to share innumerable pieces of nonsense together; he would get me into a thousand scrapes; he would make me laugh at will. Never for one moment did I doubt his friendship - nor he mine. Always, there would be Derek, Del, or just Fletch. The key in which our childhood was about to be played – sometimes sharp, sometimes flat - was never out of harmony.

Mum and her three sisters remained very close throughout their entire lives, both geographically and emotionally. In 1945, Aunt Violet and her husband, Uncle Fred, lived at No.3, with my older cousins Fred, Doreen, and Audrey. Next door, at No.5, Nanny and Grandad Clark resided with my Aunt Joan, who would not marry until her early 30's. As a result, my cousin Elaine was still a long way off and would be the last edition to the Clark clan. In the back gardens of these three houses, a "hole in the fence" allowed free movement by the sisters into each other's homes. If Aunt Eileen and Uncle Ray were not exactly down our street, their home at No.40 Elizabeth Road - every bit of a five- minute walk away – ensured that they were regular visitors and very much part of the clan. Their son, Clive, and daughter Val were still a couple of years away from entering this family fray but, when they did, they fitted into the family pattern as easy as winking. So, when it came to being family orientated, I didn't have a prayer. The stage was set.

CHAPTER THREE

EDUCATING STEPHEN

Education seems to have got so damned complicated nowadays – it's certainly beyond my comprehension. We are told that standards are higher, more young people go to university, and everyone has a fair chance to obtain a first class education. Now this may well be so but, frankly, I have some questions about it all. There seem to be too many areas where, for me, the jury remains distinctly out. It was a long time ago but when I heard that my cousin Fred had "matriculated," I thought he'd done something naughty. What price ignorance?

Education in my time went something like this. You did two years of primary education, followed by another four of junior syllabus. At the end of this period, you would be set an examination – by the time that I took mine, it had graduated from "scholarship" to "11-plus." Dependent upon the outcome, the road would divide to allow the top scorers to progress at grammar school, whilst the remainder headed into what was perceived as a less demanding secondary modern syllabus. It was the way of the world.

The secondary modern menu would last for a further four years at the end of which time, most scholars would enter into the world of work. Grammar schools called for a further year of education during which battle with the General Certificate of Education Ordinary Level (GCE) would commence. Examinations would be taken in a range of subjects and if you managed to get 45%, then you passed.

At the end of the five years, many would declare their education complete and join their secondary modern chums out in the workplace. Students of a more academic leaning opted for two more sixth form years with a view to obtaining up to four subjects at the GCE Advanced Level. Those who were successful were, frequently, exceptional. They were held in awe as they gained places at universities across the land. There they would obtain degrees, doctorates and all manner else, equipping them to do rather well in life. All pretty straightforward, if you ask me, and I don't recall any kid kicking up too much of a fuss about it. If anyone had not done themselves justice at the 11-plus and later showed appropriate inclination, transfers would take place between secondary modern and grammar school education. It did happen – both ways.

And then, in the late '60s, some ne'er-do-well decided that this wasn't very good at all. Everyone should have access to the very best in education – want it or not - and out of the corridors of power, came boffins mumbling the mantra, "comprehensive, comprehensive, comprehensive." All was thrown into chaos. Grammar school kids along with a not inconsiderable number of teachers felt that standards were lowered whilst most of the secondary modern scholars – who, let me say, were not fools – just looked on in astonishment and greeted the whole sorry mess with a resigned, "yeah – whatever."

Since then, nothing has been the same and I still wait to be convinced that we have raised standards. No, it's "all shall have prizes" and the world and his wife must go to university. Yet a staggering proportion of "successful" graduates struggle with simple arithmetic, are alien to punctuation, can't recognise the need or value of a paragraph, and think that a split infinitive requires a hospital appointment. However, I digress and, after all, it's only my opinion. In the next few years, we would be "Educating Archie." Later yet, we would have a go at "Educating Rita." So, having clarified that, let me tell you about Stephen's turn.

The thought of going to school held no fear whatsoever for me. I knew it was going to happen, as sure as night followed day. Naturally, there were some who, for whatever reason, didn't want to go and resorted to tears and tantrums. But it didn't work for, one way or another, we were all going to have go to school and get our heads filled. No, all I knew was that, come September 1948, I would be packed off to Shaftesbury Road school to begin my formal academic education, and I really looked forward to it.

The school was situated, as the crow flies, something less than a couple of hundred yards from Walpole Road. From my doorstep, above the roofs of the houses in St. Stephens Road, I could see the bell tower. Shaftesbury Road ran parallel to St.Stephens, and there were two options available for reaching the school. Option one was to follow St. Stephens to Katherine Road, do a left turn for a further couple of hundred yards to Shaftesbury Avenue, where another left turn brought you to the school itself. Alternatively, a walk to the other end of Walpole took you to Plashet Grove and onto Green Street. Beyond the yet-to-be-renovated Carlton cinema, you reached the other end of Shaftesbury Road and crept up on the school from that direction. For some reason that I never quite fathomed, I always felt that only "nice" kids took the Green Street route. If ever there was nonsense in the air, it always seemed to take place on the Katherine Road route. So, local society having assessed me as being a "good little boy" and anxious to avoid any sort of conflict, I readily settled for the Green Street passage. Anyway, Derek used Katherine Road, so there had to be something "iffy" about it.

Shaftesbury Road school itself was a ground and two-storey affair, standing in the shadow of the Trebor sweet factory, which stood on the corner of Katherine Road. A sweet aroma of sugar and flavouring constantly wafted across the playground, and the tall chimney, which released smoke from the kiln, looked down on us all like some brick sentry. Whenever maintenance work was undertaken. I marvelled at the workmen, casually sitting on the lip of the chimney, taking their lunch or tea break. Heights have never been my strong suit, and perhaps it was Trebor's chimney that started it all off. Two playgrounds were available, east and west of the building – one for infants (ages 5 to 7) and the other for seniors (ages 8 to 11). Each playground included a covered area that we kids referred to as "the shed." In the event of rain, hail or snow, they provided ample protection for a good number, thus ensuring that we got our regular dose of fresh air, even in times of inclement weather.

Playground toilets were of the open-air variety and, as far as the male quarter was concerned, always seemed to smell of urine. I hated the blessed place. Natural need dictated that I would have to use the channels provided for water works but there was no way I was ever going to go into one of those cubicles designed for more serious business. I had something about taking my trousers down in what, for me at least, was tantamount to a foreign land. The wooden doors to the cubicles left too much room at the top for would-be *voyeurs* whilst the space at the bottom offered naught for your comfort – and this was long before the popularity of limbo dancing. Just to compound the general unpleasantness, the urinals provided a stadium for idle recreation, commonly known as "peeing over the wall." Standing just a foot or two back from the surrounding wall, boys of all ages, shapes, and sizes would seek to gain such trajectory as necessary to send a urinary arc of water over the wall and onto any poor unfortunate who happened to be passing at the time. Prompted by Derek (of course), I gave it a go myself, but when falling short by about a foot, I quite rightly gave it up as a rotten job.

Opposite the main entrance to the school was Ashley Road, which linked Shaftesbury Road and Dorset Road. One each corner, two shops know by all and sundry as "Ted's" and "Len's" respectively, after their proprietors. "Len's" was run by Mr. Bunn who was quiet, immaculate, and a gentleman. "Ted's" on the other hand, was a bit more down market, specialising in sticky sweets, gob-stoppers, bubble gum, and peashooters. These latter weapons of crass destruction comprised a narrow tin tube with a protective lip. Loaded with a mouth full of pearl barley, you were armed to fire these "peas" at any poor old soul that trolled by, which was a dangerous game, if you ask me. It wouldn't have taken much for a stray pea to have caught someone in the eye and I am mildly astonished that it never happened.

Mr. Bunn maintained his distinct edge through the quality magazines and comics that he stocked. Around 1950, a group of Christian writers decided that what post war youth needed were some real heroes to compete with what was perceived as dodgy influences imported from the States. As a result, the "The Eagle" became a massively popular boys comic, and retained that position before merging with "The Lion" in 1969. Through its pages, boys were introduced to the likes of Dan Dare (Pilot of the Future) and his sworn green adversary, the Mekon; friendly "bobby", P.C.49, along with Harris Tweed, a bumbling detective with a jutting chin – ably assisted by "the boy." Jeff Arnold provided the obligatory cowboy and even historical and Biblical characters got mass airing through the comic's pages. In the centrefold, there was always an "exploded" drawing – some piece of transport engineering with the protective layers stripped away to reveal what went on inside. If ever there was a "class" comic, "The Eagle" was it, and I would challenge anyone to provide evidence to the contrary. One morning, having purchased the latest edition, I became so engrossed in reading it that I walked into tree! So successful was the formula that a version for girls soon followed suit, its only drawback being the rather unimaginative title of "The Girl." Never mind, I'd sooner my grandkids have had the chance to read either "Eagle" or "Girl" than the shallow "celebrity" tosh on the market today.

But back to the school. The ground floor was the domain of the infants department for all children, shiny and brand new, from ages five to seven. Mixed classes existed until we moved into the juniors at age seven, there to go our separate ways, and never mix educationally again….and I mean never. Life in the infants was all about play, stories, singing, coming to terms with the alphabet, and dispensing with your fingers when counting. It didn't take me too long to slot into the routine and I can say categorically that I really loved school. My first teacher was a lovely lady - Miss Brownsell. I always found it funny and rather quaint, this unwritten rule that all female teachers were addressed as "Miss." It was not until I reached secondary school, in 1954, that I ever heard a female member of staff addressed as "Mrs." – but she was the school secretary, so I suppose that didn't count. For sure, I know that "Miss" Brownsell was really "Mrs." Brownsell in disguise, because she wore a wedding ring and her daughter, Susan, was in our class. It couldn't have been easy for either of them and my first memory of school discipline is the time when Susan strolled into class a couple of minutes late, with all the airs and graces. Dear Miss Brownsell was having none of that, and duly re-aligned her daughter's thinking on the matter. Susan was never late again.

With my first year completed and everyone ready to move into the class next door, I hardly thought that things could get better. But get better they did, for I came under the care of the gorgeous Miss Doughty. Now she might well have been a *bona fide* "Miss" but, if so, it could only have been due to her youth. She was dark-haired, extremely pretty, had a warm caressing voice, and was kind beyond measure. Don't tell everyone, but I looked at her with every bit of passion a six-year old could possibly be aware of. On her desk, she kept a calendar. Apart from the essential dates, it bore pictures designed to capture the attention of little children. Sometimes it was a seaside scene, other times a city, a ship, oh, all sorts. At the beginning of each month, Miss Doughty would randomly select one of us to come to the front and talk about the new scene. It was a wonderful exercise for thinking on your feet, and I shall never forget my first turn.

"Well, boys and girls. There is at least one young man who is going to be thrilled at this month's picture. Stephen, would you like to come to the front, and tell us all about it?"

Standing in front of the class, I flipped last month's data over to reveal..... a coloured photograph of a steam locomotive. But not just *any* old locomotive. Just a year or so earlier, the wonderful Stan Laurel and Oliver Hardy had re-opened a stretch of line on the narrow gauge Romney, Hythe, and Dymchurch Railway, in Kent. Their photographs had been all over the press and, from that moment, I positively ached to be taken to see the engines for myself. Miss Doughty allowed me to gaze for longer than she should at No.7 *Typhoon*, green and glistening, standing in Hythe station. Uncle Harry's tutelage came in very handy and I was able to give a full – very full – account of what lay before me. I was mesmerized and, throughout that week, there would be more than one occasion when an "earth to Stephen" call was necessary from my beloved teacher. Hard to think that, as I write, Miss Doughty is probably approaching ninety. If she is still alive – and I hope that she is - and ever reads this….."I love you, miss! I really do."

Those early and affectionate attachments to the Misses Brownsell and Doughty remain a pleasure to recall. But the next teacher waiting in the wings to continue gently shaping my development, I very nearly missed out on. When told that I was to leave the educational bosom of Miss Doughty (sigh), and be allocated to Miss Churchill, I was filled with horror. Miss Churchill was tall and rather austere. I felt sure that tender compassion, on which I thrived, was not going to be available at her hand. I grizzled, moaned, and genuinely felt frightened over the prospect.

"But, she's too tall for me!" was the best reason I could muster for avoiding Miss Churchill.

Given that I was probably not too far above four feet high myself, I could have levied that complaint at any one of the staff. Anyway, it didn't wash, and I'm so glad that it didn't. You see, I had confused Miss Churchill with Miss Humphries, and the former was an entirely different kettle of fish. In fairness, time and experience proved Miss Humphries to be tall but far from austere. She was as fine a teacher and as good a person as any other on that splendid Shaftesbury rota.

But it has to be said that Miss Churchill was something else - akin to your favourite granny. She was probably around fifty, wore her slightly greying hair in a tight bun, was plump, cuddly, and, oh, just so nice. Kindness oozed from every pore and my education flourished under her tutelage. In fact, I stayed in her class for the remainder of my time in the infants, before reaching out to higher things both in terms of academia and altitude on the top floor of the school. During my time with Miss Churchill, I witnessed her kindness give rise to an incident that amuses me still. It *did* happen, I promise you. It did!

As the '40s metamorphosed into the '50s, there was one topic on everyone's lips - Russia's own Bolshoi Ballet Company was visiting these shores. Don't ask me how, but it seemed that every child in the country – let alone the primary of Shaftesbury Road

School - knew they were visiting. Little kids, no more than six or seven years old were uttering the mantra "Bolshoi Ballet in England. Bolshoi Ballet in England." As this was a few years before media saturation, the visit had to be something pretty special to make that sort of impact. We were all snuggled into our class seats when Miss Churchill introduced the topic.

"Now, boys and girls, I wonder if anyone can tell me the name of the famous ballet company who are touring in our country this week? Hands up, please."

Like thirty skyrockets, thirty hands shot into the air, restrained only by being firmly affixed into shoulder sockets. Failing this, some might have disappeared out of the window, never to be seen again.

"Miss! Miss. Oh, miss!"

Frenetic pleading filled the air, every one of us anxious to be the one to answer the simplest question of the week. Miss Churchill was well and truly spoiled for choice.

Now, Raymond Hatton was a chunky little "British bulldog" sort of a boy – someone who I always felt would be one to have on your side in a scrap. Not wishing to be unkind, but Ray was not the brightest lad in the class and, notwithstanding the general "give away" nature of the question, there was really no guarantee that he would have the right answer. Sorry, Ray. Please don't beat me up.

But this time, along with the rest of us, there was Ray, for the first time in our short living memories, adding his voice to the pleading.

"Oh, miss. Please, miss, please."

It fair broke your heart.

Miss Churchill, queen of all she surveyed, rested her compassionate eye on Raymond. This was his moment. Even he couldn't get this one wrong. Her kindness overflowed, and she smiled in his direction. Comes the moment, comes the man, and this was Ray's moment.

"Raymond," she invited. "Would you like to tell us the name of the Russian ballet company touring our country, at this moment?"

The little fellow puffed up his chest, positively fizzing. He was born for this moment.

"Please, miss. It's the Bullshit Ballet!"

A short pause preceded a communal shriek of laughter. Raymond had disappointed no one.

"Bullshit" was pretty powerful stuff in a 1950s primary school classroom, although not necessarily a hanging offence. Poor Raymond just sat there, straight faced and wide-eyed, oblivious as to why his answer had been greeted by such mirth. After all, as far as he was concerned, he was right. But you could see what had happened. Back at chateau Hatton, his dad – all East End and Gor' blimey – had, no doubt, been referring to the Bolshoi in those less than complimentary terms all week.

"Oh, yeah Bleedin; Bullshit Ballet. That's all you 'ear abaht these days!"

Poor Ray had no idea that it was all a send up, and walked straight into it. The incident remains my abiding memory of him as, like a meteor, he flashed across my sky just this once, before disappearing without trace. The kindly Miss Churchill, perhaps, felt much the same.

During those two years of primary education, I can recall just one male teacher - Mr. Ganderton. He was a tall, balding, grey-haired man with a deep, rich voice, somewhat akin to the late, great Kenneth Horne in both appearance and tone. Perhaps he was just a support teacher, coming into school as and when there was a shortage of permanent staff. In that I only ever recall him reading us stories, I guess that may well have been the truth of the matter. He it was who introduced us all to the wonderful Uncle Remus stories. My little heart warmed to the antics of Br'er Rabbit putting it over Br'er Fox, and I was always thrilled when Mr. Ganderton came into class to continue the sagas. For the duration of his lessons, I was transported from the classroom into the world of those marvellous characters. All the way home, I would play them out in my imagination, and couldn't wait for Christmas or a birthday to come around.

"Please, Mum. I'd like any book with Br'er Rabbit in."

I can look back on those stories as an early step in my literary awakening. I enjoyed a vivid imagination, which enabled me to convert my bed into anything from a steam engine to a deep-sea diver's suit. Imaginary conversations were freely scripted and my love of words must surely have been in its embryonic stage – and this from a bloke who never read a serious book from cover to cover after leaving school until he was twenty-three. Honest! Set Mr. Ganderton down as another on the ever-growing list of those to whom I am in debt.

Those primary school years prepared me well for the ensuing four in the junior school. At age seven, boys and girls went their separate ways; girls to the first floor under the redoubtable headmistress, Miss Fettis ; lads to the top floor under the relatively newly-appointed Mr. Level, successor to the recently retired Mr.Hickling. Access to the upper floors was via two stairways and several landings, where prefects were stationed to ensure that we all went up and down in a reasonable and safe manner. Anyone committing the ultimate sin of doing two steps at a time would be "pulled out" by an ever-vigilant monitor. Once he felt you had done your penance and learned your lesson, you would be released, when most of us simply carried on in the same sweet way. From some landings, doors led into spacious rooms, serving in the main as storage areas, although one or two doubled-up as music rooms for violin and 'cello lessons. At the top of the stairs, we entered a hall from which four classrooms were accessed from the area. A further four were squashed away in each corner, and I assume this must have been duplicated on the girl's floor - boys were never allowed to tread such hallowed ground. Funny that. I cannot recall ever seeing a female – scholar or teacher – trespass on the upper floor. Doubtless, the protocol was similarly and strictly applied to the male of the species in Miss Fettis's domain.

The layout of each classroom was pretty standard and, even in 1950, still rather Dickensian. At the front, the obligatory chalkboard and easel, positioned at the side of an imposing wooden desk for the teacher. We kids would have our own wooden desks, set out neatly in rows, with space to accommodate two pupils. The desktops had two holes countersunk into them to contain white inkwells, alongside of which were grooves for us to rest our pens, for we were now about to enter the fray of grown-up writing. Not that the pens helped – cheap and cheerful would best describe them. Most of us, when dipping them in and out of the ink for the first time, positioned our little fingers too close to the nib, and could be counted on to return home with fingers smothered in ink. The four corner classrooms differed from the others in that the desks were sited on four or five wooden tiers, giving the occupants a full and unrestricted view of both chalkboard and teacher. And that was about it. None of your flip charts, overhead projectors, PowerPoint, or suchlike. You were there to be schooled in the "Three Rs," so listen up – and listen up good.

Each day began with the entire school congregating in the hall for morning assembly, presided over by Mr. Level. Prayers, notices, updating of house points (of which more later) and, on Monday mornings only, reports from the captains of the football teams (or cricket in the summer) on the previous Saturday's encounters were trotted out. Frankly, I couldn't have given a carrot about most of it – even the mechanical prayers. Where my attention *was* grabbed, however, was when assembly provided the stage for what was tantamount to "public execution," and the naughtiest of the naughty were brought to the front to receive two generous swipes of the cane across each hand. I hated having to watch it and always looked down at the floor when someone was being walloped. Even when boys that I disliked were taking their well-deserved medicine, I couldn't bear to watch. The process was, of course, designed to be a lesson to all of us and it certainly was for me. But the regularity with which some boys appeared "front of house" suggested that it was not much of a deterrent for them.

It was at this stage of our education, we were introduced to the concept of competition, and what a can of worms that has become. The promulgation of the concept that nobody can fail is rife and making anyone a loser is, simply, not on the political agenda. And what is the price we pay for all of this? By the time that teenage years have arrived, sweat shirts with logos such as "Winning is the only Option" get bandied about, designer gear is essential, and a little lad who lives in Exeter, rather than cheering the Grecians on, is transported off to see Manchester United, or Chelsea. Why? Well, they're winners, and Exeter aren't – yet! Real life isn't, never was, and never will be like that. In the '50s, we were honest about our abilities, who we were, and what we could and couldn't do. It was received wisdom that I would never beat Raymond Faires at boxing ; Ken Sayers would always dribble past me in playground football; Ken Hinds was always going to do better than me when it came to academia. It was no sweat. After all, I was the only kid in the entire school who could recite the numbers and names of all the Southern Railway's "Merchant Navy" locomotives in numerical order – *No.35001 Channel Packet; No.35002 Union Castle : No 35003 Royal Mail; No 35004......* so, what do you think of that? It never bothered me that there were brighter, fitter, and more gifted kids in the school than me. When, on our first day at junior school, we were allocated into "houses" and classes (graded "A" to "D"), nobody, as far as I can recall, was traumatised by being assessed nearer to the bottom of the pile than the top. As it was, I was rated "A" so, perhaps, there is a little bias in my opinion.

In this environment, I learned to love the concept of being in a team, with everyone working together for the common good, and it has stayed with me all of my life. Allocating each child to a "house," created more than just *esprit de corps* - it was a valuable motivational tool for everyone. Throughout the term, house points would be awarded for sporting prowess, academic achievement, or outstanding behaviour, which meant that everyone was in with a chance to contribute something, somewhere along the line. On the other side of the coin, points would be docked for misdemeanours and the announcement of the cumulative scores at Monday morning assembly was an exciting way to start the week. At the end of each term, points would be totted up and a shield awarded to the house accruing the largest number.

There were four "houses" at Shaftesbury, the options being Crusaders (red), Templars (yellow), Foresters (green - surprise,

surprise!), and Vikings (blue). I was deemed worthy enough to become a Templar, which, by common consent and consistent lack of success, was deemed fit only for wimps. Even the colour suggested cowardice and my four-year tenancy contributed little and was rarely noticed. Crusaders it was who usually carried all before them, although Vikings would consistently run them close. Yet regardless of ultimate success or otherwise, there was genuine pride in winning points for your house and I am still waiting to hear a convincing argument that this well-managed competitiveness was not the best way for things to be. Read any Harry Potter novel and you'll see that the concept still has legs.

Although not being in one of the "big two," I was well compensated by my place in the "A" stream, which suggested that I might not be the dumbest kid on the block. Quite how the allocation took place, I am by no means sure for, as time went on, there would be transfers between streams in both directions - but they were the exception rather than the rule. Basically, where you started was usually where you finished.

The new headmaster was a colossus and did a fantastic job with that school. Stocky, smiling Mr. Level looked as though he might have done a few rounds in the boxing ring in an earlier life. He struck me as a man on a mission and nobody was going to prevent him from making Shaftesbury a great school. His enthusiasm and encouragement became, well, bywords for enthusiasm and encouragement. At one of my first assemblies, he proudly announced that he had chosen a motto for the school.

"Quit ye like men," he beamed.

"Quit ye like men?" I wondered.....we *all* wondered. What the hell does that mean? What sort of a motto is that? Mr. Level put us straight....or should that be level? No matter.

"The word "quit," boys, is really an abbreviation of "acquit."

I was none the wiser.

"Acquit yourselves like men," he enlarged. "Acquit....behave. In all things, behave like men."

Got it! Well, I think so. After all, I was only seven and manhood was a threat that I was many years from confronting. But time has passed, and I think it was – and remains – a brilliant motto.

Discipline was never a problem. Most of us acquiesced to a general concept of respect for our elders and betters. Policemen, teachers, neighbours – we wouldn't dare take liberties with any of them. Routine misbehaviour at school would be met with the order, "Hands on heads!" Medium level, and you might be sent from the classroom to "Stand on the Line," the line being the joint between the slabs making up the stone floor of the hall. The risk here was that Mr. Level would come by and want to know the ins and outs of why you were there. Gosh, what cruelty! We dare not go back to those dark days. You had to seriously misbehave to earn either a couple of strokes of the cane, or a smack behind the ear. But it happened and when it did, the job was over and done with. You never went whinging to your mum or dad. As likely as not, you'd only be dealt out another dose for good measure. Human rights didn't come into it – we were too busy behaving ourselves.

The staff taught every subject under the sun - Arithmetic (none of your fancy terminology like numeracy), English, History, Geography, Art, and Music. Talk about Jacks of all trades! But if Mr. Level was to achieve his objectives, he would need some outstanding men and, by heavens, he had at least one. Mr. Ivor Jones was a thin, red-faced Welshman, aged somewhere around his mid to late forties. Immaculately dressed in a dark brown pinstriped suit, he had it all in spades - a warm smile, a very ready wit, and a totally transparent commitment to all those under his care. I am sure that he had a soft spot for me. He always referred to me as "Stevie," which would have sent Mum ballistic. I can hear her now – "His name is Stephen, if you don't mind." But Mr. Jones spoke to all of us kids with that sort of affection and respect, and didn't we love him for it?

Like everything else about him, Ivor Jones's discipline was humorous and effective. He had devised a particular delicacy, which he referred to as "Knuckle Pie," which became part of my staple diet.

It wasn't that I was a naughty boy. There were quite sufficient little herberts in my class far more worthy of a portion than me. My chief misdemeanour was talking in class. No change there, then. In the midst of some lesson or another, I would be holding forth with one of my friends on any subject unrelated to Mr. Jones's lesson when, suddenly, the voice of reality would disturb my lack of concentration.

"Stevie!"

The voice was loud, but never threatening. Mr.Jones reached for his wooden ruler and invited me to join him at the front of the class.

"Come on, Stevie. Come and have a slice of knuckle pie."

"Oh, sir."

Out I would go to Mr.Jones, who would take my right wrist in his hand.

"Clench your fist, Stevie."

Thus done, the ruler would beat a staccato rhythm on my knuckles. On average, it lasted about ten seconds and I seem to recall grinning at Mr. Jones during one helping of pie. I'm sure that he grinned back at me for, in truth, it didn't hurt a bit.

During my four years of primary education, Mr. Jones taught me in all but three of them. One particular day stands out for me when, perhaps for the first time, he recognised a glimmer of potential. With nearly sixty years worth of hindsight, I think that I astonished myself on that red-letter day.

We had been reading poetry. I can't recall the piece, but I do know for sure that it was written by William M. Thackeray. The name at the end of the poem in the poetry book said as much.

"Now, boys," said Mr. Jones. "Twenty house points to whoever can tell me what the "M" stands for in Mr. Thackeray's name."

Twenty points! It was a king's ransom. Usually, we would be talking ten at the most and, more frequently, twos and fives.

Anyone who could come up with the right answer would be a hero for weeks to come. Instantly, arms went up, flapping in the air.
   "Please, sir. Me, sir."
   Mr. Jones decreed that each boy should come forward to whisper their answer, well out of earshot of everyone but him. One by one, they went forward. John Fillery, a studious lad; Bobby Sydes, not the brightest bunny down the warren; John Sarling, another bright boy; Ken Sayers, far more likely to win points on a soccer pitch than in this rarefied atmosphere. Each and every contestant had his answer greeted by Mr. Jones's staccato, "Nope!" During all this, I was reasoning with myself. Surely, it couldn't be an obvious one. Otherwise why was Mr. Jones putting up twenty points? Rule out Malcolm, Mark, Maurice, and Michael for a start. While I was racking my brains for something a little more imaginative, a hand went into the air, and I knew the twenty points were about to be snaffled. Alan Trehearne, by general consent, the brightest boy in the class, was ready for heroism – and Mr. Jones was as confident as the rest of us.
   "Come on then, Alan. Come and whisper the answer."
   Alan strode confidently up to the base and deposited his answer in Mr. Jones's ear. We held our breath.
   "Nope!"
   Nope? Nope!!! The name is so difficult that even Alan Trehearne doesn't know it. What chance was there for us mere mortals? Alan resumed his seat, having disappointed us all.
   The fun had gone on long enough. Mr. Jones was going to emerge triumphant, with the twenty points still in his wallet.
   "Right, boys. I think that's enough. If there are no more guesses, then......."
   "Oh, sir!"
   An urgent, impassioned yell echoed round the classroom and a lone hand shot into the air. Eleventh-hour stuff. Mr. Jones looked out incredulously, eyebrows raised, jaw sagging, over a sea of thirty-eight faces to the owner of the hand.
   "Stevie?"

Steve Derby

His face and voice were a mixture of surprise, shock, and astonishment, in no particular order. Don't ask me where it came from but, in my heart, I knew I had the right answer. I must have read it somewhere and it had lodged itself in the deep recesses of my subconscious, alongside the names and numbers of the "Merchant Navies".....No.35004 Cunard White Star; No.35005 Canadian Pacific; No.35006 Peninsula & Oriental S.N. Co....... What was more, I had a sense that Mr. Jones knew I was going to get the twenty points. Teacher and scholar moved toward their destiny.

Announcing that mine would be positively the last guess, he invited me down to the front. My heart was pounding. I'm right, I'm right, I know I'm right. For the first time in my young life, I was totally certain of imminent triumph. I'd be mentioned in despatches during school assembly. Never before I had I known such a surge of excitement. Mr. Jones smiled. We both so wanted me to be right. As it was the last guess, we dispensed with the formalities of whispering in his ear.

"Right, then, Stevie. Tell us all Thackeray's middle Christian name."

"Please, sir. It's "Makepeace.""

Around the class, there were a few giggles. Makepeace? I ask you? What sort of stupid name is that? Yet, from the sight of the gaping mouths of most of my classmates, I think they knew that I had hit the button. For a second or two, I waited to hear a resounding "Nope!" It never came.

"Stevie, my lad," said Mr. Jones. "For once, instead of covering yourself with mud, you've covered yourself in glory! Twenty points to Templars."

It was a great lesson in motivation and, from that moment on, I craved the sort of praise Mr. Jones heaped upon me. I had been confirmed as not just a trier, but one who might just, every now and again, bring home the bacon. To this day, I haven't a clue where or when I had read that "matey boy" was William Makepeace Thackeray. But it didn't matter. I'd got the twenty points.

74

Yet if we all loved Mr. Jones, there was, stalking the corridors of power, his very antithesis. If Ivor Jones was a Welsh gentleman, I struggle to find grace in recalling his colleague from the valleys. I will refer to him as "Mr. Owen" – not his real name. My first brush with him was unforgettable – in fact, probably everyone's first brush with Mr. Owen was unforgettable.

The previous Christmas, Mum and Dad had bought me a Bonzo Annual. Bonzo – a chubby little dog with a big smile - was the creation of George Studdy and had been on the scene since the 1920s. Never quite made it as big as Mickey Mouse, Donald Duck, etc., but he nevertheless had his fans – Dad amongst them. One title in the annual really caught my imagination – "The Ghost of Grey Gables" – so, when Mr. Jones asked us to compose a story, I did the title the favour of using it for my own work. I can't remember anything about the plot of my little tale, but I do remember Mr. Jones telling me that it was, "a very promising piece of work, Stevie. Very promising." So far, so good, but into my light was to come some darkness.

Every class had what I shall call a natural born "go-fer" – some kid who would ingratiate himself with the teachers by offering to run errands between one class and another. In the case of Class 1A, we were represented by little Derek Fryatt, by general consensus, a bit of a pain in the bum for always trying to feather his nest, but basically harmless. Shortly after my "Ghost of Grey Gables" triumph, our lesson was interrupted by the arrival of a similar specimen from Mr. Owen's class, with a message for Mr. Jones, who was seated at his desk. Little was I to know that the missive involved me.

"Stevie, my lad. Mr.Owen has asked if you will go and see him after playtime."

I froze. How had he got my name? What had I done wrong? Mr. Jones read my body language.

"Perhaps he's going to make you his class captain next term, Stevie."

Yeah! Like as. Humour I didn't need. I dreaded everything that the visit might entail. I would have much preferred that the meeting be replaced with an appointment at the dentist for root canal filling, rather than have any sort of *contretemps* with Mr. Owen. All through playtime, I kept myself to myself. It might have helped had I known what I was being summoned for and the fifteen minute play break passed all too quickly. We lined up in the playground and, class by class, snaked toward the door, up the stairs, and into the assembly hall. While the masses filed into their classrooms, I was left alone outside the door of Mr. Owen's educational emporium where, from behind the green door of the room which housed Class 2A, I could hear him rasping out his orders, his clipped sentences all so precise and reeking of Welsh. I noted him as a dapper man, around forty-ish. His dark hair had just begun to gain some grey flecks around his temple, and spectacles perched on his nose made him appear owl-like and quite formidable. Add all of that to his reputation, and you'll have some idea of my trepidation. I moved toward my Nemesis, and knocked at the door.

"Come in!"

It was like the welcome of a shark inviting you to take a swim in its aquarium. A Welsh shark with a "sing song" accent, at that. I opened the door and walked toward Mr. Owen's desk. The eyes of every kid in that class were trained upon me.

"Yes – and whooo are yoooo?" he sang slowly, accompanied by what I am sure was a totally involuntary sneer.

Cheshire Cat, he was not. He had a voice that I found harsh and unkind.

"Please, sir. I'm Stephen Derby. Mr. Jones told me that I had to come and see you, sir."

"Ah, yes. Derby, isn't it?" the lilting valley accent continued.

Isn't it? 'Course it is – I just told you that. I never had the courage to put my thought into spoken words.

Mr. Owen looked at his class.

"Right, then, boys," he snapped, quickening the pace of his delivery. "You can all carry on reading your books until I have dealt

with........" – another sneer and back to the slow drawl – "......
Mister Derby, here."

As everyone settled down into "hear-a-pin-drop" silence, he
called me over to where he was sitting. On his desk, I could see that
he had my story.

"So, tell me, Mis-ter. Der-by," he said, emphasising the first
syllables. "Tell me, is this all your own work?"

For a brief moment, I thought that he might have seen the
title before, and assumed that I had merely copied the story. Surely
he didn't have the Bonzo Annual, too. There was no way I was going
to tell him anything other than the truth, the whole truth, and nothing
but the truth.

"I saw the title in a book I had for Christmas, sir. I liked it a
lot and when Mr. Jones asked us to write a story, I used it."

Mr. Owen paused, the customary straight line of his mouth
turning up, ever so slightly, at each end. This, I suspected, was as
close to a smile as those tightly pressed lips had ever managed, or
ever would again. I waited for him to say something. When he did,
it was in a softer, yet no less threatening, tone. For a second, I
thought I liked him – but only for a second, mind you.

"Very good, Mister Derby. Very good, indeed. You show a
lot of imagination for such a lit-tle boy."

The syllables were emphasised and, so it seemed to me,
sneered.

"Thank you, sir," was all I could say and, indeed, it was all
that I was expected to say.

"You can go back to Mr. Jones now, Derby."

The formality of "Mr." having been dispensed with, I moved
toward the door. Just before I opened it, he called for my attention.

"I shall look forward to you being in my class next year."

"Yes, sir. Thank you, sir"

Once on the other side of the door, I quaked at the thought of
leaving genial Mr. Jones behind to suffer at the hands of Mr. Owen.
It was an experience I was not yet ready for. Perhaps he was only
pulling my leg and I would be with some other, more mild-mannered
teacher. He wasn't. At the end of July 1951, our class was told that,

next term, we would all masquerade as Form 2A, which had been duly allocated to Mr. Owen. For the first, and probably only time in my school career, I would have willingly swapped the privilege for a place in the "B" stream...or the "C" or "D" for that matter.

Now, you might be expecting me to say that life under the tutelage of Mr. Owen turned out to be nowhere near as bad as I had anticipated. And you would be right. I have to say it – it was a bloody sight worse! I suppose I could forgive him for his "daily mental" exercises. Those sessions were nothing more than having ten mathematical problems regimentally barked out that we were required to solve in our heads. No notes – certainly no calculators - and a pretty short time to get the answers. Starting at the "Add two and two" level, my confidence abounded and I coped quite well. But when we launched out into deeper waters with cube roots, adding four pounds, eleven shillings and three pence farthing to twelve pounds, one shilling and four pence, I couldn't work out the answers, even if my life had depended on it. Daily mental became my nightmare and, sometimes, I prayed that Mr. Owen would forget it. He never did.

One incident, to this day, I can scarcely believe happened. But, I assure you, it did.

Returning to school after a couple of weeks' sickness, I was thrust immediately into a wide selection of tables. My bete noire went around the class choosing, at random, one table or another for a scholar to recite. Poor old Bobby Sydes, from Chester Road, got lumbered with the "nine times table" and his attempts beyond "four times nine is thirty-six" were distinctively slower in forthcoming and, when they did arrive, distinctively wrong. I was filled with anger at the way he was treated. The more he struggled to move up the table ladder, it was clear to all and sundry that he just didn't know the rote. So what did Mr.Owen do? Only smacked him on the back of the legs! And the invective that he applied as he sought to "encourage" Bobby to do better, was positively shameful.

"Come along, "duffer" Sydes."

He spat out the table into poor Bobby's face, staccato and rhythmic – a forerunner to Sir Alex Ferguson's "hair-dryer" treatment, perhaps. It was a lesson in humiliation and one that would have him up in front of the beak in these days. I felt terror on behalf of poor Bobby. Had I been in a different situation, for sure, I would have cried. But perhaps I would have done better to save my tears for another poor miscreant.

"Now, boys. What about the weight tables?"

Here I felt totally secure. Had I been on stage for the nine times table, I would have romped home. Mum and Dad, in addition to leading me through prayers before I went off to sleep, had also seen fit to choose a table at random, for me to recite. As a result, I was fluent in anything up to multiples of twelve. But, having just returned from a couple of weeks' sickness and, as a result, missed the necessary learning input, the weight table was tantamount to speaking in tongues for me. I waited for the announcement of the poor wretch who was going to be put through it and just hoped and prayed that he was going to prove a bit more fluent than Bobby.

"I think Mr. Stephen Derby is the best one to help us here."

What! Was I dreaming? I hadn't the first clue of where to start so, thank God, I had my defence.

"Please, sir. I've been away sick for the last two weeks and I don't know the table."

Pretty reasonable, you would have thought. But not for Mr. Owen - he was having none of it.

"Don't be silly, Mr. Derby. Up you get onto your hind legs and sing for us."

Indeed, a chorus of "Knees up Mother Brown" might well have been more appropriate for, as sure as hell, I was more familiar with that lyric than the wretched weight table. But there I was, left struggling and mumbling. It was clear for all to see that all was not as it should have been.

"Come on, duffer Derby. Let's hear what you have to say."

Adding insult to injury, he began to slap me on the back of my legs - this was in the days of short trousers, you have to remember. Good-natured knuckle pie, it was not.

I have taken care to try and look for the best in all those that I remember but, to a little boy, it was hard not to wonder if Mr. Owen saw some sort of satisfaction in humiliating pupils. I am truly sorry if this is unfair but, certainly, I can find nobody who recalls his classes with anything other than fear. There never was a teacher that I disliked as much and, personally, I can't trace a single benefit that he brought to my education or, as far as I am aware, anybody else's. With the avuncular Mr. Jones and the redoubtable Mr. Level, we were in the educational custody of men with tremendous personality, character, and the gift of encouragement. But, for me, I'm sorry to say that I found Mr. Owen a rotter of the first order and, having survived that year of purgatory, Class 2A were all rewarded with a return to Mr. Jones's fold for the remaining two years of junior school education. Cocooned once more, to the best of my somewhat limited ability, I flourished.

Many years later, I would come across Mr. Owen again. It was the mid-1970s, and my little daughter's headmistress was one, Mrs. Owen. Under her predecessor, the school had suffered from a rather slapdash, liberal approach, which resulted in the whole show all but collapsing until Mrs. Owen - arriving like the cavalry – pulled it round and restored it to its former greatness. One Saturday afternoon, whilst shopping, my wife and I ran into Mrs. Owen. It took me all of a couple of seconds to realise that the man at her side was her husband, none other than the notorious architect of my 1951 misery. The temptation to tell him just what I thought was certainly there, but intervening years had matured me and, by now, he was nothing more than a little guy pushing seventy. I satisfied myself in reminding him of my pleasant recollections of Shaftesbury school, emphasising the wonderful work of Mr. Jones. There was, I am sure, a distinct reticence on his part to discuss the subject in any depth so, at least, he might have had some sense of shame. If only he had been able to boast the tutorial excellence of his good wife.

I need you to keep in mind that I was, basically, a good little boy. I nurtured a passive nature and this, along with a general terror about stepping outside the boundaries of good behaviour, worked well enough to ensure that I was rarely in real trouble. Yet once - just once - I did manage to get the cane. David Ruddock was a little blond-haired tear-away, with a natural penchant for getting into trouble. If ever one was accused of anything untoward, it was a fair bet that, if you said, "It was Ruddock's fault, " you instantly had not just an alibi, but a cast iron defence to go with it. Chances were that it probably was his fault anyway.

On my way home one lunchtime, Brian Lacey, from Elizabeth Road, and I happened to see David, chucking stones at some younger kids. Ever the good Samaritans, Brian and I took the foolhardy step of "suggesting" to Ruddock that he ought to pack it in. The response was instant and, had we been brighter, entirely predictable for, suddenly, the pair of us became subjected to our own personal bombardment from David. Well, what would you do? Brian and I picked up a few convenient missiles and hurled them back at the little herbert.

Just then – doesn't it always happen – round the corner came.....Mr.Level! He'd consistently drummed it into us that there was one school rule that he would not have broken under any circumstances. Guess what? Stone throwing.

"Right, you boys. Report outside my room before the beginning of afternoon lessons."

No further explanation was required or given, as he cycled off toward the Green Man, where Katherine Road bisected Plashet Grove, for a liquid lunch.

"Yes, sir," we chorused, in his wake.

Brian had a lovely nature and was another of several who could get the giggles out of me. He was certainly not best pleased with the sentence just pronounced on him.

"You know, Ruddock. You're a right little twerp. Now we'll all be for the cane."

Ruddock shrugged his shoulders. The cane was stock-in-trade – an occupational hazard - as far as he was concerned.

All through lunch, I was too terrified to tell Mum what had happened. With the benefit of considerable hindsight, I guess she would not have quite exploded – more likely, she would have seen it as an opportunity for encouraging me to take my medicine. Certainly, she would not be marching up to Mr.Level to plead my case. It was an unfortunate shindig but, on the bottom line, I'd been caught throwing stones against Mr.Level's edict, and that was that.

Just before 2'o'clock, Brian, Dave, and I gathered outside the head's office, and heard Mr. Level's heavy, determined step pacing up the stairs. When he came into view, there was a look of mystification on his face?

"Well, what do you boys want?"

Oh, grief! He's forgotten. We needn't have bothered to turn up. But we could hardly say, "Well, we were just passing by and we thought we'd like to say "Good afternoon, sir." Each of us looked at the other, until one fool reminded him.

"We were throwing stones at lunchtime and you asked us to come up and see you, sir."

Brian and Dave looked over at me with looks of utter disbelief. But it was too late. I had prompted Mr.Level's memory cells and he started to look for his black cap and cane.

"Oh, yes. The stone-throwers. Well, you know my rule about stone-throwing."

Certainly did! Brian got a crisp stroke on each hand, which, of course, I couldn't bring myself to watch. Then it was me. Eyes closed, I took my medicine which, strangely enough, wasn't particularly painful. And then, Ruddock. A couple of hearty thwacks that were clearly water off a duck's back to him. Nothing more than another couple of notches on the gun.

Brian, tragically, was later diagnosed with a brain tumour, and he died somewhere around the age of eleven. It was the first time that death had visited one of my contemporaries and I missed him and his sweet nature. We all did. I'm sorry about the cane, but rest well, my old friend.

The school had a policy – as, I guess, did most of them - whereby it was deemed a matter of course that every scholar should be encouraged to take up a musical instrument early on in their junior education. Many opted for the recorder, which, personally, I thought was the easy option. Whatever persuaded me in my choice remains a total mystery. Perhaps, it was just that the offer came from Mr. Jones.

"Would you like to learn the violin, Stevie?"

My response should have been, "Why would I want to do that, then?"

But, again, the good, passive heart, and desire to please was my un-doing. Snatching defeat from the jaws of victory, I managed to say, "yes" when I so clearly meant, "no." From that time on, each Tuesday afternoon, along with Terry Hart, John Fillery, Walter King, and John Cole, I would traipse into the stock room to be taught the fine art of scraping the old cat's innards by Miss Campbell. Miss Campbell was blond, slim, petite, thirty-ish, and despite eyes that bulged ever so slightly, rather pretty. However, one incident caused me to revise that assessment.

General lack of interest in the lessons enabled me to over-exercise the one skill that I had in spades.....talking! On this particular afternoon, Miss Campbell's patience ran dry.

"Right, Stephen. You can pack up your instrument and go back to your class....now!"

Instant sobriety and compliance.

"But why, miss?" I appealed.

"Talking all the time. I'm trying to teach, and all I can hear is your voice chattering away. Leave now, and I'll tell your teacher. I'll write to your parents, too."

Now, that did get me focussed. No matter how I pleaded and cried – yes, cried – Miss Campbell was having none of it. There I was, just a little kid who had hardly committed a hanging offence, for whom the thought of his Mum and Dad reading a letter of complaint was just a bit more than he could take. So, packing my violin into its case, I slouched out of the room like some old hobo taking his guitar to catch the next freight out of town. If I returned to my class as instructed, Mr. Jones would want a full and unexpurgated account of the goings on in the stock room. He would feel let down and I never wanted to do that to him. Much worse, the spectre of that letter hung over me like the Sword of Damocles. What was I to do? Rightly or wrongly, I opted to go straight home. Nanny Clark would let me in whilst Mum was at work, so I concocted some old "cock and bull" story about "coming home because I didn't feel very well." It worked a treat.

Well, Miss Campbell never did write that letter. Neither did she report me to Mr. Jones. God was back in His heaven and all was well, except for the fact that, more than ever, the violin and I treated each other with suspicion. It had the better of me and we both knew it. Despite persevering for more years than I should have done, if I were to have any sort of passion for music, I would have to find another instrument. The time would come when I did just that. But I never forgot Miss Campbell's treatment of me, her unwillingness to forgive, which resulted in nurturing the seeds that would ultimately turn me off the instrument completely.

Granted, my musical progress was severely hampered by an unwillingness to practise. The little "half size" violin never saw the light of day from one Tuesday to the next. I did manage a couple of scales, came to terms with the key of "C" having no sharps or flats, whilst its relative - the key of "D" - had four of the blessed things, but that was about it. Mr. Jones did his best. No mean player himself, he would, every so often, haul me out in front of the class to play a couple of fiddle duets. It was an excruciating experience for me, exceeded only by that of those who had to listen.

But Mr. Jones remained undeterred. Unaware of the incident with Miss Campbell and having found what he perceived as some sort of a protégé, he continued to do "violins at three paces" with me. On Friday afternoons, when we were allowed to either draw or take comic books to read, Brian Lacey always brought along a generous selection from his well-stocked library of American comics. Good soul that he was, he lent them out to all and sundry. But while all this was going on, there was Mr. Jones taking full advantage of the opportunity to put me through my unwilling paces with the damned fiddle. He must surely have known that I had neither talent nor inclination and that I was far more interested in what Captain Marvel might be up to.

Now, when it came to matters of physical exertion in those early years, generally, it was another area where I was neither gifted nor inclined. However, the school went to great lengths to teach us to swim, and this I found far more to my liking. Each Tuesday morning, a single decker, green bus arrived to ferry us to the East Ham Municipal Baths, alongside the Town Hall. The building housed two pools dubbed, rather obviously and boringly, as "major" and "minor." As under-10s, we were conscripted to the minor version, which was probably just as well. On my first visit, the bus parked in Nelson Road, and we alighted to queue up outside the double door entrance. The initial whiff of chlorine in the air became more powerful when we entered the baths proper. The pool was no more than twenty-five yards (in old money) long but, to me, it might as well have been twenty-five miles, and as we walked alongside the deep end, I sensed a little trepidation. After all, if I were to fall in, just under seven feet of water was there to either welcome or drown me. Non-swimmer as I was, it wasn't difficult to see which way the wind would blow. Consequently, I much favoured the use of a changing cubicle nearer to the shallow end, where a depth of three feet would, at least, give me a fighting chance, should I plop in. Diving platforms were situated at the deep end – I guess the highest might have been somewhere around ten feet, the lowest three feet, and the third somewhere inbetween. Can you imagine the health and safety militia allowing a dive from ten feet into seven feet of water today? Neither can I – but kids did it and, to the best of my knowledge, never came to harm.

Stripped down to our swimming trunks, we lined up alongside the water's edge to be greeted by our instructor, Mr. Aplin. He carried a military bearing, with smart grey hair combed back neatly. His voice rang with authority and I will never forget his initial introduction, rasped out with military precision, befitting his bearing.

"Now then you boys, we have just four weeks in which to learn to swim."

Four weeks? Blimey! One or two of our number had already mastered the art but, for the life of me, I really couldn't imagine myself reaching that standard in just four short weeks. But Mr. Aplin was nothing if not determined. He taught us how to sit on the side of the pool and slip into the water without going below the Plimsoll Line. Then, a build-up of confidence to put one's head underneath the water - I know adults who are still twitchy about doing that but, personally, I found it easy. Exercises where we held on to the pool bars and allowed our legs to float up behind us helped the rehearsal of leg movements, whilst squatting in the water with our chins on the surface helped us get the arm movement right. Technically, it was all very sound but, after a couple of weeks, I felt no nearer to being able to swim. I lived only for the moment when Mr. Aplin announced "play time," the length of which would vary, dependent upon how successfully we had carried out our exercises. Whilst those who could swim were allowed to demonstrate their prowess in the deep end, the rest of us generally mucked about, splashing each other and pushing over all and sundry. It was great fun and certainly guaranteed that I would grow up with no fear of water.

I never did understand why "first-timers" were schooled in the breast stroke. To be honest, I found it difficult to master and when I ultimately achieved buoyancy, it was through the infinitely simpler dog paddle. Once I found that I could keep off the bottom of the pool, my confidence grew and, with it, proficiency in not just the dog paddle, but also the breast stroke, and the front and back crawl. Perhaps I mis-heard Mr. Aplin's forecast of four weeks because it took me all of four *years* to learn to swim.

Dad, bless him, had a try at weaning me off trains and injecting something a little more rigorous into my repertoire. He loved boxing partly, I suspect, because one of his workmates, Harry Bevan, had a couple of boys who showed a very early talent for the sport. Not that he thought that I would prove to turn out to be a challenger to the Bevan boys but at least, he must have reasoned, it could give me enough nous to deal with anyone who tried to bully me. Alongside East Ham Police Station, in High Street South, a prefabricated building played host to the East Ham Boys Boxing Club and, without a by your leave, Dad signed me into the organisation, along with Derek, and my school friend Alan Self.

The building was a bit ramshackle to say the least. Members waited outside in all weathers until the doors opened at around 6'o'clock, when we would make our way into the cubicles to change into vests, short, and plimsolls. One or two of our fellows had managed to get themselves a pucker pair of boxing boots, and really looked the bee's knees but Del, Alan, and I had to settle for the basics. As with Mr. Aplin, the leader of the band was a real committed enthusiast.

Mr. Craddock was a policeman, with sharp features and a billiard ball head – a total hair-free zone. Undoubtedly a fighter, he was in remarkable physical condition and woe betide any criminal coming into contact with him, I thought. He rasped rather than spoke. Our first routine was skipping, designed to increase the pulse and generally loosen us all up for frays yet to come. Now this, you must understand, was not the skipping that I would see the girls occupying themselves with in Walpole Road. No, this was concentrated, rhythmic pounding on a wooden floor at a goodly pace. The sound of several feet stamping out the beat, punctuated by the slap – slap – slap of the rope against the floor, was inspirational and I loved making my nine-year old contribution. Each skipping session would last for about two minutes and as the final seconds ticked away, Mr. Craddock would bellow out, "Twenty seconds to go." This was the signal for us all to redouble our efforts and go for broke. As we went as fast as we could, Mr. Craddock pushed the pace.

"Bangy, bangy, bangy, bangy, bangy," he rapped out, in time with the sound of our tired little feet hitting the deck.

After fifteen minutes of this ritual, we were ready to move on to the heavy punch bags, which were suspended from the girders that ran across the hall. Safe in the knowledge that punch bags never hit back, we ducked, weaved, and generally danced around, smacking the bag with a salvo of punches, confident that, had our opponent been human, he would have been laid out good and proper.

If there were more boys than bags, then a spot of shadow boxing never went amiss, where safety was further guaranteed by the unlikelihood of the shadow ever hitting back. Derek, Alan, and I danced around like demented fairies, swiping out at will, convinced of our invincibility.

Then, finally, we faced the greatest challenge of all. The hall contained a small boxing ring, elevated slightly above ground level. Each boy would be required to climb up and don the gloves for just three minutes of punch up with one of his compatriots. Here it was that one's mettle was truly tested, because you might be matched with some lad who really knew what he was doing. I usually managed to avoid that scenario and my matches were always with either Alan or Derek. Alan was even less inclined to violence than me and I usually managed to give him a thumping. Derek, however, was a tad more crafty, although I always felt that our skirmishes finished honours even.

With all of this experience behind me, I was somewhat pleased to hear that, back at school, Mr. Level had decided that a bit of boxing wouldn't go amiss for the older boys in school. I reasoned that I would have a head start, and so it proved. Devoid of the apparatus available at the boxing club, we were restricted to skipping and shadow boxing and, without wishing to boast, I looked a class act in both disciplines. So much so that, at one session Mr. Level, called a halt to proceedings.

"Boys, I want you to watch this young man," he said, moving toward me. "He has got it absolutely right. Go on, Derby, show them how it's done."

And off I went, prancing around my imaginary opponent, tapping him a playful one on the conk, before bursting into action with a volley of vicious uppercuts that threatened to see my arms removed from their sockets. Mr. Level congratulated me again. My schoolmates offered polite applause. No one would want to face me in this form – this kid can really box. So, when it came to the serious business of putting on the gloves and getting down to three minutes-worth of the real stuff, the players to avoid were my goodself and

Raymond Faires, who really was a good fighter, despite his lack of inches. The draw matched me with Roger Coe, a stocky lad, who lived in Elizabeth Road, and seemed completely blasé about the whole business.

Roger took just over a minute to sort me out. Initially, I kept a respectful distance until a point arrived at which I must have had a leakage of common sense. Folly persuaded me to move within his range, which heralded a thundering great swing from his right hand, prior to a peach of a punch landing right in the middle of my face. There and then, I wanted to withdraw from the whole rotten show. But there was yet more to endure. Roger punched me at will – first to the right ear, then to the left. Then the right eye and, to maintain a policy of equality, the left. By the time that he found my hooter with a straight left, I was in tears, and wanted nothing more than to go home to Mum.

Mr. Level, mercifully, stopped proceedings before further damage could be done. My long term assessment of any future involvement with boxing was.....sod that! And I did.

I make no excuse for confessing that, by the time 1953 rolled around, I was already burning to reach East Ham Grammar School for Boys for the next step of my education. My cousin Fred had prospered there, so why shouldn't I? One spring evening, when Derek and I, along with a few friends, were sat together on the wall outside his house, an appalling piece of gossip was being circulated, so outrageous that, for many, it was considered as "probably unlikely." The word was out that some kid at Sandringham Secondary Modern, had actually told one of the teachers to "bugger off!" Commonplace – and worse – is the order of these modern educational times but, in 1953, it was tantamount to revolution, blasphemy - or both. Oh, Lord. If I were to end up at a school where such things happened, how would I survive? I was the kid who couldn't bear watching someone get the cane in front of the whole school, so what would become of me in a place where teachers were sworn at? It would be so contrary to my nature as to be hell on earth. I *had* to get a grammar school place – I just had to – and, there and then, I committed myself to such hard work over the next year as would ensure that, when the eleven-plus examinations came around in Spring 1954, I would win a coveted place at East Ham Grammar.

It is not my intention to discuss the merits, or otherwise, of the eleven-plus as a means to decide what was perceived to be the most appropriate secondary education for each and every eleven-year old. Detractors will tell you that the examination was tantamount to "separating the sheep from the goats," that it was disgraceful, and unfair. Every child, it was argued, had the right to the very best education available, so why this wicked, divisive examination? The creation of "second-class citizens" at such an early age could not possibly be right. Yet I am sure that to have put some of those lads of the Shaftesbury "C" and "D" streams into an arena where they would be doing battle with French or Latin would, in many cases, have been a very real and unpleasant struggle, and entirely against their natural inclination. The secondary modern late developer could be transferred to the grammar school if it became clear that his – or her - potential, ambition, and inclination began to lean toward a different curriculum. Should a struggling grammar school scholar opt to move in the opposite direction, then that too, could be arranged. For the life of me, I really can't recall any scars being worn by either camp. No correspondence will be entered into on this subject, dear reader!

So, for me, everything began to focus on May 1954. When the week of the examination arrived, the ordeal proved nowhere near as fearful an experience as I thought it might be. Everything happened in the familiarity of our classrooms and with the tests spread over five days, I arrived in my class on the first day as focussed as any eleven-year-old had reason to be. Knowledge and ability in each subject was about to be ascertained through straightforward enough questions on arithmetic, history, geography, and general knowledge. English gave me licence to produce one of my essays and at the end of the session, I felt very confident that I had come up with something sufficiently fluent to catch the examiner's eye. My reasoning was that, if I didn't do too well on the sums, literacy would compensate and come to my rescue. By the end of the week, the show was over and there was nothing to do but wait for the results.

There were three possible outcomes. Firstly, for those at the top of the marking stratosphere, there was no doubt about it. You would pass "Go," collect £200, and tell mum and dad to start counting the pennies – pounds – necessary to kit you out in East Ham Grammar togs at Fosters, in High Street North. On the other hand, should you be at the other end of matters, it was a case of "Good night. God bless, and the very best of luck at whichever secondary modern school was most convenient for you." But there was a third scenario – a "re-sit" - which smacked of, "Can't quite make up our minds about you." It did, however, provide the comfort that you had been close, weren't entirely out of the frame, and there was an opportunity for another shot at goal. Surely, I'd get into that group...at least? When Mr. Jones came into class a month or so later with a piece of paper in his hand and a smile on his face, I was all optimism. It was rather like waiting for the lottery results to be announced.....surely, this week, it is my turn!

Well, the results didn't quite match my optimism, for just three of our number had made it first time. It might have been four, but Alan Trehearne had left the school a year or so prior to the examinations. Doubtless, wherever he was, he'd be doing fine. To the total astonishment of us all, Ken Hinds, who was becoming an ever-closer friend and *was* bright, didn't get into the final. Like the majority of us – me included - he would have to settle for a re-sit at which the whole jolly dance would be waltzed again. But, at least, I was still in there fighting.

The format of the re-sit was identical to first time around and, on completion of this "try again," I had a strong sense that I had done rather better. This was confirmed when the results arrived for me to find that I faced just one more hurdle before achieving my objective. I was definitely bound for a grammar school, but which one? That was the question and the longed for place at East Ham Grammar might not yet be mine to cherish. I could finish at Parmenters, Coopers, or Raynes Park - all of them fine schools, no doubt. Yet I wanted East Ham so badly that consolation prizes were not on my agenda. In order to determine our ultimate destination, those of us finding ourselves in this educational limbo were required to attend "an interview."

The process entailed each boy having a face-to-face with the redoubtable headmaster of East Ham Grammar, Dr. J. L. Whiteley. From these, "Joe" would select those he perceived as most likely to benefit from education at his school - and it truly was "his" school. He had a reputation and was immensely proud and protective of the record of the school – and rightly so. Several young men of quality, having received their secondary education under his leadership, went on to make their mark in sport, politics, and the academic world. On the law of averages, a few would slip through the net but, by and large, the school's record up until the time when the rules were "comprehensively" changed stood alongside the very best. Parents were invited to the interview and, years after, I twigged that "Joe" was giving them the once-over every bit as much as his potential intake.

Leading up to the interview, Dad was constantly haranguing me to, "speak properly" – whatever the hell that meant.

"Say, "do not" instead of "don't"."Will not" instead of "won't".

It was as cumbersome to say as I find it cumbersome to write. Yet if that was going to get me my place, then that was the way it was going to be.

Back in 1952, the school had been situated next to East Ham Town Hall alongside the cavernous Methodist Central Hall. Fit to bust, a new site was essential and duly procured at Langdon Crescent, where three modern schools were built - Burges Manor Secondary Modern for Girls; Thomas Lethaby Secondary Modern for Boys and, the Grammar School taking up the available space. All three provided facilities that were quite magnificent. Football and rugby pitches, tennis courts, running tracks, long and high jump pits, along with internal gymnasiums, complete with wall bars, vaulting horses, climbing ropes, and all the trimmings. Workshops for both wood and metal craft, and we haven't even started talking about the academic facilities. Tarmac paths ran between well-manicured lawns throughout the site and, dominating everything, stood a tall clock tower, with distinctive white markers, denoting five-minute segments of the hour. At night, these lit up in red and could be seen for miles around. At the foot of the clock tower, a two-storey building housed the library on the upper floor, and the school dining room on the lower. It was here in the latter - a rather unlikely setting - that the interviews were set to take place.

My interview was set for early evening, and a route 689 trolley bus took us from Plashet Grove to East Ham Town Hall, from where a ten-minute walk down Nelson Road and through Sussex Road brought us to the entrance gates. The short walk straight ahead took us to the dining hall. There we were directed by a sixth former to a table where other anxious parents and offspring were awaiting their turn. At the far end, Dr. Whiteley and another colleague were in action. Unlike a couple of my contemporaries, I was very excited about the whole process. Having improved on my initial 11-Plus shot, from somewhere deep down, I had a sense that I was going to make it. I was on a roll. What's more, I hadn't said, "don't" or "won't" for all of a week!

Dr. Whiteley was a Lancastrian, who had earned a distinction in languages during his sojourn at Manchester University. He was the joint author of a textbook for Latin students, which had become standard fare for scholars taking the subject - a nice little earner, some might say. If rumour were to be relied on, he had no sense of humour, was a stickler for the rules, and you crossed him at your peril. Whatever, Dr. Joseph L. Whiteley had that indefinable quality - "presence." His dress was always immaculate and sober, in keeping with what one would expect of a distinguished head master. His dark, wavy, and neatly combed hair had begun to be liberally streaked with grey, which added to his aura. A small neat moustache and light-framed spectacles topped him off nicely. Along with all but a couple of his colleagues, he wore an academic gown, which was something entirely new to me – I'd only seen them in "Tom Brown's Schooldays." It all reinforced the belief and reality that I was coming to a very special school indeed. I didn't need to be sold on that concept. Dr. Whiteley was perfectly well equipped to take charge of 600 pupils and a teaching staff of around forty.

Either the interviews themselves were brief, or the excitement of it all made the time pass that much more quickly. Watching other lads take their turn just seemed to fire me up even more about going through my paces. When it came to Mum and Dad escorting me to the table, I was busting to put on a show.

Names and a few details were taken down, and administrative details checked, before Doctor Whiteley spelled out what would be expected of any boy gaining a place in his school. Integrity, willingness to work hard, ready to be part of the school society......oh, yes please. It was all going to plan so far. Now for the fast balls. The Doctor asked me about my interests, what my best subjects were, and why it was that I wanted to go to the school.

"I like steam engines, sir. And I always enjoy English. I think I can write some very good essays. And I just want to come to this school so badly, sir."

And that was about it. Dr.Whiteley explained to Mum and Dad the commitment that all three of us would have to show to my education and totted up the financial investment for books, uniform, and mathematical equipment. We all nodded.

"You will be advised of the result in the next ten days. Thank you very much for coming."

He shook hands with Mum and Dad, and glanced down at me.

"Well done, young man," was all he said.

Rightly or wrongly, I took that as a portent for the outcome. Perhaps my "wanting to come to the school so badly" had scored me Brownie points. Perhaps he could see that that was no orchestrated answer and had come straight from the heart. Now it would be a case of waiting for the next ten days to pass.

Mum and Dad had booked our annual holiday at Leysdown Holiday Camp, on the Isle of Sheppey. If you want to know what that was like, fish out an episode of "Hi-Di-Hi!" for a perfect reflection of what holidays could be like before we all decided that we ought to have a bit of sun to go with it, and opted to fly off to the

Costa whatever. One morning, as all of us "campers" congregated in the dining hall for breakfast, Arthur - a very popular entertainments organiser - came to the microphone to outline the events planned for the day, as was his wont. He had with him a small wrapped parcel, from which I assumed that it was someone's birthday. It happened all the time.

Having completed his routine, before vacating the stage, Arthur had just one more message.

"Now then everyone. It's very special day for one young man. Would Stephen Derby, on Table 14, like to come up and join me?"

My jaw dropped. Perhaps the parcel was for me. But what for? Nervously, I made my way to the front and stood along Arthur.

"Stephen," he said. "I'm delighted to tell you and everyone here that your mum and dad have received this letter."

He unfolded it and held it up to the public gaze.

"It reads, "I am delighted to tell you that your son Stephen has been selected to begin next term at.....East Ham Grammar School for Boys.""

I don't remember much else. He handed me the parcel, which was a gift from Mum and Dad - a fountain pen that saw me through the rest of my education *and* my early working days. It was nice, but excitement got the better of me. All that mattered was....I was in! There was a round of applause as my parents looked on at the simultaneously elated and embarrassed me, with eyes full of pride and love. Up to that date, no experience had given me so much joy, and I walked back to my cornflakes. Well-wishers and strangers patted me on the back.

"Well done, son."

"Best of luck, boy."

It was magical and, for the rest of that day only, I was a minor celebrity.

Mr. Jones was, of course, delighted for all of us who had made the grade at the second time of asking. Alan Self, Stuart Knock, Bobby Garn, Ken Hinds, Gerry Benjamin, John Fillery, and Ron Wyatt, were the boys that I recall moving on to East Ham

Grammar. When the time came, in July 1954, to leave Shaftesbury behind and, along with it, the splendid Mr. Jones, it was always going to be an emotional wrench.

"Now, Stevie," he counselled and empathised. "Concentrate on the job in hand….not too much talking, and you'll do splendidly."

"Yes, sir. I'll try. I really will."

He nodded. He knew that I would give it my best shot and, at the end of July, I left the comfort of Shaftesbury Road for the last time before taking up the challenge of East Ham Grammar. I recall it being an emotional parting and scribbled out a little poem that reflected the value I placed on the years I spent at Shaftesbury. Mum and Dad suggested that I sent it to a magazine with a view to it going into print. I did – it didn't!

Some months after joining the grammar, I followed the tradition whereby old scholars returned to Shaftesbury to see former teachers and update them on progress so far. So it was that, in November, the pleasantly rotund Ron Wyatt and I reported back to Mr. Jones, resplendent in our grammar school uniforms. He greeted us in silence as we walked into his class. Without a word, he turned toward me, raised his eyebrows, and lifted his hand to shoulder height, indicating that I had grown since he last saw me. He made a friendly scowl at Ron, spreading his arms wide to indicate that Ron had put on a few more pounds since leaving Shaftesbury. We all laughed. I never saw him again after that return visit and that was a bad mistake that I deeply regret. By now, he is probably long since dead. Yet if there is some way that he is looking over my shoulder from a celestial armchair, fiddle at rest, and a slice of knuckle pie at his side, baked to perfection with just me in mind, I just want to say, "Thank you, sir. You were brilliant and I owe you so much."

So, by the time I reached the age of eleven, I felt that I wasn't doing too badly at all. Who can say? Perhaps I was a few steps ahead of where anyone had expected me to be at that stage. Life at Shaftesbury School had been a wonderful journey, the tyrannies of Mr. Owen being the only blot on the landscape – and they soon passed. Ivor Jones had been the hero of the show, but the fact that I recall the Misses Brownsell, Doughty, and Churchill with such respect and affection surely tells me that solid ground work had been done for him to build on.

Wasn't I a lucky kid to have had such a fabulous first school?

CHAPTER FOUR

PLAYING IN THE STREET

*I want to take my leave for a moment from the serious matter
of education in order to indulge in a little nonsense. A little?
Probably an oversize portion.*

*There was greenery available to us Walpole Road kids at
Plashet Park, where we could avail ourselves of swings and enough
open space to enjoy football, cricket, or athletics. The trouble was
that it was a ten-minute walk away and, of course, another ten
minutes back again. Who wants to walk for the better part of half-
an-hour when that time could be invested in what was far more
convenient and, it has to be said, more fun? Our playground was the
street where we lived.*

*I have "dined out" more times than I could possibly count
on incidents and accidents from my childhood play. I have sprinkled
and spiced this narrative with recollections that made me laugh and,
I hope, will make you laugh and help you recall similar riots of your
own. I swear to you that they really did happen exactly as I have
written them.*

*So, before senility robs me of their memory some way along
the road, I want to share them with you here. Del Fletcher and a
supporting cast are waiting in the tunnel, ready to trot out onto the
pitch and orchestrate their own brand of mayhem.*

I suppose it must have been when we reached the age of six,
or thereabouts, that parents were prepared to let their offspring meet
out of doors with other boys and girls in Walpole Road. The age of
the motorcar was still a good five years or so away and,
consequently, there was hardly a motor vehicle parked down the
street. Granted, Mr. Watts parked his oil tanker outside No. 26 next
to the eel yard but, apart from that, traffic down Walpole Road was
confined to the very occasional motorcar, the slightly more frequent
push bike, the United Dairies milk float (horse-drawn), and the rag-

and-bone man. We had all been taught the rudiments of road safety through visits to our school from Safety Sam, a character dreamed up by the local police, who would regularly visit schools and enact scenarios designed to impress upon us the need for vigilance when crossing the road. In Walpole Road, such expertise was hardly needed ; the roads were open spaces where we could play in comparative safety.

Once allowed the freedom of my erstwhile-cocooned existence, I moved out to explore and encounter the whole range of personalities and characters who lived down Walpole. Firstly, there were those of a more genteel nature - lovely people who lived their lives peaceably and encouraged their kids to do much the same. Into this bracket came the Eatons, at No. 1, who were charming. Their son, Albert, was a pleasant little boy who, at a very early age, underwent some serious surgery on one of his legs. It was the first time that I ever saw a scar of significant proportion, and I sympathised with the guy. I have never wanted anybody to suffer. The family moved away shortly after this, which was a shame for I have a feeling that the pair of us would have ended up good friends.

Lynda Tring, at No.4, was a polite, quiet little girl, and always friendly. I suspect that, as the years passed, she would like to have kicked over some traces but, perhaps, her mum and dad took one look at Derek and decided, "Not for you, young lady." In addition to her cousin John's family sharing the house (as we did with the Polyblanks), Lynda was related to Mrs. Wright, who lived further up the street, which served as further evidence as to why the community spirit in Walpole was so strong. If the people who lived there hadn't gone to school together, well, blow me down, the chances were that they were related. Doreen Steele, at No.6, had already made her mark with me, whilst John Theobald, at No.16, was another quiet lad who moved on before I really began to know him.

At the St. Stephens Road end of the street, lived pretty Connie Hanson and her brother Rick (who was both deaf and dumb), and a year or two older than me. Eileen Filer - also very pretty - was well versed in calling a spade a spade. I'm sure she didn't think much of me. Granted that my front teeth protruded slightly and I loved trains, but I don't think I deserved to be tagged as, "that goofy little sod who watches puffer trains." Although Trevor Sealey was not strictly Walpole Road material - his official address being St. Stephens Road - nevertheless, he tagged on to us and we willingly accepted him. Strangely, I recall something of a divide between this little group and those situated at my end of the street. Everything seemed to change once you ventured into the territory beyond Gricks' eel yard. Although the two groups did mix and play with each other, I always felt a deeper intensity amongst those pitched around the lower numbers of Walpole.

You will not be surprised to learn that the leader of this particular band was Derek, but even he needed some foot soldiers. Like the trip to Widdicombe Fayre, he was accompanied by Dickie Culver, Terry Young, Alan Scarlett, Georgie Brewerton, John Round, and old Dickie Collins an' all…. and old Dickie Collins an' all. Various brothers and sisters came into the frame and, in their own unique way, provided me with companionship and laughter, with a bit of fear thrown in here and there. As friends and neighbours, they were a hard act to beat.

Kids today grow up with sophisticated play stations, I-Pods, mobiles, and such like, that I have yet to understand. In 1950, these gadgets were not even dreams on the drawing board and we made do with much simpler fare to pass our time. Thank God, say I, when I see my grandchildren hunched over a computer keyboard, or immersed in some piece of kit encouraging them to beat their previous score. Amusement in Walpole Road was very much home-made, spawned from vivid imaginations – simple things beyond the capabilities of nobody.

The age of the cigarette card was all but over. For years, cigarette manufacturers had included a picture card with their wares, depicting monarchs of England, sportsmen and women, coats of arms, forms of transport, and goodness knows what else. They were issued in series and although the main thrust of the marketing moment had virtually passed, in the '50s, there were still enough of the things around to collect. Each of us would have our own sets and compete with one another with a view to increasing personal stock.

The rules were simple enough. Each player would hold a card between first and second fingers, and flick it as far forward as possible. The card that went the furthest would entitle its owner to claim the card(s) of the vanquished. Subject to pre-match consent by all parties, you could play "no keeps," which allowed everyone to hold on to their cards, even in defeat. But "keeps" was just what it said, and the dividing line was akin to that between professionalism and amateurism. I always played "no keeps."

Marbles provided a further opportunity for those not wishing to exert themselves beyond any reasonable limit. Just like cigarette cards, virtually every kid down the street had a collection of round, glass marbles of varying shapes, sizes, and colours. These could be bought in local shops and battles would commence in the gutters of the street. The first player would bowl his or her marble along the gutter, leaving the second player to bowl and try to hit his opponent's marble. Success meant that you would be entitled to collect both your own and your opponents marble. A miss, however, meant that it was the first player's turn to try and hit your marble and, if successful, they took the thing into their own collection. It could all get a bit complicated when more than two combatants were involved in the fray. Arguments would break out about whose turn it was, which marble belonged to whom, and whether or not so-and-so had had one go more than everyone else. At this point, most players lost the will to live and the game gave up the ghost. Another area where I deemed it best to play "no keeps."

The simple game that I enjoyed most was "Five Stones," or "Gobs." How on earth it attracted the latter name, I have never been able to fathom – nor has anyone else, as far as I am aware. All you needed to play was five small square stones. The trick was to throw the five stones into the air with one hand and try to catch as many as possible on the back of the same hand. Stones thus caught were then thrown up again from the back of the hand for as many as possible to be secured in the palm of the same hand. If no stones ended up being caught, the turn passed on to the next player. However, if at least one stone was caught, the dropped items were collected up through a varied range of techniques, such as throwing one stone in the air,

101

picking up the stray, and catching the original before it dropped to earth. You'd repeat the dose until all of the stones were back in your possession.

As we became more skilled in the game, further permutations and challenges were there to be mastered. For instance, clapping hands before doing the pick up or, perhaps, slapping both knees. Variations were numerous and I always enjoyed doing as many of them as possible, before coming to a grinding halt when failing to pick up the required stones. Many of the girls were quite brilliant at this little game. Perhaps they were being subconsciously schooled to believe that the female was far better equipped than the male to do more than one thing at once, a conviction that they would carry with them into adult years. It was simple fun and a useful lesson in co-ordination.

All calm on the western front so far but, inevitably, the moment would come – and quite quickly at that – when we looked for something a tad more robust. "High Jimmy Knacker" met that very requirement and invariably ended in both laughter and/or tears. Here's how it went. One kid would be elected to stand with his – or her – back to a wall. In front of this sentinel, a chain of perhaps four kids would make an extended "back" by bending over leapfrog style, with head resting against the backside of the kid in front. Once this construction was safely (?) in place, the first "contestant" would run from the opposite side of the road to leap as far forward onto the extended "back" as possible, carefully avoiding head butting the poor soul with their back to the wall! And so the process would continue. The objective was for every contestant to land safely on the backs and for the whole edifice to remain standing, while everyone sang out a piece of doggerel, "High Jimmy Knacker, 1,2, 3," to the tune of "London Bridge is Falling Down." Of course, it was rarely achieved before the whole mass came tumbling down. We would end up in heaps, laughing at the sheer fun of it all. Those less fortunate and at the bottom of the collapsed pile, would grizzle and go off to their mums for consolation.

"Tin Can Copper" required nothing more technical than a tin can. Players met in the middle of the road – remember, this was long before the time when every household had a motor car parked outside - and someone would be chosen to be the "chaser." One of the boys – invariably a boy, because, although it had been proven that girls could do more than one thing at a time, blokes could throw further – would hurl the can down the street for the "chaser" to retrieve as quickly as possible, and return to base. While this was going on, everyone else scarpered to find a suitable hiding place, more often than not in someone's front garden. On return to base camp, the "chaser" would have to "spot" each competitor. If you were "spotted" – "Derby in Mrs. Scarlett's front garden!" - you had to own up and come out of hiding. Apart from a few whinges and appeals, it always worked that way. It was a matter of honour.

The girls joined in with all of this, but they had their own games that macho seven-year old males wouldn't touch with a bargepole. Skipping, for example, although I think most boys secretly admired the ingenuity and skill of the girls. Conventional solo stuff was no big deal. Neither was skipping backwards and, despite a singular lack of grace, even I managed to master both disciplines. But when it came to the more complex manoeuvres, I was lost along the wayside. Most impressive was when a long rope was stretched across the street and twirled around by two girls, one at each end. This in itself was no mean feat. Then, one by one, others would join in the skip so that, by the time the game reached its zenith, there could be as many as eight girls - all skipping in unison. Songs would accompany this exercise and, at an agreed word, every girl would jump and face the other way, with no interruption to the skipping rhythm whatsoever.

All in together girls
Never mind the weather girls
When I count to six
We all do the splits.

It was amazing stuff, like some precursor to line-dancing. From memory, the poor soul whose ankle, elbow, bum, or anything else that got in the way and stopped the rope was never maligned, although there was a very distinct sense that the offender had let the side down.

But there was one game that I loved best of all, 'though it truly filled me with terror – perhaps that was why I loved it. After all, it involved doing something naughty and, as I have said, I was a good little boy who, by and large, didn't do "naughty." "Knock Down Ginger," involved knocking at some poor soul's door and running away to hide. Out would come the occupant, look up and down the road, before coming to the realisation that they had been had.

Derek was constantly badgering me to, "Go and knock at old Muvver Finch's."

As you might well imagine, I didn't have the guts to knock at anyone's door, much less that of the redoubtable Mrs. Finch. She must have been around seventy at the time and was an East End woman, typical of many. Carrying more weight than was probably good for her, she was rarely seen without an apron protecting her frontage. What made her particularly fearful to me was that she had a few teeth missing and could be quite terrifying if she lost her rag – or smiled.

Mrs. Finch had a cat called, descriptively enough, "Fluff." Each evening, she would come to her door and call down the street for the moggie to return for the night.

"Fluff, Fluff, Fluff, Fluff, Fluff," she would holler with, probably, several more "Fluffs," thrown in for good measure, all spat out with the speed and rhythm of a machine gun. It usually did the trick and got her feline companion in. Derek could mimic this effect to perfection.

One day, fed up with my unwillingness to knock at her door, he performed the deed himself, the pair of us running into hiding behind the wall of Mrs. Young's house – directly opposite Mrs. Finch's. Out she came to answer the "phantom knocker." Looking up and down the street and seeing no one, she quickly concluded the truth of the matter and started back indoors. But Derek couldn't just leave it there.

"Fluff, Fluff, Fluff, Fluff, Fluff," he whispered, loud enough
for her to hear.
She turned in her tracks, her dander well and truly up.
"I know that's you, Derek Fletcher. I'll bloomin' well tell
your mum when she gets home."
The only response the threat drew from Del was a long,
loud, and fruity raspberry, at which point I totally blew our cover by
roaring out laughing. Mrs. Finch had no trouble in guessing who
Derek's accomplice was.
"And you, Stephen Derby" she retorted. "You should be
ashamed of yourself."
Secretly, I think I was.

The hardy annuals of football and cricket were fully catered
for. At that stage of my life, I had neither interest nor ability for
either discipline. When we all stood against a wall for teams to be
"picked," you could all but guarantee that I would be the last man
standing. It never really bothered me.

There were two "stadia" for football. One was situated at the
St. Stephens Road end, between the two high end-terrace walls,
where Mr. and Mrs. Roast lived opposite the Sealeys. The second
was far closer to home. Outside No. 11, a lamppost and stench pipe
sufficed for games which used only one goal. This meant one poor
soul being elected to keep goal, whilst combatants of both sides
endeavoured to out score each other. It was a quaint arrangement
that enabled those in possession of the ball to attack and instantly
metamorphose into defenders once dispossessed. The only loser was
"Billy No-Mates" in goal – he got it from all angles. In nine cases
out of ten, we used a soft tennis ball which elevated control to a real
art and, doubtless, honed the skills of those with a natural inclination
toward the game to a fine degree. Before the 1950s were out, the
Frido ball had come onto the market, a red plastic item that wasn't
quite thick enough to withstand a small thorn. As long as it was fully
inflated, it served its purpose admirably, although, when deflated, it
quickly became as hard as a rock, kicked or headed at the players'

peril. No, it was the common old tennis ball that we cut our soccer teeth on, and it would remain so for many years.

If football was beyond my interest and application, when it came to cricket, I was an even bigger plonker. The lamppost outside No.11 served its purpose as our wicket. Across the road, outside Mrs. Finch's, a coat was placed from where where the bowler did his stuff. On a good day, a swipe by a right-handed batsman could send the ball flying up the street, across Plashet Grove, and into Crescent Road. This would enable the batsman to scamper back and forth across the road for as many runs as he could amass – and it wasn't limited to six. Georgie Brewerton was a year older than me and lived with his mum and his sister Carol at No. 24, next to the eel yard. He was a bit of a bruiser was George, but, nevertheless, always one of the gang. On one occasion, when he was at the crease, he produced such a perfect stroke as to send the ball flying up the street, deep into Crescent territory. Plashet Grove was thick with traffic at the time and retrieval of the ball took all of two minutes. In the meantime, back and forth across the road Georgie went, accumulating runs at an alarming rate. Somewhere at the back of my mind, the figure "thirty-eight" rings a bell.

Well, of course, such a state of affairs couldn't be allowed to pass without comment or appeal. George was adamant that the rules of the noble game permitted him to keep running until the ball was returned. The more academic declared his opinion to be untenable, whilst the outspoken element assessed the standpoint as having little more credibility to it than "cobblers." What John Arlott would have made of it all is not on record. Anyhow, at precisely this point, George took umbrage that his judgement and knowledge were being held up to such fine scrutiny and, as a result, punch up stopped play.

It was amazing that so few windows were broken as a result of our street football and cricket. The occasions on which it happened over a ten-year period you could count on the fingers of one hand. Whether or not something subconscious kicked in as we struck or kicked the ball, I can't say, but on those rare occasions when a window was smashed, there was a strong sense of having done wrong and a need to make restitution. Mums and dads usually coughed up but that wasn't always necessary. On the bottom line, neighbours were neighbours and if they had had a window broken, well, they repaired it and got on with their lives. That was the Walpole Road way of things.

Terry and Ricky Young lived at No. 11. Mrs. Young, from my earliest memory, was a single parent, having been widowed early in life. She was a tall, bespectacled, red-haired woman with a ready smile and a voice that could, sometimes, ward shipping from the rocks. She was a good soul, having grown up in the street with her parents – Mr. and Mrs. Holmes – who lived opposite, at No.8. Her two boys were as different as chalk from cheese. Terry, the older by a couple of years, was a good-looking lad, and nobody's fool. He had a knowing way about him and if something, or someone, ever gained his displeasure, he adopted a superior demeanour of both face and speech. I suspect that he grew to be a man who did not suffer fools at all – let alone gladly. His younger brother Ricky was very different and everybody loved him. He was a round-faced – not fat - little chap who had inherited his mum's smile. His unkempt curly auburn hair fell over his forehead, and he spoke with a slight whine. His sight in one eye was weak, requiring him to wear spectacles with a black patch shielding the stronger eye, thus making the weaker eye work just that bit harder and, hopefully, correct itself. Del couldn't let that go and whenever Ricky came out to play, we got a rendering of "Pretty Little Black-Eyed Suzie," a "hit" for Guy Mitchell, in 1953. In response to this, Ricky always laughed, and whined, "Oh, Fletch! Don't!" But Fletch always did.

Ricky had the gift of being able to absorb brickbats with such good grace that I can truly record that I never knew anybody who disliked him. He had something other-worldly about him that we all recognised and loved. If anyone were going to put their foot in it, you would have staked a month's pocket money on it being Ricky. By now, he has probably matured into a six-footer, is chairman of some public company or another, and doing a darned sight better than me. But, back in the fifties, other-worldly it was.

Steve Derby

Del had a maroon bicycle with an arched cross bar. It was his pride and joy, and Mrs. Fletcher must have had to save pretty hard to buy it for him. One warm summer evening, the two of us were involved with some minor engineering work, dismantling the machine in order to do I forget what. Nut by nut, bolt by bolt, each part was carefully and lovingly placed on the edge of the kerb where Del was working.

Suddenly, the sound of an opening door, and out from No.11 came Ricky. He closed the door and began to walk across the road, with that slow, lolloping gait. To be fair, he provided us with ample warning, hailing us both.

"Wotcha, Steve. Wotcha, Del."

It was warning enough for Del. Standing to his full height, he raised his hand like a policeman on traffic control duty.

"Stop! Stop right there," he commanded. Ricky, grinning sheepishly, did just that.

"Don't move until I've picked up this lot."

With that, he carefully took up each nut and bolt that had been placed so assiduously on the kerb, and transferred them to higher ground on the wall outside his house. Task completed, he gave the green light to Ricky, who resumed his eccentric way toward us.

Quite how Del missed it, I will never know. Sitting close to the edge of the kerb where the drain hole resided, was one solitary nut. In truth, neither of us noticed it for, had one or other of us done so, we would surely have rescued it. It was de rigueur that Ricky wouldn't see it, being – as he was - intent on nothing other than joining Del and me to assist the pair of us in doing damn all for the rest of the evening. But, this was Ricky – and Ricky was no ordinary mortal.

Casually stepping onto the kerb, he placed his foot in the one spot, at the one angle necessary to a) find the nut b) make contact with same and c) hoof it straight down the drain hole, never to be seen again! I laughed like a drain – sorry about that one – as Del and Ricky eyeballed each other. Silent contempt was all over Del's face as Rick became more sheepish by the second.

108

"Sorry, Fletch," was the best the miscreant could manage. *During what seemed an endless period of staring, the Fletcher brain assessed the apology for a suitable response to both this sad state of affairs and its perpetrator. Quietly and deadpan, with just the right blend of contempt and derision, Del delivered his two-word verdict.*
"Wanker's doom!"

Now, you might wonder quite why it is that I have recalled this incident and its accompanying curse. On the other hand, you might not. Either way, I had better tell you. For an eight year old to dredge up just two words implying that boys who persisted in mucking about with themselves would, in the long run, receive nothing better in life than to become good-natured, accident-prone coves seemed quite clever to me. Never again did I hear Derek – or anyone else for that matter - use the expression. It was his and his alone and, I suppose, marked him out as a bit of an innovator. Anyhow, that's the way I saw it. We'd better get back to the street.

The Collins family, at No. 19, boasted a team of real characters. In our largely peaceful environment, if ever there was a bit of aggro to be had, chances were that it would originate from No.19. They appeared a tight-knit little unit and, for some reason I never quite fathomed, a little distant from other families. Perhaps it was that, to my knowledge, they were the only family in Walpole who went to church regularly – the Roman Catholic St. Antony's – one and the same place frequented by the Derby side of my family some twenty or thirty years earlier. I hope I do them no dis-service by reflecting that it often smacked a bit of, "go to church on Sunday, and back to naughtiness on Monday." Couldn't say for sure. Although Mrs. Collins could be a bit "loud" on occasions, she wasn't unpleasant. By comparison, her husband was incognito.

They had four kids. The eldest girl, Paddy, being a good few years older than any of us, was never really part of our little gang. Dickie – just a couple of years my senior - tended to mix with his school friends at the faith school of St. Bonaventures, whilst still managing to maintain a presence in Walpole Road. The youngest two – Joanne and Billy - were, by and large, on the periphery, playing with whoever would have them. Yet we were to have our moments.

Whatever sparked it off, I can't recall, but there was one occasion, which required me to cross swords with Joanne. Even back then, the opposite sex remained a mystery to me, but not, I guess, as much as I was to them. Anyhow, there had been a fracas, and Joanne was spitting venom. She was going to give it to me good and proper.

Whatever other attributes Mrs. Collins might have had, to my eye I don't think it would have been unfair to say that she was not endowed with what one might call classic good looks. On the other hand, my mum was. Call me biased, if you will, but as best as an eight-year old could make out, Walpole Road at large saw Mum as a real "looker." Joanne loaded her gun and commenced fire.

"Your mum, Derby. She's only good-looking because she wears a ton of make up," she shouted at me.

"Your mum, Derby. Do you know what she'd look like if she took all her make-up off? Do you know what she'd blinking well look like?"

It was world-class hollering, born of total confidence that my annihilation was no more than an insult away. Never count your chickens.

"Yeah," I came back. "Your mum.....with all her make-up on!"

I was proud of that and Joanne, unable to handle my return of serve, stomped off indoors. Mind you, I remained a bit uneasy for a while. There was a mantra in the Collins' household, which ran along the lines, "I'm gonna get my big brother on to you." Six-year old Billy, in particular, dined out on it. On those occasions when Dickie complied with requirements, out from the house he would roar, full of fire and angst, to find his sibling's tormentor and apply some above average slapping. Spiked as effectively as she had been, I wondered if Joanne would let this one pass. She did, and I can't ever recall having another conversation with her, other than just passing pleasantries on my way to school.

But young Billy was a completely kettle of fish. A whinger of the first order, it would take just the slightest issue to reduce him to tears. How slight? Well, what about this?

Throughout one Christmas holiday morning, Derek had been teasing him unmercifully about virtually everything that the little soul turned his hand to. Bill had been teetering on the brink of tears throughout and, ultimately, he got pushed just that little bit too far when Del burst into song, to the tune of "The Blue Tail Fly."

"Billy Backside, and I don't care,
Billy Backside, and I don't care......."

And just to give the whole scenario a warm-hearted festive spin, to the tune of "Good King Wenceslas,"

"Brightly shone the Billy backside...."

He got no further. It was more than flesh and blood could stand and, mingled amongst the hoots from us Fletcher acolytes, Billy's tearful voice outlined his game plan.
"I'm gonna get my big brother onto you, Fletcher."
Derek sent him on his way indoors with a verbal kick up the bum.
"Bleedin' good job, then! Send him out here. I don't care"
With the benefit of hindsight, a modicum of care might not have been misplaced. Yet the times Billy had gone weeping and wailing indoors to utter similar threats to no avail, were legion, and Derek had relied on that. Yet, this was that one step too far, the fate of all who push their luck. Within seconds, Dickie roared out of the house and held his face no more than an inch or two from Del's. He was furious.
"Fletcher. Billy's just told me that you smacked ' im one. Nobody does that to my bruvver!"

Actually, Dickie had that wrong....everyone smacked Billy. Slapping Billy around the head was a "rite of passage" for kids in Walpole Road. A bit like losing your virginity, only less fun - marginally.

Derek appealed.

"I didn't touch him, Dick. Honest."

We witnesses for the defence supported the appeal, but it cut no ice. Dickie was beyond control and began to lay into Derek, rolling him on the ground, and pummelling body and ears in a fearful manner. Billy, in the meantime, emboldened by the contribution of his minder, sat on the wall, sneering his approval.

"See, Fletcher, you sod. You won't do that again."

The bashing seemed to go on and on, until our mate from No.20, Dick Culver, his delicate senses offended by the injustice of it all, saw fit to plough in and lend his assistance. It was more than I was prepared to do. Not a fighting man, you see. For his pains, hostilities were transferred from Derek to Dick, and there, in the middle of the road, Dickie Collins focussed his attention on smacking eight bells out of the would-be knight in shining armour.

This gallant intervention, on the credit side, gave Derek time to recover marginally from the contretemps. However, on the debit side, his temper was burning and revenge was in his eyes. He looked about for some means of exacting retribution. In Mrs. Finch's front garden were some excess wooden struts which, in another life, had been a fence in her back garden. Amongst them were a few cricket bat size items, easy to handle, smooth yet firm, and Derek saw the potential they offered. From my vantage point, watching the whole pantomime from the cowardly periphery, it seemed that God himself had made those struts available to his unworthy servant.

With tears of anger still streaming from his eyes, Derek took one of the struts and marched purposefully to take a position behind the aggressor. Dickie was still totally committed to the task of beating his prey to pulp, completely oblivious to the military build up just a yard or so to his rear. Derek raised the strut back over his shoulder, with all the grace of a golfer about to hit the longest of long drives. With all the force he could muster, he brought the thing down through an arc to make accurate, sharp, and painful contact with the protruding posterior. The slap of wood against trousered bum echoed down the street, round the block, and back from whence it came, seemingly before the first shriek of pain emanated from the Collins mouth. Long before the 2003 attack on Baghdad, Walpole Road witnessed its own version of "shock and awe."

Once again, the pecking order at the top of the Collins hit list changed. The cat suddenly had another fish to fry. However, Derek - with a head start - had manoeuvred himself behind a parked car close to his house. Limping – one could scarcely call it running – toward Derek, Dickie was oathing all manner of obscenities and blasphemies against his protagonist. Old Father what's –'is – name down at St. Antony's was going to need a bit of overtime if he was going to give proper attention to Dickie's next confession.

"I'm gonna 'ave you, Fletcher," was about the only curse vaguely acceptable from a good Catholic boy.

But Fletcher was not for the 'avin'. Separated by the vehicle between them, no sooner did Dickie moved round one way, than Derek moved the other, a jolly fandango that continued for the thick end of two minutes. You could see that there was only going to be one winner - Derek knew it – and so did Dickie. But to reach the sanctuary of his home, Del would need to get his opponent caught on the wrong side of the car, allowing a free run straight through the open door of No.12.

In addition to inventive curses, the Fletcher repertoire contained a seemingly endless set of ploys, designed to aggravate antagonists beyond the norm. The most successful of these was what he used to call "the lurgy," a name originating from the wonderful "Goon Show" series on steam radio. The effect was achieved by Derek keeping his elbows at his side, lifting his hands chest high and crossing one wrist over the other. Facially, he dropped his jaw, half-closed his eyes, and peered at you down his nose. The more Dickie fussed and cussed, the more Del was determined to maintain his stance. For observers of the process, it was hilarious. If you were on the receiving end, it drove you barmy!

Sooner or later, Dickie's patience would run out, he'd lose his presence of mind and chance a straight dash for his tormentor. Being in such a state of high dudgeon, judgement was almost certain to fail him and, sure enough, it did. Frustration motivated the mad dash that Derek had been waiting for and, as Dickie came flying around one end of the car, Del had his clear run. The hound, in hot pursuit, had no chance and as soon as Derek had crossed his threshold, he slammed the door behind him. He was home and dry.

In the times we live in today, Derek would have been considered anything but "home and dry." That door would have been kicked down, bricks would have been thrown through windows, and all kinds of similar mayhem created. But this was the '50s, and that sort of thing wasn't done. Derek might have obtained sanctuary, but Dickie was still blowing a gasket – more so.

"Come out here, Fletcher. Come out and fight like a man."

Never could understand that enjoinder when it was directed at an eight-year old. Fighting was the last thing on Derek's mind, especially as it looked to me as though he had won already.

The flap on the letterbox opened and his two wide, innocent eyes stared out.

"Fletcher, I'm gonna beat you up when you come out."

Two deliberate, exaggerated blinks did nothing to calm Dickie.

"I mean it. Get out here and I'll smack 'ell out of you."

Not a word, just two more blinks. You could sense that Del wasn't much taken with the offer made, and the letterbox flap closed.

During all of this, I had been nothing more than innocent bystander. It had been right royal entertainment to witness the Collins bum soundly smacked, the proprietor of same ridiculed, and all it had cost me was a laughing spasm.

"What you laughing at, Derby?"

"I can't help it, Dick. It's just that Fletch makes me laugh so much."

Underneath it all, I think he understood.

Suddenly, the main player appeared in the bay window of his downstairs living room. Dickie's lips tightened and, although he sensed that his opportunity had passed, he fired a final, if resigned, tirade.

"You can't stay in there forever, Fletcher. When you come out, I'm gonna beat you up."

Non-plussed, Derek pulled the curtains to, and I wondered what on earth he was up to. I didn't have to wait long to find out. A drawstring operated those curtains and, when pulled, they would part like theatre curtains in front of the stage. A moment passed before Derek pulled the string and there, in its full glory, the bare Fletcher backside was displayed, trousers and underwear around his ankles, metaphorically telling his antagonist that he'd been done over. I laughed 'til I could neither laugh nor cry any more, and even Dickie couldn't help but grin at the sheer effrontery of it all.

"I will get you, Fletch," he whimpered, more in hope than determination.

But, in that moment, I think all three of us knew that it wouldn't necessarily happen. Doubtless, some future misdemeanour would bring the pair of them into confrontation, but not this one. Life would carry on at it's own communal pace, down in Walpole Road.

Georgie Brewerton lived with his mother and sister Carol up at No. 24. Being a year or two younger than Georgie meant that he was always likely to be odds-on favourite to come out on top in any bout of fisticuffs that involved me. Quite what it was that I did to incur his wrath and a punch in the face is lost in time. Off I went indoors, crying and snivelling to Mum who, believing whatever tale it was that I came up with, stormed up the passageway into the front garden, with me dutifully following.

"Georgie! Come here!" Mum called out.

Sheepishly, he ambled away from the crowd gathered outside Mrs. Young's to the gate of No.7. I think he knew he was in for it.

"What's been going on? Stephen's just come in here crying and I want to know what's been going on."

He looked down in the mouth and rather sorry for himself.

115

"I hit Stephen," he mumbled.

Before Mum had a chance to put her two penn'orth in, full of tears, temper, and tantrum, I leaned over the garden gate and lashed out, catching Georgie a resounding slap on the side of the cheek. It was just the adrenalin talking.

"There now," I said. "Now Stephen's hit Georgie!"

I felt triumph and vindication. In modern parlance, my opponent was gob-smacked - in both senses of the expression. But Mum was livid and, dragging me inside, gave me another wallop, and sent me to my room.

"Don't you ever do that again when I'm trying to sort out a problem. Do you understand?"

Eventually, I knew I would have to go back into the street, and had my doubts as to what reception I might receive from Georgie. Bless him, he never said another word about the matter and we both got on with our lives as though it had never happened. Whatever he might or might not have been, vengeful he wasn't, and those who witnessed the incident recognised that the mouse had roared – or, at least, whimpered loudly.

Whilst Mrs. Finch continued to prowl around in the downstairs accommodation of No.10, the upstairs flat was occupied by Mr. and Mrs. Scarlett and their two boys, Michael and Alan. Mrs. Scarlett was Mrs. Finch's daughter and, sadly, both she and her husband suffered disabilities, which caused them both to limp. Mr. Scarlett's profession was, I am sure, "white collar." He was a quiet man, who kept himself very much to himself. I had great sympathy for them both because they truly were decent people and it seemed bitterly unfair that they both had to struggle in the way that they did. But, my goodness, they gifted us all with a couple of boys who were heaven sent for laughs.

Michael was a couple of years younger than me and comparatively quiet. Perhaps he couldn't get a word in edgeways, once his grandmother was in full throttle. He didn't have a contentious bone in his body, which was probably just as well, as younger brother Alan more than made up for the deficiency. Whereas Michael could polish up quite nicely with the application of a little soap and water, Alan was one of those snotty little fellows, whose noses frequently dripped and who didn't give a damn about remedying the situation. A world-class nose picker to go with it, too.

One afternoon, during a long, hot summer holiday, we devised a game to help pass away our weeks of idleness. Simple enough, we would all sit on Terry and Ricky's wall and, in turn, choose some celebrity, announce his or her initials, and leave the rest of us to guess the identity the mystery guest. Hardly taxing, but in my own mind, I had some doubts about Alan's ability to cope with it all. Yet, sho' 'nuff, he insisted on having a turn and poor old protective Michael, as always, acted as his advocate.

"Oh, go on. Give him a chance."

We all knew about the pressure that Alan could put on Mike, so, against our better judgement, we gave him his chance. There in front of us, the snotty one provided the initials of the figment of his imagination.

"B. D. C."

Blank faces all round. B.D.C? No matter how we sliced it, none of us could come up with anything that remotely fitted. Michael, sympathetically, reached out to help his brother.

"Are you sure that's right, Al?"

He hadn't the slightest doubt and said as much, getting close to the edge of tears, which caused Michael to beat a hasty retreat. Alan was far from averse to running indoors to accuse - falsely - his brother of enough "crimes" as would land him in the remand home.

Okay then, Al. Let's hear it for "B.D.C."

"Yeah," says six-year-old, full of self-satisfied importance that confidence in a potential result inspires. "I knew you wouldn't get it. It's............Billy der Kid!"

Billy der Kid! I ask you. At least he could say it a bit better than he could spell it – but only just. Our laughter reduced Alan to tears. For the life of him, he couldn't work it out. His logic told him that, as we couldn't work it out, he'd won - hadn't he? So why does all the hilarity tell him that he's lost? Mike put a consoling arm on his brother's shoulder.

117

Steve Derby

"Never mind, Al. We'll let you have another go later."

Oh, Mike. What the hell are you thinking of? Isn't one go enough? He'll never improve on his first shot.

And so the game went on, with us all carefully and deliberately avoiding Alan's "another go." But completely stupid he wasn't, and it didn't take him long to work out what was happening, and positively demand his human rights. Gentle reasonings and wise counsel from Michael moved the mountain not one inch. It was his turn and, by the cringe, he was going to have it. Out he went.

"Okay.......A.C."

Come on, serious now. We all put our thinking caps on in the hope and belief that Alan had got this one right. Even Ricky came out with a couple of names that fitted the initials. Trouble was, nobody had ever heard of them. On further questioning, it transpired that Ricky hadn't either. Derek chastised him as only Derek could.

"Ricky, why don't you shut your gob?"

"Right-o, Fletch!" said Ricky, and with typical good nature, duly shut his gob, and faded into the background.

In the meantime, we all continued dredging the depths of our brains to solve the conundrum. A.C? A.C? Hmmm. It became clear that Alan was going to have to come to our rescue once again. Please God, let him have this one right.

"Come on then, Al. None of us can get it. Who is "A.C?""

Puffing himself up to his full four foot six, all was revealed.

"'Arry Secombe!" he triumphantly announced.

What followed was akin to choreographed mayhem. Eight of us involuntarily stood up from the wall to prevent a laughing seizure, which might have left us permanently transfixed there. Terry Young wandered up to little Alan, who was close to tears yet again, and still none the wiser as to how he had caused this cacophony. Terry looked down his nose at Alan with all the scorn and distain a ten-year old could muster.

"You're nuts, Scarlett. Bleedin' nuts!"

For once, even Ricky was on safe ground and mustered sufficient confidence to add his own two-pennyworth.

118

"Yeah. Bleedin' nuts."
And with that, the pair of them put their noses in the air,
assumed superior smirks, and disappeared inside No.11. It was as
though neither could remain in the presence of such perceived
stupidity
Michael placed his arm around the disconsolate Alan.
"Come on, Al. We'd better go in."

It was pitiful to see Mike lead his younger brother gently across the road. With great dignity, he escorted him through the green front door, and closed it gently behind them. Out of the sight and sound of laughing playmates, Alan would be licking his wounds and receiving an alphabetic education. One thing baffled me still, though. How on earth did Michael manage to stop laughing himself at two such classic goofs? Perhaps he thought Alan *had* got it right – it's the only explanation I can come up with.

Poor Mrs. Finch continued to be the butt of some prank or
another of Derek's. At the end of her back garden, in common with
many others in Walpole Road, she had constructed an old wooden
chicken coop, with a door at each end, each secured by a wooden
strut. One day, looking over the fence that divided his garden from
Mrs. Finch's, Derek watched her stoop and clamber into the hen
house to collect the eggs. Alan was at play in the garden with his
cousin, Raymond, and Derek just simply could not resist.
"Here, Al."
Al trotted over to the fence where Derek was standing.
"Wodga want, Fletch?"
"Why don't you go and lock the door behind yer Grandma?"
Why not, indeed? Although it wasn't the smartest thing in
the world to do, the plan had the distinct advantage of Alan not being
the smartest kid in the world. Sho' 'nuff, he did the deed, sliding the
struts at each end of the coop into the locked position.

Mrs. Finch went berserk, stomping around like some demented King Kong, amidst a maelstrom of clucks and squawks, with feathers, dust, and bodies flying up all over the place.
"Let me out, you little buggers! I'll tell your mother when she gets home."
The boys were terrified and knew that if they released their charge, they'd each be in for a thorough good hiding. So, allowing discretion to be the better part of valour, they exited the scene. Derek did much the same.
Outside in the street, about an hour later, Del told me what had happened.
"So, where is she now, Del?" I asked.
"Still there, as far as I know...or bleedin' care!" he laughed.

The aftermath of war had left sufficient devastation around as to unintentionally provide children with playgrounds that would not be tolerated now. On the corner of St. Stephens Road and Green Street, stood the remains of the "high" – theologically – and mighty St Stephens church, waiting for a demolition team to come and raze it to the ground, after it had been hit by a bomb in 1940. In better times, alongside the church had been the family recreational garden for the vicar of the parish and, since the end of the war and several years beyond, the couple of acres that lay unattended became known as "the vicar's garden," which, of course, is exactly what it had been. Now there were bricks, crushed tin cans, wooden planks, thistles, and bushes, all spread out on the unkempt grassy ground. In short, it was paradise for games of cowboys and Indians, war scenarios, hide and seek, and plain mucking about. We took full advantage for hours.

Just a hundred yards or so from the site of the church, on the corner of Green Street and Plashet Grove, stood the "Duke of Edinburgh" where my maternal grandfather took successful steps to eradicate the family fortune. It had, like the church, been reduced to a shell. Nowadays, the area would have been fenced off within minutes but it was many years after the cessation of hostilities before access was denied. We wandered at will amongst debris where great steel supports remained in place. If we wished, we could walk across them, although this was only for the daring or foolhardy. I had neither quality. In the bowels of the place, there remained rooms for exploration, and games of "Hide and Seek." With so many options, you could conceal yourself for the better part of an hour, and still not be found.

Unsurprisingly, Mum and Dad were not particularly fond of me playing in "The Duke," but rarely admonished me, even when they knew perfectly well that I had been down in the depths. Behind the pub, on the walkway that linked Plashet Grove to Green Street, was a large iron wheel in the midst of all the chaos. I was never able to ascertain what it was all about. Nobody ever offered a reasoned explanation, so we just climbed up on it and slid down on the seats of our pants. A further mystery was how nobody ever got chucked in the horse trough that stood alongside the pub – or perhaps I just got away with it. I'm realist enough to know that if anyone was going to get a soaking, it was very likely to be me – or, perhaps, Ricky.

Despite the necessary walk to Plashet Park being sufficient excuse for us lazy herberts to stay fixed in Walpole, we were not total strangers to it. There would be occasions when, in need of a little variety, we would stir from our lethargy and stroll along St. Stephens, Katherine Road, into Chester Road, past the Congregational church, and then on to Shrewsbury Road. Just a block along was the entrance to the closest excuse for greenery to be found on our doorstep. Personally, I really wasn't that fussed about going to the place, knowing that the purpose of the trip was likely to be football and/or cricket, and, at that time, I didn't do football and/or cricket. I would have been far more content to go somewhere and watch a few trains. As ever, the driving force that got me to the park was Derek, who assured me that we could," have a few laughs" and having a few laughs always appealed to me. Invariably, it was worth the effort and we would enjoy swings, slides, and greens, whilst the most adept, inclined, and energetic would play football and/or cricket.

It was, and remains, a nice little park. On entering it from Shrewsbury Road, we were immediately greeted by a couple of tennis courts to our left. Straight on was a large green used, in the main, for football. Over to our right, another large green expanse, reserved for cricket and family picnics - the two tended to go together. Where the park bordered Plashet Grove and Woodhouse Grove, was an extremely tasteful floral area, with immaculately kept lawns. The flowerbeds were, in season, a blaze of colour and it crossed none of our young minds to vandalise them in way, shape, or form. A small cafeteria was convenient for picnic-less parents to enjoy refreshment whilst keeping a close eye on their offspring in the play area. "Going on the swings," we called it.

The swings always made me feel that I was going to throw up and I can't remember being one of those keen enough to wait for my turn. A small wooden roundabout was more my mark, where we all pushed the thing round and, when it was going like the clappers, jumped on to the platform to sit on the main body of the contraption as it spun round. This, too, made me want to throw up, but it was so much fun getting the thing going as fast as you could, that I was willing to suffer for my art. My favourite recreation was a structure of vertical and horizontal metal bars which, from a distance, looked like a mathematical figure. You could climb up them, through them, hang from them with your knees hooked around the top bar, or fall off the thing, which was no uncommon occurrence. Crikey! The risks that we ran did nothing more than make us careful.

But the most dangerous and, by default, generally most popular ride was a contraption referred to as "The Jazz." Here's how it went. Imagine the framework of a rather large tent, with four iron-angled supports at each corner, and you're on the way. Adjoining iron struts along the top reinforced each support. Within that construction, a substantial wooden plank, some fifteen to twenty feet long, was suspended. The joints were fitted in such a way that the swinging plank always remained parallel to the ground and riders would pile onto the thing to get it swinging back and forth. Higher and higher it would go, aided and abetted by two kids standing at each end, clinging on to the supports and shifting their balance to maintain and increase swinging momentum on what passed for a white knuckle ride back in those days. It probably was the cause of as much damage to underpants and knickers as it was to knuckles. It was always a battle to get a turn on the thing and, sometimes, it went at such a pace that I swore the riders would be thrown off the end, like a shovel depositing a load of dung on the roses. Yet, apart from minor scrapes, it never happened. Health and Safety had we none – and we were none the poorer for the lack.

There was one particular fascination about "The Jazz" that was shrouded in mystery, until Derek enlightened me. Noticing how frequently he kept shinning up the support poles, holding on at the top, before sliding down to earth, I wondered why it was that he always seemed more keen to climb up the poles, rather than taking his turn for a ride. One day, all was revealed.

"Here, Stephen. If you climb up that pole and wrap your legs around it, it makes your willy feel funny."

This I had to investigate and, sure enough, he was right. No more did we worry if we couldn't get a seat on the Jazz. Give us a pole and we were happy as Larry. It was probably our initial sex lesson, even if we didn't have a clue about what was happening. It made your willy feel funny, and that was about it.

Playing in the street continued to be a vital part and parcel of our young lives for some time yet to come. It would only begin to change around the age of thirteen, when friends made at our secondary schools or uniformed organisations came onto the scene. They weren't so much replacement as enhancement, for the early relationships were so well grounded that we would continue to share our lives, albeit at somewhat different levels. Kicking a ball around on concrete lost its appeal as we began to stretch our areas of influence further afield. Bush Wood, alongside Wanstead Park, was no more than a short cycle ride and a trip there gave us the opportunity to create hiding places amongst the trees. And just for a little naughtiness, a whole gaggle of us would congregate at Wanstead Park, paddle across the shallow lake to one of the two islands, where we would smoke our first cigarettes. As infant smokers do, I left my matches in my jacket pocket once, and faced fearful retribution when Mum found them. She threatened to tell Dad, but what was he going to do about it? He was a twenty-a-day man himself!

The social climate down Walpole Road began to change as a family or two moved away. Mr. Longhurst, of course, stayed exactly where he was – no more venturing out to 'Awnchurch for him and his family. I seem to recall Mr. and Mrs. Collins taking the first relocation - we could survive that. Yet when Mike and Alan Scarlett announced that their parents were about to rent a newly built flat on the redeveloped site once occupied by St. Stephen's Church, well, this was something rather different. Their new home was little more than few minutes walk away from Walpole, so there remained a sense that they were still part of the gang, even if the loss of regular contact with young Alan cost us dearly in the currency of laughter. Derek lost no opportunity of taking advantage and having one last hurrah.

It was another of those interminably long, hot summer holidays, where putting one foot in front of the other was about as much as you could manage. Our morning had been pretty uneventful. Too hot for football, too tired for cricket, we just sat around the street talking, and taking the occasional ride around the block on our bikes. We needed something. We craved adventure and exploration.

Nobody had ever had the pleasure of entering the Scarlett residence, at No.10. But now that they had a new house, it was deemed only right and proper that we should all have the chance to view it properly. Well, that's the way Derek saw it.

"Can we come round and play in your house, this afternoon, Mike?"

"Well, I'll have to ask me mum," Michael drawled.

Mrs. Scarlett was a million miles from daft, and the thought of her brand new flat being occupied by all and Walpole sundry in her absence, would not have been particularly high on her wish list. Moreover, if Derek was going to be there, the chances of something going awry were pretty high. Mike must have got pretty short shrift for, having popped round to his mum, he returned with the reply to Del's kind offer to "take wine" at Châteaux Scarlett.

"Me mum said "No! Not bloody likely!""

Under normal circumstances, that would have been the end of the matter. But circumstances this time around were not quite normal. Derek was as streetwise as they came.

"Look, Mike. Doesn't your mum go off to work in the afternoon?

Mike confirmed that it was so.

"Well, when she's gone, we'll all come round. We won't mess the place up. She'll never know."

Poor Mike was on the back foot with this one. On the bottom line, he was a decent boy and would not want to do anything that his parents had forbidden. He hesitated between "yes" and "no." "No" because of obedience; "yes" because he knew that Derek had the power to put him under just enough pressure to make him crack. Sure enough, within a few minutes, Del had his wicked way. We were all going to Mike's at quarter past two, and none of us were to say a word to our parents.

Mike had to swear Alan and Raymond to total and utter secrecy.

"Now, Al. You mustn't let Mum know that we've been in."

"I know," said Alan. "What do you think I am? Stupid?"

Somewhere in my imagination, I could have sworn that "Billy de Cid" rode past the far end of the street.

So it was that, with Mr. And Mrs. Scarlett out of their flat, at around 2.00pm, a small group of us knocked to gain entrance. Already gathered were, of course, Michael, Alan, and Raymond and, one by one, we trooped through the door to augment their number. Leading the parade was Derek, followed by the Young brothers, Terry and Ricky. The hunting party was completed by Dickie Culver, John Round, and myself. John had red hair and his mum used to go ballistic if anyone called him "Ginger." His elder brother, Fred, was two years older than us and, beyond question, highly academic. Over the years, I gained a healthy respect for Fred, for he was a really was a very clever bloke. John was droll but, being under ten, I didn't have that word in my vocabulary. He was just funny and I was content not to know why.

Michael issued the battle orders.

"Look, if my mum finds out we've been in here, she won't let me come out to play for weeks. We'll have to be out before five, 'cos that's when she comes home from work. Agreed?"

Agreed.

In the middle of the living room, Michael had set up his miniature snooker table. Dickie Culver suggested that it might be a good idea if we had a knock out competition, so he wrote everyone's name on slips of paper, folded them, and placed all of them in a bag for a draw.

"It's like the draw for the F.A.Cup," observed Mike.

As competent with the cue as I was with the cricket bat, I was neatly disposed of by Dickie in the first round - and I can't say that I wasn't glad. Not only couldn't I play snooker, but also I didn't understand the game. As for Derek, who should he get drawn with but....Alan! Drawing Al was as good as a bye into the next round, but Mike took time to coach his younger brother.

"Look, Al. All you've got to do is your best. Fletch can miss a shot just like the rest of us."

Fletch lurked in the background, occasionally grinning over at me. He knew – we all knew – the result was a forgone conclusion and Mike was only doing the brotherly thing – damage limitation, if you like.

"And please don't cry if you lose, Al," Mike went on. "After all, it's only a game."

But as far as Derek was concerned, it was a darned sight more than a game. It wasn't just a matter of winning - it was all about rubbing Alan's nose in it and laughing for the sheer joy of the exercise. The thought of poor Mike seeking to bring solace to the vanquished Alan was all the motivation he needed. The stage was set for the "match of the round" – Del Fletcher, the bookie's favourite by a mile, against Alan Scarlett, the bookie's favourite for last place by several light years!

"Don't forget, Al. No crying if you get beat. It's only a game."

In his heart, Mike knew that he was wasting his breath.

The whole thing went down the pan from the very first stroke. Del had agreed that Al could break, which he did, sending the white scooting around the table, touching all sides, but never coming within close proximity of a red ball. As the white came to rest, Del moved over to the scoreboard.

"Right. That's four points to me."

He chalked them up and took his turn at the table. From the next shots, we knew that we were about to witness a mammoth score. Red followed by the black. Another red followed by the blue. By the time that Al came to the table again, he was already a cricket score behind, and you could see the confidence draining from the little chap. But, to be fair, he was going to give it his best. This time, with his first effort, he managed to hit a ball - a red, which cannoned all over the place before coming – conveniently - to rest right at the mouth of one of the pockets.

"Oh, hard luck, Al," said Mike.

"Yeah, hard luck," the rest of us chorused, laughing inwardly and knowing that nobody – not even me – could miss the next shot. Al said not a word as Fletch sank not only the red, which had been gifted to him, but also plonked the pink into a pocket for good measure.

And that was how it progressed. Al did manage a couple of reds, but it was all rather more luck than judgement. We could all see that he was fighting back tears, nobody more than Derek. There were moments when I thought he was going to make one of his trade mark comments, to ensure that the waterfall Al was trying so hard to contain behind his eyes came flowing down. But he didn't so, perhaps, he had more heart than I gave him credit for. It was Mike who pulled the plug. With the game finished, leaving Del to face Dickie in the final, Mike put his arm around his vanquished little brother. Just one word out of place, and Al would sob for a fortnight. In fact, Mike managed nine words, every one of them out of place!

"Cheer up, Al. You only lost by ninety-five!"

He might as well have said a million and ninety-five, for all the comfort it was to Al. A cry of tortured anguish erupted from the little guy, as he shook himself free from the fraternal embrace. Tears bottled up for the better part of the last ten minutes were given free reign, leaving frustrated anger the only means of expression.

"Sod off, Michael. And you, too, Fletcher. Get out of this house. Go on, Mike. Tell Fletcher to get out!"

Poor old Mike stood there dumb-founded. After all, he'd seen it coming and done his level best to take all necessary precautions. And for what? An invitation to leave the stage....and take Fletcher with him. Even Del looked aghast as, flushed with rage, Al stomped out of the room. We heard the toilet door slam, followed by the sound of the lock being applied, which provided us with sufficient clues as to his whereabouts.

"You are a twerp, Mike," said Dickie. "You could see that he was near to tears. Only lost by ninety five!"

The final began with an uneventful couple of shots, and quickly faded into insignificance when, from the hallway, we heard the sound of banging – heavy banging. It was as though someone was hitting wood with a mallet, intent on some serious damage. It didn't take Sherlock Holmes to work out that whatever was going on, Alan was at the root of it. The whole gaggle of us congregated outside the locked lavatory door, from where the banging was coming. Mike got a chair to stand on and looked through the fanlight to see what was going on inside the karsy. Stepping up, he gasped with horror.

"Please, Al, please. Please don't wreck the joint."

"What's he doing, Mike?" I asked.

Exasperated, Mike invited us all to, "Look for yourselves."

Although not inclined to look at people sitting on the toilet, I decided to make an exception on this occasion. Alan was sitting on the side of the bath, with his heels resting on the wooden seat of the toilet. At regular intervals, he viciously slammed his heels down onto the wood. It wasn't going to take too much of that sort of treatment before either the wood cracked or the blessed seat came away from its hinges. But what were we to do? How could we get him out and prevent the Scarlett residence from accumulating evidence that would prove to Mr. and Mrs. Scarlett that we had all been in creating mayhem, not to mention the cost of a repaired bog seat. Pleading with Al did us no good at all.

"Get Fletcher out of here," was the un-negotiable term he offered us. Until Fletcher left, he would stay put. The incumbent was adamant. It looked pretty watertight with Alan holding all the aces.

The kicking stopped, and we heard movement behind closed doors. By climbing onto the side of the bath, Al was able to keep one foot on the side and rest the other on the door handle. Holding onto the sill of the fanlight, he steadied himself and peered down at us. And there he stayed, confident in his own security, insisting that Del kindly left the stage, and firing insults at the lot of us. If he had been within reach, every single one of us – me included – would have choked him. But as so often befits tyrants, there was an Achilles Heel that would ultimately lead to Al's down fall – in this case, literally. Simple really, but only Del saw it. By having his foot on the door handle, this tyrant had made himself both accessible and vulnerable. Without fuss, Del sharply turned the handle downward from our side of the door. Equilibrium on Alan's side was immediately undermined and anything – or anyone - relying on the door handle for balance had misplaced their faith. His overconfident, grinning face changed instantly. His eyebrows shot up, his eyes widened, his jaw dropped, and so did he! Newton 1, Scarlett 0. We shrieked at the sound of the crash as he hit the floor. All, that is, except the self-satisfied Derek, who just stood there, grinning.

On the other side of the door, Al was crying fit to bust. Now he needed us, and the lock on the door was released. Dear old Mike, ever the dutiful brother, picked him up and tended, as best he could, to his wounds. It was a pointless exercise. All Mike got for his troubles was a couple of kicks, a threat that he would "tell Mum and Dad what you've been up to," and several more volleys of, "Get Fletcher out of here," spiced liberally with, "the sod."

Whether or not Mr. And Mrs. Scarlett were ever made aware of the afternoon's shenanigans, I couldn't say. The last I heard of Mike was that he made a very successful career for himself in Barclays

Bank. Good for him – he deserved it. As for Alan, the page remains blank – but I'll bet he did alright somewhere.

Playing in the street would, eventually, begin to grow up. Tin Can Copper, Knock Down Ginger, and other such larks were all very fine when you were under the age of ten, but as we approached and invaded our teenage years, changes, unavoidably, took their toll. Other threads of interest and activity intertwined with our "playing" and wove their distinctive patterns into the tapestry of our lives. The street would continue to be our playground for some years to come yet, although in a somewhat more mature format. So, if I take my leave of it for a short while, I ask you to take my word that, like General MacArthur, I shall return.

CHAPTER FIVE

WHO MADE GOD?

At the commencement of the 21ˢᵗ Century, religious sensitivity is high on the agenda. Islam has received bad press not least as a result of the New York atrocities of September 2001. In July 2005, horror hit the streets of London when bombs were detonated at various points of London's transport system. It was a painful time for many of every shade and hue of faith. Yet I believe that peace will come and, when it does, the core values of belief will be at the heart of reconciliation and healing.

Once was a time when the voice of the church was listened to with more attention than perhaps it is today. Listened to, mind you – not necessarily acted upon. For whatever reason, the whole business of faith was paid far more than a modicum of respect in my childhood. Now it is in the market place, along with several rather flaky creeds, available to be embraced, mocked, or ignored. During my upbringing in Upton Park, it was never quite like that.

I have to set out my own personal stall here. One way or another, there has never been a time when I didn't believe in God. Although neither my Roman Catholic father nor Anglican mother proactively practised their faith, it would be wrong to say that they were not believers. They were Christian with a small "c" and, right from the start, took pains to ensure that I was well catered for when it came to what I prefer to describe as spiritual up-bringing.

Stepping back a generation from my parents, it will come as little surprise to learn that there were, as far as I am aware, no strong religious leanings amongst the Clarks - dinners chucked up the wall and support of the "Duke of Edinburgh" providing ample evidence. But on Dad's side of the fence, the temperature and theology was somewhat higher. My great grandmother clearly stood out and

Uncle Jack gave me some clues as to where my spiritual tendencies might have originated.

"My Gran was the grown-up I loved best of all. She had the small back bedroom upstairs, and I would climb up to see her as often as possible.

"Don't go in if Gran's at her prayers," Mum would snap. Sometimes she was, but I crept in just the same.

Gran must have spent hours on her knees by the old armchair with the crucifix above it on the wall, talking to her God or the Virgin Mary. She prayed for help for every single one of her big family, for those passed on as well as the living; for remote cousins, of whom I had never heard, and even for those to come, like the baby cousin Hannah and her husband Danny were expecting. It took a long while to get round to us all. For herself, she asked nothing but forgiveness for her sins, although I cannot believe my saintly Gran ever hurt or sinned against God or any fellow human in her life."

I'm sure I would have liked great grandmother. Despite my ultimate destination of Methodism, I like to think that we would have got along fine. She wouldn't have let a little thing like that stand in the way. Or, there again, would she? Dad often recalled the time when a team of Catholic missionaries came to St. Antony's to conduct a week of mission. Perhaps some of the Collins family were there, too. Anyhow, these guys really went out into the dark and dismal places of the world to propagate their faith and, every night, Dad would be down the church, lapping it all up. Yet, did it bring him into the fold? Well, not quite as Gran would have wanted.

"Marry yourself a nice Catholic girl, Joey," she would exhort. Uncles Jack and Len would get the same advice. Blow it if she's got a temper, swears like a trooper, and has been round the block more times than the old tom cat – as long as she's a "nice Catholic girl," everything'll be sweet and dandy. As it was, none of the boys went down that particular route when it came to their choice of wives and I, for one, am mighty glad about it. Had Dad taken Gran's well-meaning advice, I would have been denied the best mum a bloke could ever have had. Whatever it was that she believed in, I adored her.

Funnily enough, they weren't alone out there in Walpole Road and the surrounding area when it came to matters of faith. Perhaps it was the outbreak of peace after six long years of war that made parents in the 'Forties and 'Fifties feel they "owed God one." I couldn't say for sure, yet you couldn't help but notice the significant number of children who attended Sunday school in those post-war years. Playing in the street on a Sunday was strictly taboo and only Mr. and Mrs. Pitman – the confectioners in Plashet Grove – opened for business on that particular day. I would be allowed to go and buy a bottle of Tizer from them to go with lunch, but that was about it. Sunday was special and you could see it in the quiet streets. Nowadays, young people who attend church regularly can be looked upon as a bit quaint. Worse, they can be subject to all manner of harassment by other kids who haven't got the first idea of what it's all about. But, in the 1940s and 1950s, even if parents didn't go to church themselves, a more than significant number saw reason enough to make sure that their children did. Fair enough, one viewpoint was that it "bought" parents an hour or so of peace and quiet on a Sunday afternoon, but I'm not totally convinced that that was all there was to it.

Perhaps it was the result of some compromise between an exclusively Roman Catholic or Anglican input, that Mum and Dad sent me to a little Anglican Sunday School, run by an order of nuns, on the corner of St. Stephens and Waterloo Road. I am indebted to the recollections of Connie Hillsden (nee Hanson) for being able to put a little more flesh on the bones.

"In addition to running the Sunday school lessons in the front room of the house at the corner of St. Stephens and Waterloo Road, the eight nuns who lived in the house ran on Tuesday nights a meeting called, "The Coral League." Kids would attend to hear stories about Africa. The girls knitted dish clothes and socks for sending out to the Dark Continent. They took me on my very first holiday when I went with Sister Marie Clair and Sister Anna, who

took some of us to a place in Kent. We stayed with a family who were very kind to us, but I missed my home so much that I couldn't wait to get back to good old Walpole Road.
I remember when we all had to go to St. Michael's church in Rutland Road. My brother Ray pumped the organ on Sundays and I played trains with the hymnbooks along the pews. Often I would create a stir when I had gathered so many into my "train," they all fell off onto the floor at the end of the pew. Still, blond hair and blue eyes got me out of a few scrapes!"

Being neither knitter nor holiday-maker, I remember little of those afternoons, save for one occasion when Irene Filer wandered into the front room, loudly announcing, "I want to see Jesus." Physically, of course, he was not "in da house," so Eileen was disappointed. Since the bombing of St. Stephens' church, the nuns had transferred their allegiance to St. Michaels, in Rutland Road. Liturgically, it stood somewhere between high Anglican and ultra-Roman Catholic. Given the choice, I have a feeling that the clientele of those days would like to have kicked the Archbishop of Canterbury firmly up the backside, caring not a jot that his surplice was in tatters, his mitre skew-whiff and dangling over his eyes, in order that a more papal flavour might prevail. Indeed, St. Michael's liturgy was so "high" that I swear the worshippers risked spiritual vertigo. Incense wafted through the aisles and up to the rafters. Sometimes, you had to peer through the mist to catch sight of the altar!

It was into this house of mystery, once a month, we little ones would be jerked from our comfortable Sunday school and trooped round to Rutland Road for service. It promoted a nauseous feeling of insecurity within me and despite Mum assuring me that the vicar – Father Butterfield - would tell us some lovely stories, I had serious doubts. Anyone over the age of twenty was construed as "old" in the eyes of a four-year old, but I'm sure that Father Butterfield was the "real deal" and seriously old. His gargling, "spit and gob" voice frightened all kinds of hell out of me and if he had some lovely stories to tell, well, I don't think I heard them. Don't get me wrong - I am sure that he was a good and holy man, but I can only say that now, armed with the defence of maturity. Anyhow, whenever it was announced that we would all be meeting at church next week, I would tell Mum and Dad that I didn't want to go. Theatrically, I performed symptoms of a wide range of maladies designed to ensure that, come Sunday afternoon, I needed to be wrapped up warmly in bed. Clearly, a re-think was necessary, were I not to be lost to the Good Lord forever. Salvation came from the most unlikely quarter.

At the junction of Whitfield Road and Plashet Grove, stood the Assemblies of God Full Gospel Hall. Probably not missionary zeal inspired by profound spirituality, Derek had become a Full Gospel Hall-er and was always badgering me to "come and join *our* Sunday school." As far as this sensitive child was concerned, snotty old Father Butterfield was fast approaching his sell-by date so, with the encouragement of my friend, I "converted." It signalled the commencement of eight of the most happy – and influential - years of my life.

The church then, as now, is a two-storey affair. The top storey was reserved for worship, and reached via stone steps leading up from Plashet Grove. In the downstairs section, accessed by a short flight of stone steps at the Whitfield Road side of the building, Sunday school classes were conducted. Unlike at St. Michael's, we weren't required to ascend to the "holy of holies" on a regular basis and, initially, I was relieved about that. Visions of incense and Father Butterfield still raged within whenever the word "church" was mentioned, and if that had been what was on offer "upstairs," it would probably have seen me off for good. Instead, I was allowed to learn at my own pace and find my own level through the sensitive and informal leadership of the church. Being taught by a friendly man in a suit was far more to my taste than being growled at by some bloke dressed up like a pantomime dame.

The first step in my education led me to understand that "full" in this context had nothing to do with "bums on seats," despite the fact that there were a considerable number of seats accommodating an equally considerable number of bums. No, the concept was that the Christian Gospel, in all its fullness, was the order of the day. Punches were not pulled and eternal destiny was clearly mapped out. Teaching was fundamental with total emphasis on what the Bible said and what God was looking for from you, devoid of the harshness I had associated with the high atmosphere of St. Michael's. In its stead was genuine care and commitment, totally commensurate with the family and community spirit that I had been - and continued to be - doused in.

Every child was issued with a blue "Star Card" which, I suppose, was somewhat akin to a passport. On it was our name and address, whilst inside, a grid provided a square for each Sunday throughout the year. Just before three'o'clock each Sunday, about one hundred and twenty of us – maybe more – dutifully presented our cards to be stamped in the appropriate square, to "prove" that we had been present and correct on that particular Sunday. If you managed a minimum of forty-five stars – yes, forty-five – over a twelve-month, you got yourself a prize. It might seem alien in these days of too many kids having too much, but I can tell you that the prize was a real motivator. If you were on holiday but managed to attend church somewhere or other (as evidence, a letter from parents), you still got your star. If you didn't, then you lost out. During one year, I managed to get my card bashed fifty times. The two missing ones were due to holiday and me not making enough effort to find somewhere to worship. But I was far from the only one who regularly made that magic half-century. What was on offer was really that good.

Each Sunday afternoon, in the main body of the hall, seats were set out in circles for groups of between six to ten scholars, with segregation of boys from girls a matter of high priority. As we had become used to this at primary school, I can never recall anyone finding anything particularly weird about this. Perhaps being the shy little souls that we were, we even felt comfortable with it. I know for sure that, for my part, it created an air of mystery about girls, which I've always been glad about. Even at my advanced age, I still like the ladies in my life to have some "mystery" about them. At the front of the hall was a small raised platform from where the superintendent, Mr. Ted Crick, would conduct the afternoon's affairs. Behind him, a raised stage fronted by a blue-curtained handrail, whilst across the wall at the back of the stage, were written the words "Jesus who loved me and gave himself for me." Each group had its regular teacher and, from the time that I joined the Sunday school to the time that I left, I was privileged to come under the tuition and guidance of some outstanding men. Mr. George Viles who, memory tells me, used to work for the corporation hygiene department; Mr. Fred Haselgrove, a quiet, thoughtful man who went on to become church treasurer; and my favourite of them all, Mr. Dan Crick.

Where do I start to do that man justice? When I leave this earth, if St. Peter has enough reasons to let me pass the gate, it will be in no small measure due to the influence of the quiet, saintly Mr. Crick. The longer I continued learning from him, the more I marvelled at his kindly, controlled patience with the lot of us. Derek, to the surprise of no one, did his level best to try him sorely. Each week, he would come out with the same old question that gives this chapter its title. Regardless of the topic that we had been talking about during the afternoon, Derek looked for the earliest opportunity to play his ace. For example, if we'd been discussing, "Thou shalt not kill," this is the way the script went.

Mr. Crick - "Any questions?"
Fletch - "Who made God?"
Or what about Adam and Eve?
"Any questions?"
"Yeah. Who made God?"

You get the picture?

It was a verbal tennis match with Mr. Crick doing his best to return every would-be ace the maverick sought to serve. Never once did he lose his cool as, I suspect unwittingly, he continued to lay the foundations of my faith.

Superintendent Ted Crick was a short, bald, tubby man, facially rotund and a dead ringer for Mr. Pickwick. He and his wife Hilda were totally committed to the church at large and, in particular, their young Sunday school charges. A couple of Sundays absence were never allowed to go by without one or other of them taking the trouble to make a visit. Once, when I was in bed with measles, Mrs. Crick came almost daily, just to make sure that all was well and that I was making progress. It was never intrusive and perhaps there was something about me that made her feel that I had potential. Anyhow, my parents were impressed so much that Dad went as far as to observe that this sort of care had never been shown to him throughout his entire Roman Catholic up bringing.

I've thought long and hard about the way that that church did Sunday school, and why it resonated with me. The closest I can get is that it was fun. I'll say that again – it was fun! Despite the set format, the whole thing was never boring. Once we were all in our places, passports stamped, Ted Crick would call everyone to order, and conduct a session of choruses. Short, simple stuff, very rhythmic and tuneful, designed to air our young lungs and, as a by-product, come to terms with some basic Christian ethic.

There were a couple that were always popular: -

"Joy, joy, my heart is full of joy;
Joy, joy, my heart is full of joy.
The saviour dear is ever near,
That's the reason why my heart is full of joy."

Simple, huh? Okay, try this one.

"Deep and wide, deep and wide,
There's a fountain flowing deep and wide.
Deep and wide, deep and wide,
There's a fountain flowing deep and wide."

Now, I'll grant you that these little choruses are neither Charles Wesley, nor, indeed, Graham Kendrick. However, where the fun came in was the actions that accompanied many of the choruses. "Deep and wide" provided a superb vehicle to catch out the unwary and those not paying full attention.

"Deep" - raise one hand as high in the air as you could and the other as low as you could.

"Wide" - arms apart, as far as you could stretch 'em.

"Flowing" – wave your hands from side to side, as though you were playing an invisible piano.

So far, so good.

But, having been lulled into a sense of false security, the trap was laid for when we repeated the chorus. Then, every time the words "deep," "wide," and "flowing" came up, you were not to sing them, but simply do the actions!

Thus, vocally, you had: -

"..........and.........
............and.........
There's a fountain............ and................

Every time, without fail, someone would lose the plot and offer a lusty "deep" when they should have remained silent. Self-righteous prigs who had not fallen foul looked at the miscreants with a knowing air. Mind you, whilst doing that, they took their eyes off the ball with the result that when we hit "wide," they fell straight into the same trap. "Wide, wide as the ocean," where arms were flung as far apart as possible, was another winner. If you knocked someone's block off in this process, so much the better. Silly stuff, I know, but truly it was a lot of fun.

Goodness, there were so many others. Nearly sixty years on, I can still remember all the words and melodies. "It is no Secret what God can do"; "Round the Walls of Jericho"; "Jonah and the Whale"; "Only a boy called David; "In my Heart there rings a Melody; "Give me Oil in my Lamp." Simplistic they might have been, but they served to give us kids a basic knowledge of Bible stories. Some contestants on modern TV quiz shows might have done a darned sight better than they did had they been exposed to the same material.

Oh, and the music. I'll never forget the accompaniment. There were a couple of teenage girls in the school who could play the piano brilliantly. They seemed like grown women to little me whereas, in reality, they were probably only fifteen or sixteen, at most. But, boy, could they play! The piano was augmented by anything up to half a dozen senior girls who drove the rhythm with their twirling, ribboned tambourines. Not your standard "chink, chink, chink" on the beat, but true artistry. Listen to Scottish military drummers. They don't just keep a beat. Instead, they chatter their own peculiar syncopation, adding colour and pace to all that they touch. That's what the tambourine girls at the Gospel Hall did, par excellence. The whole thing was magic and even we lads used to sing our guts out. We just couldn't help it.

Having set the agenda with something like ten minutes of choruses, it would be time for prayers. Ted Crick would quieten the atmosphere, reminding us of the serious nature of the business that we were about to undertake. As a prelude, he would ask if there were any people that we ought to pray for, any situation, or personal needs. Given such licence, out it would all tumble - sick relatives, sick animals, what I'd like for my birthday and, "please Lord, stop that rotten Henry Sherman beating me up." Sometimes, I felt that the Lord shouldn't have been bothered by some of the things we prayed for. Yet they all meant something to someone in one way or another, so perhaps it was okay and I'd lost the plot somewhere. Having drawn up his menu, Mr. Crick would invite one of the teachers to, "Lead us in prayer, brother or sister whoever" whilst, at the same time, throwing down the gauntlet to any of us scholars to add our own efforts - should we feel so moved.

Remarkably, there were more than a few takers. In particular, I remember the gangly John Barrett. Over the years, John became a regular contributor and, although not the most lucid of speakers, he gained my admiration simply because he had the guts to put his head above the wall. God would surely not have worried about his tendency to mumble whatever it was he had to say. Neither would He bother that John constantly spiced his celestial appeal with the word "Lord."

"Lord, we thank you for being able to come here this afternoon, Lord. And, Lord, we pray, Lord, that you will help us,

Lord, to understand more about your care, Lord, for us, Lord." That sort of thing.

On and on John would go, bobbing and weaving, ducking and diving in and out of the "Lords," slave to this verbal mannerism apparent to all, save for dear John. Derek, of course, was onto it like a shot. As brave John battled through his prayer, Derek would be nudging me, mimicking every word and, although I knew better, I struggled to contain my laughter. My face would flush, perspiration dampen my forehead, as tears rolled down my cheeks, in an attempt not to burst out laughing. As soon as the final "amen" was said, I felt at liberty to explode with laughter. Dan Crick would reprimand me gently.

"Come along, Stephen. It's not like you to mis-behave during prayers."

He was right – it wasn't. Pointing at Derek, I defended desperately.

"I can't help it, Mr. Crick. It's Derek. He just makes me laugh, and I can't help it."

Mr. Crick was far from daft and knew full well the true state of affairs and who the culprit really was. But it was no good. Derek just sat there, with the face of an angel – butter wouldn't melt in his mouth. Surveying everyone and everything with a look of disbelief that his behaviour could be held up for scrutiny, his face reflected pure hurt. I never quite worked out how he did that.

Choruses and prayers done, it was time to turn to our individual teachers for instruction in the Bible, delivered with a thoroughness that cannot be over-emphasised. As a result, by the time I reached teenage years, my knowledge of the life and teaching of Christ, alongside a basic understanding of more than a sizeable portion of the Old Testament was deeply ingrained into my thinking. I don't think that I was alone there. Certainly, I would find it hard not to believe that the vast majority of my contemporaries at that school had anything other than a very firm grasp of what was considered right or wrong. That is not to say that we were necessarily particularly good at keeping to the straight and narrow, but we did, at least, have a set of guidelines that provided us with

some clues. I find it sad that in this day and age, too many young -
and not so young - people don't seem to have those guidelines or
commitment to them.

Before the afternoon was over, there was just one more piece
of business to attend to. At beginning of each year – or whenever a
new member joined - we would receive a small stamp album to save
the stamps distributed each week by our teachers. The stamps – or
texts, as we called them - comprised a simple Biblical scene, along
with an appropriate scriptural quotation and reference. If you didn't
turn up on a particular Sunday, you would forego your text and, as it
was not payable in arrears, you could get to the end of the year with
gaps in your album. I have a slight recall of big-heartedness raising
its head when, if you were only a few missing at the end of the year,
the deficit would be made up. I can't be sure about that but, if I am
right, it would be totally in keeping with the ethos of the Full Gospel
Hall.

For many years, I kept at the side of my bed a simple card
that had been given to me, bearing the words "God is Able." As the
years passed, it became increasingly dog-eared, but I couldn't bear to
part with it. Resting alongside it was a particularly conservative
picture of the face of Christ with the powerful words of "One
Solitary Life" on the reverse. Copies of this had been issued to
servicemen during the war, Dad having originally given his to
Grandad and Grandma Vanner. On the reverse, in his distinctive
hand, is written, "To Mum and Uncle Tom, 28th July 1945." As you
might guess, it is precious and still with me all these years on.

Once the texts had been given out, a couple more choruses
were sung, during which we took up "the collection." before a final
prayer and dismissal. At 4'o'clock, the Gospel Hall would spew us
all out onto the street - but we'd be back again next week, that's for
sure.

Now you might be thinking, "Well, that's a pretty formal old
routine," and, to an extent, I can understand that. But, about every
six weeks or so, the format would change when we entertained a
"guest speaker." On these occasions, chairs would be set out theatre
style and although the afternoon would follow the tried and tested

format of choruses and prayers, in place of our lesson, the guest would speak to us all. Their names have faded from my memory, save for one that we all loved like mad.

"Uncle Arthur" was a riot on two legs. He was the first person that I encountered in church who not only had a sense of humour, but actually traded on it. I suppose his style might be described as "manic" today, but it was all so beautifully orchestrated. A very competent accordionist, he would take the stage and begin his set by getting us all singing along to his accompaniment.

"Now then, boys and girls. What's my favourite chorus?"

We all knew it.

"Wide, wide as the Ocean" we'd yell, with the passion of Old Trafford's Stretford End. And off we'd go into a frenzied rendition, complete with actions.

But it was his presentation that put Uncle Arthur in a league of his own. All the other speakers were sincere, mostly soft spoken but, invariably, rooted to both floor and desk. Not Uncle Arthur. He was frenetic - all over the blessed place! If a character in his story was required to hide, there he would be, behind the piano, peeping over the top, blinking at us like a frightened rabbit. We shrieked. Occasionally, I wondered if he was a frustrated pantomime artist, but ultimately concluded that he wasn't. What he had to say was steeped in the Christian Gospel and, whatever it might have looked like, his was no performance. It was nothing more nor less than a man using his gifts to convey the love of God to kids and, I can tell you, it worked a treat for so many.

Many years passed when – delightful surprise - I met him again. I was in my thirties and had undertaken responsibility for marking the local Scripture examination papers. Once the results were known, a sizeable rally took place at which awards and prizes were distributed. At one of these, I spotted Uncle Arthur sitting in the congregation. He was older – we both were – but instantly recognisable, with the twinkle in his eye still present, and every bit as bright. At the end of the rally, I went over to him.

"Hello, there. How are you?"

143

He courteously returned my greeting. After a space of twenty-some years, he was hardly likely to recognise me. We shook hands, and he thanked me for the work that I had been involved with. "I know you, don't I? You're Uncle Arthur."

His eyes positively shone and his smile broadened as I told him about my memories of him speaking at the Full Gospel Hall. When I told him that I remembered his favourite chorus was, "Wide, wide as the Ocean," he was clearly moved. He called over to his wife – I can't recall her name, so let's call her "Mary."

"Mary, it's one of my boys from Plashet Grove. Come and meet him."

"Aunty" Mary was lovely, just the sort of lady I would have expected to cope lovingly and patiently with Uncle Arthur. I'm not sure quite how I qualified as "one of his boys," but I wasn't going to argue the toss. I was just so happy to see this good man enjoying the moment. At the back of my mind, I hoped that, one day, some middle-aged guy or girl might come up to me and say, "I remember you. You're Steve Derby. You spoke at our church when I was twelve. I've never forgotten it." Well, I can dream, can't I?

We live in times when overseas holidays are the norm rather than the exception. In the 1950s, such extravagance was virtually non-existent, and a trip to Southend, or Canvey Island was a very special treat. An adventurous trip to the hop fields of Kent could provide a working holiday, and pay for board and lodgings, all at the same time. For me, the ultimate was a week or two at one of the holiday camps situated around the coast, and here I was luckier than most. As soon as we were all re-united after the war, Mum and Dad regularly booked holidays on the Norfolk coast, between Great Yarmouth and Lowestoft. Three years on the bounce at Golden Sands, followed by another three at Corton Beach, where the cliffs, sand, sea, and organised mayhem *a la* "Hi-de-Hi," were marvellous and memorable fun.

In the wake of more austere times and with an eye to those unable to make the pennies stretch very far, every year, the Church organised an outing to the coast, which was always a riot. Three or four coach loads of scholars, teachers, parents, and supporters would head to somewhere within comparatively easy reach of East London for games, swimming, singing and, in Derek's case, general mucking about. Our favourite destination was Maldon, on the River Blackwater, a little way beyond Colchester. I loved Maldon. It was a quaint little Essex backwater, with a park and marina containing all manner of delights. The river meandered through the town en route for the North Sea from the tiny harbour on the outskirts. Distinctive sail-powered, cross-channel barges glided elegantly up and down on their business. Alongside, the river fed a deep pool, one end of which was dedicated to tiny pedal and rowing boats, whilst the other was reserved for swimming. A small sandy beach skirted the pool, behind which was a grassy slope that provided space for picnics and a vantage point to watch over kids playing in the water.

The depth of that swimming area was, I swear, unfathomable. Although from the beach to the opposite bank was less than thirty yards or so, by the time you had waded out no more than a few yards from shore, the deep sloping shelf ensured that all those under the height of, say, five feet, would be submerged. Dangerous, or what? The diving platform situated just a few yards from the shore remained beyond attainment to me until I had learned to swim. On the riverside of the pool were some ramshackle changing rooms from which a wooden walkway provided access to a springboard and, for the more adventurous, a high diving board. The thing must have been about three metres high but when the time arrived and I had the necessary confidence to dive off the top board, I swear that never once did I manage to touch the bottom. Perhaps there was no bottom!

Past the promenade alongside the riverbank toward the sea, was a small grassy play area, which was always the focus of my Maldon activities. A narrow gauge steam locomotive, designed along the lines of a "Royal Scot," chuffed its way up and down an hundred yards of line, and virtually every penny of my spending money went on this entertainment. On one of our outings, John Barrett managed to work his way into the driver's favour and spent the whole day assisting with the sale of tickets *and* getting free rides.

Perhaps God had answered his stuttering prayers and put me to shame into the bargain. If so, we both deserved what we got.

The promenade continued beyond an inlet where some extremely run-down small ships were moored. They looked as through they had been involved in conflict, although I was never able to prove this beyond reasonable doubt. There was a ghostliness about them that fascinated me and, doubtless, if we could have got on board, we would have had a high old time. But we never did and, given that even Derek couldn't come up with a route for access, I guess that there was nothing that could be done.

Terry and Ricky Young – inevitably – made their contribution.

We had enjoyed a wonderful day, and late afternoon saw us all getting ready for our return. Loads of parents had made the trip and something like sixty of us were sat on the bank alongside the swimming pool. Mum and Mrs. Fletcher sat with Mrs. Young.

Time was moving on and Terry and Ricky had dried and dressed themselves after their dip. Mrs. Young told Ricky to go down to the poolside and rinse out his swimming trunks, so off he went down the sloping grass bank toward the water. Between the beach and the water had been built a protective wall – don't ask me why. What it did mean, however, was that, in order to gain access to the pool, you had to step from the little sandy beach, over the wall, to put your feet onto the bottom of the pool. Nothing more than a couple of feet, I'd say. Nevertheless, as Ricky leaned over, squeezing the water from his swim wear, he lost his balance and fell in – fully clothed!

Grizzling pitifully, he squelched back up to where we were all sitting – and laughing. Turning to Terry – who could be relied upon to do a proper job – Mrs. Young awarded him Ricky's damper than ever trunks.

"Go and wring these out, Terry," she instructed, adding a parting shot, "And don't you fall in."

All eyes followed Terry as he made his way to the poolside. It was as though the script for the next moments had been written long before any of us existed, and I doubt if there were any amongst us who didn't have some sort of premonition that we were about to be entertained royally. Terry started confidently enough but his brain must have been contaminated by his mother's instruction and, for a brief, but significant, moment, he lost his concentration. Perhaps there is something to this telepathy lark. Despite there being nobody within yards of him, he reached forward, lost his balance and, with arms twirling in a singularly unsuccessful attempt to maintain equilibrium, plopped ungracefully, fully clothed, into the drink!

If Ricky's baptism had raised a shriek, it was nothing to compare with the sight of Terry, drenched and bedraggled, coming toward us. Over the cacophony, Mrs. Young's voice could be heard, like some banshee wailing for its lost little ones.

"Oh, my Gawd!" she yelled in disbelief.

Ricky was totally exonerated and enjoyed the laugh against his brother every bit as much as we had enjoyed the laugh against him.

"Somebody pushed me," Terry claimed, meeting with even more hilarity from all of us who had seen that there was no one anywhere near him when he toppled. The lesson to be learned was, if you are in a hole, stop digging!

Neither Ricky nor Terry had any spare dry clothes and the poor guys had to endure the embarrassment of spending the next half-hour and the journey home clothed in nothing more than their raincoats. Derek, of course, couldn't leave it at that. The remainder of his day was dedicated to lifting the back of the raincoat of whichever brother came within reach, with fervour akin to discovering just what Scotsmen really did wear under their kilts. Those outings to Maldon were great fun.

The church's syllabus of Christian education and encouragement was nothing if not comprehensive. Each October, Mr. Crick would remind us all that, very shortly, we would be having "The Demonstration." On first hearing, the term flummoxed me, but I soon got the gist. Simply, it gave teachers and staff the opportunity to put us kids through our singing and recitation paces. At the event itself – usually a Monday evening - parents would come in their droves and provide very real support. I carry two incredibly special memories of those events.

During the weeks leading up to the event, Mr. Winch, who lived just opposite the church, in Whitfield Road, would coach us to perform a hymn outside of our knowledge and, indeed, comfort zone. To my eternal gratitude, he opted for "Peace be Still." Look for it in most of the mainstream denomination hymnals today and you will find it not at all. But in 1951 and to this day, it remains for me one of the greatest hymns ever written. The theology was rock-solid, and the tune magnificent. Each verse comes across as a "movement" in a classical piece, and the whole thing left me with no other option than to sing at the top of my voice. It is well worth searching out.

The second memory was far more personal and had far-reaching effect. The theme chosen for the Demonstration (there was always a theme) was "Road Signs" and it was here that I made my public speaking debut, reciting a little poem entitled "Hidden Turnings." I never had an ounce of nerves and, in truth, couldn't wait to get up on my hind legs and go through my paces. Put it down as a "starter for ten" that I would be an incurable public speaker throughout my life. Folk who heard me that night in 1951 couldn't say that they weren't warned!

But I want to go back to Sunday afternoons and another practice that made an indelible mark on me. In 1954, a blond, dashingly handsome and charismatic American evangelist came to these shores with his entourage. Dr. Billy Graham created a national stir with his preaching and regular invitation to his hearers to, "Just get up out of your seat and come to the front," as a sign that they were ready to embrace the faith. Those that responded were greeted and guided by trained stewards to take early, faltering, steps in the Christian faith. Many thousands responded, amidst opposition cries of "Foul!" It was claimed that it was all about emotion and these "conversions" had no hope of being permanent. "Cassandra," of the "Daily Mirror," - an acidic, yet highly competent old hack - invited Billy to a war of words at a local tavern. Graham accepted and Cassandra proved big enough a man to recognise that there was more to Dr. Billy than he had given him credit for. After their meeting, he wrote, "I never realised that goodness could cudgel us sinners so darned hard." Not all were similarly convinced and, it has to be said, churches did not immediately fill to overflowing, as response numbers suggested they ought to have done. Yet many lives were, unquestionably, changed.

The Full Gospel Hall had been ahead in this game for many years. I can't recall a Sunday when Mr. Crick, or our guest speaker, would not invite, "any of you boys and girls who would like to give their hearts to Jesus, to meet with us in the side room." My learning, experience (such as it was at that stage), and convictions almost guaranteed that, sooner or later, I would do something with this fast ball. The teaching of the church did not short change when it came to conviction about discipleship, the hereafter, and the theology of judgement. Christianity had been presented to me in such an attractive, relevant, and challenging way as enabled me to make some reasoned judgements and, as each Sunday passed, I sensed a mounting compulsion (or was it curiosity?) to get myself sorted with God – whatever that might entail. So, one particular afternoon, when I must have been about ten or eleven, I took the plunge. Along with Harry Crick (Ted Crick's nephew) and, of all people, Derek, I trespassed into the holiest of holies to see what it was all about.

Mr. Crick closed the door quietly and eyed the three of us with suspicion, perhaps aimed more at Del and Harry than me. I suppose I was a bit of a favourite with a number of teachers at the school and my presence had, perhaps, been long awaited. Derek and Harry came, if you will, out of left field.

"So, you boys have come to do business with God, have you?"

Oo-err! Funny way of putting it, I thought. But having jumped from the high board, there was no turning back and the three of us knelt before our mentor, as he began to pray for us. Truthfully, a lot of what Mr. Crick had to say went over my head in every sense. He pleaded for the forgiveness of our sins, that Jesus would wash our hearts clean, and that the Holy Spirit would fill us. Hardly surprisingly for one so young, I'd never really thought of myself in reprobate terms. To the best of my knowledge, I'd never done anything particularly untoward, led a life of debauchery, threatened to shoot the Pope, or anything like that. Lust was patiently waiting in the shadows a good five or six years into the future, so the slate was clean on that score. Granted, I had laughed when Derek had blown a raspberry at Mrs. Finch, and I wondered if that counted as sin?

There is a scriptural account of early Christians experiencing a sense of the presence of God so profound that they began to speak in different languages – "other tongues," as the Book of Acts puts it. Up to that point, the only "other tongues" I'd heard were at Christmas parties, when Uncle Ray and Dad were in their cups. But, I knew the theology. Suddenly, without a by your leave, the fireworks started, and Mr. Crick launched out in a language that meant diddley-doo to me. I couldn't understand a word, and began to feel rather uneasy. But worse was to follow.

"Come on, boys," he urged. "Speak out as the Spirit fills you."

Oh, no! Speak out?! I was sweating, and even Derek had been stunned into silence. The longer the three of us knelt there speechless, the greater the pressure. Talk about "I'm a ten-year-old – get me out of here!" wasn't in it! Then, amidst the turmoil and desire to be anywhere else but where I was, Harry starts mumbling. Don't ask me what he was on about. I was pretty sure he was doing nothing more that imitating every utterance coming from his uncle's lips, but maybe I was wrong and the Spirit really was doing its stuff on old Harry. Ah, well, if you can't beat 'em, join 'em. So off I went, imitating Harry as best I could, dragging Derek along with me in my wake. There were the four of us, one undoubtedly genuine, along with three others who didn't have a clue. Whenever I think back to that afternoon, I'm convinced that the good Lord was up there somewhere, looking down on proceedings, laughing His head off.

When we gained our freedom, I quizzed Harry.

"Here, Harry, was that genuine?"

"'Course it weren't. But if I hadn't done it, Uncle Ted would still have had us there now!"

Frankly, I was a bit disappointed about the overall outcome. As a sensitive little boy, I had truly wanted something wonderful to happen and, as far as I could tell, nothing of the sort had. I had genuinely tried to "give my heart to Jesus" as requested, yet from where I was sitting, He didn't seem much bothered as to whether He had it or not. Maybe, just maybe, I was booking my ticket for something that might happen in my life further on down the road. Yeah – I'm sure that's it.

Somewhere around the age of thirteen, along with Harry, John Barrett, and Derek, I progressed to a new level. In a room accessed from the back of the downstairs hall, a Senior Bible Class was conducted every Sunday afternoon – sort of Sunday school for adults. There must have been the better part of thirty in that group, with ages from thirteen upward represented and, this time around, no segregation of the sexes. Mr. Davies, the leader, I liked. He was a very smart, white-haired gentleman of somewhere about sixty, who positively exuded passion for the faith. This was a far more formalised meeting than I had been used to in the Sunday school, although the spirit of freedom was still easily recognisable. Instead of the fun choruses, we sang hymns that had a good swing to them. Prayers followed the same format whereby individuals could contribute "as the Spirit leads," – quote Mr. Ted Crick. Teaching was offered by Mr. Davies himself, or some other duly appointed member. I can't recall guest speakers getting in on the act – certainly not Uncle Arthur. Shame!

Anyone was free to make a contribution. In fact, Mr. Davies positively exhorted us to do so. The easiest option here was during hymn-singing, when someone would often read out the words of the verse about to be sung. Bystanders would punctuate this with a few "Amens" or "Praise the Lords," and being the new kid on this particular block, I found it a strange and rather rarefied atmosphere. Where my attention was grabbed, however, was by the large number of individuals able to put together some tale or another about answers to prayer, guidance, healing, and a host of other blessings. It came over so naturally that I had not the slightest reason to doubt that the stories were the truth, the whole truth and nothing but the truth. After my "Demonstration" triumph, I suppose it was inevitable that, sooner or later, I would say something, although I knew not what. Just by way of warming up, I had a bash at reading a few verses of hymns but, I asked myself, would I ever have anything original or – more important – genuine to say? Only time would provide the answer.

But just as things were bubbling along quite nicely for me, changes began to occur in my life. Other interests and other people began to invade my territory, and although I still enjoyed the Sunday afternoon meetings, holes in my attendance record started to appear. My Aunt Joan had married Sid Rogers and we both had interests in common. After lunch, somewhere around 2'o'clock, I would drop into their flat next door at No.5 to chew the fat on a range of issues. We would become so engrossed that, often, 3'o'clock came and went, with me still listening to Uncle Sid - or yattering. Initially, pangs of guilt compelled me to bid a fond farewell, and rush round to the church in time to take most of the meeting content on board. But I knew that that was not the way it was supposed to be. As the weeks passed, I was at church less and less. There had been a time when a missed Sunday seemed certain to earn me a celestial reprimand - two might produce something of a more serious nature. Yet when this number stretched to three, four, five and counting, it became clear that I had reached some sort of spiritual watershed and the time for moving on was drawing close. Perhaps it was just a case of the people at that church having done their job. For something like eight years, they had given me a spiritual education *par excellence* and, as the years passed, I would remain eternally grateful for that.

By the time that I reached my fifteenth birthday, I was no longer part of the Full Gospel Hall. Moving on in no way dismantled my belief in God, and I remained sure that it would have impact on my life for a darned sight longer than a few months. But, for now, it was time to draw breath and wait to see what happened. Well, I can tell you that, eventually, something spiritual *did* happen, to the astonishment of all and sundry, not least, myself. A time was not too far distant when I would frequent other places of worship, and profitably so. Yet it would be totally impossible to deny the fact that I could never have received better example, teaching, and encouragement than I did from the Full Gospel Hall, and all those associated with it. Thank you, each and every one of you.

CHAPTER SIX

ESTHAMEIAN – ARISE!

It has been said that anticipation is better than realisation. I have to take issue. From that moment at Leysdown Holiday Camp, when my secondary educational destiny was sealed, starting grammar school was scarcely out of my mind. I just couldn't wait. Reflecting as I do now on my years at the East Ham Grammar School for Boys between 1954 and 1959, the wait was worth every single second. I had already made friends with a couple of older lads, who already attended the school and, to a degree, knew the ropes.

"So you're going to be a new fag, are you? You know that you'll have your head put down the toilets and flushed, don't you?" they warned.

If that threat was designed to frighten me, then it didn't work. "Fag" was the term used in "Tom Brown's Schooldays," to describe any new young fellow-me-lad. Whereas Thomas Hughes' notorious Flashman might have set the standard for bullying at Rugby, times had changed and I couldn't imagine Dr. Whiteley putting up with that sort of nonsense. And anyway, as for the ritual of head down the toilet, what's a face wash amongst friends?

No, my own enthusiasm was more than sufficient to keep everything on the boil and overcome any attempt to un-nerve me. But there was more to it than that, much more.

Early in August 1954, Mum and Dad received that letter from Dr. Whiteley, congratulating them on the fact that their son had gained a place at his school, along with a list of items that I would need to make my stay profitable in every sense. Geometrical instruments, rulers, and pens were understandable and quite acceptable. Others had me a bit nonplussed. I mean, what was train-spotter supreme going to do with football boots, shorts, cricket whites, and suchlike? These were accessories linked to physical endeavour which, as I have made clear, was not at the top of my favourite activity list. Still the stuff had to be bought, so it was off to Fosters, the general outfitter in High Street North, who had a monopoly on the sale of school uniforms and sportswear. The introductory letter left little doubt that Fosters were the only store to do business with and, as a result, summer trade was "Christmas come early" for the little shop, with every one of the new intake rolling up at the door with what was tantamount to a command to spend money. Whilst the sports side of the bargain might not have been of any real interest to me, when it came to the school uniform, well, that was another matter. Once I had that, I would truly belong.

Dr. Whiteley was red hot on smartness and nothing less than a full complement of uniform would be tolerated. A black jacket and white shirt, a black and white diagonally striped tie, together with a dark grey pullover. On the breast pocket of the jacket, the school badge - a replica of the East Ham Borough crest, outlined in the colours of whatever house you were allocated to. In those same colours, the letters "E H G S" arched over the crest. For your physical denominator, grey trousers which, at the unequivocal command of the headmaster, were to be of the short variety for all first year students. Someone told me that this policy had something to do with a shortage of materials available to the nation at large, although I've never managed to verify that. Anyhow, long trousers were strictly for the second year upward and although there were some dissenters to this, I can never recall them being called to account. Socks were grey, with two black hoops, separated by one white one, turned over at the top.

Oh, and lest we forget (as if we ever could), the crowning glory.....the school cap! It came in a variety of styles and fashions. For the minions, it was a simple black affair, with the East Ham crest embroidered at the front. Should your school career lead you to the dizzy heights of prefect, then you got the same version, only in velvet, if you please. School and house captains would be entitled to have a tassel affixed to their velvet caps, which made them look like high-achieving nancy boys – but I wasn't going to tell them that. Not during my first year, anyway.

From the very start, an ethos of good control was established amongst the first year intake. So that we knew what was going to be expected of us, the School Rules were presented to us. Brief and to the point, they were, I suppose, the forerunner of a staff handbook – or Health and Safety policy. Or both!

What about this?

EAST HAM GRAMMAR SCHOOL FOR BOYS
SCHOOL RULES

1. *All boys will wear School Uniform (inc. Cap) to and from School and when representing the School in any activity.*

2. *All articles of wearing apparel must be clearly marked with the owner's name, on suitable name tabs.*

3. *The Sixth Form only will be allowed to enter School before 8.55am.*

4. *All boys other than SIXTH Formers will remain in the Main Playground during mid-morning break and the Dinner interval.*
   OUT OF BOUNDS: Stage; Changing Rooms; that part of "B" corridor extending from the Secretary's Office to the end of the School; Hall and Grand Piano.

5. *All milk will be consumed under the Covered Way in the Main Playground.*

6. *Sandwiches and ice-cream must be eaten in the Playground and wrappers deposited in the waste paper baskets. Boys who bring sandwiches for lunch will be allowed to use the Dining Block.*

7. *The lavatories must not be used as an extension of the Playground.*

8. *Balls which go on to the roof must not under any circumstances be retrieved.*

9.   *The Main Entrance will be used by Sixth Formers and Staff only.*
10.   *Only those boys who have permits will be allowed to bring Cycles to School. Cycles must be padlocked and cyclists must dismount to wheel their cycles to cross the Barking Road.*
11.   *The Cycle Track must be used by Cyclists only. Other boys must use the Sussex Road Entrance.*
12.   *Boys will not open windows or operate sun blinds or partitions without the permission of a Master.*
13.   *Boys will WALK on the RIGHT of the corridors.*
14.   *Boys are not to remain in the school premises after 3.40 unless they are taking part in a school activity.*

Reading them again after so long, I am surprised at the inconsistent usage and surfeit of capital letters in the document. We were a grammar school, for goodness sake. Shouldn't we have known better? Anyhow, whatever the grammatical rights and wrongs of the document, rules were rules, and all scholars were required to live and die by them.

By the time that my first day at school arrived, I was well primed. With every item of uniform pristine and in its right place, I set off for the bus stop on Plashet Grove, satchel over my shoulder. Irene Phillips, from No.23, followed just a few yards behind me. She was a couple of years my senior and, I always thought, very pretty. As I stood at the bus stop, she walked past on her way to the girls' grammar school, situated at the junction of Plashet Grove with High Street North. She said not a word, but her raised eyebrow and slight smile seemed to suggest that I had not scrubbed up too badly. I felt so proud.

My bus took me along the same route to East Ham Town Hall as I'd travelled with Mum and Dad, when I went for my interview. The option was to either walk to the school along the Barking Road or, alternatively, follow the hordes down Nelson Street (alongside the fire station), toward Sussex Road. Time and experience would persuade most to opt for the latter as, on the corner of the junction with Napier Road, there was a sweet shop. Like Fosters, they must have done a roaring trade and it was the preferred way to and from school. On their first day, all new kids ran the gauntlet of being pointed out and taunted as "fags" by lads who, just a year earlier, had been at the receiving end of precisely the same treatment. By the time that boys entered their third year, evidence suggested that they had grown out of the habit – but we didn't know that at the time. I'd been made so aware of the practice that, to be honest, it didn't really bother me and I had built up an inner resistance.

I'd set out on my journey alone but, as I drew closer to the school, I recognised a number of former Shaftesbury friends. Perhaps it was a need to cherish this particular moment that made me decide I would stay a one-man band for the time being. At the school gates, I reflected on the time just a month or two ago when I had walked through them and onto the site for my interview. Then, it had been a case of wishing and hoping. This time, I looked over at the school buildings, with the all the all-dominating clock tower straight ahead, and knew it was for real.

The school was a two-storey, red-bricked affair, set out roughly in the form of a letter "F," with an impressive frontage, the East Ham Borough crest set over glass doors, which led into the administrative area, and Dr. Whiteley's office. The longer arm of the "F" was designated "B Corridor," with the two off-shoots being "A" and "C" corridors respectively. Between corridors "C" and "A," double swing doors provided access to the school hall, behind which, separated from the main building, stood a well-equipped gymnasium with changing rooms. Metal and woodwork facilities were housed under the same roof. Given the facilities for sports and games, handicraft, not to mention academia, by any stretch of the imagination, we were extremely well catered for.

On that first day, along with all the other first years, I was ushered into the hall, which was pretty well filled with wooden seats. This time around, for one performance only, we would have the luxury of a seat although after our induction, we would have to make do with sitting on the parquet flooring. A hum of busy conversation filled the air as those that knew each other shared this new, exhilarating, yet slightly scary experience. Ken Hinds had been at Shaftesbury with me and we sat alongside each other. Intelligent and bespectacled, Ken had great drive for one so young and was one of the nicest guys that I knew. There and then, the pair of us decided that we would stick together as a two-some, rather than create some kind of Shaftesbury Mafia with others from our old school. We conducted our own reconnoitre of the surroundings. Before us, a raised stage, reached by way of half-a-dozen steps, where grey curtains were pulled back. A single desk held central place. To our right, tall windows looked out on the playground whilst to the left, we were separated from the flats along Barking Road by one of the paths that lineated the entire site. Thick grey curtains – the same hue as those for the stage – hung down, protecting the windows. Behind us, a balcony which, we were yet to discover, housed the more senior scholars on assembly days and suchlike. The hall was perfect for school plays, examinations, orchestra performances, and assemblies.

Suddenly, there was a deep hush subduing all, heralding the arrival of Dr. Whiteley. There could be no doubt that this was the headmaster. He strode purposefully to the front of the hall and mounted the steps to the stage, before turning to survey his new intake. He impressed me every bit as much as on our first meeting at my interview. Lord of all and whom he surveyed, he stood there, gently exhaling breath upward through his moustache. We fags didn't dare speak a word, and it was left to him to break the silence, with a firm, yet civil, welcome. For the next fifteen minutes, he set out a few wise "do's" and "don'ts" that we were already reasonably familiar with, having read the school rules. Nevertheless, it did no harm to have a reminder. Yet Dr. Whiteley went deeper than that, emphasising the importance of "doing your best" and "being a credit to the school." Do this, and all will be well. It was almost spiritual and I, for one, wouldn't have dreamed of doing anything other.

Whilst all eyes had been fixed to the front, most of us had not noticed the five teachers who had taken their places at the side of the hall. The Head introduced them as "those appointed to be responsible for the first year classes," and it didn't take a genius to

work out that there were going to be five streams, "A" to" E."
Certainly, I wasn't expecting to be at the top of the food chain,
although I hoped I wouldn't be assessed as lowly as "E." When the
class lists were read out and my name came up, I found myself
allocated to Mr. Cox in Form 1D, so I started with no
misapprehensions as to where I stood in the academic stakes. A final
exhortation from the Doctor to work hard and behave, before Mr.
Cox trooped twenty-eight of us out of the hall and along to "C"
corridor, where our desks awaited us in room C6, neatly ranked in
front of his desk and chalkboard. The anticipated scramble for seats
next to favourite mates bypassed Ken Hinds and me. We'd done our
deal, made our pact, and simply shrugged our shoulders before
finding a couple of desks near to the front of the classroom.
Throughout our grammar school years, Ken and I invariably sat
together – always at the front. He would always be around to
become a very good influence on me, well capable of harnessing and
encouraging the dreamer.

By the end of our first week, it seemed as though we had
known our new classmates for a lifetime. Gerry Benjamin and
Bobby Garn had come from Shaftesbury, so we were cool there.
Dave Philpott was from Brampton school and proved to be a pretty
useful sportsman, and good-looking to go with it. At the back of the
room, sat Stan Gibbons, the tallest boy in the class, with a mass of
blond hair. Stan not only looked funny (in the best sense of the
word), but *was* funny, as time would prove. He was a fine footballer,
too, and the time was not far distant when he would turn out for
England Schoolboys at Wembley, no less, (a 3-0 win over Scotland
Schoolboys) alongside another of the new intake, Ron Boyce, who
was destined to make a name for himself in the professional game
with local club West Ham United. When it came to electing a class
captain (yes, you did read that right, we had a class captain), without
rhyme nor reason, we opted for Mike Apostolidis. Dave Philpott
mumbled something about being, "elected on the strength of an
outstanding name." Nice bloke as Mike undoubtedly was, Dave was
probably right.

Mr. Cox was medium height, probably somewhere around the age of thirty, and proved to be an excellent teacher and form master. Very aware that he had a group of novices, he sensitively inducted us into rudimentary matters that we would need to give our best attention – particular wearing your school cap when off the school premises. What I really liked was that, when a master entered the room, we were all required to stand until bade to sit. Now that *did* feel special and much more like the Rugby of Dr. Arnold. It imbued a sense of respect for the staff, although some of them, it has to be said, were not terribly fond of the practice. Left-wingers were getting in everywhere. Mind you, it got the better of Mr. Cox on one occasion.

Entering the class, he waited by his desk until every boy was on his feet. It took a moment or two, but time was on his side. Unfortunately, Mr. Cox's chair was not as robust as he had every right to expect and when he sat down, the blessed thing collapsed beneath him. Twenty-eight eleven-year-olds laughed – momentarily. On coming up for air, we could see that he was not best pleased.

Mick Barber was one half of the Barber twins, his brother Les being in 1E. They were quiet boys, very dark of skin, jet black of hair, and as honest as the day they were born. Fate decreed that Mr. Cox's eye should fall on Mick.

"Barber!" Mr. Cox uncharacteristically bellowed.

"Yes, sir?"

"Come out here."

Poor Mick took the walk of shame.

"Did you think that was funny, Barber?"

"Yes, sir."

And with that, Mr. Cox gave Mick a thump right across the back of the head.

The unfairness of it all was far from lost on any of us. Mick had only told the truth, the whole truth, and nothing but the truth. A teacher – albeit a nice one – had finished up on his backside. It *was* funny, we'd all laughed, and who wouldn't? So getting a wallop for telling the truth seemed quite beyond the pale. Somewhere at the back of my mind, I am sure that Mr. Cox apologised later, which would have been all that I grew to expect of him.

When we got down to the real business of learning, Mr. Cox's friendly, efficient manner worked wonders. During the first six months of my schooling, he introduced me to the mysteries of mathematics, algebra, and geometry, and the "sums" I had grown to hate under Mr. Owen, at Shaftesbury, quickly became quite good fun – especially algebra. Mr. Cox was talking sums, but not as I knew them, Jim. Despite never excelling mightily at the subject, thanks to Mr. Cox, I managed to take one giant leap forward and grow to love mathematics.

A well-organised agenda for each day was already established and, at 9.00am each day, we were expected to be in class for Mr. Cox to call the register and establish who was and who wasn't there. Thus duly logged, we paraded to the hall for assembly. Jewish lads were exempt and allowed time apart to study their own Scriptures, for there was an unequivocal Christian emphasis in assembly. The gallant six hundred filed into the balcony and main hall seating area, whilst we "fags" sat cross-legged on the floor at the front. These introductory proceedings were overseen from the stage by the Deputy Head, Mr. Ingram, a studious, bespectacled Scotsman with greying hair Brylcreemed to his bonce, and neatly parted off-centre. Once he was satisfied that all was good and ready, he issued the command, "All stand," which we did, to welcome the procession of teaching staff, led by Dr. Whiteley. Up the steps to the stage, where the Head took his place behind the centre stage desk, whilst his colleagues sat on the rows of chairs ranked behind him. And there we all were, scholars and teachers, facing each other, and ready to do battle.

The assembly format was basic and never varied. A hymn would be announced and sixth-former Brian Rayner, at the grand piano, would thump out an introduction before accompanying us through however many verses it took. Amazingly, there was hardly a boy amongst us who didn't give it his all. Then, a Sixth Former (usually) came forward to read a passage from the Bible, a role

162

viewed by the nominee as anything between an honour and a chore. I can never recall anyone making a complete botch of it. No homilies were offered, and once we had done the Lord's prayer, it was considered that we had reached a point where we could be considered sufficiently spiritualised. Dr. Whiteley read such notices as were essential for our attention during the coming days, along with - when appropriate - a few salutary warnings about behaviour and rule-abuse. Thus, with business done, the stage party left in the same grand style in which it had arrived and, if all went according to plan, we were ready to disperse to our classes, ready for a 9.25am start to lessons.

On those very few occasions when things didn't go quite to plan, for whatever reason, there could be a delay before we vacated the hall. Invariably, this was the cue for Fred Mills, one of the Gymnastics/Sports teachers, to usurp a role of responsibility. I'm sure he was a frustrated Head, and equally sure that he knew, in his heart of hearts, that he would never make it. He just got it where he could. Fred was Yorkshire, tried and true, very thin, and with a pencil moustache. Surveying the remnants, he would be on the look out for signs of misdemeanour and if and when he found them, we all knew what was coming.

"Aaarrrrrr…….."

Whatever Fred had to say, he always prefixed it with this gargled and drawn out introduction. Small wonder that every kid in the school picked up on it on first hearing and could impersonate him to perfection. It never failed to get a laugh. At the time, I thought he was a bit of a plonker but, many years later, one or two of his colleagues told me that Fred was one of the kindest and best of men. You live and learn.

Teaching sessions were arranged in blocks of forty-minute periods, with four in the morning, separated by a fifteen-minute break at 10.45am. At 12.20pm, we broke for lunch, either to go home or attend one of the two luncheon sittings held in the school dining room. Studies resumed at 1.40pm, when a further three sessions took us through to 3.40pm. After that, we were free to do as we pleased, attend other school functions, or, if it was Friday, stay for detention. There was little or no change to that format during my time at the school. Well-organised and secure, it provided a powerful base for the team of teachers – amongst whom, there were some tremendous characters - to do their stuff.

For the first time in my life, I had no option other than to stay for school dinners. Over the years, they have received a pretty bad press but, I have to say, I found the fare served up varied, and pretty darned good. Okay, cauliflower cheese wasn't entirely to my liking, but that was a case of preference rather than quality. There were ample alternatives. The dining hall comfortably seated something like an hundred and fifty scholars and teachers, each sitting being overseen by a teacher who would call and dismiss diners in and out of the hall, as and when appropriate. One long table was set apart for the staff, who sat with their backs facing the windows, looking out at us all like judges on the bench. Somewhere around sixteen tables were strategically set out, with diners allocated to them in multiples of eight, including a senior prefect who performed the role of table monitor. Kitchen staff wheeled their trolleys around the hall, depositing dishes of the day for the monitor to "play mum," so to speak, and ensure that each boy got his share, fair and square.

My first monitor was Jim Campbell - a tall well-built, quiet, scholarly, and very likeable bloke who did his job with precious little fuss. Sitting directly opposite me was Pete Roberts.

Now, Pete was built to be funny "ha, ha." His teeth protruded slightly, and he always seemed to be smiling. During one early sitting, he picked up his dessert plate and licked it clean of custard – a practice neither documented nor recommended in the "J.L.Whiteley Guide to Good Table Manners." Jim brought him smartly to attention.

"Roberts! What the hell do you think you're doing?"

Pete looked up from his trough.

"Well, I've paid for it, so I'll eat it," he responded with logic beyond response - or so I thought. Jim was not quite so submissive.

"Well, why don't you stick your head in the jug and lick that out? Your head and that jug, Roberts - they're the same shape!"

We looked at Pete, then at the tapered jug, and imagined his face - protruding teeth and all – sitting on his shoulders, in tapered format. Laughing broke out around the table, and even Jim's threat of detention for the lot of us made precious little impact. Further hilarity arrived the following day.

It had been a very civilized and event-free luncheon. Main course completed, the dinner ladies were serving up our dessert – figs and custard. Pete was tucking into his when I shared a confidence with him that, with hindsight, ought to have either stayed with me or been shared outside of the dining hall.

"Pete, do you know how figs get squashed flat like that?"

He took another mouthful and shook his head.

"No idea."

"Well, my Uncle Fred told me that Japs put them between the cheeks of their bums and squeeze."

The contents of Pete's gob – custard an' all – shot straight back into the plate from whence it came, leaving the pair of us in a fit of uncontrollable laughter. The thought of some big, fat sumo wrestler with half a pound of figs decorating his nether regions was just more than we could cope with. Jim's calls to order, accompanied by threats, cut no ice with either of us.

But we tried – God knows we tried. Each of us looked down into our plates as the only practical way we could avoid eye contact. But we both could hear the other fighting – almost choking – to contain our suppressed laughter. Just when it might have been reasonable to suppose that we were all laughed out, I looked up to see if Pete was faring any better than me. Right on time, he felt the same need to see if the coast was clear. It wasn't, and as soon as our tear-filled eyes met, off we went again. Only when released into the playground were we able to howl and release the pent-up laughter that Uncle Fred's international cuisine know-how had caused.

From that moment, our future was marked. It only took someone to spread the word that figs were on the menu for Pete and I to know what the outcome was going to be. In the midst of one such attack, "Gabby" Hayes – one of the science teachers, - came limping by. Wire-framed glasses, a mop of frizzy hair, he required the help of a walking stick for some support. Whilst I was lost in uncontrollable mirth, Gabby crept up silently behind me. Suddenly, I got a sharp smack on the nut from the walking stick, which resulted in instant sobriety.

"Just behave yourself, boy," said Gabby, moving on out of the hall with a handful of his colleagues.

By and large, I did – but never when figs were on the menu.

My first year was all about basics and my end of term report accurately confirmed much of what I had expected. By the time that the first year ended, Mr. Cox had handed over the reigns of Form 1D to Peter Kelly, a young, friendly teacher. He summed me up with this end-of-term commendation – "A satisfactory first year's performance. He should make good progress. A pleasant member of the form." I was none too disappointed with that, or with most of the other assessments of my efforts. As expected, English Language and Literature served me well and Mr. Barnes noted, "He writes a good composition. He has done quite well." The theme was continued in mathematics where the horrors served up by Mr. Owen continued to fade into insignificance.

French saw me ranked a surprising seventh in the class and - goodness knows how - I was awarded an "A Plus." Our teacher was Mr. Holmes, nicknamed "Hitler" on account of his toothbrush moustache and swept over hairstyle. He might well have looked like Hitler, but there the similarity ended. He was a lovely, gentle man. I'll never forget the first time that I "spoke" French. Mr. Holmes invited us all to stand, point to the window, and repeat after him, *"Voila la fenetre."* Round the room we went, voila - ring everything in sight. If it was present, it got voila-red! If the object were closer to us, then we slipped into *voici* mode. The thought that I, Stephen Derby, of Walpole Road, had taken the first steps along the bi-lingual road, made me smile with delight.

Yet there had to be some debits in my first year and, sure enough, there were. Mr. Peyton observed that, in history, I had to,

" learn the idea of absorbing and retaining facts." But the *piece de resistance* was handicraft – woodwork, to you and me – where Mr. Hanley summed me up with, "Careless and erratic. Must make an effort to get down to his work." Well, he got that right. I hated the rotten subject from the start and, to this day, am totally incapable of knocking a nail in straight. Overall, though, I felt that I hadn't done too badly at all.

Now, I don't want to get too involved in the long-running argument about the merits or otherwise of streaming and grading students according to abilities, potential, and whatever other criteria might be served up. I can only say that, for me, all of this assessment, marking, and league table placings stuff provided a valuable yardstick by which I was able to measure my progress. Competition was not perceived as a dirty word and each boy knew where he stood in the overall and specific scheme of things. You were able to identify whether you were likely Premiership material, or in danger of slipping into the nether regions of a lower stream. The vast majority were able to adapt accordingly. My efforts during that initial year, which saw me achieve ninth position out of a complement of 28 in the class, enabled Dr. Whiteley to comment on my report, "Satisfactory progress – good." You can imagine, then, my delight at finding myself in the "C" Stream for the start of my second year. Not a spectacular elevation, but, at least, moving in the right direction. Save for a couple of promotions and relegations, Class 2C turned out to be pretty much Class 1D. It was the start of a period of discovery, where I would begin to understand what I was really good at. Oh, yes. At long last, I graduated to long trousers.

In that second year, English continued to be my best subject. From Year One, we retained the teaching services of Mr. Barnes, commonly known as "Gripper"(I never did find out why). A fast mover, was Gripper, always in a hurry, as he charged down the corridors, his black gown flapping behind him like an academic Batman. Aged probably around thirty, fair wavy hair crowned a face that seemed to carry a permanent scowl. I can never recall him laughing or, indeed, smiling. Fools he suffered not at all. I will always associate him with a schoolboy classic and a teacher's *faux pas* of monumental proportions.

At the beginning of each full term, we were presented with a list of books that we were expected to read throughout the year. As each year passed, we would receive fresh lists of books that had been assessed as suitable reading for boys of our age. I can't recall getting through more that six at most (there must have been a total of thirty), but those few must have had some influence.

In our second year, Herman Melville's classic "Moby Dick" had been set for us to read during the term. You know the one, with Captain Ahab deficient in the leg department to the tune of one, as a result of a contretemps with the great white whale. There we all were, seated at our desks, waiting for the grand entrance of Mr. Barnes.

As he burst into the room, as a man – or a boy – we all stood. Gripper was one of those who never seemed in tune with this practice and, after muttering something undecipherable under his breath, ordered us to sit down hardly before some of us had got up. His opening gambit was unforgettable.

"Right you lot. Get your "Moby Dick"'s out!"

Well, the shrieks from nigh on thirty twelve-year-olds must have echoed throughout every corridor in the school. I ask you. Get your "Moby Dick"'s out!

A sneer came to his lips.

"Oh, you smutty little boys!" he said disdainfully.

I was never convinced that Gripper hadn't planned the entire mischief deliberately. Think about it. He surely could see what was coming and, all these years on, I have the suspicion that he knew precisely what he was doing. A later cameo convinced me that I was right.

Classroom reading sessions were regular, where each of us would read out loud a passage from whichever book, play, or poem we were studying. Greg Seymour - a tall, rangy lad - sat alongside

Stan Gibbons at the back of the classroom. Clearly, the "Moby Dick" plot wasn't holding his full attention, and he had been casually browsing and reviewing forthcoming pages. Suddenly, he launched a Chinese whisper that started to go around the room.

Greg had found, in the next couple of pages, the word "bulwarks." Given the nautical flavour of the novel, this should hardly have come as any great surprise to anyone. Most of us literary coves couldn't understand why Greg should be grinning and silently mouthing the number of the page on which the word appeared. Maritime was clearly not at the top of Greg's "can-do's", and, due entirely to this deficiency, his pronunciation of the word "bulwarks" would have definitely come into conflict with that of any self-respecting able seaman, let alone admiral. In fairness to him, he was probably not alone, for there were several grins and giggles going on.

In this atmosphere of uncertainty, the selection of readers had now become something akin to Russian roulette. About half-a-dozen lads were silently praying that they wouldn't be selected to read the paragraph containing the wretched word. Ron Wyatt was competently leading us nearer, ever nearer, to the "bulwarks" section and, given that Ron knew full well the correct pronunciation, it looked as though the catastrophe would pass. But, no. Ron's erudite flow was interrupted by Mr. Barnes.

"Thank you, Wyatt. Very well read. Now, Seymour would you take up the story?"

Whether or not Gripper was aware of what had been going on, I couldn't say. But it did seem a remarkable co-incidence that, out of the lot of us, he opted for Greg. Here was an opportunity for revenge, if ever there was one. Poor Greg's face was a picture of shock/horror. The word was in the second paragraph designated for him to read and as we all had, on average, five paragraphs to plough through, the lot had fallen – very substantially - upon Jonah!

He started confidently enough, but it was like a small ship approaching an iceberg - you knew that disaster was impending. Sailing ever closer, Greg's delivery slowed until, there confronting him, was his nemesis. He paused, he hesitated......

Gripper's deadpan features and superior manner focussed on Greg for full effect.

"Oh, come on, Seymour. Just say the bloody word."

The worst thing he could have said! This was licence to kill, for Greg could only assume that his presumed pronunciation was correct. Hadn't the encouragement implied as much? He took his courage into both hands.

"Bollocks," he announced.

Thus put out of our misery, we were all free to celebrate. Everyone cheered and applauded. Greg Seymour had said "bollocks" right out loud in class.

Gripper? Well, he just sat there, smug as the cat with the cream. It had been a personal triumph.

As my love of language grew, my passion always favoured prose. Poetry passed straight over my head unless it was in the nature of easily understood doggerel – boys standing on burning decks, and that sort of stuff. I don't think that I was alone. As one unwilling to be beaten, in an attempt to make good the deficit, Gripper offered a prize to the boy who produced the best interpretation of a poem of their choice. Now that was more like it. My earlier public speaking debut at the Sunday school demonstration gave me a head start. All I needed was the right vehicle.

In amongst the Shakespeare, Yates, Keats, Milton, and, of course, William Makepeace Thackeray, I found a dramatic piece by Christopher Marlowe about this guy Faustus, who had sold his soul to the Devil. A midnight appointment had been made in order to complete the transaction, and Faustus, thinking better of his earlier decision, was seriously contemplating that his deal might not have been the best career move he'd ever made. For a couple of weeks, I studied the text in an endeavour to understand – feel, even – the emotions and tensions that such a situation would induce. By the time that performance date came around, I was, as they say, up for it. My name was drawn to be the last performer of the day and, not wishing to sound cocky, listening to most of my unprepared and unconvincing classmates, I grew ever more confident that I was going to win the prize. What was more, I wanted it, and that can be more than half the battle. I stepped up to the crease.

Slowly at first, I tried to convey the spirit of regret, fear, and trepidation I had sought to understand. Gripper sat to the side, and I could see that he was well impressed. Well, at least, there was a hint of a smile about his lips. When I brought the piece to its close and my Faustus had changed his address to that of a considerably warmer clime, the whole class burst into applause. I was so proud. It didn't matter that the prize turned out to be nothing more than a manky bar of Cadbury's Milk Chocolate. Did I care? Not a bit. A prize is a prize, where I'm concerned.

And so to music. Our teacher was Charles "Charlie" Collins, a diminutive, dark-haired, pleasant little cove, who struggled to maintain any sort of discipline. That he loved music was beyond question and, my, how he tried to encourage us. Under his tutelage, we would learn key signatures, timings, how an orchestra was conducted (bit like semaphore without the flags), in addition to listening to recordings of some of the great classical works. I might just have been able to put up with this but when he started encouraging us to sing, life became nothing short of pure hell. Mind you, we did adopt one favourite – although not for any musical content. A charming little ditty entitled, "Where the Bee Sucks, there Suck I." If we managed to get past that opening line with its all too obvious and freely applied adaptation, the next one would see us off completely. "In a cowslip's bell I lie." Short of dressing as fairies and skipping round the room, you could hardly find anything more likely to make a self-respecting twelve-year old lad squirm. The refrain of, "Merrily, merrily, shall I live now?" served only to twist the knife. And who wrote this piece of tosh? Only Shakespeare! Good job he hacked out "Macbeth," "Hamlet," and a few other tasties.

Charlie was a very competent pianist and would accompany us on the upright piano situated in the corner of the room. Now this would have been fine had it not for one or two small things. The first was that, had the instrument been a grand, he would have had unimpeded vision to see what was going on in class. However, the

171

upright obliterated and separated him from whatever we chose to get up to. The second small thing was, unfortunately, Charlie himself, who was decidedly deficient in the "feet and inches" department. As soon as he went behind the bunker to sit and play, so the mice would come out to turn music lessons into a breeding ground for revelry.

Gerry Benjamin and Joe Brown sat together at the desk immediately in front of the piano – the last place that poor Charlie was likely to be able to see and monitor to any real effect. Joe was another funny guy and once brought with him to school a bit of an old gas balloon, with the corners cut off. One good blow through the mouthpiece and the sound of escaping air through the cuts produced the most perfect and voluble "fart" that schoolboy-kind could muster. So, as Charlie settled to tinkle the ivories by courtesy of Beethoven, Mozart, Chopin, and others of that breed, thirty seconds or so into the piece - give or take a bar – Joe would let rip! The melody would come to an abrupt halt, and round Charlie would come to confront the hordes.

"Who did that?"

Thirty blank faces failed to provide an answer.

Drawing himself up to full height – somewhere about five feet six, Charlie issued his ultimatum.

"If there's any more of it, the boy responsible will be sent to the headmaster."

He looked around the class, trying for all his might to look severe. There wasn't an ounce of malice in his body and, to be honest, I was sure that I could detect the edge of his mouth fighting against a grin. Back he went to recommence battle with the maestros. But as soon as he had set himself down, the sound of another almighty trump filled the air. Poor old good-natured Charlie didn't know what to do.

"Was that you, Brown?" he accused.

Joe's ruddy complexion was enhanced intensely when he blushed, and blush he did. His response had all the body language of a guilty party.

"No, sir."

Unconvinced, Charlie asked him to turn out his pockets. Well, of course, by now the implement had been handed around the class under cover of desks. Body search complete, a second verbal warning was issued to Joe, and Charlie returned to his instrument. But no sooner had he got into his flow than the recital was dealt a mortal blow by another mighty sound bite from the other side of the room. At this point, having been exposed to this barrage of artificial farting, he lost the will to live and the performance was over and done for the day.

To my musical dismay, I hadn't yet found the courage to rid myself of violin playing. I had hoped that a new school would see my name disappear from the agenda, but no. The wretched fiddle dogged me even yet. Data must have been passed from Miss Campbell – damn her eyes - to the grammar school, noting that, for four years, I had been playing the instrument – and playing it very badly indeed, let me tell you. Anyhow, I found myself press-ganged into the second violins of the school orchestra, which I enjoyed not one bit.

The burden of being in the orchestra rested heavily upon me in the classroom scenario for, periodically, Charlie encouraged each boy to stand in front of his peers to sing, play an instrument, or make a presentation on some composer or another. I wasn't going to get away with the easy option of a talk – that would have been a walk in the park. Given that he knew I could just about scrape out a bit of a tune on the violin, Charlie set me up for it. I opted to regale the masses with my interpretation of, "The Skye Boat Song" – you know, "Speed bonnie boat like a bird on the wing." It's a charming little melody to which my playing added little and deducted much. The performance drew scant applause, so thank God for Stan Gibbons.

Stan, of all people, was in the process of learning to play the piano. None of us knew this until the day he stood and offered to go through his paces. Charlie was delighted - we were astonished - and to celebrate this break from normality, the piano was pulled round to such an angle as would ensure that the audience had the best possible view of the maestro. Stan looked nervous as he took his place and set up the sheet music he had brought along with him. But within two minutes, Stan Gibbons was declared a genius as, in that classroom, he showed us all that music could not only soothe the savage breast, but also be hilariously funny in the process.

None of us recognised Stan's melody which I would best describe as a tune designed to accompany a drunken matelot swaying down the street - that's about as close as I can get. The whole class laughed, but not in ridicule. We recognised that Stan was creating something quite unique and, as he brought the piece to an end, every boy stood, cheered, and applauded.

Charlie, no less than us, was in high dudgeon.

"Highly amusing, Gibbons, highly amusing," was his assessment of the performance, and we all drank to that. "What was the piece called?"

"Entrance of the Gladiators," sir."

Well, so it was, but not as we knew it. Stan, by unwittingly altering the time signature, had converted a dramatic and rousing march into something not far short of a burlesque, better equipped to accompany an eccentric Laurel and Hardy dance than gladiators entering the arena for a punch-up. Many years later, Eric Morecombe would play "all the right notes, but not necessarily in the right order." Stan had been there before him and, indeed, gone one step beyond. He played "all the right notes, in the right order, but not in the time signature the composer intended." For sure, it was yards more entertaining than me scratching out, "The Skye Boat Song."

Never one to discourage, Charlie sent Stan back to his seat.

"Well done, Gibbons. Well done."

It was inevitable that my unhappy affair with the violin would come to an end at some time in the not too distant future. Despite Charlie's cajoling, I just did not have the heart for it. The school orchestra wasn't a bad little unit and could boast quite a few excellent players. But I was definitely not amongst their number and, increasingly, I absented myself from Tuesday lunchtime lessons, and skipped orchestra practices before giving up on the whole sorry mess. That decision was helped in no small part by the fact that, on Tuesdays, in order to attend violin lessons, I needed to switch from first to second luncheon sitting, thereby encountering the wrath and sarcasm of Mr. Elford-Gulley, who presided over second sitting goings-on. Bald-headed with a goatee beard; ruddy of face and vitriolic of humour, and a teacher of French, Elford-Gulley frightened the life out of me. Perhaps his subject inspired him to want to look continental, and he inspired some of the wittiest schoolboy humour.

"He's only got that hair on his chin because he can't grow the stuff on his head!"

"Elford-Gulley. Not only does he look like Lenin – his politics are the same. Only further to the left!!"

I was thankful that I never had to contend with him as a teacher, although rumour has it that he had a terrific sense of humour, underneath it all. Good for him, but not for me. Each Tuesday, I dreaded having to crawl in to second sitting and ask him to find me a place at a table. Scowling, he would look down on me.

"What do you think this is then, boy? A bloody cafeteria?"

Now, that is what you call world-class sarcasm, for that is *exactly* what it was. With a little more courage, I would have told him what to do with his school dinner – figs, custard and all! As it was, those weekly encounters served to provide me with the courage to throw over the violin lessons and all that they entailed for good. But things were about to move up more than a couple of gears for me.

In 1955, amongst the new intake of staff, came a young, good-looking bloke, dark-haired, slim, with a pronounced Lancashire accent – as you would expect from someone who hailed from Blackpool. Quite what it was, I couldn't say, but there was just something about him. Fate decreed (oh, dear Fate, thank you at least a million times!) that he would be taking over responsibility for educating me in "1066 and all that." In his mid-twenties, Mr. Eric

Cryer related to me, and I related to him. I would not be the only scholar to feel that way.

During my first year, "Pop" Peyton had been appointed to teach me history. He must have been edging toward retirement (hence his nickname) and whereas the majority of the teaching staff could boast their doctorates, B.A.s, M.A.s, B.Econs, and suchlike, poor old Pop came with no such embellishment. He didn't help himself by telling us that "prophetic" reference was made to the school site in the Domesday Book, which noted that the land had "sufficient space for six hundred swine." At the time, the school boasted the aforesaid six hundred students. Oh, very droll. I am sure that he did his best, but he never seemed to carry the authentic academic clout of his colleagues. My first year results in history were certainly poor and on my school report for Summer 1955, he commented that I had to, "learn the idea of absorbing and retaining facts." Out of a class of 28, I was ranked no higher than 21st in the historical stakes.

But Eric Cryer was "different class" and it is in no way overstating the case to say that he became one of my heroes. His love for history was passionate and transparent. At his feet, I learned that enthusiasm, humour, and downright decency were essential ingredients for effective teaching. His commitment and enthusiasm spilled all over me and, within weeks, history began to live, homework became a joy, and Pop's comment about absorbing facts showed itself up for what it was – cobblers! I majored in writing essays for Mr. Cryer and relished his regular tests. Alongside a total obsession with history, he had a passion for classical music. When Charlie Collins was playing some piece of goodness knows what in the next room to ours, Mr. Cryer – referring to him as "Eric" remains for me, to this day, the equivalent of addressing the Queen as "Liz" - would insist that we put down our books and listen to the goings on.

"That's Beethoven." he enthused.

After class, we would check out with Charlie – Mr. Cryer was always right.

And then there was his support for Blackpool Football Club, at a time when they were one of the most feared – and loved - clubs in the land. Even I knew that Stanley Matthews was some sort of genius, and that Stan Mortenson had hit a hat-trick in the 1953 Wembley FA Cup Final. Yet I am convinced that, had Mr. Cryer been given the choice between Blackpool winning every trophy in sight, or receiving a set of Churchill's "A History of the English Speaking Peoples," Churchill would have won, hands down every time.

I thrived on Mr. Cryer's commendation and, by the end of the term, I was 16th out of the gallant 28 and, on my report, earned the accolade "Satisfactory." More to my satisfaction was a passing verbal commendation - "Well done, Derby. You're starting to show some real promise." In another six months, I was 3rd and "Very satisfactory." The rest is, as they say, history. When my tutelage on the subject passed into the hands of Pete Watkins and the wonderfully eccentric "Taffy" Davies, I hit top spot on three separate occasions. Taff described my efforts as "Very Good" on two occasions, but by the time that I did my mock "O" Level, he must have run out of ink or lost the will to live - "V.G." being the best he could manage. But I was always going to be one of the history boys.

I spare a couple of thoughts about Taff because, despite being somewhat dour, he was a character. Tall, thin, hair parted down the middle, and Pinoccian of nose, he ought to have been created by Dickens. A story did the rounds that a fight had occurred at the school gates one lunchtime between some infamous arch-thug of Thomas Letherby School and our own, our very own, Mick Walker. Mick was a reigning England schoolboy boxing champion, and he succeeded in reducing his opponent to a bloody mess. News spread through the school corridors like the proverbial wildfire and Taff became aware of the disgraceful goings-on that had gone on. Immediately after the lunch break, he launched a staggering diatribe at Mick for a full ten minutes.....school reputation etc, blah, blah, blah. When he had seemingly exhausted his vocabulary in front of a cowed and very hushed class, in the mildest Welsh accent he asked Mick, quite calmly, "Did you win?"

Whilst not a first-hand witness to this incident, I do recall him bemoaning the fact that Tommy Steele – a young man just making his spectacular way in the world of entertainment at that time – was earning an hundred pounds a week. In 1956, this was not to be sniffed at, and Taff gave us the benefit of his opinion on the differential between his and Tommy's pay.

"Tommy Steele? Tommy Steele? Paid a hundred pounds a week. Can you believe that – a hundred pounds? How much do I get paid? Not a bloody hundred pounds a week, I can tell you!"

Despite Pop Peyton having failed singularly in his attempts to school me in history, he didn't quite disappear off my agenda. Those who made such decisions deemed it fit to let him have another bash, this time, at RI - "Religious Instruction" to you, and not the politically correct RE that is served up nowadays. No, the concept in the '50s was that we would all get a severe dose of Christian education, from which only Jewish lads were excluded. At a time when the school had no Muslims, Hindus, Buddhists, New-Agers, or anything else in-between, even poor old would-be atheists were under Dr. Whiteley's party whip to attend RI. Along with Pop, there was a ripe old assortment of teachers brought in for teaching the subject. Some were able to boast a degree in divinity, others simply confessed a Christian faith, and, in the case of a few, guilty of nothing more than having drawn the short straw. The best available, as far as I was concerned, was Stephen Forrester, a tall slim man whose chief responsibilities were science orientated. Immaculately dressed – often sporting a bow tie – he chalked his notes on the board in italic script. It was pure artistry and although I tried to imitate the style, my handwriting has finished up as a bastardized version of the real thing. But Steve Forrester taught me the Collect for Purity, and for that alone, I shall be eternally in his debt.

"Almighty God, unto whom all hearts are open, all desires known, and from whom no secrets are hid,
Cleanse the thoughts of our hearts by the inspiration of thy Holy Spirit that we may perfectly love thee, and worthily magnify thy holy name."

Knock out! I use it to this day and it still works for me.

Now, given my Sunday school track record, you would have thought I would have shone at Religious Instruction. But no, not a bit of it. Without putting too fine a point on the matter, I was rarely at the races. You see, when it came to your actual Bible stories, I was well on top of the pile. But input and discussion about northern and southern kingdoms, prophets and their political significance, I couldn't have given the proverbial monkey for. I believed in God, went to Sunday school, did my best to live what I was taught – so where's the problem?

So far, so not too bad. I continued to do spectacularly in English Language and Literature, and even better in History. Capable of more than holding my own in French and Mathematics I might have been, but I was useless in anything relating to science. Add to this mix, general poverty at geography where all this wheat, barley and sugar beet stuff had me flummoxed from the start. As long as I knew enough to prevent me from booking a seaside holiday in Sheffield, what was the point of geography? So, what have we left? Ah, yes, physical education.

It would not be unreasonable of anyone taking the bother – and bother it most certainly would be – to look at the first twelve years of my life and conclude that sporting life was not within my compass. However, with the knowledge of Uncle Ernie having succumbed to cancer and Grandad Clark coughing up his lungs fit to bust, Mum was naturally very keen to ensure that my health was A1, and that I avoided the problems that beset her brother and father. As a starting point, from about the age of five, I attended a clinic at Church Road, in Manor Park, for what was described as sunray treatment. Received wisdom was that a regular dose of the rays would protect me from any lung and respiratory diseases that might be floating around. Boys and girls attended the clinic on a weekly – or should that be weakly – basis. Stripped down to our undies, we were given a pair of green tinted goggles - and what a sight we all made. For my part, a skinny little lad, white fleshed, with an even whiter pair of loose-fitting underpants that flapped around my legs like some appeal to surrender. And to cap it all, those rotten goggles made us all look like something freshly landed from the planet

Cornball. In an adjoining room, several chairs were set out in a circle around several heat ray lamps. These were probably white but, thanks to the tinted goggles, remain forever green in my memory. Once we were all sitting comfortably, the lamps were turned on to enable the healing rays do their stuff. It was warm and not unpleasant, but whether or not it did any good remained a matter for conjecture. Personally, I have a feeling that their major contribution was of a psychological nature as, gradually, I became confirmed as a reasonably healthy specimen. The educational microscope that was my school report confirmed this, where Fred Mills noted that I had progressed from "Very good work" to "Able and capable – has made steady progress," which surprised me as much as it did everyone else.

When Mr. Wallis took over from Fred, I was to be subjected to far greater scrutiny and accurate appraisal. Short, rotund, with bushy eyebrows, Mr. Wallis was a dead ringer for George Robey, the old music hall comedian. Rumour had it that he had played Rugby League to a very good standard in his youth, but he always fought shy of either confirmation or denial. Whatever, he had a great sense of fun.

In July 1956, Mr. Wallis made the following remarks about my inaugural term with him – "Steady progress has been maintained. Has occasional lapses into laughing hysteria!"

This wry observation was based if not entirely, then certainly substantially, on an occasion when, whilst lined up against the wall bars of the gym, Barry Dunn and I were enjoying a private joke. Nothing wrong in that, you might suppose. But while we were chattering and laughing, Mr. Wallis was trying to issue instructions for the enhancement of our physical well-being. Suddenly, the viper struck.

"You, boy," he hollered, pointing at Barry. "Mr. Dunn. Come out here, Simple Simon. You shall have one without a penny!" And, with that, Barry instantly regained social equilibrium and sauntered out to receive a generous portion of back thumping.

As for me, already amused fit to bust over whatever it was that Barry and I had been sharing, Simple Simon having one without a penny pushed me over the edge. I leaned against the wall bars, totally incapable of anything but laughter at Mr. Wallis's adaptation of the old nursery rhyme. Barry, downcast of face, returned to his place next to me, and Mr. Wallis returned to the fray. I guess I should have anticipated what was to follow.

"And you, Simple Simon's brother, standing next to him. Come here – you, too, shall have one without a penny."

It was as much the way that he said it as what he said. Can you imagine a thirteen-year old going forward to receive a wallop, laughing with every step? As I took my medicine, laughing hysteria knew no bounds, and his comment on my report was one of the most accurate to have ever reached its pages. The thing was – and I must emphasise this – it didn't hurt one bit.

Hence, the event was immortalised with those words, "Steady progress has been maintained. Has occasional lapses into laughing hysteria." Nothing changed there, then.

Mum's fears that physical exertion was going to be outside of my compass were about to be proved spectacularly wrong. and it all started with Roger Bannister. When he ran the first sub-four minute mile in 1954, even I could grasp that something remarkable had happened. The image of Chris Brasher leading the pack, then Chris Chattaway, before that final burst which saw Bannister striding through the tape to collapse into the arms of the stewards, made a big impression on me. Man was surely never intended to move at this sort of pace – but in a mad four-minute dash, Roger Bannister had done it, and written his name into the history books. Cool.

East Ham Grammar had long subscribed to the ritual of an annual cross-country run. In February, we would troop over to Wanstead Park, where every man jack was required to participate in a slog around the park and, in particular, the long drag up the Glade. Two races - junior and senior – were run, and in my first year, I achieved the distinction of finishing in the first 130 - just. Throughout January, Messrs. Mills and Wallace supervised training runs comprising once round the soccer/rugby pitches, out of the gates into Wellington Road, and on to Jenkins Lane. From there we moved through decidedly dodgy surrounds where untidy refuse kept company with the odd abandoned car. The whole area stunk alarmingly. Once civilisation was regained on the Barking Road, we followed the cycle path back onto the school grounds to finish down the straight from the dining hall to the gymnasium. During my first year, by the time that I reached that point I was well and truly knackered, the only thing to my credit being that that I'd got round the route without stopping. There were plenty who couldn't even manage that.

But the impact of Bannister's sub-four-minute mile had awakened something in me. I had become fascinated with the concept of middle/long distance runners biding their time through the early stages of their run, only to go hell for leather over the last three hundred or so yards in a mad dash for the finish line and glory. Now call me barmy if you must, but I began to think that I could do that. What was stranger yet - and very new for me – was that I thought I might even enjoy it! I didn't appreciate it at the time, but I was being transformed from nothing more than an unwilling plodder to a runner who might have the ability to finish further up the food chain. All I had to do was prove it physically.

So, as we approached the first training day in January 1956, I visualised the last hundred yards dash to the finish line outside the gym over and again in my mind. As Fred Mills lined us up ready to release us in groups, my eyes were firmly fixed on Dave Philpott. He had become a good friend and was a good runner. I resolved that I would beat him. Of course, all this was hidden from the world at large, as the idea of me being up front in any race was, so far, beyond the imagination of anybody. So, as the trail of would-be and wouldn't-be athletes set out from the school gates, those who had a "note from mum," - fit enough to be marshals and nothing more - could scarcely believe that I was keeping pace with Dave at the front. I am sure that Dave himself was amongst them. He upped the pace as he led us all through Jenkins Lane, but I stuck to his heels like a dog with a bone, unwilling to let go. The script read that he should be streets ahead, but he wasn't, and as the run lengthened, I began to sense fear in him.

On re-entering the school grounds before going round the school block, there was a minor buzz amongst the sick-notes along the lines of, "What the hell is Derby doing there?" I had planned to wait until we had passed the dining hall when, with seventy-five yards to go, – wham! - I'd pass Dave before he had a chance to realise what was happening. Quite properly, he had ideas of his own and was in no mood to surrender his supremacy, and as soon as we turned the corner into the final straight, he went. Oh,Lord! The best laid plans of mice and men, and all that. It was earlier than I intended, but if I didn't go now, I'd never catch him. With fifty yards to go, we were slugging it out, but I knew he was tiring. Suddenly, a rush of adrenalin swept through me and from somewhere, I found energy enough to surge forward and pass him in the last ten yards and cross the finish line ahead. It was magic – pure magic.

There we were, the pair of us, panting like old clapped-out steam engines. When we had cooled down, he was not above coming over to congratulate me.

"Well done, Steve. I never thought you could run like that."

"Neither did I, Dave. Neither did I."

That afternoon set a marker for me, and by the time that the real event came around in February, knowing that I could beat Dave, I wanted to do better than that. What about Ron Boyce, Stan Gibbons, and – the ultimate prize - the formidable Pete Judge? The run commenced by the lakeside, proceeding to an "up and over" sand hill, before skirting the bank of the lake to the fence that surrounded Wanstead Park proper. From there, the route followed a trail through the woods, before doubling back (via the long drag up the Glade) to go, once more, around the lake, back over the sand hill and on to the finish line. As with the training runs, several efforts were made to avoid the exercise, by and large by the same culprits - but it cut little ice. Those who were genuinely sick were, of course, excused whilst a fair number of those whose word was held up for scrutiny and found wanting, had to don their kit and join the throng.

One year, a small group of refuseniks found a hiding place just out of the watchful eye of the marshals. Their plan was to wait in hiding for those who had done the decent thing and run the full course, and join them for the last trot round the lake. Of course, Fred Mills and his colleagues got a strong smell of rat when examining the list of those recording quite remarkable times. Names you would expect to find up at the top of the list – no problem. But there were others that had no right. And how come those without right were finishing with not a trace of the sweat of endeavour, along with others puffing and blowing for all they were worth? It didn't take much working out and, a week or two later, the whole thing was run again. Detentions and threats were issued to the miscreants who, this time, had beady eyes focussed on them to ensure that all endured the full experience.

I came in fifth. To my regret, I never won the cross country race during my time at school – Pete Judge put paid to that every time. He never seemed to train as hard or as often as I did, but he always walked – sorry – ran away with the event. Truly, I didn't mind because he was a nice bloke and being a contender even, was giant leap from where I had been at the beginning of 1956. Taking part is more important than winning? Absolutely. But I would have liked to have won the race just once, to see what it felt like.

"Coming out" as a half-decent runner put me in the frame for other offers and opportunities. An under-14 rugby team had been formed, and I received an invitation to join. By this time, not only had I put on a bit of pace but I'd also started to fill out a bit, and it was perceived that I might just have something to offer in the scrum. I have never mastered the finer points of the game, and the only one of our number back then who had anything approaching a clue was our captain, Colin Powell. At our initial training session, we all stood amazed as the ball dropped into his arms from a great height. "Mark!" he yelled, simultaneously slamming his heel into the ground. Now this behaviour appeared extremely odd to me. You see, whilst we could rustle up a couple of Johns, Petes, Bobs, and a Steve, Marks we were distinctly lacking. However, over the ensuing weeks, I picked up enough about this ritual and other whys and wherefores of the game for Saturday morning matches to become a real joy. And, on the whole, we didn't do too badly, although there were games where we knew we were on a hiding to nothing. Westcliff Grammar and Coopers Grammar were "soccer free" institutions, where the teaching staff preferred to instruct their charges in the oval ball code. We got turned over by a cricket score whenever we came up against those two schools. What I did learn and love about the game was that, win or lose, you applauded your opponents off the pitch – and you always respected the referee. Rugby hasn't lost that tradition, and I pray to God that it never does. You know that old saying about rugby being a game for thugs played by gentlemen, and soccer a game for gentlemen, played by thugs? Well, never has that been better illustrated than by behaviour in the two codes since those days. Soccer lags sadly behind.

There were others lurking in the sporting shadows behind Roger Bannister, ready to take me to further and different sporting heights. Dad – who you might remember was a schoolboy goalkeeper of some renown - wondered why I never saw the need to go and watch a football match. Partly to please him, I made a couple of fruitless and boring sojourns to West Ham United's ground, and quickly came to the conclusion that, having tried it once (or, in this case, twice), I didn't like it. Apart from that, my only dose of professional football was injected on Cup Final day, when several neighbours would come in to our house to watch the match. In 1955, another "Wow!" moment occurred for me. Manchester City turned up at Wembley in the F. A. Cup Final to do battle with Newcastle United, bringing with them a German to keep goal. Can you imagine that? Not ten years after wartime hostilities had ceased, a former prisoner-of-war was going to tread the hallowed ground. How did he have the nerve? Well, quite simply, he had the nerve because he was a magnificent goalkeeper and a gentleman. Despite a 3-1 reverse, Bert Trautmann impressed the hell out of me with his agility and daring, as he chucked himself all round the goal, making save after save to prevent a cricket score.

Twelve months later, City was back at Wembley again, this time to face Birmingham City. With twenty minutes left on the

185

clock and his team holding a lead, Bert hurled himself at the flying feet of an opponent, and went down like the proverbial sack of potatoes. Trainers rushed on, water was splashed all over, and the brave 'keeper eventually emerged, rubbing the back of his neck, ready to carry on. Blow me down if, in the next attack, the fool didn't do the very same thing. On came the lads to patch him up again, this time sufficiently well to get him through the remainder of the game. Only after the match, which City won 3-1, did the truth emerge. Bert Trautmann had played on with a broken neck. Perhaps it was Dad's genes coming out in me for, almost overnight, I fancied being a goalkeeper. Fired by enthusiasm rather than technique, ensuing weeks saw me between the posts where, totally void of fear, I would hurl myself at the feet of onrushing forwards, fantasising that I was Bert Trautmann at Wembley. It was a conversion of heart, mind and soul.

Fred Mills wasn't slow to recognise my prowess and growth in confidence. One afternoon, he refereed a game and, true to form, couldn't resist joining in with one or other of the teams. During his time "on our side," and with the score at 2-2, Fred missed a "sitter."

"Oops! Sorry, lads," he spluttered.

From the other end of the pitch, I intuitively expressed my own annoyance – I wanted to win.

"I should bloody well think so!" I yelled.

Yorkshire drawl filled the air.

"Oh, 'ark at Derby. 'Ee *never* makes a mistake. When we've finished, you can go and report to the headmaster's office."

"What for?"

"For your damn cheek," said the bloke who'd just missed a barn door from five paces. Did that constitute a sending off?

Anyhow, once the match was over, off I went, in muddy jersey, shorts, socks, boots, hands and face to wait outside Joe's office. When the great man emerged, he looked down at me with a superior disdain that only he could muster, curious to know why such an oddly dressed specimen should be seeking to hold court with him.

"Well, what are you here for, boy?"

"Please, sir. Mr. Mills said........."

I was cut short by a roar.

"Oh, for goodness' sake. Get out of here! Get dressed and go home!"

And with that, he breezed down B corridor to deal with something, doubtless, far more important than satisfying Fred's ego. Fred regularly sent boys to him for the slightest offence, and I guess poor old Joe had just about had his fill. Back I went to the gym dressing room, got dressed, and trudged off home.

At the time of my transformation, the school boasted a brilliant Under-14 team. To start with, if you had – as we did - Stan Gibbons and Ronnie Boyce in your side, you were over halfway there. John Smith was a laid-back centre half, and in goal was Les Barber – the twin of Mick, who had caught the rough end of Mr. Cox's annoyance in my first year. Despite my novice status, I was sure that I was a better goalkeeper than Les, and yearned for the chance to prove it. But the team was so good and successful that, week after week, Les had so precious little to do that it was hard to drop him when he wasn't conceding goals. Ho hum!

I did manage just one appearance 'though, when Les went down poorly. On a sticky pudding of a pitch at Buckhurst Hill, we came out 5 – 3 winners. I'd like to say that I covered myself with glory but, in fact, the only thing we all covered ourselves with was mud. Memories of the finer details of the game have long escaped me, save for one. Somewhere in the second half, the referee awarded a penalty against us. It was a heaven sent opportunity to show the lads that Les ought to be rested on a more permanent basis. As the Buckhurst Hill player placed the ball on the spot and prepared his run-up to take the kick, John Smith called out, "When you've saved it, Steve, throw it out to me." I focussed and decided that the heavy pitch was certain to slow the ball down and that my best chance of a save was by watching the ball, as opposed to guessing and diving one way or the other. It worked a treat, as the poor kicker hit the thing straight and slowly at me. It wasn't much of a save and, come the following week, Les was back between the sticks. But, at least, I could say that I'd saved a penalty.

The school provided an amazing range of activities and if anyone was unable to find something to their taste, well, they were probably just not looking hard enough. Lunchtime chess club was where you took your sandwiches and drink along for a bit of checking and mating......not that sort of mating, boy, not that sort of mating! I managed to grasp the rudiments of the game but not to any degree of real competence. For weeks, I thought that Ruy Lopez was the Real Madrid centre-half. But, through attendance at the club, I discovered that chess is a great game, even if I was destined to be little more than a piece-pusher.

Dramatics were there for the taking. How strange that, with my passion for English and my "bring-the-house-down" performance of that Marlowe piece, only once did I venture to tread the boards. "Knock" is a satire on the medical profession in which an enterprising doctor makes a fortune through the vanity and foolishness of humanity. Well, that's what the March 1958 programme notes said. Thing was that the whole blessed play was presented in French, and at least half the audience per performance hadn't the vaguest clue as to what was going on. The same might have been said for an only just smaller percentage of the cast. I turned out as one of the villagers, along with classmates Ken Hinds, Ron Wyatt, and Vernon Appelboam (dressed in drag). All we had to do was sit in the waiting room and provide a few nasal mumbles in what we perceived to be French. Yet the school's track record for dramatic performances in the mother tongue makes for impressive reading. At random – *Julius Caesar* (1946) ; *King Lear* (1949) ; *The Merchant of Venice* (1952) ; *Macbeth* (1953) ; *Androcles and the Lion* (1955) ; and Gilbert and Sullivan's *Iolanthe* in 1957. Some quality, I would say.

The Debating Society provided a platform for would-be "stand ups" to cut their teeth. A motion would be proposed, a speaker would argue the case in favour of, whilst another would present the other side of the argument. Just in case there were areas that needed dusting up a little, each speaker was supported by the contribution of a seconder for or against the motion. After some lively questions and what passed for intelligent banter, the motion would be subjected to a vote, the result announced, and we'd all go home for tea. Again, I surprise myself that I never got involved with the Society wholesale. I'd managed to make a pretty good fist of debate in the confines of my class and exposure to a wider public might have made my school career a little more spectacular than it was. But there you are. All I am saying is that the school provided the opportunities, and it was up to you to grab them – or not, as the case may be.

And last, but far from least, I must reflect on what was, perhaps, the grandest event in the school calendar. Annually, in November, the School Speech Day was held and, among my souvenirs, I am thrilled to find a programme for the event held in the School hall, on 26th November 1959, at 7.30pm. I'm very proud to have it, for it demonstrates a quality and ambition that I shall always associate with the school and its management.

From a cursory reflection on the programme content, it is not hard to draw an analogy between Speech Day and a commercial annual general meeting. There would be a chairman, on this occasion, the Mayor, Councillor Mrs. Sutton, J.P. Alderman Mrs. W.M. Knight and her deputy, Councillor C.F.Chapman, represented local government hierarchy, whilst the Governing Body of the East Ham Grammar School for Boys (the Board, for my AGM analogy) totalled fourteen men and women, good and true. Headmaster Dr. Whiteley (the Chief Executive?) was present, along with his staff, each one named, representing middle management. Parents and scholars were the shareholders.

This grand parade of dignitaries and doings didn't stop there. Sir Eric Edwards, M.C., J.P., L.L.B. (I'd never heard of him) had been invited to address the assembly, after which the gathering was to be regaled by senior scholars with readings of works by Shakespeare, Ronsard, and James 1. The School orchestra was not to be denied, providing, as it did, "Sanctus" by Mozart, along with a taste of "Nobody knows de trouble I seen," arranged by Charlie Collins' successor, D.J.Todd. The title had me wondering if, perhaps, the piece had been selected in memory of Charlie's contretemps with Joe Brown and that piece of gas piping!

Dr. Whiteley presented his report before Sir Eric dished out the prizes awarded for all manner of academic achievements and excellence by, chiefly, those who had reached the higher echelons of the Sixth Form. If much of the goings on passed over the heads of, I would imagine, 75% of those present, prize distribution provided the *hoi polloi* of student population with an opportunity to contribute by passing judgement on each recipient. As names were announced and beneficiaries walked to the podium, cheers rang out for those who had demonstrated that they were jolly good eggs. For those not so popular, boos for their comfort, although the Chief Executive moved pretty swiftly in calling a halt to those shenanigans. The show is, as they say, never over until the fat lady sings, but with no fat lady among us, we were placed at a distinct disadvantage. The school song, "Esthameian, Arise" had to suffice in bringing closure to the event.

School speech days, in one way, passed me by. In my orchestral days, I would have been scraping away in the second violins, somewhat disconnected from the highbrow nature of the proceedings. Yet one thing could not be ignored. I had dreamed of being part of a great school, and I was. If part of the price to be paid for this privilege was sitting through the formality of one speech day a year, I was perfectly willing to cough up. It reflected tradition and I was becoming increasingly in favour of tradition and its values. If my pronounced sense of community had been instigated and fostered by friends and family, it was, undoubtedly, my schooling that lit the first flames of commitment within me.

By the time that I began my fourth term, I had become increasingly aware that success or otherwise would be measured by achievement (or lack of it) in the General Certificate of Education examinations, rather than whether or not I beat Pete Judge in the cross-country. I make no pretence to understanding the machinations of modern GCSEs, with course work and assessment levels from "A" down to Lord knows where. In 1959, the General Certificate of Education procedures required that we took written examinations under written examination conditions. Each examination comprised three hours in which to deal with questions geared to the syllabus.

Forty five per cent and over was recognised as a pass and you either got it or you didn't. It was that simple.

At the beginning of our fourth year, assessments were made of what each scholar was likely to achieve, and entry to the relative examinations approved or declined accordingly. Quite reasonably, it was decreed that I would have the greatest chance of success in English Language and Literature, History, Geography, French, Mathematics, General Science, and – would you believe it? – Additional General Science. Barring something catastrophic, I considered myself a racing certainty for the two English papers, and when it came to History, there were no questions to be asked. With only a slightly lesser degree of certainty, I felt fairly confident of French and Mathematics, although Geography would be a case of luck with the questions on the day. General Science was a decidedly dodgy area, and as for Addition General Science, well, I ask you, what was the point? With not the slightest inclination toward matters scientific, getting a pass with the conventional paper would be a miracle in itself. Going for an additional one was bound to end up in unmitigated disaster. However, eight subjects were identified for me, so eight subjects it would have to be.

As June 1959 – the month of the examination - came ever closer, intensity increased. Back in February, we had gone through the dry run of mock examinations. For the life of me, I cannot recall a single result from that exercise, but if its purpose was to give us a taster of how the examinations worked, then it was worth the effort. In the same way that I had craved success in the 11-Plus, so the desire to do well in the General Certificate of Education gnawed at me. If I say it myself, I worked damned hard during that final year, so much so that I even entertained thoughts of gaining a university place to study history in more depth. With good luck and a fair wind, I might even finish up a teacher. Eric Cryer was all for it.

"You could do it, you know. You're a hard worker and could come out of it with a very good degree."

Throughout the week of the examinations themselves, the hall was set out with desks and chairs in neat rows, placed sufficiently far apart as to ensure that there could be no cheating. On the stage, a large clock on a stand looked down on us all, acting as our point of reference for planning and pacing our efforts. Armed with my trusty fountain pen – it had come a long way since Leysdown - pencil, rubber, and ruler, each day I would take my place, ready to commence battle. I never countenanced fear about sitting examinations and truly relished being tested – the adrenalin always flowed.

The invigilator walked slowly around the hall, placing a question sheet - face down - on each desk.

"Do not turn these over until you are told to do so."

No, sir, I certainly won't, sir.

"On your answer books, write your names along with the name of the school."

Yes, sir, I certainly will, sir.

"When you turn your papers over, ensure that you read all the instructions very carefully." A sort pause, before, "You may begin."

Providing you had done a reasonable amount of work and revision, there were always a couple of questions that leapt at you from the page. The trick was to choose the ones that you felt you could do full justice, for they were the ones that would get you a big slab of the requisite 45%. Most of the examinations required candidates to answer five questions. One or two might be compulsory, but a total of five was the norm. I had worked out (it wasn't that difficult) that two good answers earning, say, eighteen marks the pair, would put you almost home and dry. If you couldn't cobble together nine marks from the remaining three questions, well, you probably didn't deserve to pass. We would not know the result of our endeavours until the results dropped onto our doormats in August.

During that two-month waiting period between completion of the examinations and arrival of the results, some of my colleagues obtained jobs, courtesy of Mr. Huxter, the Youth Employment Officer for East Ham, and were set for the next stage of their lives. Others needed to wait for their results before seeing and planning their next steps. Would it be out to work, or on to the Sixth Form? I

Love me, love my dog! Me around two years old, the dog was the first gift Dad bought for me, following his return from war. I've still got it!

Seated is Granny Derby, my paternal great grandmother. A devout Catholic, she prayed for her own forgiveness, and blessings on her family past, present, and future.

My paternal grandfather, a tall thin man with a ready laugh. Chronic bronchitis and pneumonia took him in 1922, aged just 34.

My maternal grandfather. My memories of him are as a sick old man, so this is nice to see him in his younger, healthier days.

If you have never seen an angel before, allow me to show you what they look like. This is my beloved Aunt Alice who, with Uncle Harry, cared for me and Mum whilst Dad was at war. Uncle Harry died a couple of years before this picture was taken,

My maternal grandmother Nanny Clark. She could be a bit of a firebrand but here she is in more tranquil mode.

Right: The Clark vehicle driven by Grandad Clark (L) and his brother Harry (R). Brother Bill stands on the extreme right.

Grandma Vanner (L) and Grandad Vanner (R) as I remember them best.

Dad and Mum. Not enough space or words to say how much I loved them both.

All Change for Upton Park

*Derek William Fletcher
1951. As ready for
nonsense as ever.*

*No. 35005 Canadian Pacific, from the Merchant Navy Class. Lovely engines and, at
age 8, I could recite all their names and numbers!
Reproduced with kind permission of Matt Allen of the Mid-Hants Railway.*

Steve Derby

The Full Gospel Hall Sunday School. I am in the top right corner with my head at a jaunty angle. The three scholars to the right are Harry Crick, Derek, and John Barrett (circa 1956).

There's something about a man in uniform. I'm wearing long trousers, so this has to be 1955.

Villagers in the French-spoken play "Knock." (L-R) Vernon Appelboam, Ron Wyatt, Steve Derby, Ken Hinds, J. Allen (?), Dennis Johnson, Alan Rough (?), Barry Walker.

"I don't care how miserable he looks. When I say a million lines, I mean a million lines!" Who else but the wonderful Eric Cryer.

Steve Derby

The photograph that re-united me with Derek. Summer camp at Thundersley 1954. Back row (L-R) Ollie Chester; John Barrett; George Tyler; Roger Warren; Skipper Arthur Stevens; Eddie Harris; John Kinch. Front row; John Cole; Dickie Culver; Derek; me.

The closest I ever got to being in a West Ham United team photograph. Back row on the left, I stand next to John McDowell who went on to play almost 300 times for West Ham.

All Change for Upton Park

I think I'd like to be sixteen for ever. November 1959 High Street South Methodist Youth Club. Alan Hood and Bill Hards (nice legs, Bill) dance to our little band. L to R: Keith Hollington, Brian Finlay, Steve Derby, and Tony Prince.

My first West Ham love! The wonderful side that gained promotion in 1958. Back row (L-R) Andy Malcolm; Ken Brown; John Bond; Ernie Gregory; Noel Cantwell; Bill Lansdowne; Malcolm Pike. Front row: Mike Grice; John Smith; Vic Keeble; John Dick; Malcolm Musgrove.

Steve Derby

A 12th East Ham Christmas Party! Left to right; me; Derek; Eddie Harris: John Cole; Paul Meisner; Ray Pearce (in the shadows); "Sam" Costa; Peter Tourelle; (?) Birch.

The Trophies of War. Derek and me holding on to one of the many things that unite us.

was in the latter group, but a chance meeting was about to threaten all the best-laid plans. Tony Prince had, through a lot of common interests, become a close friend. Mind you, it hadn't started that way. As part of my development as a runner, I had bought myself a natty pair of running shorts and, to avoid total and utter embarrassment, a jock strap to go with it. I wouldn't claim to be the first to have invested in this particular hammock for gentlemanly genitalia, but I know I was pretty close to the distinction. It pleased Tony not at all and he had made his stand quite public.

"Bloody big head. Who does he think he is?" was one of his more printable opinions.

As for me, I was only interested in the running and ensuring that I had the right kit for the job. Rubber plimsolls no longer did it for me, and Mum and Dad had approved the purchase of a pair of proper running shoes with spikes on the soles, to provide a better grip when running on wet surfaces. I can't recall much fuss being made about that. Anyhow, all that had passed and Tony and I were destined to become good friends for life.

Just a few weeks after completion of the examinations, he showed me a letter that he had received from the Norris Warming Company, situated in Southampton Row, London, offering him the position of apprentice heating and ventilating engineer at a salary of £2-14-0 per week - £2.70 in real money, or £140 per annum. On completion of his five-year apprenticeship, this would rise to £10 a week which might not sound much now but, believe me, it most certainly was in 1959. Heating and ventilating sounded a bit like watching paint dry to me and I didn't fancy it one bit. But when it came to £10 a week, albeit deferred, well, that had to be considered. Overnight, sixth form, university, and teaching didn't seem to have quite the same appeal. Tony was going to earn some money, and I wanted to do the same.

When I told Dad about my wish to change horses in mid-stream, he was totally miffed. For weeks, having anticipated my continuing education, he'd been filling in all sorts of tax forms and claims to accommodate the impact on his PAYE, and now it was all going to have been for nothing. Mum was a bit more philosophical about it all. I'm sure she wanted to see her son get to university - and I don't think I would have disappointed her. But she could see that my heart and head had been turned and, ultimately, Dad came round to her way of thinking. Maybe I just had too happy a home life to want to troll off to anywhere else. National Provincial Bank were advertising for junior clerks to set sail with them on a banking career that was respectable and would provide opportunities for successful applicants to play a part in the community. Goodness, how times have changed! Mum helped me with my application, which resulted in an interview at the Bank's head office at 15 Bishopsgate, in the City of London. There and then, I was offered – subject to satisfactory GCE results - a position as a junior clerk at a branch later to be advised.

When those results arrived in August, despite all the work that I had put in, I have to say that I was more than a trifle disappointed. English Language, English Literature, and History were passed handsomely, and I wasn't totally surprised to find that I had passed French. But going down on Mathematics – albeit by just two marks - was a massive disappointment. General consensus was that the geometry section had been particularly difficult, and I consoled myself with that. General Science was a surprising "near miss" with my 43% just missing the target. As for Additional General Science, well, that was all I had expected. For weeks after, I reflected on how, had I accumulated another seven marks to spread around the papers that I failed, I would have got Mathematics first time of asking (I did a re-sit later in the year and passed), along with Geography, and – wait for it – General Science. More to the point, perhaps those hours wasted trying to cram additional general science into my bonce could have been put to far greater effect in other areas. As it was, in August 1959, I had four "O" Levels, three very near misses, plus one that I would prefer not to talk about.

There is not the slightest doubt in my mind that, for five years, I was privileged to attend the finest school in East Ham. An inspirational headmaster supported by the very best of teaching staff, it is little surprise to me that I can recall so many of their names. Some never taught me, but I rarely heard ill of them. Some have already found their way into this script but I just can't move to other matters before awarding Andy Warhols's fifteen minutes of fame to a select group. All of us, in one way or another, have been inspired, guided, influenced, and, yes, reprimanded by the like of these classroom warriors.

Take, for starters, Jack Mace. He was a wonderful man and my form master during four of my years at the school. He taught French, and supported Tottenham Hotspur. I recall his habit of clearing his ear by pressing the lobe with a finger and shaking it all about – his finger, that is, not his ear. He was rarely in a bad mood but on those few occasions when his displeasure was incurred, he could stare more effectively than some of his colleagues could shout – or clout. He was a great friend of Eric Cryer - I can't pay higher tribute than that – and died at far too early an age.

Tom "Terry" Eustace, a southern Irishman and devout Roman Catholic, did his level best to sort my scientific brain out. The odds against were just that bit too long, although he met with far more success in mathematics. During my fifth year, I was given the opportunity to read the lesson in assembly – normally the prerogative of a sixth-former. It was like a knighthood, as far as I was concerned.There I was, sat at the side of the stage, in full view of the gallant six hundred, as the parade of teachers filed past me to take their place on the stage. As Tom passed close to me, he whispered, "Speak slowly, loudly, and clearly."I've done that ever since

He made a fleeting reappearance in my life many years after I had left the school. In 1970, National Provincial Bank got into bed with the old Westminster Bank to produce National Westminster. I was transferred to a City branch in 1973 where one of my new colleagues was one Eugene Eustace. Eugene proved to be Tom's son and as the family lived close to my home, he took me to meet his dad. At the time, I was sporting a beard, and had started to thin on top just a bit, not to mention the fact that it had been fifteen years since I had last seen Tom. He feigned a recognition that I thought was little more than courtesy, given the passage of years and my physical change. After welcoming me, he brought out a photograph of the under-14 school rugby team. Pointing straight at me on the back row, he announced, "There! That's you." He was dead right!

Max Seidman was a diminutive, balding geography teacher. I'm sure he was Polish by origin, and rumour had it that he had had an awful time in a POW camp. He could write on the board, starting with the chalk in his left hand and, at the point where most would move along a little, simply switched the chalk into his right hand and continued. You just could not see the join. For an encore, with a piece of chalk in each hand, he would trace out the entire coast of Africa. Starting from the northern coast, his left hand went down the west coast whilst, simultaneously, the right hand scribed the east, both lines finishing up on the southern tip at exactly thesame time. Can you believe that? It was perfect everytime.

Speaking of geography, the goatee-bearded Mr. Sandford - a great wit in his own right – frequently made me laugh, even if I was never top of the shop in the his subject. Informing us all that a quarter of world's population was, at that moment, Chinese, he concluded logically that, "one in every four people is a Chinaman."

He looked around the class and counted out four boys.

"One. Two. Three. Four. You, boy. You're a Chinaman!"

This was certainly news to Mike Goody who received the oriental dubbing.

And then there was Sam Amstell - a real Eastender - who rose to become headmaster of the school. Sam specialised in my *bete noire* General Science, and had a tendency get really excited when teaching, resulting in a tendency to spit and gob – I have witnesses who claim that he was known in some quarters as "Gobbo." An experiment with a porous pot created mayhem as, every time Sam pronounced a word commencing with the letter "P," a shower would hit the front row.

"It's a porous pot, boys. A porous pot!"

The back row couldn't resist it.

"Sorry, sir. What did you say it was called?"

"A porous pot, a porous pot."

It is a memory that I have been unable to wash from my mind – or anywhere else, for that matter, for I was in that front row!

He goes down in the annals as the architect of another classic line. Whilst trying to get a word in edgeways with an over-vocal class, frustration ultimately got the better of him.

"Every time I open my mouth, some fool speaks!"

David Zeldin - dark of features with a stooped walk that made him look like a great black crow - was, I believe, an eastern European. His harsh voice really put the fear of God into many – until a *faux pas* endeared him to the lot of us. Pete Roberts (he of fig fame) played a crucial role, for David had trouble with pronouncing his "R"s.

"You, Woberts, spell "Isosceles."

Unfortunately – or fortunately, whichever side of the fence you sat on - Pete couldn't spell the word.

"You idjut, Woberts. What are you going to do if you open your GCE paper and there is the first question, "Spell "Isosceles?""

It took a moment for him to clue into why we were all laughing. But when he did, he laughed along with the rest of us. Lovely man.

As for Dr. Whitely himself, the Head who had created this spirit of excellence throughout the school and built such a superb team, well, one incident made an impact on me for life.

I dreaded being held back for detention. Writing out lines or knuckle pie were part and parcel of my schoolboy life. But Friday detention was a real bummer. I would have to concoct some tale to explain to Mum just why it was that I was over an hour late home from school. If Dad got to hear of it, then I was likely to be up for another rollicking. What particularly embarrassed me was Friday morning assembly when those due for detention were "named and shamed" before the whole school.

On one occasion, I had been late for school three times during the week, sufficient for me to be invited to stay on after school. So, at quarter to four, on a bright Friday afternoon that cried out for a bit of football, I was stuck in a classroom with about a dozen "regulars" to the sessions. Just to add to my mortification, the master appointed to preside at the gathering was none other than

Dr. Whiteley himself! His appearance at the door was the signal for instant sobriety and order from all and sundry. Surveying his audience, he nodded at each boy with an expression that seemed to say, "Why am I not surprised to see you here?" Until he got to me, that is.

"What are you here for, boy?" he asked, failing to recall my name.

"Sir, I've been late three times this week."

"Right, then. You can write me an essay on the subject of "Punctuality."

Then round the room he went, setting each miscreant an essay linked to whatever offence that they had committed.

"Now, I have some matters to attend to, so I'm leaving you all here on trust. I'll be back at four-thirty, looking forward eagerly to reading some creative masterpieces. Any nonsense, and we'll be here until midnight. Understood?"

Despite the general assent to understanding, I don't think it was there at all for, as soon as the Head was out of the door, the high jinks started. Laughing and chucking bits and pieces around the room, there was only one person taking the matter with any degree of seriousness – me!

Writing essays continued to come easily to me and I was rather pleased with the outcome of my work. The gist was that everyone has their various gifts, citing Ron Boyce for football, Ken Hinds for academia, Stan Gibbons for music, etc. Similarly, personal qualities, such as honesty and integrity, were no less worthy. Then to the final more workaday categories, such as reliability, helpfulness, and....punctuality. I was so proud of my final sentence.

"I shall just have to assume that when God was handing out punctuality, I must have been late for the meeting!"

Dr. Whiteley returned, as promised, about three-quarters of an hour after leaving to attend his chores.

"Right, then. Has anyone finished?"

I raised my hand and took the papers to him, written out in my best script. He took a few moments to scan the opening paragraph. Was that a smile forming under his moustache?

"I'm going to read this out and I want you all to listen."

And off he went, adding all the right intonations and emphasis to make my writing far more entertaining than I believed it could be. Why, even I was all ears, just dying to hear how the story was going to end.

He reached my last paragraph and, before reading it, looked at me.

"Boy, I have a feeling that I know where all this is leading to," he said with a knowing nod.

Once he had delivered my punch line and I'd earned a couple of sniggers from my fellow detainees, he dismissed me – sort of.

"Go home, Derby. Report to my office at 9'o'clock on Monday morning – and don't be late!"

All that weekend, I lived in fear. What was I going to tell Mum and Dad? Worse, what if he wrote a letter to them saying that, not only had I been detained, but also that I had treated the matter with some flippancy. Trainspotting, football....nothing could compensate and I had the most miserable of weekends.

Well, on this particular Monday, I wasn't late and, just before nine, there I was outside Dr. Whiteley's office. I could see him at the far end of the "B" corridor, striding purposefully toward little me, waiting to hear about my destiny. Total formality was the name of the game, as he ordered – not invited – me into his room. Now I'm for it. I stood in front of his desk, on which I could see my essay. He picked it up to remind himself of what I had written. Either that, or building up a good head of steam before letting rip.

"About this essay, Derby."

"Yes, sir, " I almost whimpered.

"Scandalous, boy! Totally scandalous!."

Oh, Lord.

"Scandalous"...he paused ..."but absolutely brilliant! Keep up that standard and you'll do very well for yourself. Back to your class you go."

That was the touch of genius. He'd kept me on tenterhooks throughout the weekend to dwell on my failings. And then, just when I thought all was lost, the guy raised me onto a pedestal. That's what's called motivation and although I was never closely under Dr. Whiteley's tutorial eye, for that action alone, the bloke was magic. Mind you, another couple of weeks and I was back into the old routine!

I could go on and on about that fabulous team. In the school's Jubilee year of 1955, a school photograph was taken, and there I am, standing just behind the only female employee, Mrs. Wheeler, the school secretary. In 1959, another photograph was taken and you can't help but notice how many of the staff appear in both shots. Proof, were it ever needed, that it was a good place to work.

When my final day at school arrived, I would be telling less than the truth if I said that it left me unmoved. It wasn't that I had my doubts as to whether or not I had done the right thing in deciding to leave and earn my corn. No, it was the recognition of, and appreciation for, all that had been done for me by so many people. Mr. Cryer wished me all the best, repeating his, "You could have got a first class degree" comment. I think he was right and hated the thought that I might have let him down. Those about to depart platform 5C had collected shillings and pence to buy Jack Mace a little momento of our stay – a shirt, a bottle of brown ale, and a couple of cigarettes. All heart, we were, all heart. But he appreciated it, as we appreciated him.

I remembered how, when I left Shaftesbury some five years earlier, I had written a couple of verses to reflect my feelings at that time. Well, the muse must have remained with me for, to my astonishment, I've just found the lines that I wrote on leaving the Grammar school. Don't get excited – they're no challenge to the

Poet Laureate. But they do tell me something about myself and, if you don't mind, I'll share them with you.

17ᵗʰ July 1959

I have reached a landmark – I have left school. Our form (5C) had great fun removing doors and building barriers across the corridors. The boys became more quiet at the Leavers Service. We returned to school for our last dinner – salad. The day ended with the hymn, "God be with you 'til we meet again." Jack Mace (Form-master for four years) was pleased at our gift of a shirt, a bottle of brown, and 4 cigarettes. We had a final "get-together" in the "Duke's Head." It was hard to say "Goodbye" to people like Vic Elkington, Mickey George, Stan Gibbons, and countless others. I pray that God will keep us all safe and guide us and bring us all together, after some time, for a wonderful re-union. Now, I set out on the great adventure called "Life"...............

At the gathering for our final assembly, I can't remember a word of what was said, or by whom. But I do recall vividly singing the hymn, "Lord, dismiss us with thy blessing." Apart from the first line, the lyric did not entirely fit the occasion. Once again, Brian Rayner at the keyboard excelled himself, and I found myself too choked up to sing with any degree of gusto, knowing that I would never return as a scholar. The school song, "Esthameians Arise" followed. Its truly rousing tune, penned by F. W. Halfpenny, and E.T. Andrews' words were – and remain - nothing short of inspirational.

> *Not buildings grey nor records hoary*
> *Can make a "School" to last for aye,*
> *But souls aflame with high ideals,*
> *That will not falter by the way.*
> *Nor shrink, when effort most is needed,*
> *But fight, and fighting win the day.*
> *Let this then be our high endeavour*
> *"Esthameians" Arise! Arise!*

Though not immured in cloister'd splendour
But set amidst the hum of men,
We yet may hold a high endeavour
Before our steadfast gaze and then
Strive ever onward to attain it
And, falling, rise to strive again.
Let this then be our high endeavour –
"Esthameians" Arise! Arise!

"Say not the struggle naught availeth"-
Not everyone can win the prize;
But this we know, that each one may
Achieve the best that in him lies
And make earth better for his presence
To this we each and all can rise.
Let this then be our high endeavour –
"Esthameians" Arise! Arise!

I did a better job of getting through this one, although, once it was over, tears were trickling down my cheek. Ken Hinds was next to me.

"What's up with you, then?" he asked without overt sentiment.

"Nuffin'" I sniffed. Funny how when someone asks you what's wrong, the answer is always, "Nothing," or, as in this case, "Nuffin'." But Ken knew where I was at. He was leaving too, off to a merchant banking career with Warburg & Co. He smiled at me and rested his hand on my shoulder.

"We'll be alright, Steve. You see if we're not."

The words of the school song expressed sentiments and attitudes which, I hope, have become part and parcel of the person I have grown to be. They served as inspiration to an ordinary kid not to quit when the going got tough, to have a few worthy goals and give them his best shot, along with a realisation that, whilst not everyone can come first, he might just – just – achieve something reasonably worthwhile and make the world a little better place. I think I might just have managed the first two. The jury is still out on the third count.

Look, I am unashamedly a grammar school man. Not a snob but someone who is truly grateful for the quality of opportunities made available through my school. There I was, the son of a reluctant naval man who held down a tough manual job and a mother who machined overalls. I rubbed shoulders with blokes who would go on to Oxford, Cambridge, Exeter, oh, all over the place, and was taught that, if I worked hard and applied myself, anything was possible. Teachers taught by example and I learned that concentration paid dividends and, with my sights set high enough, I might just reach the sky.

But it was about far more than simply academic excellence. It was the place where I learned self-confidence – not arrogance – and that I did, after all, have something to offer. Along with hundreds of others, I was an ordinary kid with a modicum of academic ability, who was encouraged to make the most of his life through education. If that is not the essential part of the way to progress – socially and economically – I shall wait to hear what is. The truth is that more than a few Esthameians did, in fact, arise – and arise considerably. In my own little way, I'd like to feel that I was one of them.

CHAPTER SEVEN

UNCLE HARRY'S LEGACY

When Uncle Harry introduced me to steam engines, he could scarcely have known the direction that my interest was likely to take me. I never asked him if the railway was just a job for him or, like so many that I have subsequently met and read about, a labour of love.

Between 1946 to the end of steam in 1967, a new hobby thrived on these shores, mainly due to the innovation of a young entrepreneur. Maybe it had been there all along but it would be a brave man indeed who didn't willingly recognise Ian Allan as the godfather of train spotting. It took a little time for me to latch on but, once it did, collecting the numbers of my beloved locomotives became little short of obsession.

And I wasn't alone. Throughout the 1950s, every major station – and many minor ones - throughout the land was all but overrun with boys of all ages, armed with notebooks and pencils, watching operations and jotting down the numbers of every engine they could. It was fabulous, harmless fun and I am sure that most young boys of that era tried their hand at it at some time or another.

Now, of course, steam has long gone and even diesel locomotives are confined mainly to freight. Passenger trains - once the prerogative of great, powerful, steaming beasts - have been replaced with smooth running electrics. They may be cleaner and more efficient but where, I ask you, is the romance in that?

Where? Back in the 1950s, that's where.

I am sure that my return trip to Wellington at the end of the 1940s, lit the blue touch paper. Following a week of being mesmerized by steam overkill, there was bound to be a degree of withdrawal symptoms on my return to London. And so it was. Come the arrival of the 1950s, I became obsessed by the need to search out and watch steam engines at work, and just had to find some place where my yearnings could be satisfied. Everybody fed my addiction. When each Christmas, or birthday arrived, Mum, Dad, aunts, uncles, grandparents, would send cards and gifts with a strong strain of steam.

I must have been around six when my complaint about a twinge – it was no more than that – found me, with Mum, at the school dentist's surgery at the East Ham Town Hall annexe, situated on the corner of Barking Road and Wellington Road. In the reception hall, in addition to the receptionist's desk, were a couple of rows of wooden benches and, after recording my name with the nurse, we sat on the back form, moving further to the front as each patient was dealt with. I hadn't read "1984" at that time (in fact, Orwell had only just put the final touches to his work) but, by the cringe, his "Room 101" would have been several sights more terrifying had he had the opportunity to visit the school dentist for inspiration. The place was a house of horrors! A door alongside the receptionist led to the surgery, and one after another, kids came back through it, crying and nursing blood-stained handkerchiefs to their mouths. Hardly encouraging for the next in line, who only entered the chamber if their parent could persuade or, as in my case, force them through.

The white-coated dentist was an elderly man with not a trace of bedside – or should that be chair-side – manner. Void of compassion, he supervised matters as you were plonked in the chair, had a rubber gag jammed between your upper and bottom sets to keep your mouth open, and a rubber mask jammed over your mouth and nose for the anaesthetic gas to send you off to the land of nod. The thing was like a sink plunger and applied with all the grace one would use in trying to cleanse the toilet bowl.

The only way Mum could get me anywhere near the place was by promising to buy me a book at the London Co-operative Society Store, diagonally opposite East Ham Town Hall. Through this, I discovered Thomas the Tank Engine, then in his infancy and not the lusty infant that he has grown into. Gordon, James, and Henry were his only mates at the time but, hey – who cared? Even if they had funny faces on their smoke box doors, they were steam engines. But the price I paid for this treat was high and only when we became patients of the lovely Mrs. Rogers, in Earlham Grove, Forest Gate, did I begin to come to terms with visits to the dentist. The electric train set that Mum and Dad bought me, comprising a tank engine, three trucks, and a circle of three-railed line (the middle line carried the current to power the engine), continued to feed my interest. Dad, splendid handyman that he was, constructed a 4' X 6' board onto which he secured the track, including a couple of sets of points, which enabled simple shunting operations to take place. Before every subsequent Christmas, he would drop some hint or another about what was likely to be in my stocking.

"You know, Stephen, it would be nice if we could have "*Sir Nigel Gresley*" running around your line with a couple of coaches."

Guess what I got for Christmas? Right!

"I think the "*Duchess of Atholl*" would go really well with everything that you've got already."

And what turned up? Right again!

Mind you, they were not quite the surprises Dad intended as, like every kid, I was always searching the house for hidden presents. Once I knew that my parents' favourite gift hiding place was behind our outsize gramophone, I had been drooling over both Sir Nigel and the Duchess long before Christmas morning. Even Derek had been over to inspect the prize. Speaking of whom, train sets enabled me to witness one of the few occasions when Derek was hung out to dry.

It was a dark cold Saturday afternoon in December. The rain had prevented any of us kids going out to play and, with so little to do, I asked Mum if Derek could come over and play with my train set. She was about to go shopping with my aunts and Dad was busying himself around the house. They could see that I was bored out of my skull and guessed that Derek was much the same. They gave in.

It was great fun to watch my engines scoot around the track. One had to be careful when negotiating the curves as approaching them just that bit too fast would see the whole shebang come derailed. Locomotive, coaches and trucks would spill over onto their sides. Derek was good at this and would laugh like a drain. As for me, it wasn't funny at all. These were engines and you just didn't do that sort of thing to engines deliberately.

We must have been playing together for something like a half hour when Derek suggested that he popped over home to pick up some of the accessories from his own model railway. The Rovex No.6201 Princess Elizabeth wouldn't be any good on my three-rail track, for Rovex had opted for two-rail track, the locomotive taking its power from a contact made with the rail, just below the cab. As Derek headed for the door, Dad looked in on us.

"Won't be a second, lads. Just going over the road for some fags."

"And I'm going over home to get my signal box, Mr. Derby. I won't be long," Derek explained.

And with that, the two of them went their separate ways.

Now it's a funny old way the world spins sometimes. Dad and his elder brother, Uncle Jack, could, if seen separately, be confused as twins. Neither of them carried too much weight – or hair. That Saturday afternoon, fate intervened for, as Derek came back with his signal box and other paraphernalia, who should be standing at the gate but.....Uncle Jack, paying us one of his infrequent and unannounced visits. For no reason for which he could be blamed, Derek assumed, wrongly, that it was my Dad, and responded accordingly. Their conversation was totally logical, save for the fact that neither party had a clue as to whom they were talking. Derek first.

"I've got it, Mr.Derby."

Uncle Jack always saw the funny side of things.

"Have you, now?"

Derek began to move into the house when Uncle Jack, confronted by a stranger entering his brother's house, decided to milk the situation for all it was worth.

"Where the hell do you think you're going, young man?"

Del turned and looked incredulously at Uncle Jack - the bloke he thought was my Dad.

"I've just been over to get my signal box. Stephen and I are playing with his electric train set."

At that precise moment, the real Dad came along, puffing away at one of his new investments. And there they were, the two brothers, side-by-side, looking as near as dammit like two peas in a pod. Derek looked from one to the other – and back again.

Looking at Uncle Jack, he cautiously observed, "You're not Mr. Derby."

Well, of course, he was! But not the Mr. Derby that Del had in mind.

"Oh, yes l am!" retorted Uncle Jack.

Looking at Dad, he added, "This kid is saying I'm not Mr. Derby. Tell him that I am, will you?"

Dad could see what was going on, and played his part accordingly.

"Well, of course you are!"

"Well, who's this, then?" Uncle Jack asked, pointing at Derek.

Dad put the icing on the cake.

"I dunno. Never seen 'im in my life before!"

Ultimately all was revealed and normality restored. Like I say, it was one of the few times I could ever recall anyone getting the better of Derek.

Models were fine, but it was the real thing that I truly craved. Steam engines were needed urgently, and as close as possible, if you please. Upton Park station remains situated on the line that runs from Fenchurch Street, in the City, through the south Essex towns of Upminster and Southend, before terminating at Shoeburyness, where the Thames Estuary overlooks the North Sea. A junction at Barking allows trains to skirt the north Thames coast on their way to Tilbury, via Rainham. Since 1854, the entire network had been known as the London, Tilbury and Southend Railway which, whilst hardly imaginative, couldn't be faulted for accuracy. Whatever it may have lacked in the glamour accorded to other lines, it was never without charm.

For such a rather unimportant concern, Upton Park station, surprisingly, boasted four platforms, although by the time that the 1950s arrived, only two were used with any serious intent. District and Metropolitan electric underground services travelled in from Upminster and Barking, to transverse the City as far as, in the case of the District, Ealing. The Met, after leaving Aldgate East, took a northerly route on to Baker Street, before trespassing into open country toward Chesham, Amersham, and Uxbridge. The other two platforms had been constructed by the London, Tilbury and Southend to accommodate a time when their trains used to stop at the station. All of that was history, by the time that I came along.

Opposite Elizabeth Road, alongside the bridge that carried Grangewood Street over the line, was a set of iron railings. Conveniently, my Aunt Eileen and Uncle Ray lived in Elizabeth, so visits were frequent and Mum would always allow me fifteen minutes or so to stand by those railings and watch whatever traffic came down the line. There was plenty of it and from this vantage point, I had a full and unimpeded view up the line toward the station, situated no more than a couple of hundred yards away. A set of semaphore signals by the bridge gave ample warning of a train approaching from the London direction. The excitement generated by a dropped signal and the anticipation of an on-rushing locomotive was exhilarating, fulfilled ultimately by the sight of a tank engine with eleven coaches in tow, roaring toward me before disappearing under the bridge.

In addition to the regular passenger traffic, a not insignificant volume of freight carriage punctuated the flow. Already, I had learned enough to differentiate between a tender engine (a tender carrying coal and water being latched on to the locomotive itself) and a tank engine, where everything was self-contained. The vast majority of the engines using this stretch of line were "tankers," some with pedigrees stretching back almost to the latter part of the eighteenth century, and having spent their entire working lives on the line. My goodness, didn't those little "Jinty" 0-6-0 tanks at the head of forty or fifty wagons shudder and groan on their weary way? But if they were "light engine," that is, no trucks or coaches attached, they would scurry along the line, like some frolicsome little rabbit with its tail on fire. I loved them to bits.

Between the Grangewood Street bridge and Upton Park station, on the south side of the line, a single track departed from the main to lead locomotives into the goods and coal depot. Around mid-day, Monday to Friday, a "Jinty" would traipse a rake of trucks filled with coal into the yard for offloading alongside the offices of Shadracks, the local coal merchant. While the trucks were being emptied, the little engine and its crew would take a breather, before busying themselves shunting empty trucks for the return run. Back and forth it would go and, sometimes, if the line of trucks was particularly long, using the thirty yard spur that ran out of the yard, and parallel to the main line. It was a fascinating operation and it didn't take too long before I had an established lunchtime ritual. On my way home from school, before going in for dinner, the siren call to watch this simple shunting process was, frankly, too strong to resist.

At the back of the yard, the Electron Works made its living through recycling anything metal, long before recycling became cool. A covered section, housing tons of metal waiting to be processed, needed to be moved into the waiting trucks. But how? You could hardly contemplate moving the lot by hand. The answer was found in a whacking great magnet. Remember those fairground machines where you paid a few pence to try and persuade a crane to reach out for a toy, lift it up, and drop the bounty into a box for you to collect as your reward? The principal at the Electron Works was exactly the same. The drone of the magnet as it travelled along its support rail in the roof, bringing with it several hundredweights of metal, and the crash as it fell into the waiting trucks when the current was turned off, was as much a part of the scene as the sound of clanking trucks and fussy little engines.

My enthusiasm was infectious and it wasn't too long before Derek and Dickie Culver joined me, although neither was ever as addicted as I was. It didn't take us long to find another vantage point for watching trains. Between the station and Grangewood Road bridge, a small footbridge linked Park Road with Kings Road. If it had any purpose other than the provision of easier access for West Ham United supporters to reach the club's ground – or the local synagogue – then it escaped me. Corrugated iron sides prevented us from looking along the line for on-coming trains from either direction, so our strategy was to watch from the Kings Road side, which ensured that any passing electric wouldn't obscure our view of a steam engine at the vital moment. At regular intervals, one of us would go onto the bridge, kneel down, and squint through the gap under the corrugated iron. In this way, we could make out a train approaching from either direction, and so be ready for its arrival. By the time we went home, the three of us had cheeks smeared with dirt from the wooden struts, which formed the walkway of the bridge. Mums and dads didn't need to ask where we had spent our time!

I loved the London, Tilbury and Southend dearly - self-contained is how I would describe it. It was possible to travel its length within a couple of hours, even at the most sedate of paces. A locomotive leaving Fenchurch Street could, quite realistically, reach Shoeburyness, get coaled and watered, and be back from whence it came all within the space of a few hours. Every aspect of railway operation from start to finish was on your doorstep, and that is what appealed to me. It provided an excellent grounding for understanding some of the more complex and lengthier railway operations that I would come into contact with in later years. Despite a natural inability to understand matters mechanical, I have managed to grasp the rudiments of steam locomotive workings, albeit tenuously. Everything all fits and works together so beautifully and I now understand cut-off, cylinder cocks, vacuum brakes, and such like. But back then, I didn't have a clue how this giant kettle on wheels did its business. Nor did I want to know. All I thought the engine driver did was get up in the cab, blow the whistle, wave majestically at the envious onlookers, and off the thing chuffed. Like thousands before me, I dreamed of becoming an engine driver but, until that happened, I was more than content to be a professional train-spotter.

Ian Allan was a young man with serious entrepreneurial flair. Employed by the old Southern Railway, he hit on the spiffing wheeze of producing booklets listing the numbers and – glory be - names of all the locomotives working in Great Britain. History has it that he started the series with his familiar Southern Region but, by the time that I was seven, he had covered the lot. For less than a couple of shillings, you could buy one of his ABCs, containing all that one's little heart could desire. The price was within the reach of most who cared to buy a book, in which we underlined the numbers of the engines "spotted." Train spotting was thus born, and Ian Allan was its father.

The books were published in four volumes documenting Western, Southern, London Midland, and London North Eastern locomotives. After 1951, with the advent of British Railways' standard classes, their names and numbers would be tagged on to the London North Eastern volume. A bit rum that, for the standards ran on every network throughout the land. If the poor soul based in Plymouth wanted a list of everything, he needed not just a Western edition to cover his home territory, but also a London North Eastern version, simply for the sake of the standards. He never had a hope of seeing an LNER A4 trespass way down south. Such diesels and electrics as were around at the time were included, mainly in the Southern edition, but us professionals didn't give a carrot for them. The ultimate piece of marketing arrived when all four editions were bound into one combined volume. New editions were produced at least twice a year, with new locomotives added and withdrawn ones deleted. It was a marketing forerunner of football clubs producing different shirts for each season – we just had to have them.

Armed with a combined version, I discovered the full and varied range of steam locomotives that roamed throughout the land. My first ABC contained the numbers of everything likely to come through Upton Park. But it didn't take very long at the local lineside before I was no longer underlining numbers for the very good reason than that I had seen the lot of them. My combined provided me with firm evidence of bigger and better things. Engines had names, engines were gigantic, engines went to Scotland and back, and the thirst to search them out was upon me. But as these beasts never ventured along the London, Tilbury, and Southend, if I was to make their acquaintance, I would need to get to central London. It was all lost on Mum.

"You're not going to London until you're twelve."

And that was that. There was no shifting her. A Sunday trip to the British Museum only served to fan the flame. For some reason best known to myself, I wanted to see an exhibition dedicated to the Magna Carta. Having seen the 13th Century notepaper, I persuaded Dad to take me round to Paddington station. I was all excitement as we walked down the taxi road that led to the platforms. Being a Sunday, the place was somewhat quieter than had we visited on, say, a Saturday. But all was not lost and, to the right, in a dingy section of the station, a "Castle" class locomotive was taking its ease, having arrived with a train from goodness knows where. I remember it to this day – No. 4097 *Kenilworth Castle*. I dreamed about it for the remainder of the week.

However, my entry proper into the world of London steam came from a rather unexpected quarter. Family Sunday afternoons and evenings were invariably spent visiting Grandad and Grandma Vanner, in Lonsdale Avenue. While the adults were talking, I played in the garden, amusing myself by throwing stones at the stench pipe situated on the sewer bank, which ran along the end of their garden. A spot of tea before we all sat down to enjoy a simple little card game that we called "Three H'pence all your Life." Doubtless, it went under a variety of different names. No matter - quite often I would come home loaded with the princely sum of seven and a half pence, pre-decimalisation. Money was, of course, a strong motivator but, far more important, it revealed the competitive streak in me that would not surface fully for a few years yet.

A nice couple, that I grew up to call Uncle Ted and Aunt Peggy, would often join us. Uncle Ted worked in the Kings Cross area and told me how, during his lunch break, he would wander around the station and, if time allowed, visit its near neighbour, St. Pancras. Now, this *was* the Promised Land, and I constantly quizzed him about the engines he had seen. Sadly, his passion for the railway ran nowhere near as high as mine and I'm sure that one engine looked much the same as another to him. But imagine how my spirits soared when, one Sunday evening, he asked Mum and Dad if they would like him to take me up to the stations. Uncle Ted was totally "kosher" and the horror stories that one hears nowadays about "uncles" taking little boys for walks were not on the public agenda in the way that they are today. Mum and Dad had no problem with the deal and, a couple of Sundays later, Uncle Ted collected me from Walpole Road and we headed down to Upton Park station.

Sunday rail service was always poor. During a weekday, you might reasonably expect a train every six minutes or so, but miss one on a Sunday and you were talking about a twenty-minute wait...at least. Our journey on the District Line took us through to Monument where we changed to the Northern Line, and travelled on to Kings Cross and St Pancras – two stations for the price of one. The trip probably took around forty minutes, but that morning, it seemed to drag for hours, so excited was I about going to see some "real" engines. As we walked from the top of the escalator along the passageways to the mainline station, the station announcers metallic voice, droning out which train was for where, became ever louder. There was a very distinctive fishy, smokey, and unhealthy pong around the station, always present in all its vibrancy whenever I visited Kings Cross.

On the concourse, we were greeted by the soft hiss of steam from the tank engines that had brought empty stock into the station. My little heart was pounding in the hope that I might see one of the mighty A4 class. No. 60022 *Mallard* - the fastest steam engine in the world – was a member of the class and, had it been resting at the buffers, I swear I would have run in all directions at once for excitement. However, wherever *Mallard* was, it certainly wasn't in Kings Cross that day. My first sighting of a really big engine was A2 No.60523 *Sun Castle,* resting at the buffer stops after its journey down from the north. I was elated to note its number down in my book.

Security was very much a "by the seat of your pants" affair and only a few stations insisted that you bought a platform ticket, which allowed access to the trains. Uncle Ted and I wandered down to the end of platform 10 (just ¼ beyond Harry Potter's 9 ¾) to join a whole cluster of boys of all ages, duffle bags across their shoulder, ABCs in one hand, and a bottle of pop in the other. It was an early introduction to the trainspotting fraternity and, right from the start, I felt that I belonged. Enthusiasm ran away with me completely in this environment and, from henceforth, I would never be afraid to talk to complete strangers on matters steam engine. Uncle Ted took a back seat as, for the very first time, I did my thing.

Going up to a friendly looking lad not very much older than myself, I asked, "Have there been any A4s in today?"

"Yeah," he replied. "No. 60003 *Andrew K McCosh* left about forty minutes ago."

Andrew K McCosh. I thought that was a fantastic name. The following day at school, when my friend Alan Self asked me if I'd seen any A4s, I replied "nearly."

"Whadja mean...nearly?"

"Well, *Andrew K. McCosh* went out forty minutes before I arrived."

Alan laughed, as well he might.

As it was, I didn't see any A4s on that first visit, although I had other trophies to boast. In addition to *Sun Castle*, I drew a line under A3 No. 60053 *Sansovino*. I'd hoped for a bit more activity around the station but this was, of course, Sunday service. Future visits would find Kings Cross a very different and busier place. We spent a good half an hour at the end of platform 10, before Uncle Ted suggested that we went for a drink and a cake over at neighbouring St. Pancras.

Now, St. Pancras was an absolutely magnificent station. It had been opened for the Midland Railway in 1868 and the arched Barlow train shed was, at the time, the largest single span roof in the world. I grieve for what it has become as the major London Eurostar start point for the continent. Somewhere along the way, it was assessed as a Grade 1 listed building, but you wouldn't guess by the vulgar extension that was shoved on during the 2000s for the benefit of a rail link to the Continent. On my first visit, I was more than content with eight, was it, platforms and a neat, orderly pattern to traffic. More than any other London station, I found it akin to a cathedral. We walked along the taxi road, which ran through the middle of the station (still no ticket required) to the throat of the terminus where, on the main departure platform and ready to leave with an express, simmered my first "Jubilee" No.45620.

I squinted at the nameplate.

"North Burnes," I said, as though I was reading the letters off a test card at the opticians.

"North Borneo," Uncle Ted corrected.

Oh, yeah. So it is. This was the first sign that I was going to join the myopia club.

Something about the Jubilee class touched me more than the Eastern stuff at Kings Cross. There was smoothness and grace about them and, had they been people instead of locomotives, I would have described them as "jolly decent blokes, always smart, and with friendly faces." It is not original, but I grew up to recognise that locomotives, for whatever reason, seemed to possess personalities in their own right. They lived, they breathed, they smiled.

I was grateful to Uncle Ted for that magic morning, and my introduction to the "bigger" league of steam that was available in the capital. It provided me with a little ammunition to pressurise Mum even further into allowing me to "go solo." But, ever still, the straight bat.

"You're not going up there until you are twelve!"

So I remained grounded with the London, Tilbury and Southend for a little while longer. Yet it was further exploration of this very line that would lead me into a magic land I never knew existed. Grandad Vanner used to earn a few bob by taking responsibility for locking the Northern Outfall Sewer (now refreshingly renamed as "Greenway") gates between High Street South and Boundary Road. On our Sunday visits, somewhere around 6'o'clock in the evening, he wheeled his bicycle through the house, fitted his clips on and set off to do his job. No more than four sets of double gates were involved, and I was thrilled the first time that he asked if I would like to accompany him. Would I? Wouldn't I just! The job took the better part of three quarters of an hour, and gave the pair of us the opportunity of chatting and getting to know each other well – which we did. Although Grandad's responsibility ended at Boundary Road, the sewer bank continued tantalisingly into the distance and, frequently, I wondered where it went. I'll have to investigate this.

Cousin Barry could never have been accused of being "into" railways. In fact, I was never quite sure of what he was into. However, he too had accompanied Grandad on security duties and was as curious as I was about where the bank might lead. One Sunday morning, the pair of us decided that we would find out for ourselves what was at the end of this particular rainbow. Without a word to Mum, other than saying I was going to see Barry at his home over in Wilson Road, we met up and cycled along Boundary Road, and up the approach to the gates of the sewer bank.

It was a tremendous adventure for two little eight-year olds, and we really didn't have a clue about what we might find from our sortie. Half a mile into our journey, we came to another set of gates, at a point where the bank was transversed by a main road. Crossing over, we continued our merry way to the next set of gates, and negotiated another road. This was exhilarating stuff, as we got deeper and ever deeper into this new, unfamiliar, and forbidden territory. After a third crossing, the surroundings took on a different flavour. To our left was an expansive cemetery, at which point I think both of us were starting to wonder just how far we should push our adventure. It took all of another few minutes for me to answer the question.

In the distance, beyond the cemetery and to our left, a towering white concrete edifice rose from behind the trees. As we moved closer toward it, the sound of hissing steam reached our ears, and we saw a couple of white plumes of steam reaching up into the morning sky. We cycled on to a point where, to my total and utter delight, we surveyed a scene chock full of engines, some in steam, others cold. About half a dozen parallel lines led into a large brick building, each one packed with buffer-to-buffer locomotives. Many of them I had seen before, going about their business through Upton Park. Yet there were a couple of strangers who really ought to have found a proper home on some other line or another. The large white tower proved to be the means by which the engines were replenished with coal. But how, I wondered, could there be so many engines in one place? All I could do was gaze in awe and wonder at this Aladdin's cave of steam.

Unbeknown, Barry and I had stumbled upon Plaistow Motive Power Depot (the grand title for what were always known to spotters as "sheds"), where locomotives were housed overnight, and prepared for their runs between Fenchurch Street, Tilbury, Southend, and Shoeburyness. It had never occurred to me that 22,000 steam engines spread out across the country had to sleep up somewhere. Could I ever have believed that they just stopped in their tracks at nine'o'clock in the evening, waiting for the sun to come up the following morning, when they would continue along their merry way? No, they had to be cleaned, coaled, and watered, not to mention being "spotted" by me. It didn't take long to work out that discovering and getting around sheds was the future for my train-spotting career. Instead of getting grit in my eyes peeping under the slats at Park Avenue foot bridge, if I found an engine shed, the job could be done wholesale. Surely there were other "Plaistows," where big engines from all points of the compass lurked, waiting for me to discover them. Up until now, it had been main line London stations that appealed, where locomotives would come in and out at regular intervals. But now that I had discovered where stock-in-trade was at its most substantial, access to sheds was going to be my prime objective.

Barry and I cycled back to Boundary Road, with me busting a gut to tell Mum and Dad what I had found. Having admonished me (mildly, let me say) for trolling off on what they perceived to be a foolhardy trip, their smile told me that I hadn't been such a bad boy. I couldn't wait to get out and tell Derek about it all and, the following Sunday, we both made the same trip...and again, the week after that. It was the beginning of many sorties to Plaistow.

Within a couple of weeks, Derek and I were to make another discovery. The local traffic through Upton Park was chiefly the prerogative of tank engines. All right, there were occasions when some old boneshakers with a tender attached would rattle through at the head of a goods train, but romantic they were not. I wanted to see named locomotives without having to travel up to London, where "namers" lurked and had their being. I envied kids in other parts of the country who would do their spotting alongside some line saturated with standard green engines at the head of a long line of "blood and custard" coaches. Why couldn't we have some of that close to our own doorstep?

Manor Park station was a couple of miles from Walpole Road. On one particular Sunday, Del, having recognised that we had had our fill of seeing the same old engines at Plaistow, came up with another adventure.

"Why don't we go down the Bridle Path?"

Now the Bridle Path ran between the former Great Eastern Railway out of Liverpool Street on one side, and the City of London Cemetery on the other. It was a time when Mum and Dad were warning me about not taking sweets from strangers, which was as wise counsel then as it is today. As far as my parents were concerned, the Bridle Path was another "out of bounds" territory and I was not to go there under any circumstances. Perhaps strangers who handed out sweets had been found down the Bridle Path - I don't know. But what I did know – and, by now, so do you – was that Derek always had the upper hand with me. If he suggested that we ought to go down the Bridle Path, well, that's where we would be going.

We cycled along Plashet Grove, turned into High Street North, and on to Manor Park. Sunday traffic was sparse in those days, public transport all but non-existent, and a couple of kids could travel along the road in comparative safety. Even this was in direct contradiction to Mum's orders that I should only ride along the pavements - but what's a boy to do? Over the railway bridge at Manor Park station, a sharp right turn into Forest View Road took us to the gates of the cemetery and the entrance to the Bridle Path, just across Aldersbrook Road. The path sloped down toward the line, turning sharply left to run parallel to the tracks for something like a quarter of a mile. It provided a superb vantage point for viewing the goings-on on no less than six lines that formed the permanent way.

Up and down main lines linked Liverpool Street with Ipswich, Norwich, Southend, and Clacton ; additional up and down lines for electric trains to shuttle between the London terminus and Shenfield. These four tracks were sandwiched by two seldom-used lines for freight when the going got particularly hectic on the main passenger routes.

As with the road, Sunday rail traffic was very much at a premium and, for something like half-an-hour, sweet nothing travelled along any of the lines. Del and I, as much to relieve frustrated anticipation as anything, rode further down the path, to the fly-over that took the electric service over the main lines, prior to dropping down into Ilford station. To our left, the path continued into some leafy route skirting the cemetery and we decided that it would be a spiffing wheeze to see where it led. Yet just as we were about to begin our trek, we were halted in our tracks (no pun intended) by the sound of a shrill whistle, coming from the London direction. You couldn't see us for dust as we scampered back to see what was coming down the line.

In the distance, heading slowly toward us, was a large green locomotive, unlike anything we had ever seen at Upton Park - or Plaistow, come to that. As it shushed its way ever closer, we could see that it carried a tender, to which was attached a short rake of trucks. But there was more. Above the middle driving wheel, we could see a curved metal plate that told us that the locomotive had a name. No more than an hundred yards before reaching us, the driver opened up the regulator. Sharp, determined barks came from the chimney, as his engine picked up speed. It swaggered past us, as we read from the nameplate *Honingham Hall.* It happened to be No. 61610, but that was nothing more than detail. The joyful realisation was that, for the sake of a fifteen-minute bicycle ride, I could see "namers."

The Bridle Path remained my favourite spotting place until Mum lifted her "not until you are twelve" edict, and no wonder. British Railways - formed through nationalisation in 1948 – had begun a major building programme, which resulted in the introduction of standard locomotives. Having enveloped the major regions under one umbrella, the engineering fraternity were able to draw on the best engineering brains available, and several new classes took to the rails. Of these, none came anywhere near matching the magnificent "Britannias" and I shall never forget seeing my first - No.70001 *Lord Hurcomb* - pounding along the line on its way to Norwich. This handsome green monster, with its smoke deflectors and high running board, took elegance to new heights. The chime whistle stated loud and clear that here, indeed, was a locomotive to be treated with respect.

My desire for discovering yet more engines was becoming all but tantamount to an addiction. Upton Park would continue to have my affection but now my focus was on Plaistow engine shed and the Mecca that was the Bridle Path. I was reaching into a world of engines I had only seen in picture books. Namers were being seen on a regular basis and it wasn't long before I could recite them – along with their numbers – as fluently as I had managed my times tables in school. *No. 35008 Orient Line; No 35009 Shaw Savill : No. 35010 Blue Star*......oh, what a future lay before me.

"You're not going up to London until you are twelve!"

Nuts! I knew there was something that I had forgotten. Mum was still sticking her heels in. Twelve was lifetime away. Each Monday, schoolfriends who had long been allowed by their parents to go up to the London termini, would come into school and show me the numbers they had logged during anything up to eight Saturday hours on the platforms. At Liverpool Street alone, not only were they seeing everything likely to romp through Manor Park, but also engines *en route* for Cambridge and Enfield, which inconveniently turned away from the main route at Bethnal Green. I pleaded with Mum, explained, appealed, and grizzled – as kids still do – that all my mates were allowed to go, so why couldn't I? After what seemed like months of haranguing and manoeuvring, I finally managed the breakthrough - in reality, it was probably only a couple of weeks. No matter, long before my twelfth birthday, Mum pulled the lever, the signal dropped, and I embarked on one of the greatest adventures available to boykind during that magical period. I was allowed to go to London, as long as I behaved myself.

It has to be said that London-based trainspotters, in the 1950s, had the very best of virtually every world. Those living anywhere other than the capital would surely have paid a king's ransom for the ready and convenient access that we had to Paddington, Kings Cross, Euston, Waterloo, Victoria, Liverpool Street, and other marginally less important termini and junctions. Having been granted leave of absence by Mum, a Saturday morning ritual was established whereby Alan Self, Stuart Knock, and myself - occasionally, Walter King – met outside Upton Park station, ready to reach Euston by 10'o'clock to see the "Royal Scot" commence its journey to Glasgow. But why Euston? And why the "Royal Scot?"

Well, ever since I had acquired my Hornby-Dublo model of No.46231 *Duchess of Atholl*, I yearned to see the real thing. It didn't register with me at the time, that the engine was based at Polmadie shed, in Glasgow, and sorties down to London were few and far between. The Duchess would do most of its work north of Birmingham and Carlisle, but should it ever decide to venture further south of the border, then Euston was where it would turn up. If and when it did, there was every chance that it would head the "Royal Scot" - the crack Scottish express – so, Euston it had to be.

Arriving at the station via the District and Northern lines, we emerged from the underground between Platforms 2 and 3, to be greeted by at least one locomotive with its train from the north. It could be anything – a "Royal Scot," "Jubilee," "Patriot," or a "Princess Coronation" – all namers. If we were unlucky, we could be greeted by a couple of "Class 5s" for, excellent engines that they were, with 842 of them on the prowl, they were too common to get excited over. As departure time grew closer, we headed for the end of Platform 3, where officialdom allowed us to congregate with Lord knows how many other lads, to have our fun.

The departure of the "Royal Scot" was always nothing less than an event. Through the road bridge that spanned the throat of the station, we had a view of the 1 in 100 incline that was Camden bank. A mile or so beyond and out of sight was Camden Motive Power Depot, and excitement always rose when we saw a locomotive backing down Camden Bank. It would pause to gain clearance

222

before gently easing its way into the station to collect its train. Somewhere just before 9.30am, the locomotive designated to take the "Scot" would come off shed, and regally reverse down onto its 450 tons worth of train. Slowing to gently buffer up to the coaches, the safety valves positively screamed excess steam into the north London air, telling the world that the boiler was full beyond the pressure it was constructed to take. More water injected into the boiler would close the valves because, with a 300-mile romp to Carlisle - where another "Princess Coronation" would take over for the final 100 miles to Glasgow-, there was no point in wasting precious steam.

It was always the prerogative of the "Princess Coronation" class to haul the "Royal Scot." They were painted in what was termed Brunswick green, lined in black and orange and, to my eye, totally magnificent. In earlier - and in some cases later - years, they had been adorned in either blue or red, but green was always my favourite. However, forget the colour - what impressed me was the image of overwhelming latent power, for they were, truly, big engines – 105 tons of big engine. Everything about them was right. Some of the class had once been streamlined until the casing was removed in 1946. Those who had undergone this treatment could be identified by the bevel on the top of the smoke box, just in front of the chimney. It made the locomotive look like some American footballer, with its shoulders hunched, ready to do battle with whatever, or whoever, got in its way. Their massive oval buffers looked like fists. The express locomotives of most other regions had round buffers; all very pretty, but no match for this monster. Half way down the long boiler was the straight nameplate – all the "Coronations" were named, and appropriately so. None of this namby-pamby tosh that you see on power cars today. No, there the engine stood, lord (or lady) of all it surveyed. It seemed to say, "I'm No. 46242 *City of Glasgow*, Jimmie. Don't mess with me 'cos I mean business, so jes' watch ye'self." Behind, a tender carrying 4,000 gallons of water was loaded with 10 tons of coal, crammed in and heaped high. Everything spoke of muscle and power.

At 10'o'clock, right on time, the guard sounded his whistle from the dark depths of Platform 13; a deep hoot from the locomotive's whistle, fractionally before the driver lifted the regulator to release the enormous power of super-heated steam into the cylinders. The front of the locomotive would be swathed in clouds of steam and water released through the cylinder cocks before the first blast came from the chimney as the entourage of engine and fourteen or fifteen coaches began its journey. The pistons began to slide back and forth into the cylinders, slowly at first, but building momentum to a point where it resembled punching an opponent into submission. Camden Bank and the Glasgow road didn't stand a chance. All was steam, noise, power, and drama.

Under the road bridge, the engine began the daunting climb up the bank, and even a "Princess Coronation" would not turn down a little assistance. As it hunched its shoulders to tackle the job in hand, the fifteen coaches slowly followed, before the final part of the drama unfolded. From the recesses of the station came the sound of another locomotive, working every bit as hard as the giant up front. The tank engine that had brought in the empty stock, having been uncoupled from the train, found its work was far from over. Failure on the bank was unthinkable and, as the coaches cleared the platform, up comes this tough little tanker, pushing the train with all its might. By the time it disappeared under the bridge, it was thrashing about alarmingly, totally committed to ensuring that the unthinkable never happened. And, to the best of my knowledge, it never did. We would see it negotiating the curve, half way up Camden Bank - and then it was gone.

I never found departures from other main line London stations quite as dramatic and spectacular as they were at Euston. Oh, yes, they would have their own particular style and I'm not saying that they were not exciting. Paddington's "Kings" and "Castles" enjoyed the luxury of some rear assistance, but as the route out of the station was virtually flat, I always felt that this extra push was more for show rather than effectiveness. Locomotives leaving Kings Cross travelled little more than an hundred yards before disappearing into the tunnels at the throat of the station, where all the drama and spectacular hard work was shielded from the ears and eyes of trainspotters. Despite the exit from Waterloo being little more than a downhill ride, the Bulleid "Pacifics" could - and did - slip and slide all over the place before getting a grip. They all had their appeal, but for fireworks and volcanoes, Euston was the only place to be.

I continued to enjoy end of platform conversations between those of a like mind about what had been in during the day, comparison of ABCs, and suggestions as to where the next port of call might be. We were all brothers in steam (I can recall just a couple of sisters), and there was a certain something that set us apart from enthusiasts with other hobbies. Even walking to a station, the world at large would see us, nod sagely, and think, "There goes a trainspotter." It was the uniform that did it, you see. Mackintoshes with the belt tied rather than buckled; duffle bags slung across our shoulders containing a few sandwiches; a bottle of some sort of pop; a chocolate bar (my favoured delicacy was "Punch," - toffee and fudge covered by chocolate), and our notebooks. Some of my mates took their ABCs with them, but I preferred to keep mine pristine at home where I would mark off new sightings at the end of a day's activity. As my travels became more frequent, I found that I only needed to note down the engines I was not sure about having seen before. With brain-training of that quality, no wonder dates and numbers still stick easily in my mind.....*No 35015 Rotterdam Lloyd; No. 35016 Elders Fyffes ; No. 35017 Belgian Marine........*

Gerry Elvin was a prefect at East Ham Grammar, and lived just a few doors along from Grandma Vanner, in Lonsdale Avenue. A good six years older than me, he had failed to rid himself of the trainspotting bug. When he showed me his ABCs, my jaw dropped. Numbers were lined all over the place – even locomotives based in Scotland, terrified of venturing any further south than Doncaster, or Crewe, for fear that their kilts might be lifted, or some other such engineering embarrassment. Gerry told me his secret.

"I go on excursions where they take you around all the sheds in a particular area. But you can still see loads of stuff in the London sheds. Most of them are dead easy to bunk, and you'll get loads of cops."

Interpretation of these particular pieces of train spotting jargon for the uninitiated might not go amiss.

"Bunk": the active verb for visiting any railway operation without permission, usually a shed. Frequently referred to as trespassing.

"Cop"; verb to describe the initial sighting of any locomotive. Not to be confused with a member of the railway police that you were likely to encounter whilst bunking. Also a noun, describing engines seen for the very first time.

Cops were what it was all about. Part of our ritual when we spotted a locomotive for the first time was to yell, "Cop!" In contrast, the appearance of a regularly seen engine would be greeted by, "Scrap it!" I had witnessed immaculate giants thunder through stations to be greeted with such defamation. If only we had known what history had in store for them all during the next ten years, maybe we would have shown a little more respect. However, back to Gerry, who instructed my friends and me in the art of shed bunking.

"Try something easy to start with," he said. "Kentish Town is a piece of cake – no one ever gets chucked out of there. You'll see everything that goes in and out of St. Pancras." Alan Self and I took Gerry at his word and decided to give it a go.

Kentish Town underground station was on the Northern Line. The entry to the shed was no more than a five-minute walk along Highgate Road, where a side alley led down into the shed. Despite Gerry's confidence and endorsement about Kentish Town being "a piece of cake," we still needed to take care, for the bane of the trespasser's life was always the shed foreman. He had the power of life and death as far as we understood it. Catch him on a good day, and he would be likely to turn a blind eye. On a not so good day, you might be invited to "Sling yer 'ook," thereby terminating your little adventure.

On our first attempt, Alan and I walked tentatively down the slope to the edge of the rails. Looking to our left, we could see a plethora of steam engines that made us want to rush up to them, books and pencils in hand, giving not a damn about shed foremen and their ilk. Straight ahead, across a couple of tracks, was the entrance to the shed, where locomotives were resting. I could see a couple of "Jubilees," which tempted me to take a premature plunge. But from the adjoining administrative offices, staff had a perfect view of anyone thinking about taking such a chance. Patience was the name of the game and best policy to wait for a moment when all backs were turned. Then, and only then, would we make our mad twenty-five yard dash into the safety and sanctuary that the shed provided.

We waited....and waited...and we waited until, suddenly, the moment arrived. Perhaps it was tea break and the staff had started to head down to the canteen. Whatever - we didn't care. Eyes were temporarily and briefly diverted from their vigilance, and that was all we needed. Like little bats from hell, we took our courage in both hands, and belted across the lines into the shed where we were safe, and ready to begin the first of so many magical tours around a main line steam engine shed. Kentish Town was a wonderful experience and, over the weeks, our ABCs began to fill up. Gerry Elvin was right. Kentish Town was easy. Or maybe it was just a case of railway staff in those days being perfectly content to let kids collect the numbers as long as they did nothing daft. Yes, I think that was it.

Access to many London sheds was, indeed, a piece of cake. But there were others something akin to Fort Knox or, at least, they were for me. I never managed the gigantic and local Stratford, with its allocation of four hundred plus. Camden, bristling with "namers," I got round just the once when, on a Sunday morning, I attached myself onto a visiting party. Was *the* duchess resident? She was not. Willesden required neither courage nor expertise. A walk from the station to the road bridge that crossed the Grand Union Canal, before turning right and along the drive into the shed was all it took. Ducking beneath the official windows (as you do), spotters were able to edge deeper into the complex until they were at the throat of the shed housing, as it did, a myriad of dirty, work stained freight locomotives.

Yet although my early preoccupation with shed bashing focussed on the Midland, there was absolutely no doubt about my favourite London depot. I don't think I would be alone in the opinion. After "doing" Willesden, it was back to the road bridge and over to the other side of the canal, where we followed the footpath alongside the water. A few hundred yards along, a break in the wire fencing allowed access to a grassy bank. Slide down it, and you found yourself alongside the mighty edifice that housed the four turntables of the ex-Great Western's Old Oak Common. The place was a smoky cathedral and the sheer expanse of the shed overwhelming. Wherever you looked, there were engines. "Kings," "Castles," "Halls," panniers, freight – Old Oak had it all in spades. And the yards were just as populated, chock full of locomotives returning from Paddington for servicing in readiness to return and pick up their trains for a run to Penzance, Birmingham, or Wolverhampton. Who knows? I might even have stood alongside *"Something Hall."*

Smaller in scale – but by no means less enjoyable - were Cricklewood for freight on the St.Pancras line; Bricklayers Arms for Charing Cross; and a delightful hike across the allotments alongside the North Circular Road to reach Neasden shed – always good for an "A3 Pacific, with the twin towers of Wembley Stadium standing sentinel on the horizon. Any trainspotter could tell you tales about them all but, if you don't mind, I'll stick with my two greatest triumphs.

Walter King shedded with his parents in an upstairs flat adjoining Moores the Builder, just around the corner from Walpole, in Plashet Grove. He was a nice lad was Walter, inoffensive enough for even me to clout without fear of reprimand. He had an accent as Yorkshire as it came, which sounded very much out of place amongst the East London "gor blimeys" in which it found itself. Yet Walter was the envy of us all. You see, he was the only spotter out of the lot of us that had seen representatives from classes that never ventured south of Doncaster. There were some of our number who, if not downright unbelievers, were, at least, agnostic.

"Where'd yer see this stuff then, Kingy?" Thus spake the disbelievers

. "Oop Yorkshire, when Mam and Dad took me on t'olidays." Thus responded the King.

It was a very good reason and, truth be told, I think everyone believed him. It was just that we were all green with envy.

Anyhow, Walt and I set out during one school holiday with the objective of finding Stewarts Lane, which serviced the engines for Victoria, not least, the magnificent and immaculate "Golden Arrow." We took an electric to Battersea Park station, situated right next door to Battersea Dogs Home. A little further on to the right, we found Stewarts Road, so we guessed that we were likely to be on to something. Sure enough, alongside the road were several tracks, veering away to the right and, by way of affirmation, a "King Arthur" crawled around the curve, tender first, en route for Victoria. The driver looked at the pair of us from his cab, knowing full well what we were up to.

There were other kids coming in our direction, armed with note books, dressed in anoraks, carrying duffle bags – same old uniform, common as the old surplice, mitre and crook are to Archbishop what's- 'is-name.

"Is this the way to Stewarts Lane?" I asked.

A gruff, despondent lad replied.

"Yeah. But you'll never get in. That foreman's a right bugger."

Well, you can't say fairer than that, now can you? We passed each other on our different merry ways. However, Walter and I had come too far to give up now and, between the arches and bridges that the lines threaded through, we gained the first glimpse of Utopia. Rising steam, smoke boxes of all manner of classes from Bulleids to Maunsells. Oh, hold on, boys. Your favourite son is coming to you.

Access to the shed was over a footbridge, situated at the end of Corunna Terrace. It was a long bridge that stretched over several lines to where a flight of wooden steps led down into the yard. Perched all along the thing, like a set of crows ready to take flight,

229

were something like thirty kids, armed with all the necessary train spotting paraphernalia. Locomotives were moving in and out all the time and if you never went to anywhere else during the day, time spent here would have been well worth the investment.

But it was in the darker recesses of the shed where the real treasure was to be had. To reach it, we would need to take our courage in both hands, walk down the steps of the bridge, brazenly pass the shed master's office, before hot-footing it for the shed itself. Stewarts Lane was not Kentish Town, where you could furtively hide until the right moment arrived. Everything was completely open and, as soon as anyone put so much as a foot on the footbridge stairs, heads in the office would turn, faces would smile, all minds with a common thought, - "Here comes another dopey pair."

So, what were our options? So far, every effort by our predecessors had been thwarted. Time after time, would-be invaders were repelled and sent back from whence they came. Tales of derring-do about how various ingenious attempts had been made to get into the promised land were shared ad nauseam. These ranged from running and hiding alongside moving engines, to entering the complex from a fence a little further along from the bridge. Nothing had worked. If there was a way in, then the combined brainpower on that bridge had failed to work it out. But I hadn't come all this way not to give it a go.

"Look, Walt. This is the deal," I told him. "We're going down to ask permission go round the shed. I'll tell the shed master that we've come from Ipswich and didn't know that we needed a permit and would he mind if we had just a little look around before we went home."

The pair of us knew that it was just about the worst plan that could ever have been cooked up in the circumstances. But could he tell me a better one? Was he up for it?

"We'll never get past, Steve. It's not worth risking it. The foreman might even chuck the lot of us off the bridge."

"Look, are you up for it, or not?"

Walter was clearly mulling it over. Like me, he was keen as mustard to get round the shed and his reply took all of fifteen seconds.

"Oh, all reet,"he reluctantly, and unconvincingly, concurred.

So, courage in both hands, we took our first steps down. Dutifully, the heads in the office lifted and smiled at the next two sacrificial lambs. The crows on the bridge all yelled and laughed like crazy.

"See ya in a couple of minutes, yer daft sods," was about the most printable encouragement that we received from the older boys.

We reached the cinder path leading to the foreman's office. To our surprise, nobody came out to order us back from whence we came and it all began to feel rather surreal. On reaching the door of the office totally unmolested – can I believe this? – we walked in as though we owned the place. Past the grinning staff at their desks, and on to a door that looked official enough to protect a shed foreman's office. Tentatively, we poked our heads round.

"And what can I do for you boys?"

Now this was certainly not the greeting we had expected. In fact, the bloke looked and sounded perfectly pleasant and reasonable. Perhaps we should have been encouraged but, suddenly, blind panic kicked in when I realised that I didn't have a clue as to what an Ipswich accent sounded like. Come to think of it, I wasn't totally sure that I knew where the blessed place was. It was then that I thanked my lucky starts that it was Walter who was sharing this adventure with me. In what I could swear was nothing more nor less than pure Yorkshire, he spoke with a confidence that certainly hadn't been in evidence before our walk to destiny commenced.

"Please, mister. We wondered if y'd let us have a look round t'shed. We've come down from Ipswich, and didn't know we needed a permit."

What a line! I stood amazed as our appeal was heard by a bloke that, surely, could differentiate between Yorkshire and Suffolk. And expecting him to believe that we didn't know that we needed a pass - well, that was just too unreal to believe. We were on our way out. Thanks very much, Walter.

But he looked up at us from his desk, his expression unchanged, unchanging.

"Well, okay, then, lads," he said. "Only, look very carefully about you. The shed's a bit full today and there's a lot of stuff lying about. If anyone stops you, you can tell them that you've been in to see me. Only half an hour, mind, and come and tell me when you're leaving."

Walt and me, we couldn't believe what we were hearing. Here we were, at the shed where "Golden Arrow" locomotives were buffed up to gleaming perfection, chock full of steam and, beyond our wildest dreams, with full permission from the boss to go round. For the life of me, I can't remember saying thanks, I was that excited. But I'm sure we did. As for Walter, what could I say?

"Walt, you're an absolute marvel!"

On the footbridge, the crows were perched, awaiting our return. They were to be disappointed. It would have been a bit churlish to wave to them. We just made our way to the shed, notebooks in hand, taking proper care to avoid danger. I'd bunked sheds before, but this was the first time that I had ever gone round with the full authority of the foreman. There, amongst the mighty, and not so mighty representation of the old Southern region, along with its allocation of standards, Walter King and I lived the dream. We took our half hour before returning to the shed master and, this time, I did thank him - whoever he was. We walked up the steps of the footbridge to where the green-eyed fraternity reigned. No.34104 Bere Alston was just around the corner, out of sight from prying footbridge eyes. It was a mighty "cop" for me. Our notebooks were the envy of all, and even those that comforted themselves with staccato outbursts of "seen it" couldn't disguise their envy. There was just one question on all of their lips.

"What on earth did you tell him? We've been trying for weeks and got nowhere."

When we explained our strategy, the general consensus of opinion was that it was too far fetched to be true. Maybe so, guys.

But the proof of the pudding and all that. Walter King and I, for the only time in our lives, had "done" Stewarts Lane.

Despite having moved on to greater things, I continued to frequent Plaistow shed. It wasn't difficult. Off the train at West Ham Manor Road, turn left into Durban Road, at the end of which a cinder path took you past the foreman's office and on to the shed proper. Of course, the likelihood of a "cop" in Plaistow was long passed, but I liked the familiarity of my local shed – there's the old community thing rearing its head again. I was never thrown out and, come to think of it, my dismissal occurred at only one shed when some officious railway policeman at Old Oak Common threatened to tell my Dad that I had been trespassing on railway property.

School summer holidays were long and the euphoria of their commencement soon passed. After I had been on holiday with Mum and Dad for a couple of weeks, it was a case of playing in the street, mucking about over Wanstead Flats or Plashet Park, and train spotting here, there, and everywhere. I don't think there were many kids who, by the time that September rolled around, weren't more than ready to get back to school. I know I was. Alan Temple was one of my train spotting converts. There would be many over the years, whose interest was stirred by my unyielding passion and commitment to the creed, for I promoted train spotting with something exceeding missionary zeal. Toward the end of one summer holiday, I took Alan along to Plaistow. He'd never been to a shed before and the responsibility of initiating him into the mysteries weighed heavily upon me. We followed the old familiar route through Durban Road.

"Now, Al," I counselled. "We just walk in, keep a weather eye out for anyone who might look as though they might be in authority, and make for the shed. Once we're in, we can stay as long as we please."

That had been my modus operandi, time and time again and, once more, it worked like a charm. Under the covered section of the shed, the pair of us walked up and down amongst the ranks of passenger and freight tank engines, him scribbling every number like fury and me – who had seen them all before - simply drinking in the delight of being amongst so many old friends. Yet there was to be a shock and surprise waiting for us, that I would never have anticipated.

At the back of the shed, on the siding closest to the drivers' mess, stood a gleaming example of a Whitlegg "3P" 4-4-2 Tilbury tank. These engines had been around since 1923 and been designed specifically for the London, Tilbury, and Southend line, although as time passed, a number of them would be sent to do service in other parts of the country. Nevertheless, I had logged a more than respectable percentage of the class but I'd never seen one of them quite like this. The engine was immaculate and had just returned from Bow Works, up the line, following a full overhaul.

Suddenly, whilst Alan and I were gazing at the machine, from the mess room, authority appeared, with all the trimmings; a gnarled old mechanic, with attitude.

"What are you boys doing in here?" he asked.

It was, of course, the dumbest of questions. We weren't there for a picnic and he knew darned well that we were trainspotters. We said as much and he mellowed just a little.

"Have you seen this one before?" he asked, pointing to the pristine black tank engine.

I told him that I had but, of course, it was new to Alan.

"But not like this, I'll bet. Come on lads, I'll give you a tour."

And with that, he took us up onto the footplate, carefully explaining the functions of each lever, dial, and wheel in the cab to two mesmerised thirteen-year olds. And he didn't finish there. Climbing back onto terra firma, he took us down the steps into the inspection pit, underneath the engine itself.

"Mind yer 'eads," he cautioned.

And there, in that dingy corner of an East London engine shed, the pair of us beheld motions and workings far too complex for our tiny brains to comprehend. No railwayman was ever thanked so profusely as that good bloke. I couldn't speak about anything else for days afterwards. When school recommenced, and we were invited to write an essay on "The Highlight of my Holiday," guess what I wrote about? And guess who got a commendation for his essay? Right first time, both times!

I continued to crave the *Duchess of Atholl,* who, determinedly, continued to elude me. But there was something in store for me that more than made up for the lack – probably the highlight of my trainspotting career. When it happened before my very eyes, I thought I was dreaming, but I swear to you that this story is true. One Sunday morning, in March 1956, for no particular reason other than having nothing better to do, Derek and I thought we'd go over to Plaistow. On this occasion, rather than cycling, we opted to take the train for a visit to the shed that proved every bit as uneventful as expected. The glittering Tilbury tank had long returned to its duties and was probably covered in grime by now, so this was nothing more than a morning out for the pair of us before dinner and Sunday school. On our return to Upton Park, in keeping with our usual pattern, we stood by the door next to the main line, just in case anything came hurrying through. It was a Sunday, so we were scarcely optimistic. However, it so happened that, for whatever reason, our train was delayed in Plaistow station for something like five minutes, and I started to have concerns about cold dinners and not being back on time. Yet without the loss of those vital minutes, I would certainly have been at the table on time, but would have missed the sight of a lifetime.

As our train eased into Upton Park, we heard the soft sound of escaping steam, coming from the East Ham direction. Instantly, we were all attention and focussed on the main line. To our total astonishment, shuffling through the station, coupled together in the lightest of steam, were "Britannia" No.70038 *Robin Hood* and "A4" No.60022 *Mallard.* The fastest steam locomotive in the world (126 mph, on 3rd July 1938) - not flying though Doncaster, Grantham, York, Darlington, on its way to Edinburgh, but, with the air of having a casual fag, drifting through sleepy little Upton Park with his mate, *Robin.* Derek and I looked at one another incredulously. Even he knew that this was a real red-letter day. True to form, when we told all our mates, not a soul believed us – and why, indeed, should they?

Only after a couple of weeks did the mystery become unravelled by an entry in "Trains Illustrated." The Saturday prior to our sighting, celebrations had been held for the centenary of the London, Tilbury, and Southend Railway. During that afternoon, I'd been at Liverpool Street, to witness the arrival of *Thundersley* – Tilbury tank No. 41966 in disguise - fully regaled in traditional colours, hauling a restored coach from an earlier period, together with a train of more up-to-date stock. While all this was going on, down at Tilbury itself, as part of the shenanigans, *Mallard* and *Robin Hood* were guests of honour. What Derek and I had witnessed was the two locomotives on their way back to their home territory. Ultimately, we were both believed and deeply envied.

Perhaps it was inevitable that the hobby of collecting numbers would, ultimately, dim for most boys at some time or another. As the sands of the 1950s seeped away, it became increasingly clear that the writing was well and truly on the wall for steam. Even before Dr. Richard Beeching went about his review of the rail network and its efficiencies (and otherwise), familiar scenes began to change irrevocably and, hard as it was to accept, steam and all that it had stood for would shortly be no more. As time has passed, platforms overcrowded with lads taking both numbers and risks in order to underline a couple more numbers in their books are seen no more. And as for "bunking" sheds, well, forget it. The Health and Safety oligarchs and jobs-worths have put an end to that once and for all. At the time, I was unable to comprehend life without locomotives. The thought that over 20,000 mechanical miracles were about to disappear was totally beyond me. Buildings, big ships, and steam engines, - they went on for ever, didn't they? Well, the short answer is "no" and before the decade was out, the cull had begun.

When I reflect on those times, I am amazed at how my addiction came, quite painlessly, to a halt. Make no mistake, I have never escaped the spell that steam engines cast over me – it was too deep for that. Whenever a signal was up, I scurried to find a vantage point to see an engine pass. Nowadays, preserved lines around the country give veterans like me the necessary reminder and opportunity to taste, see, and support a mode of transport that once claimed the attention of virtually every little boy at some stage of life or another. So it was, chiefly, the number collecting aspect of my interest that came to a halt almost overnight. Other interests and opportunities were being added to my life's agenda and, at age thirteen, the transition to those "other things" was joyful enough to ease any pain that might have been incurred by putting my ABCs to rest.

But how grateful I am to my dear old Uncle Harry for providing me with such a wonderful legacy, dividends from which I continue to draw to this day. Have I any disappointments about those trainspotting days? Well, yes, just the one. I never, ever saw the *Duchess of Atholl!*

Steve Derby

CHAPTER EIGHT

THAT'S ENTERTAINMENT!

Frankly, I have little truck with much of what is promoted as comedy these days. Young men dressed as though they had just wandered in off the building site (no offence, builders), full of foul and offensive language, under the impression that if they shout loudly enough and adopt enough poses, then they are funny. What worries me is that so many of their audiences seem to agree! Even the great and talented Billy Connolly needs calling into order. How, I ask you, can a man as gifted as this give a powerful, dramatic, and totally believable performance as John Brown, the widowed Queen Victoria's consort, only to get in front of an audience, "effing and blinding" to his and his audience's hearts content?

I have to accept that comedy does evolve and what I find funny goes completely over the heads of my children – certainly, my grandchildren. Yet it doesn't stop me from wondering what might happen if, during some offensive rant by one of these comedians (by definition as opposed to repute), some little – or not so little – innocent, stood and declared, "You know, folks, I don't think this is very funny at all." I have a vision of the laughter stopping and, one by one, the entire audience admitting that they didn't find it particularly funny either.

"So, why are you laughing?" our innocent asks.

"Well," comes the reply, "Everyone else was, so I thought I'd better join in!"

An interesting twist on Andersen's "King's New Clothes."

*The late Ronnie Barker (now there **was** a funny man) once remarked that alternative comedy is just that. - an alternative to comedy. Of course, we all have our favourite comedians and shows but, on the bottom line, I think we all know what is genuinely funny. Not only does it tickle at the time, but it enjoys the blessing of longevity. You ask the man or woman in the street where, "Don't*

238

tell him, Pike!" comes from and a substantial majority will give you chapter and verse. You can't get away with asking for "Four candles, please," without everyone within earshot bursting out laughing. I'm not saying that there isn't some good quality laughter being made nowadays. It is just that I would like it served with a shade more subtlety.

Right, I've set my stall out. Now I can revisit the entertainment that came my way in my infancy.

When the day drew to its close and all the playing in the street had been done, I would retire into the living room of No.7, with Mum and Dad. Were it possible for you to join me, the first thing anyone born before, let's say, 1955, would notice is that there is no television. Perhaps it's in another room, you reasonably think. Yet you would be wrong, for – horror of horrors - we have no television, no moving wallpaper, no focus for our being. In vain, you would look for some gismo or another on which to play your CDs, but there would be no point - the little discs are still a good thirty years away from the market. A home computer for the 1950s family was the stuff of fantasy, and pretty far-fetched fantasy at that.

Our living room comprised a couple of armchairs, a dining table with three chairs set round, a mantelpiece arching over the fireplace (we hadn't worked out central heating either), and a small radio set. These were available in all shapes and sizes, and Mum and Dad chose a rather compact item. Radio stations were selected by turning a knob that moved the indicator displayed on the face of the machine to the appropriate frequency. And don't start on about BBCs 1, 2, 3, or 4. Back then, Sky was that blue stuff over and above all our heads, and we were years from the proliferation of choice available today. Just two main radio services provided us with most of our options. The Light Programme commenced broadcasting mainstream light entertainment and music in 1945 until closure in 1967, when it was replaced by Radios 1 and 2. 'Heavier' programming – news, drama, and discussions – was to be found on the Home Service. The rogue-ish Radio Luxembourg was around and would eventually open a wider door to more teen-orientated material and weave its way into young lives. So, the radio was our prime source of home entertainment in the early 1950s, and provided much for us to discuss when playing in the street.I am quite clear about the first radio show to catch my childish attention, for it seemed that everyone had a soft spot for "Educating Archie." Archie was, in fact, Archie Andrews – a ventriloquist's dummy - and we rarely missed his weekly half-hour adventures. As far as Walpole Roaders were concerned, Archie was no dummy but a real life kid, just like us, and it would take the advent of television before a dark secret was revealed. It was this - Peter Brough (the guy with his hand up Archie's shirt) was unquestionably the worst ventriloquist of all time - wooden Archie had far more talent in one of his splinters. Yet, having said that, Brough must have had some sharp advisors, as "Archie" merchandise flooded the shops and, doubtless, made him a wealthy man - but no better a ventriloquist.

The day following airing of the show, on the way to school, Derek, Dickie Culver, and I would not only talk about Archie's escapades, but re-enact the script, with all its catch phrases. Max Bygraves, would arrive on set with the pronouncement, "I've arrived and to prove it, I'm 'ere!" Should Archie come up with an idea of even the most miniscule proportions, Bygraves would greet it with, "That's a good idea – son!" with emphasis on the last word. Those expressions, and others like them, slipped easily into our developing vocabularies. Astoundingly, the artists who cut their broadcasting teeth on the "Educating Archie" roster sounds like a "Who's Who" of entertainment greats, rather than a little cast whose star was a carefully crafted lump of wood. In addition to Max, at one time or another, the cast would enjoy the services of Robert Moreton, Hattie Jacques, Tony Hancock, Alfred Marks, Sid James, Dick Emery, Harry Secombe, and even old "All right, my loves?" himself, Bruce Forsyth. A little thirteen year-old girl soprano named Julie Andrews was the resident vocalist. The list goes on. At its height, the show attracted 12 million listeners, which is pretty good going for a ventriloquist's doll.

The commencement of my love affair with laughter and comedy must have had its roots in "Worker's Playtime." I can't see how it could have been otherwise. This simple touring variety comedy and music programme became part of the national fabric, and I, for one, always tuned in to the lunchtime half hour. The show would be broadcast live from a factory canteen "Somewhere in Britain" and, as part of its *raison d'etre* was to support the war effort, the Ministry of Labour chose which factory canteens the show would visit. Government always sticks its snout in somewhere or other, but this was one of its better efforts. Before my time, I know, but I understand that Ernest Bevin (the Minister of Labour and National Service), occasionally appeared on the show to congratulate the workers, and exhort them to greater efforts. When the War came to its conclusion, "Worker's Playtime" continued to raise the morale of the workers, whilst the Government busied itself in rebuilding Britain and its economy. The BBC, for their part, were very happy to maintain the successful format, even if it meant transporting crew, cable, microphones, two pianos, a producer, and a bunch of variety artists up and down the country three times a week. I am deeply grateful for those decisions and those who made them and, remarkably, the show ran on to 1964.

As with "Educating Archie," the list of performers on "Workers Playtime" is stunning for the depth of talent represented – both established and up-and-coming. Comedians "Cheerful" Charlie Chester, Peter Sellers, Tony Hancock (again), Frankie Howerd, Morecambe and Wise, Bob Monkhouse, Elsie and Doris Waters, and the magnificent King of Knotty Ash, Ken Dodd, all did their turns. My goodness, even the controversial yet brilliant, "Cheeky Chappie" Max Miller was not averse to making an appearance, although I'm sure he was told to take his gags from the red book as opposed to the blue one. Amongst the singers were Ann Shelton (who worked with no less a personage than the great Glen Miller), Eve Boswell, Dorothy Squires, and, once again, Julie Andrews who, having graduated from "Educating Archie," was starting to reach out for that elusive commodity, Superstardom. Julie - who was to become Mary Poppins, and ever more shall be so - got there. Novelty acts also made themselves a pretty useful living and Percy Edwards made his by duplicating the sound of any bird or animal that you could think of. Being totally unaware of the difference between a lesser-spotted what-not and a racing pigeon, my judgement on Percy can only be on the grounds that he received hearty rounds of applause - so he must have been good. Peter Cavanagh was an impressionist, billed as, "The Voice of them All." Now here, I *could* make a judgement when he had a shot at those voices with which I was familiar. I recall his efforts at the diminutive, bespectacled Liverpudlian, Arthur Askey – Mum's favourite - with his "Hello, Playmates" and "Aye thank yew," - but even I could do a passable attempt at him. No matter. Peter was on the radio far more frequently than I was, so he had to have had something.

The death knell had not quite sounded for the music hall tradition, although first hints that its lifespan was drawing to a close were apparent during those early post war years. Over many years, British music hall had featured rousing songs and comic acts in theatres up and down the country, which gained their own reputations. Many cities and towns throughout the land were able to boast a "palace" or "theatre," where stars of the day came to perform for the locals. As with radio, music hall had spawned a host of "household names," who had truly earned their spurs by withstanding some of the harshest and severest examinations across the land, with honourable mention of the Glasgow Empire. By all accounts, Friday night's second house could be a graveyard for the careers of any up and coming talent. Yet the net result of this sort of treatment compelled performers to hone their material and presentation to such a fine degree that they could survive audience wit and insult, which was sometimes as professional as that of those on stage. I am amazed how, so often, the first I hear of a new comedian nowadays is that they have been awarded a television series of their own. It reminds me of that magnificent observation by Kitty Muggeridge on David Frost - "He rose without trace." There are a lot who have done just that and it wouldn't have happened back in the 1950s, I can tell you. Back then, you really had to pay your dues.

Having heard the radio performances of these troopers, I thirsted to see them in the flesh, so to speak. At the corner of Burges Road and High Street North stood the Palace Theatre, and many of the artists that I listened to on radio appeared on the East Ham Palace stage. Once – just the once – Mum and Dad took me to see Archie Andrews. It was okay, but that singular lack of ability by Peter Brough was there for all to see, and the wheel fell off somewhat. But there were others who stood out far more prominently. Dad had been going on about some bloke called Frankie Howerd, and the three of us were booked in to witness this promising newcomer. Not quite sure of what to expect, I sat through the prancers, dancers, and singers, waiting to hear and see what all the fuss was about. I can tell you, it was worth every second of the wait, and you must remember that I couldn't have been much older than seven. Frankie Howerd captivated me completely. When his name was announced, the place went bonkers. He took the stage, bowing and smiling to his audience and, before he had even uttered a word, he had us all in the palm of his hand. There was something awkward about his manner that told you he was going to be funny but, of course, I didn't realise quite how funny Howerd's funny was going to be. No technicolour suit a la Max Miller; nor anything akin to Max Wall's black tights; none of Ken Dodd's air of manic madness. No, Frankie was just a bloke who lived up the road, dressed in a normal suit, and who had a few tales to tell. From the start, I fell in love with that delightful informality and lack of airs and graces. If you didn't know better, you would have sworn that he was making it up as he went along.

"Good evening, ladies and gentlemen. Oh, I've had a rotten week this week (laughter). No, I really have."

More laughter, because we knew that he was going to let us in on the intimacies that had caused his "rotten week." Some of his material probably went over my young head, but there was ample for me to get my teeth into. As he unravelled his stories, there were moments when he seemed to hesitate, as if searching for words that just would not come. The narrative became seasoned with "ums," "errs," "yerses," and "well, no, here, listens." It would have appeared shambolic had you not known – as I later discovered - that every word (even the interjections) had been carefully scripted. Can you believe that? All those little asides that I thought were *ad lib* had, in fact, been nothing of the kind.

A few yards behind Frank on stage stood a grand piano where sat a lady of mature years, a shade overweight, dressed finely, and displaying more than a touch of "mutton dressed as lamb." Patiently, she sat there as Frankie went through his patter until, with a double take, he noticed her. All camp and condescending, he explained to us, in stage whispers, about what a sad life she'd had, providing if not chapter and verse, at least enough to set her up for ridicule.

"Deaf as a post, you know. Can't hear a word."

The audience laughed, whilst the accompanist just sat there, nodding and smiling, oblivious to anything that Frankie might have said. Rubbing his hands and arms as if to keep himself warm, he raised his voice - as one might, if someone is hard of hearing – and, smiling, addressed the object of his scorn.

"Chilly, dear. Chilly."

She screwed up her eyes and turned her head in an effort to hear what had been said.

"I said, it's chilly," Frankie all but yelled. She smiled benignly and nodded her agreement to whatever she thought he had said.

Back to the audience, "Poor old soul."

And as we laughed heartily, but not unkindly, he added the immortal words.

"No, don't laugh. It's wicked to mock the afflicted."

But that was, of course, exactly what Frankie was doing, and we were all laughing as he did it. What comedian ever encouraged his audience not to laugh? We hooted. The ladies who undertook that accompanist role – and there were several - were fantastic and provided an inestimable contribution in making Frank the jester that he truly was.

Frankie Howerd lasted the course – and then some. Despite realistically sensing that his time had come and gone after a successful stint in the television sitcom "Up Pompeii," he came back bigger and better than ever in the twilight of his career through the unlikely medium of the Debating Chamber of the Oxford Union. From the heights to the shallower water, and then back to the heights again. There were a lot of people who were very glad about that remarkable comeback of a quite remarkable artist. Count me among them.

The Palace played host to another artist who was to escort me further down the road of laughter. At the end of the Second World War, Norman Wisdom hit the ground running. Totally different from Frankie Howerd, Norman was all about the clown. When he took the stage at East Ham, before he had uttered a word, we all roared at this little guy wearing a tweed flat cap askew, peak turned up; a suit a couple of sizes too small; a shirt with a crumpled collar along with a mangled tie. You couldn't help but draw comparison with Charlie Chaplin's creation "The Tramp," and it would come as no surprise when, some time later, Chaplin nominated Norman as his "favourite clown."

His talents were widespread. Not only was he a first rate slapstick artist, but he could move you to tears when, in some sketch or another, things were not going his way. When he appealled to his audience with those sad old bloodhound eyes, you instantly sided with him. And when matters took a turn for the better, and the smile returned, he hopped about the stage as light a cork on the ocean. Oh, yes, he was a damn fine singer, too. In 1954, his recording of "Don't Laugh at Me" reached No. 3 in the popular music charts. It was fully deserved.

Norman Wisdom endeared himself to me with a routine that he performed the night that I saw him. In the midst of one of those "everything's going wrong for me" moments, he wandered disconsolately around the stage, mumbling we knew not what, as he was "off microphone." Then, with exquisite timing, he passed the microphone for his voice to be picked up.

"Especially tonight," was all that we, the audience, heard.

The little clown's eyes lit up, and his smile returned. You could see his mind at work. "That was fun," he was thinking. He walked back toward the microphone and, when he was within range, repeated, "Especially tonight" into the thing. There was no stopping him now and for I don't know how long, he performed a sequence demonstrating how many various ways he could pass that microphone, saying just those two words. Different accents, coming at the microphone from different angles, and best of all, a run from one side of the stage to the other, leaping past the microphone like Nuryev and, in mid-flight, treating us all to a generous helping of "Especially tonight!" It was hilarious as he went into one of his laughing fits – it sounded like the braying of a donkey - for sheer joy at what he, the little clown, had done. He had triumphed and we were thrilled for both him and ourselves.

Norman was another who went on to greater success. His light-hearted comedy films were well received and, almost bizarely, he became a cult favourite in Albania, of all places. In 2000, when he received a knighthood, his little comic creation must have laughed fit to bust when the news broke. In 2005, at the age of 90, he decided to call it a day and retired. Well, you would, wouldn't you? He left us to our memories on 4th October 2010.

With the slow but sure decline of music hall, the Palace came to a rather sad and undignified end. In an endeavour to regain some custom, the management decided to promote nude reviews. Delightful young ladies willing to display their attractive figures on stage, on the strict condition that they didn't move, replaced Archie, Frankie, and Norman. In that the Palace closed for business in 1958, you could only assume that East Ham mankind was not yet ready to come out of the shadows and pay good money for that sort of stuff. By that time, the male hormones had started their work on me and, as I walked past the Palace on my way home from school, I struggled not to look at the photographs of the "artistes" displayed outside. I had this awful guilt feeling that if anyone caught me oggling, I'd be grounded for weeks. Derek was much the same – I think!

During the radio week, we could choose from a number of half-hour comedy shows. Ted Ray presented the splendidly titled

"Ray's a Laugh!" with Kitty Bluett, as his radio wife. American Ben Lyon did equally well in his family-orientated, "Life with the Lyons." Jimmy Jewell and Ben Warris were a double act that set the stage for the advent of Morecambe and Wise. All provided good, clean, simple fun. Yet if I had to pick my favourite, "Take it from Here," with the wonderful Jimmy Edwards, Dick Bentley, June Whitfield, and a pretty brunette singer, Alma Cogan, would take the prize every time. The segment of the show that featured the Glum family was nothing short of pure genius.

Mr Glum, a rumbustous character, played to perfection by Jimmy Edwards, would set up the plot, chatting to the barman in his local about something that his dimwit son Ron (Dick Bentley), had got up to with his fiance of long-standing, Eth (June Whitfield). Eth of the whiney voice was a docile, not very bight lass, which made her the ideal partner for Ron! The scene having been set thus, a short couple of bars of music transported us into the Glum's front room, where Ron and Eth would be sitting on the sofa. I can hear it now.

"Oh, Ron... "

"Yes, Eth?"

And then the week's story would begin in earnest, Ron being blank and deadpan, which was the ideal state to be in, if you were going to get optimum laughter from such magnificent lines as this, for example.

"Oh, Ron. Is there anything on your mind, beloved?"

Pregnant pause.

"No, Eth."

"Oh really, Ron, do you expect me to just sit here, like a lemon?"

"No thanks, Eth. I've just had a banana."

The high quality of the script writing was hardly surprising, given that it was in the hands of Frank Muir and Dennis Norden. Crikey! Even I could be funny with those two blokes writing the lines. When, as happened in every episode, Ron started to try his luck with Eth - who was resisting as all good girls should - who should burst through the door, fresh out of the boozer, but Pa Glum.

"Ullo, 'ullo, 'ullo. What've we got 'ere, then?" followed by some sarcastic piece of innuendo.

Ma Glum was only ever heard in the background. When Pa wanted the benefit of her opinion, a loud call up the stairs to where she was, presumably – hopefully, - working.

"Muvver!!!!"

The response was a gargled, unintelligible set of syllables, honked through the nasal passages. It took a long time before I was convinced of the truth that "Ma" was none other than the stunningly beautiful Alma Cogan.

Many years later, a short appreciation of the show was presented on the radio. I tuned in, fully expecting that time would had endowed cobwebs to the style, presentation, and humour. Oh, how wrong could I be? For half an hour, I laughed and admired the witty scripts. The show could still be a hit today for, make no mistake, quality lasts.

In 1951, a show hit the airwaves whose influence would reverberate from the time of its conception to this very day – and that will hold true no matter what the date might be when you are reading this. Inspired and created in the main by the brilliant Spike Milligan, "The Goon Show" was unlike anything that anyone had ever heard. Scripts were a mix of ludicrous plots, puns, and catchphrases, spiced with an array of bizarre sound effects. Aided and abetted by Harry Secombe (you remember - A.C.), Peter Sellers, and – briefly - Michael Bentine, Spike and his team provided a host of eccentric characters. This pioneering work has been described as "sound cartooning" and that feels about right. Listeners were allowed to conjour up their own images of each of the characters, and there was no one to contradict you. The humour itself was as sharp as a knife.

Harry Secombe was thinly disguised as Neddy Seagoon, and virtually played himself throughout the series. Between the pair of them, Milligan and Sellars gave us the never-to-be-forgotten imbecilic, but lovable, Eccles; the simpleton Bluebottle; Major Denis Bloodnok, an over-the-top military incompetent ; Neddy's arch enemies, Grytpype-Thynne and his sidekick, Morriaty, not to forget Henry Crun and Minnie Bannister - an elderly pair, whose type could easily be found frequenting Eastbourne – even today! Sorry, Eastbourne. I just couldn't resist it.

Sixty years on, the quality of the scripts still stand up well.

Neddy Seagoon: "I'll have you know, I'm as intelligent as the next man."

Eccles (in the dumbest of voices): "I'm the next man, folks!"

Then a wonderful scene, opening with the better part of a minute of clocks striking the hour. A short pause before.......

Bluebottle: "What time is it, Eccles?"

Major Bloodnok's entry was always heralded with the brass section of the studio band blazing out a march. BBC's Radiophonic Workshop had created an effect to represent the sound of Bloodnok's digestive system in action, comprising a variety of inexplicable gurgling and explosive noises. At the end of the introductory march came a mighty explosion, clearly intended to indicate that the Colonel had passed wind with gusto.

Bloodnok: "Ooooohh!! No more curried eggs for me!"

The beauty of the Goons was that, somewhere along the line, everyone could have a share in their repertoire. Words and phrases from the show became common parlance and I doubt if there was a kid in the entire country - let alone Walpole Road – who couldn't do a more than passable impression of one or more of the show's characters. Eccles was, by far, everyone's favourite, and I never knew any kid who, at one time or another, hadn't a mate who'd "got the Lurgy." Derek had gone so far as to create a visual version of the ailment, as presented for the benefit of Dickie Collins.

The talent of that trio knew no bounds, even to the extent of producing records that made the popular music charts – Top Ten, mark you. "I'm Walking Backwards for Christmas (Across the Irish Sea)"," Bloodnok's Rock and Roll Call," and everyone's favourite, "The Ying Tong Song." What a glorious piece of nonsense that was. Get a copy, download, beg, borrow, steal – anything. But in the name of all that is good and funny, don't pass on from this world without having heard it.

Yet our radio fare wasn't confined to laughter. Between 1946 and 1951, "Dick Barton – Special Agent" was required listening, with its fifteen minute episodes broadcast at 6.45pm every weekday. Introduced by Charles Williams' memorable theme, "Devil's Gallop," ex-commando Dick, with his assistants, Jock Anderson and Snowy White, solved all manner of crimes, escaped from the most hopeless situations by the most contrived routes, and saved the nation from disaster, all before bedtime and Ovaltine. At its height, the little show attracted a listening audience of 15 million and provided good entertainment for listeners – old and young alike. Until, that is, something far more imaginative hit the airwaves.

Youngsters nowadays take space travel in their stride. They grow up knowing that, in 1969, man reached the moon and any future expeditions, no matter how wonderful, are going to be perceived as old hat. Satellites buzzing around our globe are the norm and Richard Branson is close to making space travel reality for the man in the street (dependent upon which man, which street we are talking about, and whether or not he's got the necessary "readies"). You could be forgiven for feeling that, if we ever discovered life on another planet, we would be more likely to check the football results before turning our attention to such a mighty – and unexpected - turn of events. You see, there's not enough mystery, nowadays.

But boys of my generation, looked at the moon....and wondered. It was too early in our infant lives to have encountered H. G. Wells, with his "Time Machine," "First Men on the Moon," or "War of the Worlds." Georgie Brewerton was of the opinion that there *were* little green men out there. Terry Young was a little more sceptical. Derek and I didn't have a clue. Yet the time was right for us to be inducted into the mysteries of space travel, and "Journey into Space" was the ideal vehicle for the purpose. Half-hour long weekly episodes were written by the splendid Charles Chilton, who was also responsible for Dan Dare in the "Eagle" comic. Jet Morgan was Chilton's Dan Dare character, aided and abetted by Doc Matthews, Mitch Mitchell, and everyone's favourite, Lemmy Barnet. Despite the strong and attractive character of Jet, Lemmy was always popular because he came over as the frightened, yet realistic, member of the crew. If there was a funny line in the dialogue,

Lemmy would always get it and we loved him for it. When David Kossoff, who played the part to perfection, decided to move on, Chilton and the BBC made an inspired choice with Alfie Bass. You could scarcely see the join. The plots began to convince us that there really could be men from Mars, and each episode ended with the standard "cliff-hanger," such as having only ten minutes oxygen left for a journey of several days. Surprise, surprise! They always found a solution - just in time!

"Journey into Space" became immensely popular on a far wider stage than simply the United Kingdom. The programme was translated into several different languages and shipped all around the world. The final series was destined to become the last radio programme to attract a larger evening audience than television, when television turned up on our doorsteps. And should you need further endorsement, "Journey into Space" was listened to avidly by no less a personage than the renowned scientist, Stephen Hawking. You have to take a science programme – albeit a fictional one - seriously if he is amongst the punters.

Sunday listening came in a different package, which I enjoyed immensely. At noon, families all across the country would tune in to "Two-Way Family Favourites," a music request programme designed to link families at home with British Forces serving in West Germany, or elsewhere overseas. The rather lovely theme song, "With a Song in my Heart," introduced the programme, prior to Cliff Michelmore and Jean Metcalfe reading the requests and playing the records. My early musical listening habits had yet to be defined and refined, but I do remember my lovely cousin Audrey charging out into her garden, announcing loudly to neighbours that, "Bing's on the radio." For all I knew, Bing could have been the cat - but he wasn't. He was the magnificent Bing Crosby – what was called a crooner in those days – and the more I heard of his warm, velvety voice, I found that I really liked the guy. Certainly, he pleased me more than the other super star of those years, Frank Sinatra. "Family Favourites," then, was my earliest introduction to popular music, albeit of a more refined nature than what was to come just a few years into the future.

But then, having been peacefully soothed by the dulcet tones of Cliff and Jean, and lulled into a false sense of security, came the one'o'clock assault on the eardrums, when any soul enjoying a bit of peace and quiet would be jerked savagely into consciousness by the cry, "Waikey, Waikhaayy!" And as if this were not enough to revive unpleasant memories of the Blitz, the clarion call was followed by disorganised mayhem with a dance band bashing out, "Somebody stole my Gal", accompanied by several loonies yelling and screaming in the background. Welcome to the Billy Cotton Band Show! I only have to recall that voice and the madcap introduction to positively smell the roast beef.

Billy Cotton, the father of the late BBC Head of Light Entertainment, was a character of the first order. By the time that I was aware of him, he was aged around fifty, bespectacled, and bald, with a rotund, beaming face that exuded good fun. His band was highly rated, and provided music to reflect the post war spirit of London. "Maybe it's because I'm a Londoner," and "Friends and Neighbours," might sound a bit saccharine sweet to the modern listener, but they certainly caught the mood of the post-war public. And Billy was shrewd enough to balance these with "Knees up Mother Brown" stuff like, "I've got a lovely bunch of Coconuts," and suchlike. Kathy Kay was the excellent female vocalist, who dealt with the sensitive and tender parts of the repertoire, whereas Alan Breeze could do the lot. Ballads and comic songs – he coped with them all admirably. As a spin-off from their novelty hit, "Two Little Men in a Flying Saucer," the show featured a brief slot when, to the perceived sound of a hovering flying saucer, Breeze would call out, "Hey! You down there. You with the glasses on!" This, of course, was aimed at Uncle Bill, and a bit of "witty "repartee would follow.

There is the story of the almost tragic occasion when Alan Breeze could have lost his life. It was during an open-air performance in Jersey, when part of the act was for Alan to be playing a piano, which, at a given moment, was designed to explode. Had it been well controlled, as intended, it would have been hilarious. But some clot must have put in more explosive than

252

necessary, resulting in the thing going off like a bomb. Breeze was seriously injured and photographs show smoke wafting around the deck-chaired audience. I'll bet there were a lot who thought it was all part of the act and laughed for a fortnight! Fortunately, Alan lived to tell the tale. Born in West Ham, he was truly one of our own.

But change was bound to come, and television was waiting in the wings although it never really got into its stride until the mid-1950s. The family of my school friend and trainspotting buddy, Alan Self, was the first that I knew to have a set. Household Derby joined the clan in 1953, just in time for the F.A. Cup Final. Very few of our friends were in the same privileged position, so Alan and I were able to continue swapping notes in the way that we all did with radio shows. We began with reflections on Muffin the Mule, a string puppet who trotted on and conversed from the top of Annette Mills' piano top. A decent sort was Muffin, which could hardly be said of the show's other character, Peregrine the Penguin, a right surly herbert, if ever there was one. Always complaining about something or other, frowning for England, and his beak flapping up and down at a rate of knots. Dear Annette's charm always created an atmosphere of calm, which allowed these two very different characters to rub along rather nicely. Alan and I frequently burst into song with the show's theme song, "Here comes Muffin, Muffin the Mule,"

The epitome arrived when on Saturdays, at teatime, – between 1951 and 1956 - "Whirligig," came to town, hosted by the excellent Humphrey Lestocq (conveniently and lovingly referred to as "HL"). Armed with an infantile catchphrase, "Goody, Goody Gumdrops," and a sidekick puppet, the bossy Mr Turnip, HL orchestrated a selection of competitions and short features that, as with the radio shows, gave several artists their first lucky break. Steve Race went on to considerable fame in music, but began as the unlikely companion and ventriloquist for cowboy puppet, Hank. The old varmint (Hank, that is, not Steve) entertained us weekly through confrontations with his archenemy, Mexican Pete. Despite being primarily a musician, Steve Race was a damned sight better ventriloquist than Peter Brough. Rolf Harris introduced us to

Willoughby, who, once sketched onto a blank sheet of paper, moved and spoke with Rolf. Small beer in this technologically advanced age, but in the '50s, it was rocket science. As with Muffin, the distinctive theme tune was on everyone's lips – even those whose access to television was through the kindness of some neighbour or other who had set. It ended with the creed that, "One hour of Whirligig is the hour for me!" and with all due respect, dear Annette Mills and Muffin the Mule just couldn't compete with that.

I'm quite amazed - and not a little frightened - that both television and radio are now "on tap, 24-7." In the early years of my childhood, distinctive time slots were allocated for children's entertainment. "Children's Hour" was typical. Starting at 5.00pm, it did what it said on the tin and, by 6.00pm, the show was over. Much the same principle was applied for children's television shows. Come to think of it, it was the same for adults. Long before the wee hours, an announcer – dressed to the nines, as though in readiness for an audience with royalty – told you that programmes for the day were complete, the National Anthem was played, you stood to attention and saluted (if you felt so moved), made your cocoa, and sauntered off to bed. Now we are over-exposed to music, sport, soaps, reality shows (anything less like reality I find hard to imagine), and I just can't help feeling that the "less is more" allocation of time in the '50s provided better quality entertainment than youngsters of today – and adults, for that matter - are fed with.

Right, I feel better for having got that off of my chest. I can't recall the last time that I went to a cinema. It's not that there aren't films out there that I'm sure I'd enjoy. Rather, it's just that getting up out of a comfy chair to drive a dozen miles to my nearest cinema doesn't have much appeal. Non-attendance may be very much my loss.

Yet in post war years, cinema – or "the pictures," as we called it - was every bit as essential as television, texting, and Facebook have become today. "Celebrities" emerged through the medium of radio, but "the pictures" set the bar higher. The films that we watched fired our imaginations, and the games we played in the streets were re-enactments of what we had seen on the screen. Actors and actresses became household names and, thus, very much part and parcel of our everyday conversation.

Today, there is a more professional slant to the cinema, where two - or sometimes three - high profile films are available in separate studios, all under the one roof. The 1950 version was a very different matter.

There were four cinemas within easy reach of Walpole Road. The Odeon, in Barking Road, next to the Boleyn public house; the Granada, further along Barking Road, toward the Town Hall; the Gaumont, on High Street North between the station and Town Hall; and the Carlton, in Green Street. The latter had lain dormant since 27ᵗʰ January 1945, when it took the full force of a V2 rocket. The Gaumont enjoyed something of a dual personality in that, whilst most referred to it by that name, others would talk about it as the Premier. Apparently, the cinema had originally opened as the Premier Cinematographic Theatre, until that company was bought out by Gaumont British, in 1929. Hence, Gaumont or Premier. Take your pick. The Coronation was over at Manor Park, but why troll over there when you had enough choice in your own backyard?

Each of these auditoriums displayed a certain grandeur. Capable of seating between 1,500 to 2,500 souls in stalls and balcony combined, they were often filled, and a trip to any one of them was an event of which we never tired, although the format was virtually identical, whichever one we chose. The front-of-house kiosk sold you your ticket, before an obligatory stop at the confectionery stall to stock up on as much tuck as you (or your parents) could afford or allow. Going to the pictures without tuck was, well, *infra dig,* and its purchase was all part of the ritual. At the door to the auditorium, a uniformed usher or, more often, usherette, inspected your ticket, and told you where your seat was.

"Go to the left, and then down to the second row, dearie."

I always resented the "dearie" bit, especially if it was a bloke clipping the tickets.

Still, off we went to where another usherette (this time, it always seemed to be a female) would shine her torch on your ticket and escort you to your seat. It was guaranteed that you were going to have to get other patrons to stand as you made your way to your place. This part of the process was best dealt with as quickly as possible, for those already *in situ* and deeply engaged in the plot, would greet you with such East End pleasantries as, "Oi! I'm trying to watch this bleedin' film," or, "Sit down, for Gawd's sake." But it was a temporary attack and, once you were comfortably seated, the baton was passed on and you were thus authorised to inflict similar curses on the next poor souls trying to find their seats.

There was precious little variation in the programmes offered by each cinema. The "big" film – the "A" feature – was accompanied by a "B" grade offering which, as might be expected, tended to be on the mundane side. As a result, you could be entertained by, say, the epic, "Gone with the Wind," only to find it in bed with some low budget western, featuring Ronald Reagan. And, before you ask – yes, the same Ronald Reagan who occupied the White House between 1981 and 1989. Sandwiched between these were short advertising features and, if you were really lucky, a cartoon or short comedy. Brief "trailers" for forthcoming films were shown, in a usually successful endeavour to maintain regular attendance, and the entire package was, conveniently, shown in a loop. The result of this was that you could sit there until the whole show had run back to the point at which you first arrived. Derek often boasted about sitting through the entire programme twice, there being no one briefed to check your arrival time or kick you out when you had out-stayed your welcome. Personally, I thought it somewhat immoral to have two doses for the price of one, but that was just my better nature showing through once again, I guess.

The Granada added one interesting variation to this agenda, although quite what the history of it all was, I am not sure. There was an orchestra pit in front of the stage at the Granada, from which a "190 Granada Special Wurlitzer" organ would rise "before your very eyes." If you were lucky (or, indeed, unlucky), you would be "treated" to an half-hour of variety which, from memory, was not much good - definitely a case of, "never mind the quality, feel the width." Yet, in every other way, the Granada fell in line with its competitors.

My personal introduction to the world of cinema was through the good grace of Nanny Clark. Nanny's picture house of choice was the Odeon and, on most Thursday afternoons, she would be there, come what may. If I was on holiday from school, and Mum was working, Nanny would take me along with her. Although many of the films that we saw together have dropped off my memory radar, two still come to mind. "Halls of Montezuma" starring Richard Widmark, was a war film, focussed on American derring-do in the Second World War. It was a jolly good action film, with a stirring theme tune that provided me with a valuable reference point for the next time we played soldiers in Walpole. More emotional was "My Foolish Heart," with the lovely Susan Hayward in her pomp, and described by one critic as, "a soggy love story." No matter, every time the director deemed it necessary for tears to be squeezed out of his audience, the theme song was played. Whenever I hear that line about lips being much to close to mine, I start to blub. I've started now.

Personally, I rarely had any great desire to go to adult cinema of my own volition. Dad was a little more proactive and thought it would be a jolly fine idea for the pair of us to go and see, "King Solomon's Mines." Loosely based on Rider Haggard's novel, it was my first introduction to Stewart Granger, who took the role of Allan Quatermain. Deborah Kerr played a female character that you will scour the pages of the novel to find not at all. Dad was never a prolific reader, but he must have had a go at this particular book, as he provided a pre-film briefing, effective to the point that, even before the film started, I knew Umbopa was the good guy, whilst Gagool was a right old villain. It was all right, I suppose, but nowhere near as good as "The Titfield Thunderbolt," all about a railway line that was going to be closed down, and the efforts to save it. Being about steam engines, you will understand that, given the choice between good old Umbopa and the Titfield Thunderbolt, there was going to be only one winner. "A Ticket to Tomahawk" also featured a steam engine, so I had to go to that as well. But what a sad case I must have been, for Marilyn Monroe starred in that film - and I didn't even notice!

"Star Wars" was still several light years away and, apart from the wonderful "Quatermass Experiment" - not due until 1954, and on television at that – our appetite for science fiction remained the preserve of "Journey into Space." Derek and I were crying out for something weird and wonderful from beyond to find its way onto the silver screen and frighten the life out of us and, in 1951, we got it! "The Day the Earth Stood Still," had every young pulse racing. With hardly enough plot to plant a potato, the story centred around a visitor from outer space travelling 250 million miles – give or take a yard – to tell us all that, unless we lived peacefully with one another, earth would be destroyed to protect the safety of other planets. Michael Rennie took the lead role and was about as alien as a bank manager wrapped in Bakofoil, with a pumpkin on his head. But – and here was the selling point - he came accompanied by a giant robot, Gort. "The screen has never conceived a creature like this," ran the promotional blurb, which was probably about right for the time. Hoardings displayed this gigantic silver robot with the torso of a man and a tin helmet of a head lacking facial features. It looked as though it had been constructed out of outsize silver cigar containers but, hey, who cared? This one we had to see.

Down Green Street, the management of the John Lewis store hit on a novel promotion idea. A week or so before the film was due to be shown in Upton Park, a Gort replica was created and set down just inside the main entrance to the store. Amazingly, when you spoke to the thing, it spoke back! How'd it do that? After school, we would all make our way to Lewis's and quiz Gort about his life, past, present, and future. We were totally blown away as he answered all of our questions. We were only eight, you understand.

I suppose it should come as no surprise to learn that the curious mind of Fletcher soon enlightened – and disappointed – the whole lot of us. In a little cubicle, just a few yards from Gort, one of the Lewis's staff sat, with a microphone. Cut off from view of the general public by nothing more than a thin curtain, he could easily hear our questions, see some of our movements, and respond accordingly. It was as simple and obvious as that. Derek wandered over to do no more than lift the curtain and reveal the "Voice of Gort" in mid-flow. You could see that the "voice" wasn't best pleased.

"Oi!! Bugger off!" he yelled.

Not an unreasonable response in the circumstances, you might suppose.

Unfortunately, the "voice" had forgotten to turn away from his microphone, and little ones, waiting for an answer to their innocent enquiries, thought that it was poor old Gort himself issuing the ultimatum.

"How old are you, Gort?"

"Oi! Bugger off!"

Tears were shed, screams were heard, maiden aunts fainted, and the poor old boy in the cubicle could only look on red-faced, and mumble a genuinely penitent, "Oops! Sorry." Gort said that as well!

As for Derek, he wasn't seen in Lewis's for many a long day after that.

It didn't take too long to grasp that I was not quite yet ready for grown-up films. Something more akin to our tastes, inclinations, and innocence was required. Well, I guess local cinema managers across the country were one step ahead of us there for "Saturday Morning Pictures" suddenly became an accepted part of our staple social diet. For the grand sum of six pence – that's 2.5 pence in new money – we received, in exchange, entertainment from the likes of the Little Rascals, Tom and Jerry, Mickey Mouse, Donald Duck, the Three Stooges, Hopalong Cassidy, Roy Rogers and his fuzzy sidekick George "Gabby" Hayes, Gene Autry, Flash Gordon and – for which I thank my God each and every day – Stan Laurel and Oliver Hardy. Any theatre opening its doors to the young on a Saturday morning received a guaranteed full house. For a reason I never quite fathomed, the Gaumont decided against this sure-fire winner, leaving the coast clear for the Odeon and the Granada to clean up.

Most of our friends in Walpole Road opted for the Odeon, so I have no concrete reason why it should have been that Derek and I went for the Granada. At 9.00am each Saturday, we made our way to the Green Street bus stop at the top of Crescent Road to catch the 690 trolley bus, which stopped right outside the Granada. Between the cinema and the Church Army building on the corner of Hartley Avenue, was a piece of tarmac where we junior patrons would line up in a remarkably orderly fashion. For the life of me, I can never recall any real bad behaviour, as we waited our turn to be ushered into the foyer, pay our tanners, and join the general hubbub brewing in the picture house itself. And there we would all be - a packed house of kids (ages ranging from five to fifteen) - yelling our heads off in anticipation of the forthcoming fare. In an attempt to establish some sort of order before the main course, the manager would get the lot of us singing. Hardy annuals such as "Pack up Your Troubles," and "Maybe it's because I'm a Londoner" would make you think that there was still a war on. The whole business was rounded off with "The East Ham Grenadiers" which, although adopting the tune of "The British Grenadier," had a lyric adapted to accommodate us youngsters. Granada cinema......East Ham Grenadiers.......get it? At 9.30, the lights dimmed to more good-natured cheering and yelling, and we were off.

As with the senior show, the format remained consistent during the time that I went along to the pictures and, frankly, it worked a treat. Interest had to be captured from the moment the lights went down, and there was no better way to achieve this than with a cartoon. The face of Bugs Bunny staring out at us all from the screen drove us into the stratosphere! Sylvester and Tweetie Pie, Tom and Jerry, vied with Bugs in the popularity contests and although Mickey Mouse (just into his twenties at that time) was greeted with respect, I was always more of a Donald Duck man myself. Mick was okay, but the Duck was wild, with attitude, and deserved all he got. Pluto and Goofy had their moments but, at the final count, Tom and Jerry were always my favourites. Still are.

Temperatures suitably raised, the next feature would either allow a breather or recharge our energies to yet more fanatical heights. You see, there were some rather good travelogues and general interest features around at the time. They were accepted in the spirit offered and watched politely, accompanied by neither boos nor raspberries. One stands out in my mind. "Jeremy's Journey" was a twenty-minute reel about a little lad who was barmy about steam engines. The plot was simple – little boy dreams he was asked to drive the "Royal Scot" from Euston to Glasgow. Sheer ecstasy! Even now, I can remember the engine that was filmed – No.46253 *City of St. Albans*. Now there's anorak for you.

But far more frequently, these slots allowed comedy to be king. The Three Stooges, with their "hare 'em, scare 'em" madcap antics were always good for a laugh. So, too, were Abbot and Costello, and the Marx Brothers. But over all, I fell in laugh – no misprint - with the wonderful Stan Laurel and Oliver Hardy. It's all subjective, of course, but those guys could never put a foot wrong with me. They were not just funny - they were nice blokes to go with it. Some fifteen years on, I found myself looking at one of the duo's short features through the window of a television rental company. Alongside me, occupied in the same activity, were a small boy of about eight, and an elderly man, who must have been well into his seventies. There the three of us were, each from a different era, laughing fit to bust at the antics of the fat man and his thin accomplice. And, do you know what? I'll swear we were each laughing at different things. That's comedy greatness, and "the boys" have walked with me throughout all of my life.

Do you know that, despite my best efforts, I just can't recall seeing a main feature clearly selected on the grounds that girls might enjoy it? They turned up in considerable numbers but what for, I asked myself? Perhaps it was an early sign of sexism in society. It always seemed that boys got the better part of the deal so, being one of the breed, I felt well catered for – particularly with the westerns. Just how many films of this genre were produced during the 'Thirties and 'Forties, I could scarcely hazard a guess. Yet there must have been a fair number, and given that many of them adopted virtually the same plot, scripting costs could hardly have been a problem. For example, no western would complete without the obligatory chase with the villains (scruffy and unshaved) being hotly pursued by the good guys (pristine white hats and clothes, as you would expect after a hard day's cattle ranching). Revolvers were fired *ad hoc* and we'd cheer like stink when the "goodies" were flashing across the screen. Then the camera turned its attention to the "baddies," whose appearance provoked such reception as might welcome Madonna on stage at "An Evening of Culture and Refinement." Back and forth it went, with boos and cheers resonating around the auditorium. A successful "hit" that brought a "baddie" tumbling from his horse released unconfined joy from the masses. By and large, the "goodies" came out of it all pretty much untarnished. Of course, we were not yet privy to such intimacies as kissing. All we knew was that only cissies did that sort of thing, and when Roy Rogers and Dale Evans looked goo-ey eyed at one another, the shrieks and whistles were ear splitting. It became ritual, every bit as much as Rite B.

The morning was always rounded off with "the serial." These were cleverly crafted productions of fifteen-minute episodes of a story, shown over a twelve-week period. Each episode would end with a cliff-hanger, designed to make sure that you came back again next week to find out if the hero managed to live through being blown up in an aircraft, falling off a cliff in a car which exploded on impact with the rocks below, or avoiding some evil-intentioned herbert creeping up behind him with a carving knife the length of your arm. We were into it all wholesale. As we left the cinema, we each offered our personal explanations as to how escape might just be humanly possible. During one set of deliberations, when the hero's car went over a cliff to explode horribly, Georgie Brewerton pontificated with all the authority that only Georgie could muster.

"Saw him jump before the car went over the edge."

Well, of course he'd seen nothing of the kind. The filmmakers were careful to ensure that nothing of that nature was ever included and we told Georgie that he was talking rubbish. He knew it. Yet – blow me down - the following week when an extra clip was inserted into the film, there was matey boy, jumping out of the car before it parted company with the road!

"Told you so, " said the fully exonerated Georgie.

Anyway, those serials really did ensure that we would be back next week to check out what happened – and there were some great heroes in them. Gene Autry – the singing cowboy – found himself featured in "The Phantom Empire," a strange mix of the Old West with villains from a futuristic underground city. The acting reached the quite remarkable standard of being unadulterated pants, but eight year olds didn't know that and we couldn't wait to enact the plot when we returned to the reality of playing in the street. The American comic book hero Captain Marvel was featured, in which weedy little Billy Batson was engulfed in a cloud of smoke whenever he uttered the word "Shazam!" When the smoke cleared – there was Captain Marvel in all his finery. He could fly, defy bullets, pull trains, and doubtless, fart a becalmed galleon across the Atlantic. In order to conceal his identity, the good Captain would yell,"Shazam!" heralding more smoke and lightening - and there was Billy Batson back, with not a hair out of place.

But I don't think there would have been a kid amongst us who, if asked for their favourite serial, wouldn't nominate Flash Gordon. Larry "Buster" Crabbe it was who took the role with his girlfriend, Dale Arden. Along with the boffin Professor Zarkov, Flash set out to rescue the world from all manner of ills. His main adversary – Ming the Merciless – looked and dressed like a refugee from some oriental musical. Thin, tall, and balding, Charles Middleton fitted the bill to a tee and I never forgot my shriek of recognition when Middleton turned up in, of all things, a Laurel and Hardy short ("Beau Hunks" 1931). The scenery was appalling, with rocket ships looking like adapted Vim cans, suspended by wire. Exhaust appeared as little more than exhaled fumes from a particularly large cigar. But try telling that to those of us who sat transfixed. It was wonderful entertainment for youngsters and only on growing up did I see it all for what it was worth. Perhaps my mistake was growing up.

In 1953, the Carlton, in Green Street, opposite Neville Road, re-opened in a flourish of publicity. Since its "hit" from the Luftwaffe in 1945, it had lain inaccessible and derelict. With the auditorium now restored to its old glory, customers returned in droves to relive pre-war memories, whilst new ones came along out of curiosity. Much local advertising took place and when Del and I learned that there would be Saturday Morning Pictures, well, we converted from the Granada. It was pretty clear that others followed the same policy for, on the first morning, the place was packed out. The manager was a big, rotund man, with a small military moustache, and sleeked back black hair, named Sam Lutens. On he bounced to introduce himself as "Uncle Sam" and induct us into the new war cry that was the Carlton's theme song. Sponsored, as the cinema was, by the ABC chain of cinemas, we were all ceremoniously dubbed as "ABC Minors," and given badges to prove it. To the tune of "Blaze Away," we sung our little hearts out.

"We are the boys and girls well known as
Minors of the ABC
And every Sat-ur-day all line up
To see the films we like and shout aloud with glee

We like to laugh and have our sing-song,
Just a happy crowd are we
We're all pals together,
We're Minors of the ABC"

The tried and tested agenda was applied here every bit as rigidly as in the other cinemas. No point in changing a winning formula so cartoons, comedies, westerns and serials were served up on a regular basis. Unfortunately, toward the end of my Saturday morning picture stint, there was evidence that things were starting to become a tad more rowdy, and on one occasion, Uncle Sam lost his cool. A few kids had discovered that the silver wrapping paper from their chocolate bars, when thrown up into the projection beam, looked for all the world like lighted matches. The first time it happened, the place went berserk and Uncle Sam went flying into where he thought the miscreants were sitting. Of course, there were too many sat there in the dark for names to be named, so no one could be accused or anything proved, and he had to let it rest.

For a few weeks, peace in our time was restored. But other perpetrators picked up on the trick, and that sort of nonsense to became a feature of Saturday mornings. I'm sure that was one of the reasons that terminated my regular attendance – I really did walk away from trouble whenever it raised its head. Far more to the point, Mum had, by this time, relented on her rule that I would not be allowed to go trainspotting "up London." Once she gave me that green light, Saturday Morning Pictures had no chance - it was a no-brainer. But it had been great fun while it lasted.

It is hard to appreciate that the pre-occupation with, and manipulation of, music in our society was not always so. Perhaps it's just the grumpy old man in me again but, nowadays, I see too many talent-less pretty girls/boys being propelled to fame for a fortnight by unscrupulous record company moguls and producers whose sole aim is to make a fast buck. Extravagant publicity machines thrust "never 'eard of yer" kids onto television screens, and we are required to bow down and worship.

I am not saying that there is a complete dearth of musical talent – far from it. I might have my own personal tastes, but I can recognise quality whenever it is placed before me. Yet, too often, I fear, we are being conned. A pile of bricks is put in a museum and we are told it is art. Some fist-fingered oik crashes out a few discords on a guitar at ear-splitting level and we are told that this is original and the way ahead for music. Yeah.

My earliest introduction to music was through the family parties held at Christmas, Boxing Day, and New Year's Day. I looked forward to these events immensely, because they provided me with the chance to get together with cousins and friends that I might not have seen very regularly throughout the year. Derek was invariably present because, well, he was my mate. Uncle Bert and

Aunt Joan returned regularly with little Joan (not so little at age twelve) and Cynthia, and the parties were always jolly affairs. Dad usually reserved these occasions to get himself pickled, much to the annoyance of Mum. One night, after a "do" at Uncle Ray and Aunt Eileen's, the three of us were driven home by some party-goer with Dad in the back seat, out of his skull. Mum was livid and, on arrival at Walpole, she issued her orders to me as she made for the front door.

"Get him out of there and in here," she commanded.

What was a boy to do? I was just about tough enough to do the deed and, as Dad and I shuffled up to the house – him leaning all over me and positively reeking of whatever he'd been soaking himself in – he uttered the immortal words.

"I'm sorry Stephen. I'll never do it again."

And he never did – until the next party!

Unlike today, few families boasted of anything that might be generally described as a record collection. Rather, we'd have, at most, about two dozen shellac 78 rpm items that only got airing at the parties, after which they were allowed to hibernate until next year's party season. How those records ever survived was a minor miracle. None of your compact CDs, MP3s, or similar were on the scene, and our means of conveying musical joy was somewhat archaic. The gramophone was a chunky item of furniture containing speakers, and a turntable that ran consistently at 78rpm. 45rpm and 33 1/3rpm items were yet to hit the market and the only speed change available was an indicator that could vary the pace of the music to either "slow" or "fast." An arm about the size of a hammer, into which a metal pointed needle (or should that have been nail?) was inserted, would be lifted (thus activating the turntable) and placed so that the needle sat in the groove of the disc. Bingo! You had your music. After several plays, the needle had to be changed as usage seriously impaired sound quality, and what had begun as a clear tone gradually descended into something akin to your music being played to the accompaniment of shingle being disturbed by sea waves. It might have done the needle precious little harm but the records themselves became scratched, scarred and, ultimately, permanently disabled. Please Dansette, come to our rescue soon.

The first record that ever captured my imagination was Anton Karas's version of "The Harry Lime Theme" or, if you wish to be pedantic, "The Third Man Theme." Taken from the 1949 film, "The Third Man" featuring the wonderful Orson Welles, it was a tuneful little offering with a mix of zither and mandolin. I found it captivating and must have ruined the thing long before its time was properly due by constant playing. Conveniently, its Greek styling lent itself to party dancing and became immensely popular, alongside offerings by the like of Winifred Attwell, a Caribbean lady who hit a winning formula with her honk-tonk piano, rattling out tunes as though you were at your local. I happened to like Winnie, but I cringed at The Stargazers' "I see the Moon" and "An Old Beer Bottle." The group were, for their time, a quite completent outfit and money was surely the only reason that inflicted the pieces on the world at large. By the time they got their airing at parties, Dad was invariably several sheets to the wind and tried to get me to join in. Mum always came to my rescue.

"Leave him alone, Joe. You know how he hates making a fool of himself."

I appreciated that, even though a time would come when I thoroughly enjoyed making a fool of myself – but always on my own terms, thank you very much.

In 1954, all of this jollity was to be thrown into chaos, as popular music began its run up for a quantum leap from which it has never looked back. During that year, in amongst the Crosby crooners, Sinatra serenaders, and Billy Cotton blasters, a thirty-year old American bandleader dipped his toe into the water by releasing a little number called "Shake, Rattle and Roll." It went on to sell a million copies and entered the British singles charts in December 1954. There was something very different about this record, and it certainly didn't sit easy with the crooners and vocal groups predominant at the time. It was almost wild and abandoned and, from the lips of American disc jockey Alan Freed, we first heard the term "Rock'n' Roll." Stateside – particularly amongst the black communities – the term was a euphemism for sexual intercourse but, in our innocence, that fact by-passed us completely. Early in January 1955, Bill followed up his initial hit with "Rock around the Clock" and from that point, the fat was well and truly in the fire. There couldn't have been a soul in the land who couldn't at least kick the song off.... "One, two, three o'clock, four o'clock rock!" More than any other record, "Rock Around the Clock" set clear water between itself and the staid, largely saccarine product that had simmered gently on the back burner since the end of the war. Now young people had something of their own to get their teeth into and the media dubbed Haley as the "Father of Rock and Roll." Passing years have provided sufficient evidence to suggest that he was nothing of the kind, but in 1955, we knew no better and simply went along with it. There were, however, more shocks to follow.

Chris Barber had long been an icon for those in love with traditional jazz – and in those days, there were many. My mates Tony Prince and Keith Hollington both had a more than working knowledge of the music, regularly dredging up the names of Monty Sunshine (clarinet), Pat Halcox (trumpet), and Ottilie Paterson, a white female singer with a powerful voice reminiscent of the black blues singers, for whom the style appeared to be their prerogative. She was, indeed, rather special and justifiably one of the major selling points of the Chris Barber Jazz Band. Yet quite what Chris had in mind when, on one of his albums, he included two tracks under the banner of "The Chris Barber Skiffle Group" seemed something of a mystery – at first. Whipping his banjo player, Lonnie Donegan, out from the background and bedecking him with an acoustic guitar, Chris added Beryl Bryden on washboard (washboard?!), and himself on string bass to reproduce a simple, yet infectious little piece.

It started with strummed major chords played on the beat of the bass. Donegan narrates the tale of an illegal carriage – by train - of livestock across some US border or other, in which the driver tells the tollgate officer that all he has on board is cows, sheep, and general livestock which - we are all relieved to hear - are not subject to duty. The official duly allows the train to slip through and as it gathers up "a little bit of steam and a little bit of speed," the driver calls back down the line to advise tollgate officialdom that he's been telling porkies and that his train was really chock full of pig-iron on which - horror of horrors - he should have paid substantial duty. It remained the best "up yours" song until David Allan Coe created "Take this Job and Shove it." By January 1956, the record had caught on, and frequented the charts for the better part of four months. If there was a kid around who didn't know the lyric, then you had to wonder which planet they had been living on during the period.

John Cole, with whom I had shared Shaftesbury violin lessons, as well as being a second violinist in the grammar school orchestra, was a massive fan. He had virtually every record that Lonnie made, including his first first album – 33 1/3rpm, if you please. Included was the old traditional American folk song, "Frankie and Johnnie," all about an adulterous affair and summary revenge. I've heard the song a thousand times since, by a thousand different artists – and so, probably, have you. But I can tell you that no one, but no one, has ever topped Lonnie's version. If I might add my two penn'orth, it was one of the earliest "country-rock" records made, although that format was still waiting to be discovered the better part of twenty years in the future. It wasn't too long before we realised that Lonnie's music wasn't really new at all. In those early days, none but the most studious and well-informed would ever have heard of Huddie "Leadbelly" Ledbetter. Huddie had done a bit of murder in his time and been in custody for his troubles. The story goes that he was excused the death penalty because he wrote a song for the warden and thereby came to be considered a national musical treasure. This is the bloke who penned not only, "The Rock Island Line," but a host of others including "John Hardy," "On the Western Plains," not to mention, "Irene Goodnight," sung by virtually every old sot from Glasgow to Walpole Road.

Lonnie Donegan's impact on the male youth of his day was enormous. Overnight, the country went skiffle mad, and almost every boy in the country wanted a guitar slung round his neck and to be honking out three-chord folk songs. Every Saturday morning at

269

10'o'clock, Brian Matthew introduced half an hour of "Saturday Skiffle Club," on the Light Programme, when up and coming units got the chance to be heard over the airwaves. The story goes that Cliff Richard failed an audition although, of course, he more than made up for it over the next fifty plus years. The best of the bunch, I always thought, were the Vipers, led by the late Wally Whyton, who brought such gems as "Maggie May," "Don't You Rock me Daddy-o," and "Ten Thousand Years Ago" to our attention. It was all so simple and achievable. Get a couple of acoustic guitars, a washboard, and a tea chest bass comprising nothing more than a broom handle for a neck and a washing-line cord for a string, and anyone could be in business. Up in Liverpool, some kid not much older than me named Lennon or suchlike, was playing in the Quarrymen Skiffle Group. He was joined by a couple of mates – Paul and George someone or other – and, in the fullness of time, they didn't do too badly for themselves! My own route was far less dramatic and considerably less successful.

Just around the corner from Walpole, in Plashet Grove, there was a barber's shop. When I called in one afternoon for a short back and sides – as you do - Clem Adelman, a young Jewish lad, came in with a guitar tucked underneath his arm.

"Bet ya can't play it, Clem, "I challenged.

"Bet ya I can," he fired back and promptly took the thing up, and strummed the opening chords and rhythms of the Vipers,' "Ain't You Glad."

I was well impressed and, there and then, decided that, more than anything else in the world, I wanted to play guitar. For the last eighteen months, Dad had been paying Clifford Phillips two guineas a time for me to take weekly twenty-minute piano lessons at No.1 Walpole. It was a king's ransom. I'd even managed to get to Grade IV on the instrument and was reaching out for the next level. But it only took that encounter with Clem Adelman and it was a case of, "Forget Liberace, I want to be Lonnie!" Piano lessons went by the wayside, and Dad had our instrument all to himself, working up a lather to perfect his decidedly shaky rendition of, "Now is the Hour."

A couple of weeks later at school, Tony Prince came swaggering across the playground, guitar in hand. This time, I was far more cautious than I had been with Clem.

"Hi, Tony. Can you play that thing?"

He stopped, knelt down and rested the instrument on his knee. A little bit of tuning, a bit of strumming, and then a rendering of the old folk song, "Gypsy Davie." It didn't take the wink of an eye for me to seize the opportunity.

"Hey, Tone. My mate Keith has got a guitar. Why don't we get together and form a group?"

Not a thought about the fact that I couldn't play a note. As it happened, Tony was not too far ahead of me in expertise, and he proceeded to teach me all he knew which, to be truthful, was little more than about a dozen chords. Fortunately, the material that we wanted to play was so simple that, if you knew three chords, then you had a repertoire. Within a month or two, we had recruited Ian Fulcher and his banjo, whilst Tony and Keith did their stuff on guitars. The banjo got chucked in my direction, freeing up Ian to play drums and/or washboard. A somewhat unlikely addition was Tony's dad, Jack, who did the honours on tea chest bass. We called ourselves "The Danes" although the mists of time have obscured quite how that came about. Vocally, Tony and I harmonised and, one way or another, we have done that socially for the rest of our lives.

Lonnie Donegan continued to enjoy a string of hits. Bill Haley, too, continued down his pleasant enough route. But across the Atlantic, something almighty was stirring. A 20-year old kid from Tupelo, Mississippi, had made a record that was going to change everything. "Heartbreak Hotel" - a slow, driving blues, delivered with an almost threatening, echoed voice - was something new for the world, let alone Walpole Road. Elvis Presley had arrived and the "Rock Island Line" was firmly shunted up some siding to make way for an express train, never mind an old wheezer carrying pig iron. When Elvis's publicity photographs hit the streets, there were clearly new matters to be addressed by boykind in general, for I can't recall a girl who didn't swoon at the sleek black hair, smoldering eyes, and gyrating hips that got him into trouble with all manner of institutions. We thirteen and fourteen year old boys were instantly put in our rightful pecking order, as we were held up for scrutiny against a really good-looking guy. The Presley machine was unstoppable and Elvis continued his gallop with further hits like "Blue Suede Shoes," "Hound Dog," and the sultry, "Loving You." Many years later, Cliff Richard would go on record as saying, "Without Elvis, none of us would have made it" and I guess he was right. Anyway, throughout 1957 and 1958, we were awash with a veritable tidal wave of records and artists whose music would live on and on and on.

I was not yet old enough to go on holiday without a measure of parental control, so in August 1957, Mum and Dad tagged me along with them to Bracklesham Bay Holiday Camp, Selsey, in Sussex. It was there that I first heard one of the sweetest sounds ever known in popular music. Holiday camp dining rooms were pretty well regulated places. Tables were set out for eight or ten people to sit round for breakfast, lunch, and evening meal. Good friendships were made during the week or, if you were particularly lucky, the fortnight. Three very pretty girls sat at our table and my parents were always great supporters of young people. As for me, shyness ensured that I kept my head below the parapet, and this story provides sufficient evidence as to why that was a wise policy.

In the dance hall, the camp had installed a jukebox where, day in, day out, one record above all others was played constantly. I'd heard the Tanner Sisters and the Beverley Sisters – but these two girls were different class. Their voices were sweet as honey, and I loved the opening guitar chords. They just made you sit up and it was small wonder that their record was so popular amongst the campers. I kept asking Mum who they were, but she wasn't sure.

"Why don't you ask one of the girls on our table?" she suggested.

So, come the next meal, taking my courage in both hands, I caught the attention of the prettiest girl, in my book.

"Excuse me, Julie. Can you tell me the name of that record everyone is playing on the jukebox, and who are the two girls singing?"

She looked at me and smiled sympathetically.

"Yes, Stephen. It's called, "Bye Bye Love," and it's by the Everly Brothers!"

Oh, me Gawd! It's blokes singing, not girls. Julie, bless her, never turned a hair at my innocent little slice of ignorance. Perhaps when they got outside, she and her friends all laughed their socks off. But, in that moment, something else was born in me. As they went on to wake up little Susie, cry in the rain, face their problems, take messages to Mary, sympathise with poor Jenny, and decide that all they had to do was dream, Don and Phil Everly became heroes to me. Not too many years – months, in fact – would pass before I leaned heavily on their lyrics, particularly when I gained – and lost – my first girl friends. Problems, crying in the rain, and dreaming were all unavoidable parts of teenage years and the Everly Brothers always had just the right words for every situation. Thanks, guys.

Now there was something more to talk about than just the latest escapades at school, or imitating what we had seen in the cinema, or heard on the radio. Music cascaded into our lives, and a whole new set of heroes and heroines came to our attention. It seemed that hardly a week passed without some record or another becoming the major matter for discussion outside No.11. Elvis just got better and better and nowhere more so than on his double-sided hit "All Shook Up" and "Don't be Cruel." He would rule the roost for a few years yet, until his manager, Colonel Tom Parker, signed him up to appear in some of the worst movies that have ever soiled the screen. The fabulous Platters, a black vocal group fronted by the amazing Tony Williams produced hit after hit, ironically drawing on the music of our forebears. "Smoke gets in your Eyes" remains one of my very favourite records. Silky Sam Cooke's "You Send Me" started his ball rolling, before a tragic and untimely death in 1964. "The Killer" Jerry Lee Lewis came up with, "Great Balls of Fire," - the only thing to compete with the fabulous piano-thumping, hot gospel style of Little Richard. Richard's "Lucille," "Keep a

Knockin,'" "Long Tall Sally," "Good Golly Miss Molly" were far more rock'n'roll than anything that Bill Haley had given us – and I haven't even mentioned Chuck Berry.

The old brigade didn't disappear immediately, as the sanitised Dreamweavers ("It's almost Tomorrow), Pat Boone ("I'll be Home" and unashamed covers of Little Richard hits), and Kay Starr - backing the horse both ways with her "Rock'n' Roll Waltz" fought something of a rearguard action. Even sweet Doris Day lived to see her "Que Sera" become a football anthem. Now who would have bet on that in 1958? Meanwhile, in Lubbock, West Texas, a tornado was brewing.

One Saturday evening, I was getting ready to cycle round to spend an evening with Keith, in Sherrard Road. Mum and Dad were finishing tea and, as they frequently did, watching the television. Realising that rock'n'roll might well be here to stay, the BBC deemed it necessary to be on the bandwagon and, every Saturday at five minutes past six, broadcast the "Six-Five Special." Don Lang, with his Frantic Five, would blaze away with theme tune, before Pete Murray introduced the show with some piece of twee nonsense like, "It's time to jive on the old six-five." Dreadful. But as rock'n'roll took a firmer grip on youth of the day, releases from America received early exposure on the show. Suddenly, I was stopped in my tracks by a sound unlike anything I had ever heard doing the rounds, even in those creative days. Whereas Chuck Berry's guitar could be a bit muffled, the one on this record was crystal clear and right "in yer face." The drummer was hitting the skins as though his life depended on it, as the vocalist fired out the lyrics telling his girlfriend that she'd never say "goodbye," or make him cry. I thought the singer was a bit cocky to have the nerve to say that to his girl. But there was no denying that this was a record like no other.

Dad looked over at me.

"Now, that's what I call a good record," was his in depth analysis. I couldn't disagree with him there, and Pete Murray filled us in with the necessary details,

"That was, "That'll be the Day," the latest Coral release by The Crickets. Watch out for them – they're going to be big."

Well, I don't need to tell you that they *were* big, not least because they had Buddy Holly writing the songs, playing guitar, and doing lead vocals. Jerry Allison – Buddy's long-time school friend – hammered the drums and Joe Mauldin plonked the bass. How just three guys could make such a thrilling sound still mystifies me and, over the years, Buddy and his Crickets have been my very favourite group. No need to catalogue their work. Buddy gave every young boy hope. Elvis was so good looking that most of us lads developed inferiority complexes. But before he had a tooth job and makeover, Buddy was as ugly as the rest of us - the guy even committed the cardinal sin of wearing glasses! But the message he gave us was received loud and clear – if you're good enough, blow what you look like. No one would dare call him "four eyes" and all of us myopic bounders shot straight down to the glasses house to get fitted up. I reckon that he should be recognised as the patron saint of opticians.

The songs of that era which went on to provide lyrics to accompany and influence our adolescence have proved their worth through their longevity. Throughout the history of popular music, artists of different generations have drawn deep and successfully from the well. The Rolling Stones were sharp enough to make "Not Fade Away" one of their anthems, but it was the Crickets who gave it to the world. Cliff Richard may well have asked if you wanted to dance, but Bobby Freeman was first on the floor. When the little rascal cobbled together a popular version of "Willie and the Handjive," he left poor old Johnny Otis to lick his wounds. It happened time and time again although, to the credit of the Stones and Sir Cliff, the originators have always been acknowledged. My point is this – it was a fine time to be young and awash with such fabulous music.

So, as best I remember, there you have it. Entertainment for Walpole Road kids meant radio, films, and music. What we listened to in the early 'Fifties prepared us for the likes of "Hancock's Half Hour," "Round the Horne," "The Navy Lark," and "The Ken Dodd Show" to come and tickle our funny bones. What we watched at the cinema provided additional raw material for what we would get up to when we returned to playing in the street. And the music of that era continues to bring back memories of friends, situations, and lessons learned. Money in the bank, I'd say.

CHAPTER NINE

IRON FILINGS

In October 1956, not for the first or, indeed, the last time, I fell hopelessly in love. I didn't see it coming, which is, of course, what makes falling in love the special experience it is. Our relationship flourished for a very long time. Even now, over fifty years on, I recall our laughter, joy, tears, and sense of optimism that things were only going to get better. We are still in touch, but from a distance.

My friend's life has taken a different route from my own. Despite enjoying a moderately successful and occasionally glittering career, I have found her lacking in self-belief. Over the years, those who should have known better, frankly, let her down. A painful twelve-month spell of her life early in the current century ended with her being abused and excluded from places that, in past years, she had graced. No more was she feted and, sadly, I feel there is little that I can do for her. Perhaps she doesn't want me to anyway.

I was never tempted and always remained faithful. I cherished those times when she made me feel needed, and I wanted to be in her company – as often as possible. If she were away, I would try to join her. If that wasn't possible, I would make sure that I was intimately aware of what was going on in her life during those moments of absence. For the better part of forty years, we were inseparable. But then, she and many of those around her, changed. I don't much care for those with whom she now keeps company with, and I wonder if she ever feels the same about me.

Oh, precious West Ham United – how I loved thee!

The transformation that took place in my life with regard to football was little short of miraculous. In 1954, during a Physical Education session, I was appointed to play at right half - whatever that meant - with Fred Mills designated to referee our game. The pitch was across the road from the school on what was known as the

Barking Recreational Park – Barking Rec, for the uninformed. The rain was tipping down and I'd meandered around on the muddy pitch for twenty or so minutes with, as Chuck Berry would one day put it, "no particular place to go." Suddenly, Fred's broad Yorkshire accent burst out, pure and clear.

"Look at Derby, everyone. See where he's taken up his position. That's the way it should be done."

Given that I didn't have the first blessed clue where I was supposed to be, this was praise indeed. It was certainly a good deal better than when we lined up against a wall to be "picked" for street football, and I suffered the longest of waits before either captain sought the benefit of my expertise.

Dad continued to make ill-fated attempts to get me into football. On those rare Saturday afternoons when I wasn't pounding the beat of the major London stations and engine sheds, from our garden I could hear roars emanating from a crowd gathered less than half a mile away, as they watched West Ham United ply their trade. Every so often, the sound of singing would come wafting through the air – something or other about bubbles, or some such. He would regularly encourage me to "go over and watch West Ham" and, for the sake of a quiet life, I eventually succumbed. As a result, I can categorically state that I was present (and that's about as far as it went) amongst the crowd in January 1956 for an F.A. Cup-tie between Preston North End – a formidable outfit back then - and the Hammers. I had yet to learn that West Ham was always capable of making a mess of the formbook, and this match provided ample evidence. They turned in an astonishing 5-2 win, with a guy named Albert Foan netting a couple of goals and becoming hero of the week. Preston's established international Toms - Docherty and Finney - could do nothing about it. As for me, well, all it did was get Dad off of my back for a few more home games.

Yet those aliens who plied their trade at the ground were not entirely a mystery unto me. Through the good offices of Mike Scarlett, Dickie Culver, and John Round, I had become familiar with the names Billy Dare, John Dick, Malcolm Allison, Noel Cantwell, Frank O'Farrell, Ken Tucker, Ernie Gregory and – always whispered in reverential tones – 'Arry 'Ooper, a.k.a. Harry Hooper. It wasn't rocket science to know that Harry was the jewel in the West Ham crown. Every time we played street football, each boy (except me) would adopt the persona of his particular favourite, and there was always a to-do when it came to Harry - "Billy de Cid" managed to whinge himself into the role more often than not. You will understand, then, that there was much wailing and gnashing of East End teeth when Wolverhampton Wanderers splashed out £25,000 – a tidy sum in those days – to whisk Harry off to the Midlands. Which reminds me.

I was always curious as to why it was that John Round and his elder brother, Fred, were Wolverhampton fans, whilst Dickie Culver and his dad confessed their affection for Tottenham Hotspur. Fred and John would go on about Bert Williams and Billy Wright, whilst Dickie would eulogize about Ted Ditchburn, Alf Ramsey, and Tommy 'Armer – very likely a relative of 'Arry 'Ooper! For the life of me, I couldn't quite figure out why anyone should have allegiance to any club other than the one up the road. Many years later, the penny dropped. Wolves and 'Spurs were highly successful outfits at the time and my guess was that Fred, John, Dickie, and Mr. Culver just wanted to be on a winning side, rather than being associated with a piddling mid-table outfit outside of the top division - which is just what West Ham was in those days.

My proper initiation into matters West Ham came through the good offices of my grammar school colleague, Dave Philpott. Ever since that mad dash down the back straight in the cross-country practice – perhaps as a result of it - we had become a really good friends and, soppy pair that we were, thought that we would seal our friendship through a blood pact. I'd just read some book in which two friends cut themselves and allowed their blood to intermingle. Us two twerps didn't have the guts to do it properly, fiddle-faddling with a blunt razor blade to draw a pinprick of blood from the end of our fingers. Dave was West Ham crazy and with something akin to missionary zeal, succeeded where Dad had so gallantly and successfully failed. On 27th October 1956, the Hammers were to entertain Grimsby Town, who had just won promotion from the old

Third Division (North). Despite West Ham showing all the signs of waging their annual battle against promotion, this one was down as a "home banker."

"It's like this, you see, Steve. There are four divisions in football. The top one is the First Division; the next one is the Second Division; the next one is......"

"Don't tell me, Dave. Let me guess," I interrupted.

"Yeah, I could. But you'd be wrong. There are two Third Divisions. One the Third (North) and the other the Third (South)."

He was right – I would have been wrong. He continued the explanation.

"In that way, Hartlepools don't have to come all the way down country to play Plymouth, and Southend ain't got to go to Carlisle."

"So, what about Coventry?" I asked, knowing enough geography to see that they would have been slap-bang in the middle.

"Gawd knows," said Dave. "I guess they just play in whatever division they're told."

"So, where is West Ham, then, Dave?"

I'd clearly touched a nerve.

"Still in the bloody Second Division. Whenever they look like going up into the First Division, something always happens and they miss out. If they look like going down to the Third (South), they start to play like champions and finish up mid-table, well away from relegation. My dad says that they don't want to go up."

On the day of the match, I cycled from Walpole to Dave's home, in Henniker Gardens. From there, the pair of us walked along Central Park Road, down Creighton Avenue, and crossed Barking Road into Priory Road, used most frequently by buses returning to, or coming from, the London Transport Garage at the far end. I have to be honest and say that, for the first time in my life, I felt a tinge of excitement about the whole business.

Nobody seeing the ground in its current state – all-seater and with all sides under cover - would believe how rustic (ramshackle even) it was in 1956. Running parallel to Priory Road was a small wooden stand, always referred to as "the Chicken Run." It was aptly named being, as it was, a mainly wooden construction looking exactly like, well, a chicken run. In 1985, a similar edifice at Bradford City's ground went up in smoke, killing fifty-six people, and injuring over two hundred and sixty five others. I can't help reflecting that the Chicken Run was a similar disaster waiting to happen – thank God it didn't. Here it was that dockers from the King George V and East India Docks congregated, having lubricated their tonsils at the Boleyn Arms, situated on the corner of Green Street and Barking Road. As my visits to the ground became more frequent, I grew to love the warm Cockney wit and good-natured banter that the dockers aimed at the opposing side. Nothing violent, politically incorrect to a fault, and yet entirely without malice. And some of the players proved well capable of giving as good as they got!

Opposite the Chicken Run stood the much larger west stand, housing the administrative offices, gymnasium, and dressing rooms. None of these fancy out-of-town training complexes – professional training facilities weren't that much far removed from us kids putting down coats for goalposts. Only in the this stand could you have the luxury of a seat – the rest of the stadium was strictly "Standing Only." Until well into the 1960s, the west stand provided supporters with the opportunity to be behind whichever goal West Ham were attacking. At half time, supporters were allowed to walk through the tunnel underneath the stand to emerge at the opposite end of the pitch. Dressing rooms were situated half way down this tunnel and, if you were lucky, you could watch the players emerge and trot out onto the pitch. Attendant policemen and officials ensured that you didn't stray either onto the pitch or into the dressing rooms. The west stand survived in a slightly extended form until, in 2002, it was pulled down for the current multi-purpose structure that now occupies the site.

The two stands at the north and south ends of the ground illustrated something of a social divide. The south bank was a little more up-market in that blue-collar workers, along with their lads, could view the match in reasonable comfort. Small wooden fruit boxes were brought along for offspring to stand on in order to gain a better view and I can't ever recall anyone complaining about the practice. The great appeal of the south bank was that it was covered and, thus, provided some protection against the elements. Yet if your taste was for something a little more raucous, then it was the north bank for you, my fine fellow. If, as time passed, supporting a football club meant something more sinister than wearing a flat cap, a rosette in the favours of your chosen club, and, possibly, a rattle, then it was from the north bank population that this faction emerged. I know that is something of generalisation – there were good, fair-minded supporters there, too – but that was how it seemed to me. In the 1950s, the north bank was uncovered, and occupants of the high-rise flats behind the bank obtained a free view of goings-on for which those inside the ground had to pay! Covering the bank in the '60s put an end to that bit of nonsense.

But let's go back to the 27ᵗʰ October 1956, as Dave and I went to be part and parcel of a 17,498 crowd. We arrived about three-quarters of an hour before kick-off. Not that there was any risk of being locked out, you understand, but rather that we would able to get down the front of the terracing and situate ourselves directly behind the goal. The programme was a single sheet comprising of little more than the team line-up, some details of last week's fixtures – both first team and reserves - and forthcoming matches. The whole thing cost a couple of coppers and, it could be argued, was over-priced. Mind you, not as much as the current glossy propaganda missives.

"Got a couple of reserves out today," Dave told me, scanning his programme. "Blackburn is the reserve centre-forward and Wragg's only in because Grice is unfit. Mind you, Blackburn has been scoring a lot of goals for the Reserves, so we should be alright."

Over by the west stand, in front of the tunnel from which the players would emerge, the Leytonstone Silver Band was puffing its way through a selection of popular melodies of the day, and some unpopular ones of yesteryear. At the end of each piece, the ever-growing crowd would applaud its appreciation until, with just five minutes to go before three'o'clock, a spirit of expectancy spread round the ground. The band had finished its turn and was now waiting around in silence, like soldiers in the trenches about to go over the top. Even as a new recruit, I swear that I could feel it. Something was going to happen and I stood in awe, waiting to find out what. One of the bandsmen picked up a gleaming post horn and put it to his lips as though he was about to quaff a pint from its depths. Two sharp whacks on the bass drum preceded the sound of the post horn splitting the air with the opening three notes of "The Post Horn Gallop." The carnival was about to begin, and I was totally caught up in it.

As the band galloped into the piece, a wild cheer went up from the middle of the Chicken Run. From their vantage point, the gathered crowd could see straight down the tunnel where the home side were lined up, about to take the field. Lead by captain Malcolm Allison, ten claret and blue clad warriors took to the field, with green jersey-ed goalkeeper Ernie Gregory in hot pursuit. It was like an orgasm of humanity spilling onto the pitch with 17.000-plus voyeurs cheering like crazy! Something stirred within my soul at that moment, and from having not the slightest interest in the game, I knew that I was walking the Damascus road. I liked the colours that West Ham played in - claret v-necked shirts with blue trimmings, white shorts, and claret socks with blue turnovers. By comparison, Grimsby, with their rather plain black and white striped shirts, looked somewhat mundane and down at heel, when they took to the field to a smattering of polite applause.

Big Ernie Gregory, the goalkeeper (wearing black shorts for some reason best known to the higher echelons of West Ham management), ran into the goal in front of us, and began fielding shots fired in at him by forwards of the day. Warming up was the name of the ritual and there was something about the goalkeeping concept that held my attention. Nobody ever said much about the goalkeepers. I had, of course, by default, happened to see the last two Cup Finals with Bert Trautmann performing his miracles and heroics. Another seminal goalkeeping moment was about to have its way with me.

Dave was a wonderful mentor as he coached me through the niceties of the game, familiarising me with the players. Then, as the game was set in motion, he began to yell in a language completely alien to me. On this evidence, he and Mr. Ted Crick would bring the house down at the Gospel Hall, for if ever I heard anyone speaking in tongues, it was Dave Philpott on that October afternoon.

"Garn, you Irons!! "Oily, sawtyesself."Oh, save the goalie."

With the benefit of long experience, I am now in the privileged position of being able to interpret each pronouncement for you, dear reader. We start with, "Garn, you Irons," an exhortation that the "Irons" (West Ham's traditional nickname) might "come on" and strive toward better things.

"Oily" was the crowd's pet name for Doug Wragg, dark and balding on the wing. It then became plain...oily?....oily Wragg! Hence, the reasonable exhortation, "Oily, sort yourself out," a plea frequently directed in Doug's direction, as he was never able to cement a place in the side.

"Oh, save the goalie," served for, "Well saved, goalkeeper!"

Clearly, this language – together with more earthy encouragement - was understood by virtually everyone in the ground. A sort of soccer Esperanto, probably shared in one form or another all across the country.

Despite all the euphoria, the game took a distinct turn for the worse when Grimsby – how very dare they? – scored. I ask you. Just up from the Third Division (North) and they take the lead on our patch. General consensus was that this success would be short-lived for, surely, there was enough claret and blue firepower to turn the screw on Grimsby. In goal for Grimsby was Clarrie Williams, memorable in that he wore a royal blue jersey. Even with my limited knowledge of the subject, I knew that goalkeepers wore green. Suddenly, in a fit of agitation and action, Malcolm Musgrove cut into the penalty area from his left wing, where, to date, he had been, shall we say, insignificant. From around the penalty spot (twelve yards from goal, Dave informed me), Malcolm gained a clear view of the whites of Williams's eyes and let fly with a screamer. The crowd began to yell for the goal and, carried away with the whole atmosphere, I was preparing to join them. But Clarrie had other ideas. I watched as he took off and, seemingly five feet off the ground and horizontal, with no visible means of support, punched the ball away to safety. The crowd, as one, rose to applaud a magnificent save. Crowds did that sort of thing in the 50s – it didn't matter which side you supported.

Dave went into raptures.

"Save, the goalie," he yelled, as he would.

As for me, although I had not yet mastered the language, I felt that, in that exquisite moment, something had moved in my soul. How had this guy, against all the odds, kept that missile from ripping the net out from its supports? It wasn't natural. It wasn't possible. For the rest of my life, I would re-live and savour the moment. Musgrove unhindered, pulling his left foot back, before hitting the ball with such venom as to render anything or anyone getting in its way insignificant. And yet, not so. There was Clarrie, the last line of defence who could do something about it, throwing all that he had into the path of the cannonball. The moment was almost spiritual. No, it *was* spiritual. I remember little more about that game other than that Grimsby held on to their lead and wandered back to the north east with the two points awarded back then for a win.

On our way home, Dave bemoaned the fact that Blackburn had been useless, Foan had had his fun against Preston, and that despite all of his (Dave's) best exhortations, "Oily" had never really sorted himself out. Back at school on Monday, he was full of the match, scattering his opinions around to all who would listen – and some who wouldn't. For the first time in my life, I was in on the conversation and no one could quite make out what had happened. Last Friday afternoon, I had been all about engines and train spotting. Now, three days later, and I'm looking and sounding like a fully blown Hammers fan. The general consensus was that it was nothing more a temporary abhoration and would soon pass.

During the next couple of games, West Ham performed at a level of what passed as "normal" for them. A narrow home win against Stoke and two away defeats – one by Middlesborough, the other by Doncaster. Goals for - two, goals against - six! Something had better happen if they were not to tumble further down the table and I gave the whole business up as a bad job, and got me back unto engine sheds. Well, something *did* happen, something beyond the wildest imaginings of those that had stayed loyal to the Hammers throughout thin and thinner. Around the middle of November, Dave burst into the classroom in a state of high dudgeon indicating that, at the very least, he'd won the pools. He made for me.

"You see that, Steve? West Ham have only gone and signed Eddie Lewis from Preston!"

Eddie Lewis? The name meant nothing to me, but it was clear enough to read between Dave's lines that West Ham had done a smart piece of business that met with his full approval. This was confirmed throughout the day as holy huddles gathered, proclaiming something akin to the arrival of the Messiah. And under West Ham terms of reference, I guess that comparison wasn't entirely out of proportion. With my soccer education very much in its infancy, I had yet to learn that *the* team to watch in those days was Manchester United. Under the shrewd management of Matt Busby, a group of some of the most talented players ever to grace a soccer field had been assembled – and not by the power of the cheque book. Busby believed in giving youth its head and had scouted for – and signed - some prodigious young talents who, alliteratively, had become known as the "Busby Babes." Of course, it was inevitable that some would not make the grade and, like Eddie Lewis, slip off of the agenda. Mind you, he didn't slip too far as a transfer to Preston North End was by no means going down the pan back then – despite that 5-2 thumping at West Ham earlier in the year. Yet even at Preston, Eddie had been unable to make his mark and when the northerners came knocking at West Ham's door, saying, "Frank O'Farrell, if you please," the management looked at its options. Frank was a fine Eire international, clearly capable of competing at a higher level. Compromise was reached when the clubs agreed to a straight swap – O'Farrell for Lewis - and everybody was happy. Most fans didn't seem too bothered. Sure, they were losing a fine wing-half but, in exchange, they were getting a guy who had played for Manchester United. Hey! We could be going up a notch here.

At the end of November, Eddie was down to make his debut against Leicester City, a club who were all but running away with the division, and racing certainties to reach the upper rank of the Football League, come season's end.

"You gonna come to the match, Steve?"

"Sure, Dave. I'll meet you over on the south bank."

What was happening to me? To give this tale fair balance, I spent the morning of the game undertaking my usual tour of duty around Kentish Town, Willesden, and Old Oak Common. But instead of taking in Cricklewood and Neasden, just after mid-day, I was on my way back home for lunch and an early departure to the Boleyn Ground to meet Dave and witness the debut of Eddie Lewis. Day light was shortening and the earlier darkness served to create a more intimate atmosphere inside the ground. Grimsby might have only mustered 17,000 but the arrival of Lewis, and the presence of the league leaders, would swell the gate by 3,000 to a figure of 20,000. I looked forward to the possibility that I might witness yet another goalkeeping miracle. Whatever, I couldn't wait to be a part of that atmosphere and one of the throng. When the "Post Horn Gallop" rattled out across the ground, and the players took to the field, all eyes and cameras were focussed on the newcomer. Cameramen wandered from player to player, snapping portraits and poses as best they could. But it was Eddie Lewis they and everyone else had come to see. Strongly built, Elvis-good-looking with his dark hair sleeked back, Lewis looked every inch of what he was - a bustling, tough, centre forward who had played for two of the senior sides in the land. And now, here he was, in claret and blue, with a white "9" on his back.

The day also marked the debut of another player, who received nowhere the acclaim accorded to Lewis. The last couple of results must have tried the patience of manager Ted Fenton and he did what many die-hards thought was the unthinkable – he dropped Ernie Gregory. You might have said that he was only a goalkeeper and who cares about them? Don't count me amongst your number. Bob Wyllie had spent a number of years at Blackpool as deputy for Scottish international George Farm who, in addition, to being incredibly consistent (forget that 1953 Cup Final), was rarely injured. Ernie Gregory was a terrific player, totally loyal and held in deep affection by the Hammers fans. But, when all was said and done, he was thirty-five. There was a need to look to the future, and so Bob got his chance.

Hardly surprisingly, all the smart money was on nothing other than a Leicester victory. In their own strike force, they boasted Arthur Rowley, who had been bashing goals in all over the place. Derek Hogg was a bag of tricks on the left wing, and John Morris at right half was a former colleague of Eddie Lewis's up in Manchester. They were not just good – they were very good. As the game progressed, I witnessed the truth of the West Ham condition. Against the poorer sides (sorry, Grimsby), they were dire. Against the strongest – they were world–beaters. Where just a few weeks earlier, the Shrimpers had whipped the Hammers pants down and smacked their corporate bums, Leicester was having the devil's own job trying to contain the Lewis-inspired Hammers. Somewhere around the middle of the first half, a ball was played to the feet of our inspiration. Expectancy rose, although tight marking suggested there was precious little justification for such a state. The Leicester defence started to close him down and John Anderson, in the Leicester goal, appeared more than ready and equal to anything that might come his way. All except, that is, the piece of magic that Lewis conjured from his Manchester United repertoire. For sure, no one at West Ham would have been that switched on. The briefest look up to see that Anderson had strayed little more than a few inches too far off his line prompted a chip shot over the goalkeeper's head, which saw the ball float deftly over the goalkeeper and into the top corner of the net.

The crowd went crazy. Not just that we were one up on the probable champions but, rather, we all knew we had seen something exceptional. Grizzled dockers looked on, their jaws dropping to their chests in astonishment. One voice rang out above all others.

"You can see where he's been, can't you?"

That was how we all felt. This Eddie Lewis was a class act and, by the end of the season, he would have added eight more goals to his initial strike. Bob Wyllie was showing potential to suggest he could be a more than competent replacement for ageing Ernie, and when Ken Tucker added a second, we thought that it was a case of, "Good night and God bless," for Leicester. But Arthur Rowley was not to be denied and, in addition to his obligatory goal, almost gave Leicester a point they didn't deserve. With the goal well within his range, he whacked the ball across Wyllie toward the bottom corner of the goal. It caught the post a terrific thump, shot across to the other post, which it slapped with equal force, only to rebound back into play. West Ham 2, Leicester City 1 was how it finished up.

By the strangest twist of fate, when January arrived and the draw was made for the Third Round F.A. Cup ties, West Ham were paired with Grimsby at home once again. Of course, I had to be there, and when Clarrie Williams took his place in the south bank goal, I applauded like mad. At the other end of the scale, when the referee and his linesman took to the fray, a very serious outbreak of booing hit the air.

"What's all this about, Dave?" I asked my fount of all knowledge.

"J.G.Williams, ain't it? J.G Williams, of Nottingham."

I was totally in the dark as to what it was that J.G. Williams – and J.G.Williams of Nottingham, at that – could possibly have done to be greeted with such venom.

"He's the crook who gave that penalty to Tottenham in last year's replay."

Apparently, following Hammers' exertions against Preston in the previous season's Cup competition, a couple more successes had resulted in a sixth round appearance at Tottenham. A superb 3 – 3 draw earned them a replay back at the Boleyn where all was going well until J.G.Williams – of Nottingham, mark you – awarded Tottenham a highly dubious penalty. Little Tommy 'Armer (you remember him) was deadly from the twelve-yard spot and promptly ended Hammers' hopes of a semi-final appearance – who can say, perhaps even a Wembley final. No wonder he got booed. But once these hostilities were over, West Ham sorted themselves out to mug Grimsby by a 5 – 3 scoreline. By the most amazing of co-incidences, the October scenario between Williams and Musgrove was re-enacted, virtually shot for save before my very eyes. But that was the only repeat performance and at the end of the afternoon, Dave and I went home happy bunnies, anxious for the mid-day Monday draw when we would see who we were to play next.

There were then, as now, rituals to be learned, and none so profound as being able to join in a chorus of "I'm forever blowing Bubbles," the song that I had heard from our back garden. It was all about optimism, and ever more shall be West Ham United's song. In those days, it fitted the club like a glove. Quite where the tradition grew from is open to debate. Personally, I rather like the tale of a player from somewhere amongst the annals who had curly hair, thereby earning himself the nickname "Bubbles." It may or may not be true. What was true was that the song became inextricably synonymous with West Ham United, long before Liverpool decided that they would never walk alone. I may be a bit off-target here but it seemed to me that the song was only dragged out of the closet for F.A.Cup matches. If the side were struggling, someone, somewhere in the Chicken Run, would begin the refrain. From there it would swell around the ground until every man, woman, and child had take up the strain. Long before the advent of the "Mexican Wave," the chicken run fraternity would begin to sway in time with the singing until, ultimately, we were all caught up in the euphoria and the entire crowd – away supporters excepted - would be singing and swaying. It took on the semblance of an hymn, uniting every Hammers supporter in a shared mission with the players themselves. It frequently had the effect of raising the team out of whatever level of mediocrity and lethargy they had sunk to, into performing like super heroes. For a long time, I truly believed that just singing "Bubbles" and swaying was sufficient to turn the tide. Of course, it wasn't but as for creating a sense of family unity, it was hard to beat.

Anyhow, back to the F.A. Cup. Having disposed of Grimsby, the dream was that we would get one of the top teams to test our metal. Providence was surely listening in when, at mid-day on Monday (none of this celebrity mucking around to suit the needs of television), it was announced that, "Everton.....will play....West Ham United." It *was* a big draw. Everton was not exactly setting the woods on fire in the top division, and one might get good odds on

West Ham putting one over them, even on their own patch. Dave had an uncle who lived on Merseyside and, as soon as the draw was made, he was on the telephone to ask if we could come up for the match. There would be no need for advance tickets as, even if every supporter that the Hammers could muster attended, there would still be space in the edifice that was Goodison Park. So it was that a couple of 14-year olds caught an early morning express from Euston and, somewhere around mid-day, were walking down Lime Street station with Dave's uncle, ready to trudge through the streets to his home for lunch.

"You'll beat this lot," he confided. "Getting too old and no spirit."

Ever the optimists, Dave and I were convinced that the day was going to be ours and, in fact, it nearly was. Everton scored early in the second half, only for Billy Dare to equalise. Everything looked set for a replay until up popped their captain, Peter Farrell, to nod a soft winner over the head of Bob Wyllie. We were stunned into silence. Hammers deserved more than a second crack, but one piece of sloppiness had condemned them to be also rans. Never mind. It had been a great experience, not least because I had been able to notch up about fifty new engine numbers in my book!

Despite that disappointment, Hammers went on to rattle off five consecutive wins, including an unbelievable piece of entertainment at home to Sheffield United. Jim Iley, at left half, had been playing some magnificent stuff and it was no surprise when Tottenham paid £16,000 - a not inconsiderable sum in those days - for his transfer a few months later. In goal, the pint-sized Alan Hodgkinson, who had taken over from the equally diminutive Ted Burgin, bounced around his penalty area, frustrating all and sundry. In two months time, he would be doing much the same for England, at Wembley. With four minutes to go and the scores level at 2 –2, a free kick was awarded to West Ham on the edge of the Sheffield penalty area. John Bond accurately chipped the ball into box for fellow full back Noel Cantwell to get his head on the end of it and secure the points with a 3 – 2 win. Highly irregular in those days for a full back to venture into his opponents' half – let alone both of them! It was a ploy that Bond and Cantwell would use to extremely good effect throughout the next couple of seasons.

As week followed week, I willingly made my way deeper and ever deeper into the world of West Ham United. The atmosphere in the ground was always electric and, in a very special way, the place was becoming another of my community homes. Players seemed to be my friends, and even the opposition were in no way enemies. On one particular cold and misty January afternoon, during a game against Port Vale, I stood behind the goal and watched their goalkeeper, Ray King, arch backwards to tip a ball over the bar. I looked around a ground that was barely half full, with but one thought in my mind.

"I am privileged to be here, "

All these years on, I know that I was absolutely right.

When I look at the cosmopolitan makeup of all teams that play throughought the land, I find it almost unbelievable that, in the 1950s, you could count the number of black players plying their trade in the league on the fingers of one hand. It so happened that Doncaster Rovers were due down on 16th March and were able to boast one amongst their number. Dave filled me in about the players that I should look out for.

"Well, Alick Jeffrey won't be there. He's only seventeen and just broken his leg playing for the England Under-23s. Harry Gregg's in goal, and he's a Northern Ireland international. But there's this bloke at centre-half. He's as hard as nails. If you come at him, he kicks yer balls. If you go past him, he kicks yer arse!"

Heed the word of the prophet.

Well, Harry Gregg was enormous that day, dominating everything. For such a big man, he was immensely agile and, after Doncaster had take the lead, I could see no way around him. And the centre-half was, indeed, a force to be reckoned with. Twice he gave away penalties. The first kick was left to the normally reliable right foot of John Bond – "Muffin" to his friends. He had a kick like a mule – hence the moniker linking him to Annette Mills' four-legged playmate. Possibly overawed by Gregg's magnificence, John produced a powder puff of a shot to the goalkeeper's right, which was easily deflected. It was the first penalty that I had ever seen saved and I couldn't wait to get home and tell Mum. The second kick was thundered in by Eddie Lewis, and honours remained even at the completion of ninety minutes.

But what was it about Doncaster's centre-half? Dave had it dead right – if it moved, he kicked it! But the more we booed him, the more he laughed. He had the broadest of smiles, clearly loved playing – or what passed for playing – and established a real rapport with all the fans, Doncaster and other persuasions. Many years later, an inspired television executive decided that there was mileage in having stand-up comics doing a set of silly, clean gags. One night, there was this black guy, with a Yorkshire accent, the broadest of grins, and a boisterous laugh bringing the house down. "Well, blow me down," I thought. "It's him! The centre half! Charlie Williams!" And so it was. Born in Yorkshire of Jamaican descent, Charlie was one of the first black players in British football after the Second World War and the the first black comedian to make the big time on British TV. In 1999, he was made an MBE for his charity work and also voted Doncaster Rovers' all-time cult hero by viewers of the BBC's Football Focus programme. What I wouldn't give to see him on a soccer field again, kicking all and sundry, taking the knocks in return, and laughing about the whole blessed scenario. He got featured on "This is Your Life," and was asked what sort of player he had been. In his best "On Ilkley Moor bah'tat, he recalled, "Well, me old flower, I weren't a good player....but I were good enough to stop them that were!" Exactly! Well put, Charlie. He passed on in 2006, and I miss him still.

Come the end of that 1956 - 1957 season, West Ham had rollercoasted to a very respectable eighth position, in addition to having being a shade unfortunate to exit the Cup earlier than they ought to have done. This, in West Ham terms, was a very satisfactory state of affairs and when the season came to its close, I had become totally immersed in not just West Ham's way of doing things, but with things football in general. For starters, I knew that manager Ted Fenton was only the third man to occupy that position throughout the club's sixty-year existence. Managers were allowed to stay around for long enough to do the job, and the thought of Ted being dismissed, replaced, or anything else, never entered the heads of the supporters. I also understood that a policy of attacking the south bank in the second half was favoured. Indeed, I always had a sense that the team were at a psychological disadvantage should the opposition win the toss and elect to attack the south bank end in the second half. Opposition supporters mingled with each other on the terraces without the slightest trace of ill will. We joked with one another, supported our teams, and applauded good play, regardless of who produced it. I loved that spirit, and deeply mourn its passing.

There was a wonderful old character around West Ham in those days. We all called him "Monty" because he bore an uncanny resemblance to Field Marshal Montgomery, the hero of Alamein. Monty must have known it for, at every home match, there he would be, kitted out in khaki shorts and shirt, with a beret set at the jaunty angle for ever associated with the real thing. From his rightful place in the Chicken Run (where else?), he would stand on the wall, blaring out what passed for reveille on his bugle. It would scarcely be accommodated in today's safety-conscious society, but old Monty would get over the containing wall, and march along the cinder track, saluting all and sundry. The police turned a blind eye to the whole pantomime, because Monty was as much a part of West Ham as any of the players – and we loved him for it.

Charles Buchan's "Football Monthly" was an absolute must for any self-respecting football fan. Buchan had enjoyed a splendid career with Sunderland, Arsenal, and England and when it came to retirement, he opted for journalism, leading to the publication of this monthly essential. Articles on players were included – and not just those at the top end of the market. Arsenal or Accrington, Manchester United or Mansfield – they could all count on a fair crack of the whip. Some really informed opinion made up the articles published alongside coloured portraits of heroes of the day, again from all divisions. Best of all were the team photographs. At the beginning of a season, every club would circulate an official team photograph, showing all of their players, systematically lined up and seated, smiling and totally unaware of what the forthcoming season might have in store for them. These would be supplemented, at quite regular intervals, by updated photographs taken prior to the commencement of matches. After a game, kids armed with their copies of "Football Monthly," clamoured round the gates to where players of visiting clubs were boarding their bus. The latest team photograph would be presented with a polite request that they sign across their image which, in 99.9% of cases, they did. As a result of all this, I quickly learned who played for who and was thus able to enter Walpole Road gossip about their various merits or otherwise.

The edition that we looked forward to most came in August, when the fixtures for the forthcoming season were published. We would look for those sides that had given us a good game or a tonking, and hope for a repeat performance or summary revenge. Matches against local opposition were really special, in particular, the clashes with Leyton Orient. The "O's" were a decent little side but we usually managed to come out on top when pitched against them. As we scoured the fixtures, the last thing on any of our minds was that West Ham might do something really special – like getting into the First Division. Nah! That wasn't going to happen. Ever since the war, the side had mucked about in the Second Division in no really serious danger of either promotion or relegation. They were quite comfortable where they were, thank you very much. Better to be masters of your own destiny in the Second than to have all manner of havoc created by rubbing shoulders with the Arsenals, Wolves, and Manchester Uniteds of this world. I certainly can't recall the 1957- 1958 season being heralded with any real degree of optimism. We wouldn't go down, and should the spectre of promotion raise its ugly head, then, as always, we would fight against it with all our might.

The season began with us playing host to humble Lincoln City. True to form, we were treated to the spectacle of everything going perfectly well, save for the somewhat essential requirement of putting the ball in the back of the net. After what seemed like the twentieth miss of the afternoon, a frustrated Ernie Gregory turned to face all of us gathered on the South Bank

"Gawd Almighty!" he yelled, his big hands raised, appealing to the heavens.

And so said all of us, Ern, when at the end of the match we acknowledged, rather than celebrated, a 2 – 2 draw.

This less than auspicious start showed little sign of abating and, by early October, West Ham had suffered no less than five defeats, three of them consecutive. Derby County had just won the Third Division (North) title and their visit early in September had me biting my fingernails at the thought of what last year's holders of this distinction – Grimsby – had achieved on their visit to the Boleyn. However, spirits were refreshed with a 2 –1 victory, in which Noel Cantwell, collecting the ball well inside his own half, made for the Derby goal. Anticipating nothing special from a full back, Noel was allowed go on, and on, and on, until, from the edge of the penalty area, he fired a rocket of a shot that would have killed diminutive goalie Terry Webster, had he been fool enough to get in its way. All would surely be well now, but two days after this victory, an evening visit by Sheffield United and Alan Hodgkinson resulted in a 3-0 thumping, Alan having no need to repeat his heroics of the previous season. So, with a princely total of just ten points in mid-October, some fans were beginning to think the unthinkable – that, perhaps, it *was* possible for us to go down.

Our next fixture was just across the Thames at Charlton Athletic, and there was certainly no comfort for us in that thought. Charlton were good and, despite having been relegated from the First Division at the end of the previous season, they were racing favourites to go straight back up. You could see why. Long-serving Sam Bartram had retired (at age 42, would you believe?) and been replaced by Willie Duff, a Scottish goalkeeper (there's an oxymoron for you), who might have sounded and looked like a pudding, but was a jolly fine goalkeeper. John Hewie was a Scottish international, whilst Derek Ufton had done very brief service for England. Up front, they could still boast South African Stuart Learie and it made you wonder how they had ever managed to lose their grip on their elevated status. Few north of the river could see anything other than a Charlton win – and an emphatic one, at that - and 30,000 came to see the slaughter of the innocents. Dave and I joined them.

Well, we should have known it, shouldn't we? With just twenty minutes on the clock, little Billy Dare put us in front. What was even more exciting was that West Ham was actually playing well. The massacre might not happen and, who knows, we might even get a draw or a narrow defeat. That would be more than respectable. As the first half drew to its close, our lightly inflated bubble of hope sagged when the referee awarded Charlton a penalty. Can't recall if it was handball or anything like that - probably a dodgy tackle. Doesn't matter really, as here comes Gordon Hurst – he of the bald head and veteran of better days – to do the honours. The ball pinged from his crisp shot to Ernie's right, but the goalkeeper read it to perfection and pushed it around the post. Pandemonium! Ernie's saved a penalty! Dave and I were delirious, so much so that we didn't notice the man in black – and I ain't talking Johnny Cash – pointing to the spot again. Ernie had, apparently, transgressed by moving before the kick was taken and, according to the laws of the game, that meant a retake. Charlton could breath again. Dave provided his personal opinion on the quality of the referee's judgement and parentage so graphically that I wondered if the poor soul might be a relative of Mr. J.G.Williams, of Nottingham. But he wasn't going to change his mind. Hurst didn't dare try his luck again, so for this second bash, skipper Derek Ufton stepped up to the plate. He ran forward, and we all held our breath. Confidently, he smashed the ball............straight into the wall that surrounded the ground! The idea was, of course, to put it in the net – and some of us laughed!

That incident proved to be the turning point of the match and by the time that the ninety minutes were up, 18-year old John Smith and Malcolm Musgrove had added two more goals to ensure that woolly old West Ham triumphed by 3-0. After all the nonsense of the opening weeks of the season, I guess that is exactly what we should have expected. Yet I doubt if anyone would have anticipated what was to happen next, for West Ham were about to make a move which would transform not just their season but, in some respects, their entire future.

Big transfers were not the stuff of which West Ham was made. Throughout the tail end of the previous season, there had been rumblings that Dave Hickson, the boisterous Everton centre forward, might be ready to chance his arm down south. A fee of £10,000 had been mentioned and a state of high optimism prevailed around Upton Park. As it was, it was all ended in tears when Hickson decided to pursue his career at Huddersfield Town. But were we down-hearted? Not for long, mate!

Over the past few seasons, Newcastle's front line had been led by the lanky Vic Keeble. Having commenced his career with Colchester United, he quickly earned himself a transfer to the north east, where he was destined to be part of Newcastle's triumphant 1955 Cup winning team. With his beak-like nose, he looked every inch the predator in front of goal that he was. Word on the street was that Newcastle might be ready to dispense with his services, and the newspapers had it that West Ham had put their pudding up for treacle. This was a time, you must remember, when agents worked for insurance companies, friendly societies, and such like. They had nothing to do with football and players and clubs were entirely free to do their own grown up thinking and dealing, man to man. And there was no such thing as the barmy "transfer window." Can you imagine any other commodity being put up for sale or purchase in a restricted time frame?

"Yes, I really like the car. I'll take it now."

"That's very kind of you, sir. But I can't sell it to you until the car purchase window opens in two months time."

Back then, the freedom of transfers to take place at any time throughout the year was flavouring to every season. Were some player or another not performing, clubs were free to scout around for a suitable replacement and, once terms had been agreed, the player was with a new club. This could happen on any day throughout the year, and it was exciting to hear about potential transfers, even when it didn't involve your own club. Mind you, when one of your own was under the microscope, sleepless nights could occur, as when

'Arry 'Ooper was on the slab. But it was so very much part of the enjoyment of football in those days. Goodness knows quite what swung the deal, but by the time we were ready to entertain Doncaster, Vic Keeble was a Hammer.

Flushed with the success at Charlton and the general smell of mothballs as the club opened its wallet, we all turned up to see Vic make his debut. In a relatively short time, Eddie Lewis had fallen from favour and was to make only six more appearances in a Hammers shirt before heading off to the Orient – Leyton variety. If Eddie was watching the Doncaster game, he must have had a strong sense of *deja-vu* as Vic Keeble was accorded the same acclaim and attention he himself had enjoyed not a year ago. As the game unfolded, regular clientele could have been forgiven for thinking that they were watching a continuation last season's fixture. Charlie was still Charlie, and Gregg was still Gregg. Small wonder that the following month, Manchester United made Harry the world's most expensive goalkeeper at £24,000. When we fell behind to a breakaway goal, we feared for our well-being. Yet there was a new air of determination about this West Ham team, that hadn't been in evidence during the early season shenanigans. Shots rained in on Gregg and the swine stopped the lot! Then, just as we were starting to lose hope and the will to live, a cross came into the area destined to land somewhere around the penalty spot. Flushed with sky-high confidence, Harry launched himself out for a ball that he had no right to claim. He fumbled it straight onto the head of Vic Keeble, who nodded it into the unguarded net. A 1-1 draw at home to struggling Doncaster might not have been the best result in the world, but most of us went away with a sense that things could only get better.

And get better, they most certainly did. After years of mucking about, West Ham suddenly began to play like a real team. Players who had been aimlessly poodling along seemed to come to life and demonstrate latent talents. Cantwell and Bond looked not only the best full backs in the division but, if the press was anything to go by, in the country. Young Ken Brown had taken over from Malcolm Allison (who had commenced a frustrating fight with tuberculosis) and was the classic "stopper" centre half, missing nothing and never needing to resort to the "Charlie Williams' School of Charm" for inspiration. Most remarkable of all was the transformation of John Dick, the Scottish inside left. Notoriously left-footed, with Vic Keeble alongside him, he began to score goals for a past time. In seven consecutive matches following the Doncaster game, he netted no fewer than seven times - and this from a bloke who hadn't a league goal to bless himself with until Keeble's arrival.

Results turned, and gates grew. The football served up was irresistible, as Huddersfield and Stoke both leaked five goals at the Boleyn. During that season, both Bristol Rovers and Lincoln (on their own ground, mark you) were hit for six, whilst poor old Rotherham took the biscuit when, in March 1958, eight strikes were rattled past poor John Quairney. I almost felt sorry for Rotherham when a perfectly timed lob over Ernie Gregory saw the ball bounce on the six-yard line and, from thence, over the bar. But that's the way it goes when the fates are against you. Oh, yes. Just in case we thought that this flush of form was nothing more than a fluke, First Division Blackpool, full of quality players and internationals, came down for a Third Round Cup Tie, took the lead through an early penalty, only to go home having had five West Ham goals deposited in their net.

With results like these, West Ham became embroiled in a genuine battle for promotion, alongside some real class acts. Blackburn Rovers with the splendid Ron Clayton and Brian Douglas; Fulham with Johnnie Haynes, Tony Macedo, and Jim Langley; Liverpool with Tommy Younger, Billy Liddell, and Alan A'Court. Charlton, I have already paid tribute to. Note this – all of these players were competent internationals, plying their trade outside of the senior league. It wouldn't and couldn't happen today, more's the pity.

After the win at Charlton, for the remainder of that season, Hammers lost just three league games. Ipswich did for us 2-1 on Boxing Day, whilst Huddersfield and Dave Hickson wreaked a 3 - 1 revenge for the 5 – 2 bashing they had taken earlier in the season. A home game against our chief rival – and most people's favourite for promotion - Charlton, produced nothing more than a 0 - 0 draw. Not too bad, you might have supposed until, three days later, it was put in perspective when off we trolled for a fixture against Notts County (who would be relegated), which resulted in a 1 – 0 defeat at Meadow Lane. Those with long and not so long memories feared a severe outbreak of West Ham Disease, and that the wheel might yet fall off. However, a 3 – 0 win over Cardiff City helped to calm the nerves a little, until we looked at our next fixture – Liverpool at home – another in-form rival. 37,750 souls crammed into the ground on that day to witness Billy Liddell put the Reds into the lead, before John Bond equalised with a thunderous free kick. Yet promotion wasn't anywhere near a certainty, and it would all came down to the last matches of the season.

Hammers closing match was away to Middlesborough; Blackburn were at Charlton, and Fulham away to Cardiff. Everyone began working out permutations, which we hoped would result in West Ham taking their place in the First Division after an absence of twenty-six years. On that never to be forgotten final day, a phenomenal game at Charlton saw Blackburn gain a 3 - 4 victory, thereby securing their place amongst the elite, and leaving poor old Charlton grabbing thin air. Dad was working in the garden as I glued my ear to the radio, soaking in every goal, and computing and re-computing what needed to happen if West Ham were to reach the Promised Land during my first full season of support. By the time that the results were read at 5.00pm on "Sports Report," I was praying for a Cardiff victory over Fulham. You see, the Cottagers had a backlog of fixtures as a result of a prolonged Cup run, which saw them reach a semi-final. Were they able to maintain successful league momentum, they could still upset Hammers, should our boys to go down at Middlesborough. But if Fulham lost, that would be the end of their challenge. I could scarcely contain myself!

Biting my fingernails, I listened nervously as the First Division results were read out. Wolves were going to be First Division Champions again, but let's get down to the real stuff – the Second Division. The refined drone of the announcer reached the result that might confirm West Ham's fate.

"Cardiff City.......three. Fulham.....nil."

Three – nil! That was it! They couldn't overtake us and West Ham was certain to be promoted. I shrieked, and ran into the garden where Dad was digging in readiness for some planting activity. Never had any sense of occasion, did Dad.

"Dad! Dad! They've done it – they're up!"

In fairness, he did get a bit animated and we danced around in each other's arms, celebrating the best news that Upton Park had received since VE Day.

"So, how did they get on at Middlesborough?"

Oh, blimey. I hadn't waited to find out. All that mattered to me was that mathematics decreed that Fulham's defeat left Hammers high and dry in the First Division, even should they have lost at Middlesborough. As it happened, the team had put in a splendid performance, running out winners by 1 – 3. It was a joyous moment.

The names of the regular line-up for that season stays in the memory and embossed upon my heart:-

Ernie Gregory, John Bond, Noel Cantwell, Andy Malcolm, Ken Brown, Bill Lansdowne or Malcolm Pyke, Mike Grice, John Smith, Vic Keeble, John Dick, and Malcolm Musgrove.

Players of their quality, if available today in the Second Division, Championship or whatever old tosh they care to dress it up as nowadays, would never be allowed to stay together. Only Noel Cantwell, went on (successfully) to what might be described as "bigger and better" things, when a 1960 transfer took him to Manchester United, the till ringing at £29,500. Most of the team stayed at Upton Park until age or form decreed they should kindly leave the stage. Andy Malcolm enjoyed one last hurrah at Chelsea, whilst John Dick went across the capital to Brentford where he became something of a cult hero. Young John Smith, after an inspired decision by one of the coaching staff to move him to an attacking wing-half role, became one of the "bright young things," of whom England expected much. Ultimately, he would defect to Tottenham, with Dave Dunmore coming in the opposite direction.

However, replacing the irreplaceable Danny Blanchflower proved a bridge too far for John, and he never really fulfilled his potential. Low key moves saw him serve time at Coventry City, Leyton Orient, Torquay, and then Swindon - where he won his only honour in the sensational and shock League Cup win against Arsenal at Wembley, in 1969. But that was it and, despite brief managerial appointments at Walsall and Dundalk, by the time that 1988 arrived, he was dead, aged just forty-nine. John Smith had been a hero to us kids and I've always wondered what would have happened to him had he stayed at West Ham.

I cannot avoid recording how very special was to support a football club – any football club – in the 1950s, without drawing comparison to the same activity in modern times. Readers who were there at the time will recognise what we took for granted whilst those of a later generation will struggle to believe some of the things that went on. When reflecting on my earliest football experiences, it doesn't take me very long to realise that the game that captured and enthralled me, is no longer the one on offer today. Between 1950 through to 1980 – perhaps a few years beyond - no one would have predicted players pinging from club to club, and being paid (not necessarily earning, mind you) £120,000 plus a week in wages. I would be amongst the very last to argue that players of that earlier era weren't seriously done down in many ways, particular when it came to remuneration. But the pendulum has swung too far, and great clubs – clubs with real pedigree - are finding survival a real struggle. What I signed up to all those years ago, in 1956, is no longer available and, as a result, my interest in the game has become remote and academic, rather than passion driven.

I mourn the passing of an era when personal contact with the players was taken for granted, yet never abused. The men who wore the claret and blue each week were both our friends and neighbours. We knew that Noel Cantwell lived in Loxford Avenue and that Ernie and his family resided in a decent part of Ilford. Just around the corner, on Barking Road, Cassetari's cafeteria would play host to many of the players who met to discuss the game in depth and, ultimately, provide a generation of coaches and managers who went on to achieve no small degree of success. Autograph hunting and a conversation with your heroes were not only possible, but positively indulged in. During school holidays, any number of kids would congregate in the car park of the ground to shove football annuals, programmes, and "Football Monthly" under the players' noses. We never tired of asking and, in the main, the players never tired of signing. I can only every recall Alan Blackburn getting snotty and turning us aside. His goal-scoring exploits in the reserves suggested that he was a talent soon to be called upon. As it was, he played just fifteen games for the first team, scoring a grand total of three goals, before trolling off to Halifax, Margate, and then Wellington Town. Who wants your rotten autograph, anyway?

Supporting the reserves in the Football Combination was every bit as important as loyalty to the first team and these games were a goldmine for getting new and valuable signatures. When the first team were playing away, the ground played host to matches between the reserve sides – none of this business of going over to Chadwell Heath. The beauty of this for the autograph hunter was that an established opposition player might find himself temporarily dispensed with by the first team, and turn out for the reserves, with a view to regaining both form and position.

One Monday August evening in 1957, Portsmouth reserves came to do battle with our second string. In the last few minutes, with scores level at 1 – 1, West Ham was awarded a penalty. In goal for Pompey was the Northern Ireland international Norman Uprichard, coming close to the end of a distinguished career, and temporarily displaced in the first team by Alan Barnett. Alan Blackburn stepped up to wallop the ball high into the net. Uprichard made a mighty leap to get a hand to the ball, without deflecting it away from its target. Half an hour later, there I was alongside "Black Jake" – he really did look like a pirate - with my "Football Monthly," which he signed. Can you believe that? Me rubbing shoulders with an international!

"You were really unlucky with that penalty, Norman," I consoled.

He nodded either in agreement, appreciation, or irritation.

All of this created and fed an intimacy that the modern game has neither hope nor intent of duplicating. Up and down the country, I guess, it was the same. Wonderful players would stay loyal – or were held hostage – to their Second Division masters. Brian Clough rattled goals in for Middlesborough; Gregg stayed with Doncaster for a few seasons before Manchester United came knocking at the door; Geoff Bradford of England and Bristol Rovers – yes, Bristol Rovers - stayed and thrived in a lower division - and there were plenty more where those came from.

The seeds of my discontent were planted in 1960 with the abolition of the maximum wage, George Eastham's stand for freedom of contract, and Jimmy Hill shoving his bearded chin into anything and everything football. Now don't get me wrong. When the great – and I do mean great - Tom Finney was offered a bucket of cash to leave his hometown club, Preston North End, and abscond abroad in the early 1950s, club chairman, Nat Buck, famously declared, "You can forget all about that. If tha' doesn't play for us, tha' doesn't play for anybody." And tha' didn't. Tom remained a "one club" man throughout his illustrious career which, much as Tom loved the club, wasn't right. Twenty pounds a week "in season" maximum was all you could expect, regardless of whether you were at the top of the First Division with Wolves, or down amongst the dead men with Crewe Alexandria.

This stranglehold that clubs had over their players meant that, season after season, by and large the same old boys would be trotting out. Changes would only occur when some young upstart who had begun to show promise, forced himself into the reckoning, or some poor old soul had started to run out of steam and could no longer be counted upon to be counted upon. There might be a bit of transfer activity, which allowed new players in and others out, but, by and large, the players we saw in one season were 95% of what we had seen the previous one. There was every possibility that they would make up 95% of what you would see the next. It made for corporate identity, knowing who would be representing your opponents in the forthcoming match. Consequently, I find it easy to recite many of the 1950 – 1960 line-ups of major clubs, but wouldn't have a clue who was turning out for most of them today. Of course, players were treated scandalously and a decent above average reward for their skills was entirely appropriate. But £250,000 per week? Per-leeze!

When a side was relegated, the familiar mass exodus of the best players that we see from today's over-rated and over-paid prima donnas never happened. The reaction to relegation was, "Well, we're the ones who got ourselves into this mess, so we'd better get ourselves out of it!" Often they did, sometimes they didn't. Sheffield Wednesday used to go up and down with such regularity that they became known as the "yo-yo" club. It was great fun to make pre-season predictions of who would take the honours, and who might be relegated. Despite the occasional favourite, there was always a wide choice of possible contenders who were well capable of winning major competitions and fewer, it seemed to me, of potential toilet fodder.

Dark horses rose without trace to confound the lot of us and, although it is outside of the era I am recalling, a classic example was provided when, in 1961, Alf Ramsey's tractor boys from Ipswich Town did the unthinkable and won the Second Division title. Few gave them any chance of survival amongst the upper echelons but - could you believe it? - within twelve months, they confounded the lot of us by snatching the First Division title with a team of has-been, might-be, and never-was journeymen. Alf worked out systems to match their strengths, and off they jolly well went. Mind you, they went back from whence they came in pretty short time, but by then, Alf had moved on to transform an England side that had threatened precious little, into worthy World Champions within just four years. I am convinced that that is something we are not going to see happen for a very long time – if ever. Football is all about doing your damndest to stay in the wretched Premiership, where the money is. As for a fair shot at a trophy, well, just think yourself lucky to be in the band, and tug your forelock as Chelsea, Manchester United, and Arsenal swan off to gather what silverware is going. And they call it a competition.

On their return to the top division in 1958, West Ham, with basically the promotion eleven, adapted astonishingly well. For their opening fixture, Ken Hinds and I travelled down to Portsmouth, where a 40,000 gate witnessed the Hammers play their first match in the senior division for twenty-six years. The place was heaving and there we were, two fourteen-year olds, trying to get a decent view of the pitch, in amongst a whole horde of Pompey fans. So what happened when group of home supporters saw us with our claret and blue regalia?

"Come on, lads. There's a place for you down here."

And the waters parted for the pair of us to get a prime position and watch Hammers come up with a 2-1 win. More than the win, I remember and cherish that camaraderie. The integrity of those disappointed Pompey fans who didn't simply acknowledge that we were the better side, but also contemplated the likelihood of relegation for their own favourites by the end of the season. They were not disappointed. Oops, I meant, they *were* disappointed, as Portsmouth went into freefall. But they had seen a good game, so to hell with the result. When, in the midst of opposition supporters, did we bash eight bells out of each other? We did not. Instead, we gossiped about our respective teams, reminisced on past fixtures, and honestly expressed our opinion as to how the game would go. And when the gladiators took to the field to ply their trade, applause and cheering was not confined exclusively for those in our favours. Not a bit of it. If the opposition scored a "blinder," I applauded as loudly as anyone else in the ground.

And the wit was wonderful. Sure, there was a bit of "effing and blinding," but around the grounds that I visited, there was some quality stuff. Chelsea always seemed to enjoy a monopoly in this department, for whatever reason. They supplied me with the best terrace comment I ever heard.

The eve of the F.A.Cup Final was always a bit special, when a "full" England side took on the "Under 23s." Uncle Sid – Aunt Joan's husband - asked me if I would like to go along and I needed no second invitation. As likely as not, some of the regular England squad players would be involved in the Final itself, but there would still be the opportunity to see stars past, present, and yet to be go through their paces in a good natured, non-combative frame of mind. At centre half for the Under- 23s was Maurice Norman. Maurice was a big lad, who had come to Tottenham from Norwich in 1955, for a £28,000 fee. He was, if I might put it this way, a burly "farmer's boy" sort of a chap, which might be expected of any player who had come from Norwich. No offence. But he was a fabulous "stopper" and enjoyed a superb career. The match was an opportunity for him to set out his stall in the hope of achieving higher things.

During a bit of hectic defending, Maurice took a swipe at the ball and completely missed his timing. The result was that the ball followed an upward trajectory - and several yards up, it has to be said. As it began its descent, Maurice kept his eye steady as best he could, with a view to clouting the ball back upfield at the earliest possible opportunity. Amazingly, his timing failed him again and the blessed thing hit the ground with a thump, and bounced up to hit poor Maurice fair and square on the bum! When we had all recovered from our laughing seizures, one wag demanded identification.

"Who's that idiot?"

A friendly, protective, and sympathetic voice replied, "That's Norman."

"Norman? Norman? Norman bleedin' Wisdom?!"

Poor Maurice. At that moment he did look like a clown. But that little scenario played out up on the terraces sent me home happy, and ready to relay it to any and all who would listen.

West Ham's commencement of their initial season in the First Division saw them produce three wins plus a highly creditable draw. Following the Portsmouth result, a spectacular 7 –2 thrashing of Aston Villa, plus a never to be forgotten home 2 – 0 triumph against the previous season's Champions, Wolves. The draw was gained at the expense of Wolves at their Molyneux ground. Three points out of four from the Champions was no mean feat. Full of confidence, we waited with eager anticipation for the September night when the show that everyone wanted to see came to town. The Munich tragedy of February 1958, that took the lives of some wonderful players, meant that the fabulous Manchester United "Busby Babes" were not going to tread our green and pleasant pitch. Yet the club had retained its enormous drawing power, not least as a result of the sympathy that the country felt at their loss. On the night, 36,000 fans crammed into the ground to witness Hammers gain a 3 – 2 win, along with the debut of a big, blond teenager who had been playing absolutely brilliantly in the club's successful Youth Eleven. If you're not saying to yourself, "He's talking about Bobby Moore," where have you been all this time?

Suddenly, woolly old West Ham was very much amongst the big boys and nowhere was the evidence stronger than with the signing of Phil Woosnam, from Leyton Orient, the till ringing at £30,000. £30,000 – can you believe it? £10,000 for Dave Hickson or Vic Keeble had been more our mark to that point. Dave, Ken, and I – along with a few thousand others - began to believe that we were going to take our place at the top end of the table alongside the Wolves, Arsenals, Manchester Uniteds, and 'Spurs of this world. Come the end of the season, a very respectable sixth place had been achieved, the highest in the club's history since 1927. Everything in the garden was rosy.

The following season started as though we were going to do even better. For the princely sum of £3,000, we had secured the services of Eire international goalkeeper, Noel Dwyer, from Wolverhampton. He played like a thing possessed and, by the end of November, we had lost just four matches (that was no disaster in those far more competitive days) and completed a hat-trick of victories against Manchester City, Arsenal, and, once again, Champions Wolves. The away match at newly promoted and inconsistent Sheffield Wednesday was hardly likely to cause us any problems. But, you must remember, that this was West Ham, with a long-established tradition of being able to snatch defeat from the jaws of victory at any given time. Back in Upton Park, we could scarcely believe the score from Hillsborough….Sheffield Wednesday

7, West Ham United 0! Dwyer had been all over the shop, but we were too full of ourselves to believe that this was anything other than a temporary set back. Sure enough, the following week, a 4 –1 win over Forest put everything back into perspective, and the forthcoming trip to Blackburn held no fears. But I guess we should have seen it coming, for the defence, once so sure and certain, was leaking goals at an alarming rate and we returned from the north west, chastised to the tune of 6 -2. Suddenly, all was far from well and by the end of that season, we had hung on to First Division status by our fingernails. Ironically, it was the commencement of the most glorious period in the club's history.

The time scale of my recollections prevents me from documenting in detail all that awaited the club in the 1960s. It all began when manager Ted Fenton was shown the door in 1960, under circumstances never fully explained to all and sundry. In his place, from Arsenal came Ron Greenwood, a Championship winner just six years earlier with Chelsea. He had faffed about as a player with Bradford, Brentford, and Fulham before moving to coach Arsenal, and we wondered what the hell he knew about the game, or the West Ham way of doing things? We were soon to find out. Greenwood proved not only a coach of immense talent but, what's more, a gentleman. As the 1958 side began to age, depart, and generally fade away, the astute scouting of Wally St. Pier had provided some magnificent young players to draw on. Augmented by a few shrewd Greenwood signings, West Ham began to look like becoming a side of no mean ability, the envy of many for the quality and purity of their football. Something major was surely on its way into the trophy cabinet at the Boleyn.

Sure enough, in 1964, West Ham won the Cup for the first time, with a 3 – 2 victory over Second Division Preston North End. It was a somewhat laboured effort, but who cared - apart from Preston, that is. Tony Prince and I were there and embraced passionately when our old school friend, Ronnie Boyce, headed the last minute winner. The following season, the team battled its way to the final of the European Cup Winners Cup to be played at, of all places, Wembley. On 19th May 1965, the world watched as

Hammers played football from another planet to overcome Munich 1860 with two Alan Sealey goals. At the final whistle, I exploded with joy. With one arm around my dad's shoulder and the other around my mate John, I hooked my legs over the shoulders of John's dad, and sang "Bubbles" at the top of my voice. I never knew a better moment throughout all my years of watching football.

I know it's all history now, but I'll remind you anyway. The following year, England's only success in the World Cup was achieved with Hammers' Martin Peters and Geoff Hurst contributing all the goals in the final against West Germany. Best of all, big, blond Bobby Moore captained the side, continuing his seemingly effortless endeavour to provide a yardstick for everything good in the game. Expectations were high and, never again, would we be an unambitious outfit, scruffing around in the lower divisions. Or would we? In the ensuing years, success intermingled with failure at reasonable regular intervals. A couple more F A Cp wins, defeat in another European final, plus the club's closest shot at landing the First Division title, when they reached the dizzy heights of third in 1986 season. Great players continued to grace the shirt – step forward Sir Trevor Brooking, Billy Bonds, Phil Parkes, Frank Lampard (Snr) - and bring joy to thousands. Yet, in amongst all this, a couple of awful relegation seasons soured the whole flavour.

I recognise - and have to accept - that many of my generation still have the fire burning in their bellies. They still anticipate a time when someone other than the wealthiest of clubs will come up with a Premiership title or Cup win – perhaps West Ham's day is not quite over and done. Who knows? Well, I'm sorry, guys, but I shall have to pass, for football 21st Century style has no appeal for me. I was brought up in a different atmosphere and, nowadays, gain my greatest pleasure in reminiscing, studying, and reading about the game of days gone by. I find deep satisfaction in being able to write to an old player and, invariably, receive a kind letter of appreciation for my troubles. Letters from Alan Ball, Nat Lofthouse, Harry Gregg, Fred Else, Ray King, Colin McDonald, Bob Wilson, Ernie Gregory, and others tell me that they are glad to be remembered with such fondness. Those in the know will recognise that there are six goalkeepers in that lot. Those not "in the know" know now. I'm sure that Bobby Moore would have written to me.

Bob left this earth far too early, just short of his 52nd birthday, in 1993. His final resting place is under a little tree in the City of London Cemetry, in Manor Park, where a tasteful stone marks the spot shared with his parents, who are acknowledged. As far as the great man himself is concerned, there is no statue, no poorly chosen, over sentimental words. Nothing of his triumphs as England's best captain ever. It simply records:-

BOBBY MOORE OBE 1941- 1993

When you are a man of Bobby Moore's standing, nothing more needs to be said.

I visit that cemetery whenever I can, and when I do, my ritual is always the same. Walk round to where Mum and Dad's ashes were scattered; pop over to the rose planted in memory of my dear Aunt Eileen; and then, a quiet time with Bob, to revisit the years that I cherished most in football. The laughs, the characters, the sportsmanship, the uncertainty, the competition, the camaraderie. Oh, how I loved it. Oh, how I miss it.

CHAPTER TEN

SCOUTING FOR BOYS

My friend suggested that my choice for the title of this chapter was not a wise one. It is, of course, nothing more than the title that Lord Baden-Powell, the founder of the Scouting movement, chose for his book on the principles of Scouting as he envisaged them. My friend had a point though. Nowadays, "BP" would probably have had the thought police from the welfare society knocking at his door for, I suppose, it indicates the change of focus in today's hopefully enlightened times. Too little seems innocent anymore and too much is innuendo.

But I'm going to stick with my title, for the Scouting movement was a kind servant to my generation and remains so today, for those who will enter into its spirit. It established wonderful rapport and comradeship between young lads, and when Lady Baden-Powell set up the Girl Guides, well, she unwittingly provided a vehicle for many a light-hearted and innocent romance. Segregation of the sexes in matters of education came to an end, for me, through the Scout and Guide movements. They provided a lovely gentle introduction to the weaker sex where, on average, I enjoyed a broken heart once a month.

So I want to turn the clock back in my story to reflect on how Scouting became a vital thread, which ran through so much of my life, pulling it together like a drawstring every bit as much as Sunday School, Grammar School, Trainspotting, and West Ham United ever did.

Every so often, the peace and quiet of play-free Sunday mornings would be disturbed by a sound that brought us out of our houses, like squirrels ending their hibernation period. It began in the distance, gradually building to a level where all eyes would be focussed on the St. Stephens end of Walpole Road. Then, bringing

313

their melodious racket with them, the Boys Brigade drum and bugle band, based at the big Baptist church in Plashet Grove, opposite the library on the corner of Plashet Park, turned into our street. Young lads and girls marched by, all smartly dressed in black, with a white belt fitted diagonally from shoulder to waist. The boys wore small pillbox hats, black again, with two white rings around them. The parade was led by three side-drummers who, although young, really had mastered their art. In the second rank was a big bass drummer, who wore an apron between his instrument and person to protect his uniform. He was flanked by two more side drummers, driving the rhythm and providing solid ground for the front kettle-drummers to rat-tat-tat out their phrases. I loved it when they clicked their sticks together in time with the rhythm without breaking stride.

The drummers were followed by couple of ranks of buglers, blowing out simple but stirring march melodies. The remainder of the entourage followed on, marching in time with the music, rightly proud of the impression they made as they swaggered down the street. As soon as they turned into Walpole, Derek, Terry, Ricky, Michael, Alan, and I ran to greet them, and accompany the procession as it moved down the street. I imagined that, one day, I too might have a side drum attached to my middle and be the envy of everyone, bashing hell out of the skins, clicking sticks with the best of them, and generally showing off. When the band marched out of Walpole toward Elizabeth Road, we all returned to whichever warren we had emerged from, and waited for 2.45pm when it would be time for Sunday school.

I know for sure that it was this little scenario that gave birth to my wanting to join up with one of the uniformed organisations. The obvious one where I might live my dream was the Boys Brigade but, for one reason or another, I never ventured in that direction. A temporary craving to join the Sea Cubs was inspired by the uniform of navy blue jersey, shorts and socks, nicely set off with a white-topped sailor's cap at a jaunty angle, just like Dad's. But, for the life of me, I couldn't find a near-by branch of Sea Cubs. Given the in-land nature of Upton Park, I suppose that shouldn't have come as too much of a surprise. Yet one morning in school, Steve Hazell came charging into class and announced that he had just joined the Sea Cubs. Now this was the news that I had craved, and I quizzed Steve as to just where the outfit met, with every intention of signing on the dotted line.

"Oh, I just sent a letter off to Cadbury's, and they sent me all the badges and books," he replied.

Silly twerp! It wasn't the Sea Cubs at all. It was the "C" Cubs, an early marketing endeavour by Cadbury's (the chocolate company) to gain extra profile. Still, despite this being very much a false dawn, I joined the "C" Cubs, which, I guess, made me an even sillier twerp than Steve! It took very little time for me to realise that I was nowhere near where I wanted to be, so I cast the "C" Cubs adrift, in favour of making a serious attempt at getting into the conventional Wolf Cubs. Mind you, Cadbury's made pretty good chocolate.

Derek and George Brewerton had been Cubs for a year or so but, saddled with all of my other activities and interests, the need to follow suit had never been heavy upon me. But the Boys Brigade band had changed all that and what was more, my trainspotting buddy Alan Self had similar ideas. Received wisdom was that the 12th East Ham, who met at Shaftesbury Road school, and boasted Derek amongst its acolytes, was the pick of the bunch. The only workable alternative was the 19th East Ham, which met at Upton Park Methodist Church, on the corner of Cromwell Road and Green Street. The 19th was Georgie's pack and he was always on about their leader Jimmy Green, clearly a force of both nature and leadership. On the occasions I'd seen Jimmy about, he seemed a jolly good bloke, even if a little loud. But, as on so many other occasions, Derek settled the matter for me. He was in the 12th and given that the pack met on the premises of our school, I saw it as a "no-brainer," and decided that that was where I ought to be, although there would be a price to pay for this decision.

Despite being only ten years old, I remained a kid who took what he knew of his Christian faith seriously. I don't want to make capital out of the point, but I have a suspicion that my commitment and understanding were a tad deeper than average. In addition to being a regular attender at Sunday school, I also frequented the "optional extra" hour served up each Tuesday nights at 6.30 pm. The format was, by and large, much the same as on Sundays, with the exception that, instead of being divided into classes, the hall was set out theatre style. Visitors, teachers, and senior members of the church came and shared some aspect of Christian teaching with all gathered therein. Choruses and prayers were prominent on the menu and given that we had already had the main course on Sunday, the number who turned up for Tuesday dessert was quite remarkable. Certainly I enjoyed it, and would never miss if I could help it. However, the 12th East Ham Cubs met every Tuesday between 6.30 pm and 8.00 pm, and a slap bang collision with my Sunday school extra curricula was inevitable. There was no way that I would be able to attend both, and this conflict created an incredible emotional pull between the two meetings for me – one that I loved and one that I wanted to love.

Mum and Dad did their level best to reason with me.

"Stephen," said Dad, "I'm sure that God wouldn't mind you going to Cubs. After all, you always go to Sunday school, and you'll probably be able to go to the church parades with the Cubs."

Well this was true, and perhaps it was that loving and logical line of reasoning that nursed me gently to my ultimate decision. As the days passed, my desire to join the Cubs grew stronger, and Tuesday evenings at the church were likely to be no more. For a sensitive little chap, it was a difficult decision to make and, perhaps, another early indication that I was put together in such a way as God would always have a big say in my life. When it came to firming up on my decision, although it was not made without tears, the transition proceeded smoothly to a point where I became as comfortable at Cubs on Tuesday nights as I had been at the church meeting.

When Alan and I turned up to make our applications, we had our first encounter with Pat Stevens. Pat was a petite, slightly sharp-featured red head, in her early twenties, and responsible for leading the Cub pack. She explained to the pair of us that there was a waiting list and, as soon as a vacancy arose, we would be hearing from her. I wondered if that wasn't little more than a ploy to test our resolve to see if we really wanted to join. I was ready to stay on that list for as long as it took. Derek had let on that no one was kept waiting for longer than two or three weeks at most and, sure enough, just a couple of weeks later, Alan and I received our invitation letters. So it was that, with nine months to go before my eleventh birthday, I became a Wolf Cub.

It made sense for me to go to my first meeting with Derek and, just after six'o'clock, there was a knock at my door. I opened it and there he was, in all his finery. His uniform comprised a green jersey, black shorts, and black knee-length socks, which sported two green hoops on the turnovers. It was completed by a green peaked cap, decorated with gold braid and, on his jersey, an array of badges which he delighted in telling me were his County Badge, Tenderpad, and a couple of what he called proficiency badges, earned for demonstrating some area of expertise in social, sporting, and Cubbing merit.

"Don't worry about tonight, Stephen," he said, as we set off with me feeling somewhat underdressed for the occasion. "Everyone starts at the bottom and once you have your uniform and have been invested, you'll be up with the rest of us."

I have to say that, right from the start, I was made to feel more than welcome by Pat Stevens and her assistants. Cub leaders were dubbed with one name or another from Kipling's "Jungle Book." "Akela" was Kipling's "leader of the pack" and a pretty obvious name for Pat. Brian Ginn was a handsome, dark-haired guy who could have been anything between eighteen or twenty-three. Ten year olds tend not to have much "feel" for the ages of their peers. His jungle name was "Kaa" who, you might recall, was a villainous snake. As far as I ever knew, he did nothing to warrant the comparison. A more senior input and balance, was provided by John Pearse, who was "Baloo" the bear. John was a big, jovial man that I liked immensely and the three of them made a very good team indeed.

There was something very organised about the Cubs. It had an almost military, but acceptable, regularity about the way it went about its business. Hardly surprising, given Baden-Powell's background. Mysteries were there to be revealed and understood, and my first introduction to this brave new world commenced with a ritual referred to as the Grand Howl. Akela set the proceedings rolling with a sharp yell of "PACK!" signalling to everyone that it was time to stand still, shut our gobs, and wait for her next command. Once she was satisfied that all gobs were firmly shut, she barked out three staccato commands.

"PACK, PACK, PACK," truncating the call so that it came out as "PA-PA-PACK!"

This was permission for organised mayhem, as everyone yelled, "PAAAACK!!!" at the top of their voices, and rushed to form a circle around Akela. She stretched her arms forward, which was the signal for all (save those not in uniform or accepted into the movement un-invested) to go down onto their haunches, fingers touching the ground between their feet. It looked precisely what it was intended to look like – a pack of young cubs surrounding their leader. I made the mistake of all novices by imitating the ritual and was quickly advised that, until I was invested, this part of proceedings had little to do with me. After a proper pause (no point rushing these things), Akela turned her hands so that her palms were facing each other. This was the signal for the next step of the ritual.

"A–KAY-LA–WE'LL-DO-OUR-BEST!" the invested and uniformed ones rhythmically yelled, after which they leapt to the standing position.

Akela spoke the mystical words, "DYB, DYB, DYB," to which Cubs responded – as you would - with, "We'll DOB, DOB, DOB"

DYB, I was to discover, was nothing more than, "Do your best" whilst the response was an affirmation that the pack would, indeed, DOB - "Do our best." Simple when you know how.

Mum and Dad took the earliest opportunity to buy me my uniform that I was allowed to wear, albeit lacking badges and neck scarf. Alan's parents did much the same, so on the following

Tuesday, the pair of us turned up looking a little more like the real thing. New recruits were allocated to a Six, which was simply a group of Cubs led by a Sixer, and supported by a Second. During those initial weeks, everything was geared to training us to the point at which we could be invested. The gentle and thorough input from Akela, Kaa, and Baloo, along with my natural enthusiasm, enabled me to fulfil the requirements of learning the Laws of the Pack, the Promise, the Salute, and the Grand Howl, alongside their meanings, pretty quickly. After just four weeks, both Alan and I were ready to step up to the crease and increase the ranks of Tenderpads by two.

On the night of the investiture, with the circle of Cubs gathered round, my Sixer led me to prominence in front of Akela. My cap was laid at her feet and she began the process.

" Do you know the Law and Promise of the Wolf Pack, the Grand Howl, and the Salute?   Yes, I do," I confirmed

Akela again, " What is the Law?"

"The Cub gives in to the Old Wolf. The Cub does not give in to himself, " I told her.

"Are you ready to make the solemn Promise of the Wolf Cubs?"

I was so excited that I wanted to say, "You bet," but thought better of it. So, with the whole pack standing to attention and saluting, I promised to do my best, to do my duty to God and the Queen, to keep the Law of the Wolf Cub Pack, and do a good turn to somebody every day.

Job done, Akela confirmed that I was now a fully blown Wolf Cub, handed me my badges, put on my cap and scarf, and shook me by my left hand. Proud as Punch, I turned and saluted the Pack who responded in kind. Then, the Grand Howl which, for the first time, I joined in legitimately. The following week, I turned up with my badges sewn on, courtesy of Mum. A Tenderpad badge (wolf's head) was worn on the left breast of the jersey, with the County badge opposite. As the 12th East Ham was in the London District, the latter badge indicated as much. Across each arm, a shoulder flash, bearing the legend "12th East Ham," which gave an invaluable clue as to where we should be returned if lost. On my cap was another Tenderpad badge and, setting it all off, a linen scarf in the Pack's distinctive colours of grey with red edging.

Yet if I thought I had reached the end of the learning process, I was to be proved very seriously mistaken. A considerable part of each Tuesday evening was invested into self-improvement, as we new boys strove to gain our "First Star." A whole range of tests in a variety of competencies was presented to us, along with encouragement that we really should "do our best" and go for further honours. I thought that there was some good stuff on that First Star agenda so, if you were a Cub, let me remind you of it. If you weren't let me tell you, and you can make your own mind up.

a) Know the composition of the Union Jack and the right way to fly it.

b) Know in simple form the stories of the Saints of England, Scotland and Ireland.

c) Recite the first and third verses of "God save the Queen" and know what to do when it is being played or sung.

d) Be able to tie a reef knot and a sheet bend and demonstrate their uses.

e) Turn a somersault.

f) Leapfrog over another Cub of the same size.

g) Throw a ball six times so that a Cub ten yards away can catch it. Catch a ball, both hands together, thrown from a distance of ten yards, four times out of six.

h) Walk upright and with good carriage, carrying a solid article weighing about two pounds on his head, without using his hands, for a distance of ten yards, turn and come back to the starting point. A Cub cap may be worn.

i) Know why and how he should keep his hands and feet clean, nails clean and cut, teeth clean, and breathe through his nose.

j) Be able to tell the time by the clock.

k)   Grow one of the following:
- i)   a bulb in water, peat moss, sand or soil.
- ii)   a chestnut or acorn in water, peat moss, sand or soil.
- iii)   mustard and cress, peas or beans on flannel.

l)   Clean a pair of boots

None of this was beyond the abilities of the average lad and, in double quick time, I had completed the tests and earned my First Star. Akela presented me with the little silver star that was to be affixed to my cap, to the side of the Wolf badge. This served to indicate that I now had one eye open and could attempt some of the proficiency badges. These were external tests on subjects related to character, handicraft, service to others, and physical health, for which you would be awarded – if you were successful – a triangular badge to be worn on the arm of your jersey. Some veterans of the Pack had so many badges that there was scarcely room for any more to be sewn on!

Of course, it would have been unreasonable to expect healthy 8 to 11 year-olds to be involved in nothing else other than self-improvement. There had to be a bit of release somewhere, and there was. We were in Spring and able to get out into the school playground, for cricket, football, and rounders. This was, I have to say, long before I became a "born-again" sportsman and was thus well nigh useless in all of those areas. However, every dog has his day.

We were playing rounders in the senior playground, in the shadow of the Trebor sweet factory chimney. Sides were chosen and, once again, I was one of the last to be picked. The game progressed well enough, but no one had managed a strike of sufficient clout as to allow them to run round all the bases and collect the point. No score appeared to be the final outcome until....... comes the moment, comes the man. My previous efforts had been entirely undistinguished and I'd only managed to keep "in" by carefully plodding round, base to base, as others made more credible, if unsuccessful, attempts for the big hit. So, with light failing, bold Casey comes forward with the bat, and stands ready to do battle. My first swing produced nothing more than a swish as it travelled through the air, coming into contact with nowt. But it was the second that made my name. In one of those "once in a lifetime" moments, timing, power of stroke, and the ball landing just where a ball knows it should, all came together to perfection. I could feel it all through my body as bat connected with ball, sending it flying out of the playground, and up Shaftesbury Road toward Katherine Road. There was no way anyone was going to get the thing before I had taken a leisurely stroll around the bases to notch up what proved to be the decisive rounder. I felt absolutely great.

I never gained any proficiency badges for the simple reason that, come January, I would be elevated to the Scouts, so time was really against me. The Second Star was statistically beyond my reach, due to one of the requisites being the completion of a year's service. But it didn't stop me from achieving many of the standards required. As with the First Star, there were some pretty basic skills required and I am grumpy old man enough to believe that addressing them wouldn't be the worst thing in the world for young people to come to terms with nowadays. See how you measure up.

Before being awarded his Second Star, a Cub must satisfy his Cubmaster he can pass the following:-

a)   Swim 15 yards or skip with both feet together 15 times forward and 15 times backward, the Cub turning the rope.

b)   Use a compass to show a knowledge of the eight principal points.

c)   Be able to tie the following and demonstrate their use:- bowline and round turn and two half hitches.

d) Understand the meaning of thrift in all things and carry it out in practice. Show evidence of the care of his Cub uniform.

e) Produce a satisfactory model or article made entirely by himself in wood, metal, cardboard, clay, plasticine, or similar substance; or an article knitted or netted, woven or carved; or a set of at least eight sketches drawn by himself in colours (chalk or paint) of National flags, or animals, or flowers, with the names clearly written. Models made in Meccano or other partly constructed materials are not admissible.

f) Lay and light a fire, indoors or outdoors.

g) Make a pot of tea.

h) Run or cycle over a stated route with a verbal message of 15 to 20 words, including figures, and repeat it correctly. Be able to use the public telephone. Know where and how to ask for assistance in an emergency (ambulance, fire, police).

i) Show how to clean and dress a cut finger, cover a scald or burn. Understand the danger of dirt in a scratch. Know the simple treatment for shock (not electric). Understand the necessity for summoning adult help.

j) Observe and point out from life three birds (not domestic), three trees and three other natural things such as insects, flowers, fishes, the choice to be made by the Cub in each case.

k) Demonstrate the safe way to use a pocket knife, strike a match, guard a fire, and handle an iron. Understand the dangers of broken glass, rusty nails, and frayed electric flex. Know the safe way to plug in and disconnect domestic electric appliances; or how to light a gas fire or ring; or how to light oil stoves or lamps.

l) Have at least nine months satisfactory service as a Cub.

Can you believe that? I know that much of it has been superseded by time and technology, but you could scarcely fault the intent. All that was missing, as far as I was concerned, was to know the names and numbers of all the "Merchant Navy" class! *No.35020 Nederland Line; No. 35021 New Zealand Line; No 35022 Holland-America Line*..... Despite not achieving my Second Star, I was mildly astonished that, in such a short space of time, I was made a Second of one of the Sixes – if you follow what I mean. All in all, I guess I must have looked like pretty good raw material in Akela's eyes.

There was certainly compensation for missing Tuesday nights at the Full Gospel Hall. The Troop was affiliated to the Congregational Church in Chester Road, at the Katherine Road end. Each month, Cubs and Scouts were required to attend the morning service which, for this Sunday only, was designated as a church parade. During the worship (conducted by the Reverend Matanle), representatives of Cubs, Scouts, Brownies, and Guides paraded their flags and Union Jacks into the church. After the better part of an hour's service, the flags were returned to the flagbearers, who stood to attention in the centre aisle, as the National Anthem was sung. About turn, we all congregated outside in Chester Road, where the Senior Scoutmaster would call us all to attention before saluting and dismissing the lot of us. Although that was all there was to it, it satisfied my desire to be "seen," for church members and neighbours came out of their houses to watch the proceedings. When my turn to carry a flag came around, I really felt that I was someone.

I enjoyed my nine months in the Cubs immensely, and as my eleventh birthday crept up on me, I began to turn my mind toward the Scouts. Moving up to the Scouts excited me. Instead of a Pack, I would belong to a Troop, with slightly more emphasis on organisation, discipline, and progression. Cubs finished at 8.00 pm and by the time that we were ready to leave for home, the Scouts were already assembling in the playground, ready for their meeting on the top floor of the school. Once again, my growing belief that someone up there liked me was reinforced for, having blossomed under some fine influences, I came under the discipline of the wonderful Arthur Stevens.

All Scout Troop leaders were dubbed "Skipper" – "Skip" for the sake of convenience – and Skipper Arthur Stevens was one of the very best. He lived in Strone Road, where his building and decorating business was based. He was a big man with thinning hair, probably in his mid-fifties. In his Scout uniform you could never doubt that he was the leader, for Arthur Stevens had that magical quality that we call "presence." Never once did I hear him use bad language. The worst that he ever mustered was "thundering" this, or "thundering" that. It impressed me and when I reached the years when all the best influences to which I had been exposed couldn't stop my own cussing, it was the solid example of the unflappable Skipper Stevens that helped me back to the straight and narrow. Skipper Stevens and his family were born to be Scouters. His daughter was none other than "Akela" and his son – Arthur Jnr – was a Scouting Assistant. Like his sister, Arthur sported red hair and had the most marvellous friendly disposition. It was a family trait. Unfortunately, I didn't see too much of him during my early years, and can only assume that he had to undertake his National Service, another little matter which, to our cost, has fallen off the modern social agenda.

But even with young Arthur absent, there was able and popular support for leadership of the Troop. "Doc" Wiseman was in his late thirties, bespectacled, and bald of head. Quite why he was so popular, I can't pin down precisely. Perhaps it was because he earned his living working amongst the mysteries of the local mortuary, alongside Central Park, in High Street South. On the other hand, it could have been as simple as the fact that, like the other leaders, he was just such a nice bloke. Mind you, it struck me as odd that the moniker "Doc" was clearly linked to his profession. Can you imagine being in urgent need of medical treatment, calling for the "Doc," only to find the mortician turning up at your sick bed?

Eddie Barrow, who gloried in the Troop name of "Pasha," a name he brought back from his time in the Middle East, was another more than capable assistant. Pasha always seemed a little more austere than either Skip or Doc, but his commitment couldn't be faulted. His career had seen him as an Air Ministry photographer, and he remained part of the Troop for as long as I was a member. George Kinch was an immense character. He and his family lived in Strone Road, where, like Skip, he ran a building business. A lovely man with a gentle sense of humour, yet well capable of firing a bullet or two when Scout behaviour got a little too energetic.

The name of the investiture game in the Scouts was obtaining your Tenderfoot (note the "foot" rather than the Cubby "pad"). Once again I found myself denuded of badges, paraphernalia, and insignia until such times as I had completed the various tests that confirmed that I was ready for investiture. Since those far off days, the standards and criteria for this qualification have changed somewhat, but the spirit has not, with its concentration on practical, spiritual, and communal skills. Now, let me see if I can remember just what it was that I signed up to.

On my honour, I promise to do my best To do my duty to
God and the Queen and to obey the Scout Law;
To help other people at all times;
And to do a good turn to somebody everyday.

Oh, yes. The motto, "Be Prepared," was impossible to forget in that the words bore the initials of the founder.

Scout uniforms in the 1950s were a very different garb to the smart range of styles and colours seen today. Predominantly khaki, we sported shorts, and shirts with two breast pockets on which we sewed our county badge and Tenderfoot. Khaki socks, held up by garters with green flashes, and the 12th East Ham grey and red scarf. But it was the campaign hat that was the killer. I always thought that it looked like a jelly on a plate, with its wide circular brim. It's saving grace was that it was not a million miles from the headgear worn by the Royal Canadian Mounties, which made me feel not quite such a plonker when wearing it. The brim had to be kept flat all round and if it wasn't, Skipper Stevens would want to know the reason why not. He managed it to perfection, and there were few of us that could compete with his standard. Poor old John Barrett, from the Assemblies of God church, was a prime case in point.

"Look at 'is 'at." It could only be Derek. "Supposed to be flat, it is. Flat? It looks like a bleedin' scenic railway. Makes you seasick just to look at it!"

You couldn't fault Del for telling it how it was.

Scouts did their thing in Patrols. As part of the new intake, Alan Self and I were allocated to the Stags, denoted by mauve and black shoulder stripes. The continuing development programme was maintained as we set about to prove our worth by winning our Second Class badges. Of course, the bar was lifted by the range of skills and performance levels required from those we had been accustomed to in the Cubs. We had to turn our attention to First Aid, cooking, and camping, whilst never losing sight of the principles of the Law and Promise. All in all, we were being turned into pretty responsible kids, and I can think of very few who failed.

With this elevation, I found myself with a whole new group of boys – many of them a year or two older than me – who, over the years, became very good friends. Derek and Alan were already on my list, but I added the likes of John Cole, Eddie Harris, Jack and Bob Penfold, Terry Hart, Oliver Chester, and by far my favourite of the new bunch, Keith Hollington. Keith – a few days younger than me - was a funny bloke, with a wicked dry wit. Derek knew him from Sandringham school and, having met through Scouting, we began to spend time in each other's company. A time would come when Derek tired of the movement, but Keith never did, and this was the beginning of another friendship dominated by laughter.

But the biggest thrill of all was my first invitation to go away camping. It struck me as a jolly fine adventure, to be tented up with your mates. Cowboys did that sort of thing and I was excited by the idea of sitting under the stars with the camp fire blazing, cooking on an open fire, and quaffing a steaming great mug of cocoa, before turning into your blanket and happily snoring your way into the land of nod. A month before the Easter bank holiday, it was announced that the Troop would be taking a three day camping break, starting on Good Friday through to Easter Monday, at Gilwell Park, the

Scout headquarters in Chingford, Essex. Permission was sought from parents and, in my case, duly granted.

There was, however, a none-too-tactfully veiled threat that cast just a small cloud over the whole matter. Tales were rife about how all first-timer campers were "de-bagged," a charming little ritual whereby you were relieved of your trousers, which were then hung on a pole alongside the flag of the realm. Already, I was trying to cope with a similar wicked rumour that, should I make it to the Grammar School, my head would be stuffed down the toilet bowl and the chain pulled. At least, in that situation, my modesty would be preserved. But the thought of having my "bags" whipped off and waved for all and sundry to see seemed to me a bridge too far. It was John Cole, who set me right. Always a thoughtful and intelligent bloke, he put the business into perspective.

"Don't worry about it, Steve. It never happens."

He was right. It didn't.

Early on Good Friday morning, 1954, about eighteen of us stood outside the Plashet Road Congregational church with our kit bags packed, a chore that had been performed in the main by mums. Well, anyhow, that was the deal that I had. Spare clothes for playing "wide" games, swimming trunks, pyjamas, a couple of changes of underwear, a groundsheet to protect us from direct contract with the grass, a couple of blankets, enamel plates with knives, forks, and spoons, plus a few essential toiletries, and we were ready to conquer the world. Gilwell Park was no more than ten miles from East Ham, and we were booked to travel in George Kinch's open-backed lorry. Tents stored in the basement of the church were loaded on, together with a range of pots and pans – "dixies" - to ensure we were well fed. Hooting and yelling with scarcely a thought to kiss parents and supporters farewell, we joyfully clambered up onto the lorry to claim the best vantage points for the trip. How we all cheered as it pulled away. It was the first time in my eleven years that I had ever been away from tender and watchful parental eyes. I don't want to dwell on the subject too much because, despite being absolutely "up for it," a little niggle of homesickness was not too far from the surface.

But it didn't last for long, as it was love at first sight for me and Gilwell Park, where 108 acres of Essex countryside were totally dedicated to the Scout movement and its activities. You were never allowed entry beyond the gates without being in either Scout or Cub uniform so, right from the start, there was that sense of being special. I've got the uniform and I'm in – you haven't and you're out! Older hands pointed out the key areas as we passed them by. On entry, over on our right, the provision store – affectionately known as "The Provvy" - where sweets, groceries, and a range of product necessary for camping and survival were sold, with no emphasis on either convenience or luxury. To our left, beyond already erected tents and those in the course of so being, was the swimming pool - unheated of course.

"Just behind there," Ollie Chester advised us," is the Palace of Industry."

What? We needed Ollie to explain.

"The bogs, you daft buggers!"

Just beyond the Provvy was a medium sized lake that I suspect might have been formed as the result of the efforts of war. It was always referred to as "The Bomb Hole." Lads were building rope bridges to cross the thing and – joy of joys – we witnessed a rather plump little specimen lose his balance and fall straight in. Everyone laughed, but the strange thing was that I think we all envied him. Yeah – let's all fall in the water.

Much of our first day was about erecting the tents and setting up cooking facilities. Remember, we were totally without gas and electricity, so it really was a case of "back to basics." Skip took centre stage and showed us the art of removing a piece of turf sufficient to lay our fire.

"What you have to do, boys, is cut it out in a way that you will be able to put it back when camp is over, so that no one can see where you have been."

Throughout the weekend, one duty would be to ensure that the removed turf was kept regularly watered. Believe me, before we left Gilwell on the Monday and the turf was slotted back into place - like completing a jigsaw puzzle - you would never have guessed or found evidence that we, or a fire, had ever been there. We were tremendously proud of ourselves.

Unsurprisingly, Skipper Stevens was a past master at organising camps and gave each of us a specific responsibility, and in a very short time we were all working like a well-oiled machine. Erecting the three green tents was left mainly to those who had done camping time before. Younger sprogs were required to collect wood, and set out a little cooking area, making sure that we did not trespass onto the territory of another troop. As for me, well, I got the short end of the straw and was allocated to dixie cleaning duties. Those dixies could get pretty dirty after usage. The open-fire cooking blackened them a treat, and when their job was done, they were a swine to get clean from both the content and having been in the fire for so long. I quickly grew to hate cleaning them, which was probably the first indication that a culinary career was not going to be for me.

Ollie Chester called out to me.

"Oi! Derby! Go over to the Provvy and get a can of elbow grease, will you?"

The sheltered route that I had perambulated through in life up to this point had taken me nowhere near such areas where I might have known that "elbow grease" was a pseudonym for "hard work." At the back of my mind, I had an uneasy feeling that I was being set up for something and, not having heard the term before, was far from easy about going up to a complete stranger and asking for a tin of anything of the sort. I didn't have a clue about what it was, but what could I do? Even when Ollie told me that this commodity was provided free of charge, still the penny didn't drop.

Derek encouraged me, but there again, he would, wouldn't he? I'd have appreciated it if, as my mate, he had told me that "elbow grease" was nothing neither more nor less than "hard work" in disguise. But he didn't.

"Go on, Stephen. It won't take you a couple of minutes."

I was in no man's land and reluctantly set off for the Provvy.

When I arrived, the place was heaving with customers of all shapes, sizes, and colours. At just about five feet in height, I felt that I was in the land of giants. Still, nil desperandum. I took my place in what could scarcely be called a "queue." It was a seething mass of humanity as, one by one, customers were served by a surly old scouter, looking as though he wanted to be anywhere other than where he found himself. Any kid unsure of precisely what he wanted was treated with short, sharp shrift. A kid of fifteen would have quaked in his boots, and I was just turned eleven! By the time that I reached the counter, he was red in the face and about to blow a gasket or two. Cautiously, I pulled myself up to full height and announced my requirements.

"Can I have a can of elbow grease, please mister?"

It was the last straw and his roar was sufficient to part the crowd in a fashion not dis-similar to Moses' effect on the Red Sea.

"Get out of here, you scruffy little brat!! Go on! Hoppit – and tell your troop not to waste my time!"

The major consolation was that as dramatically as the crowd had parted, so it gathered in on me, and I was submerged in a crashing wave of scouting. Suitably camouflaged, I sneaked to the back of the crowd undetected, where I overheard just one conversation.

"What's going on down there?"

"Oh, just some little kid asked for a can of elbow grease."

The pair of them laughed fit to bust. As for me, I'd learned to be a little more cautious when being asked to go on errands for I knew not what.

My first night under canvas was unforgettable. It was like Christmas Eve, being tucked up in bed, sack all hung up, and waiting for Father Christmas (or Dad) to come and make his delivery. No kid could possibly be expected to sleep through such excitement. There were six boys in each of the three tents we had brought with us. Not totally convinced that his "bags" weren't going to be dispensed with, Derek took out an insurance policy against the process by putting his pyjamas on over the top of his uniform. The rest of us saw no such need. Groundsheets had been laid and secured, and each of us folded our blankets into an envelope – secured by blanket pins - in which we would sleep. Sleeping bags were not *de rigueur* at this time, and anyone who brought one was looked upon as a cissy. By the time that we had laughed and frolicked through the couple of hours that followed "lights out," all envelopes were open and uncontrollable to such an extent that I would have been quite happy to be labelled a cissy just for the sake of the bit of the warmth and comfort afforded by a sleeping bag.

John Kinch – George's eldest son - was a red-headed lad, a couple of years older than me and Keith. As time passed, he became a very good friend and, ultimately, I would be best man at his wedding. But that was for the future. Tonight - and for one night only under canvas - he was to be the root cause of hilarity and shrieks of laughter. At this point, I have to issue you with a health warning, for what I am about to share with you is neither more nor less than silly schoolboy nonsense. Read on at your peril.

Some of our number were on their second or third camp, and had brought torches along. Once they were switched on, leaders in the neighbouring tents took this – quite rightly – as a sign that shenanigans were about to commence. Whether they were just tired, or simply had enough experience to know that boys will be boys, I couldn't say for they never called an early halt. Perhaps they just felt that the sooner we got it all out of our systems, the better it would be for all. In the dark, over in John's corner of the tent, there was some shuffling.

"What's going on over there, Kinchy?"

No answer.

A couple more times the question was asked.

Still no answer.

Someone scrambled for a torch, and focussed the beam on John's sleeping area. As soon as the light picked him out, we almost choked with laughter, for there he was, totally starkers, posing as Atlas with his back to us. Keith – like me, an uncontrollable giggler – went into full forward drive. John began cavorting around the tent, and trying to sit on the heads any unfortunate who got in his way. We shrieked for mercy. Throughout it all, torches ensured that the whole jolly business was silhouetted on the canvas wall of the tent for all outside to see.

Skipper Stevens voice rang out.

"Will you stop that thundering row in there?"

And that called an end to the pantomime and by around one'o'clock, we were all laughed out and sleeping soundly.

Saturday night was the highlight of every Gilwell weekend, far better even than John Kinch's performance. Somewhere around eight'o'clock, as the evening shadows were beginning to fall, every soul in that camping community gathered around a roaring campfire to sing daft – and not so daft – songs, and be entertained by fellow campers, each doing their party piece. In 1931, Ralph Reader, a former Rover Scout trying to make his mark in theatre, had been asked to write a Scout-based amateur variety show to help raise money for a Scout charity. When asked for a title for the review, some kid suggested, "The Gang's all here," and it stuck. Baden-Powell, never slow to see a good thing, asked Ralph to do another show, and a tradition was born. I doubt if there is a member of the Scout and Guide movement who, at one time or another, hasn't taken to the stage to be part of their own Gang Show. Getting around the camp fire on a Gilwell Saturday night was as close as it got to re-creating the spirit of those shows.

This was where I was introduced to what were virtually the anthems of Scouting. Sing these, and everyone knew that you were a Scout. "We're riding along on the Crest of a Wave" was, and remains, a wonderful piece of gung-ho, jolly good chaps all together composition - the sort of song that compels you to link arms, or drape them around your comrades' shoulders. It was dead easy to pick up and I remember being swept along by the sheer euphoria of being out in the open, around a blazing fire, and singing at the top of my voice, with my arms around Derek and Keith's shoulders - mates forever.

But if "Riding Along" reflected the *bonhomie* of Scouting, there was another piece that surely called into question the sanity of every soul who ever sang it. Most startling of all is that it was written in 1920 by Baden-Powell himself. Thank God he got Ralph Reader to do some classier stuff further on down the line. Nevertheless, the piece of nonsense has left an indelible mark on Scouting for close on one hundred years, so perhaps we should let it have its moment. The story goes that the lyrics of "Ging Gang Goolie" were the result of Baden-Powell's recognition that, during the first World Scout Jamboree (1920), there were so many young people from so many countries, he needed a song that made no sense in any language, in order that they could all sing. Involved, as he had been, in the Second Boer War, BP was familiar with the African style and came up with this. Ready? Deep breath, and all together, now!

"Ging gang goolie goolie goolie goolie watcha,
Ging gang goo, ging gang goo.
Ging gang goolie goolie goolie goolie watcha,
Ging gang goo, ging gang goo.

Hayla, oh hayla shayla, hayla shayla, shayla, oh-ho,
Hayla, oh hayla shayla, hayla shayla, shayla, oh.

Shally wally, shally wally, shally wally, shally wally,
Oompah, oompah, oompah, oompah."

Then, as one half of the assembly carried on oompah-ing, the other half sang the whole chant in a round. I can tell you that there wasn't a boy who didn't love singing it, regardless of the fact that we didn't have clue what it was about. I'm not sure that Baden-Powell did either.

I loved camp fires. Even in later years at Troop camps, when we didn't have the benefit of a cast of hundreds as we did at Gilwell, just thirty lads around a fire, singing and doing their party pieces, produced a wonderful atmosphere. We would finish with a short prayer and you felt that God really was in His heaven and that He, too, had enjoyed the evening.

My second night under canvass was far more tranquil than the first. John Kinch had got himself under control, although Derek remained "he of little faith" by going to bed, once again, with his full uniform on underneath his pyjamas. He must have sweated the whole night through for the sake of security. Before we turned in, Skipper Stevens gave us the last instructions of the day.

"Right, now. I want no mucking about like last night. We've got to be up early tomorrow, smart and in uniform for "Scouts' Own."

And with that, we bedded down without another murmur with but one question on our novice minds. What on earth was a "Scouts' Own?"

Sunday needed an early start. The fire was lit and the designated members set about preparing breakfast. As for the rest of us, it was a case of getting ready for kit inspection, the first activity of Scouting that I positively loathed. It would remain the same for as long as I was a member of the organisation. The sides and doors of the tents had to be rolled up and secured in such a way as to get some air into the blessed things. Six lads pitched in together for a couple of nights can have a serious effect on the atmosphere – especially when flavoured by John Kinch's nonsense. A thorough scrutiny of the ground to pick up any vestige of sweet wrappers, and generally sort out my scruffy self. Maybe I was never put together for smartness.

But back to this "Scout's Own" business. In the simplest terms, it was no more than a short religious service, centred around the Christian faith. Made up of a mixture of readings, prayers, reflections, and music, the services were based on themes, such as friendship, using resources wisely, and fairness. Fed, watered, and washed, every boy on the site trooped over to the camp fire area where, not twelve hours ago, we had been ging-gang-goolying. I can't recall anyone kicking up any sort of fuss at having to go along to what might easily have turned into nothing more than an imposed Church parade. Yet short hymns, understandable prayers, and a good "talk" from someone who really understood boys, gave us the chance to laugh or applaud, and take a real interest in everything that was said. I can truthfully say that every "Scout's Own" had something of value for me.

And so to Sunday afternoon when, after lunch, we were let off the leash which, for most of us, meant swimming. Swimmers and non-swimmers alike all headed over to the pool. It wasn't a deep affair and, most certainly, was not heated. But it was nothing short of paradise for everyone who could manage to get into its crowded waters. The de-bagging myth might have long been put to bed, but there was another ritual promised; that first-time campers would be thrown into the pool, fully clothed. I'd just learned to swim and, wearing my sports shirt, shorts, and plimsolls, being chucked into the pool held no fear for me. In fact, I quite relished it. But Derek was not the best of swimmers and did his level best to avoid baptism. I can't remember who it was, but someone in our number managed to persuade everyone else that Derek was not happy about an enforced dip, and mercy was duly shown. It certainly wasn't me because I'd have had him in the drink without a moment's hesitation. Elbow grease and sleeping in your uniform, indeed!

Our last night inevitably brought with it a spirit of anti-climax. We had had a roaring couple of days, but tomorrow we would have to take down the tents, suffer yet another kit inspection, pack our kit bags, and set off for home, arriving back somewhere in mid-afternoon. Having blown ourselves out with mucking about on the previous two nights, sleep came easily, and not without a sense of sadness. In the morning, the usual chores before we loaded George Kinch's lorry with gear and, by lunch time, it was back to Chester Road. My first camp had been wonderful, and I couldn't wait to go again. And go again I most certainly did - many, many times.

As I became a more experienced camper, I always preferred a weekend at Gilwell over and above the longer break that was arranged every summer. Don't get me wrong - summer camps of a week to ten days were certainly fun. But they really took on the role of a replacement of - or supplement to - my family holiday with Mum and Dad. The essence of Scouting was present, but not to the extent that it was during those short, sharp breaks at Gilwell. As soon as you walked through the Gilwell gates onto the hallowed ground, you could positively feel the spirit. Boys from every point of the world's compass turned up, and where else was that on offer for East London boys? In contrast, longer camps with just a handful of your mates around were fun of a different order. I recall Skip taking us to a camp alongside Bread and Cheese Hill, Benfleet, which gave us the chance of a couple of glorious days in "kiss me quick" Southend. The following year, ten days in Wimborne, Dorset (at the time of the Suez crisis, which scared me to a point where I thought I might be called up at age thirteen), were equally fine. Yet, for me, nothing compared to Gilwell Park and the strains of another old Gilwell anthem comes to mind.

I used to be a Scouter,
And a good old Scouter, too.
But now I've finished Scoutering,
I don't know what to do.
I'm growing old and feeble,
And I can Scout no more,
So I'm going to work my ticket if I can.

Back to Gilwell, happy land!
I'm going to work my ticket if I can

It said it all.

We were all taken aback somewhat when, in 1955, Skipper Arthur Stevens announced that he was going to move to Benfleet. I don't think that there was a boy among us who didn't think that Skip would go on forever. Pat was about to be married, and decided that she would remain as Akela, thereby happily retaining the Stevens connection. All of us thought that Skip's retirement was well earned, after all that he had done for the Troop, but he clearly had other ideas. Remarkably, this grand gentleman of Scouting, far from hanging up his woggle, went on to receive Scouting's Order of Merit, whilst running the 2nd Thundersley Troop. Our loss was very much their gain.

With Skip's departure, the crown of leadership came to rest upon the brow of Doc Wiseman. Whilst not being the classic Scouter that his predecessor had been, he worked hard, was certainly committed, and remained popular. It was a tribute to Skip's organisational ability that he had left behind a well-organised, disciplined outfit that ran like clockwork. Camps, badge work, Tuesday nights, special events just rolled effortlessly off the conveyer belt, and everything continued much as before. You could scarcely see the join.

For whatever reason, Doc saw something in me and Keith and by the time that we were fourteen, the pair of us found ourselves as the Stags' Patrol Leader and Second respectively. Alongside the "within nine months" promotion to Seconder whilst I was in the Cubs, becoming a Patrol Leader enhanced my sense of self-worth considerably. But if Keith and I were little more than adequate when it came to teaching and training our charges in matters Scouting, we certainly created a very good spirit in our Patrol. Boys really wanted to join the Stags, because there was always laughter coming from our corner on Tueday nights. One Whitsun Bank Holiday, we decided to take a small group to sample the drug that was Gilwell. So, armed with tents, cooking gear, and rucksacks, we loaded up the trek cart, and set off with half-a-dozen lads for a three-day camp. It proved a fantastic success, as you would expect, with Terry and Ricky Young amongst our number. Keith had even started to talk about taking out a warrant and staying in the movement long term.

We had both been awarded our First Class badges, and boasted a string of proficiency badges on our shirts. For my part, I had the Musician as a result of my rather incompetent fiddle-playing; the Athlete – a walk in the park; the Swimmer – another easily attained award, and the First Aider – stick a bit of plaster on it, mate! I am not sure if the 12th ever was able to boast a Queen's Scout – the

338

highest accolade a boy could hope to achieve in the Movement. However, if one of our number ever had scaled that particular height, he would have had to have done battle with.... the Bushman's Thong. I blush at the very thought, so I'd better explain. We are not talking about a flimsy piece of concealment that the word "thong" describes these days. In fact, my dictionary makes no reference whatsoever to such a piece of underwear. It does, however, talk about "a narrow strip of hide or leather, used as the lash of a whip, or halter, or rein," and that's what we're talking about here.

If a boy were to be awarded the Bushman's Thong, he would have to be truly committed, for this was not an award given away lightly. The standards for most of the badgework have, naturally and properly, changed since my day and, if I am not much mistaken, represent a far harder challenge than they did in 1958. No matter, what we were faced with was hard enough, as far as I was concerned. In addition to having gained your First Class badge, you would also have had to acquire specific proficiency badges, leaning on the distinct emphasis of survival in the outdoors. So, I'm on the back foot for a start, right?

In the grounds of Gilwell Park was a wooden chalet known as the Mallinson Hut, quite sufficient to hold forty lads. For the thirty or so of us who wanted to give this Thong thing a go, monthly training weekends were organised at the Mallinson throughout the winter of 1957 – 1958. Somewhere around the middle of Saturday afternoons, we would cycle to Gilwell to take up our places for the weekend challenges. This time, there was no mucking about with putting tents up and suchlike. This was winter, for goodness' sake, and we were afforded the comparative luxury of camp beds in the warm and dry. Meals were cooked not over an open fire but in the hut facilities, and all we had to do was turn up at table. Much more to my liking, I can tell you.

On a couple of occasions throughout the course, I would arrive a little late for no other reason than that West Ham was at home. This would prove to be the season when the team finally came good, although none of us knew that then. They had begun to bash goals in for a pastime, and there was no way I was going to miss that. As soon as I arrived on site after a forty-five minute cycle ride, I would be bombarded with, "What was the score? Who scored? How did Keeble play? Is Ernie past it?" and suchlike. My later arrival also provided me with another valuable contact with the outside world, having had the chance to watch "Six-Five Special." In December, I was the bearer of the most joyful of joyful tidings.

"Hey, everyone. The Crickets have just put out another record."

"What's it called?"

""Oh Boy." It's fantastic. Better, even, than, "That'll be the Day."

Praise indeed.

Even at what you might suppose was a more mature age of fifteen, the first night in the Hut was ever bit as raucous as any one under canvas. John Kinch wasn't available to entertain but we were well compensated with laid-back Bill Hunt. Bill was a drummer in the 17th East Ham's band, a good looking, fresh-faced lad, with wavy blond hair falling over his forehead. One St. George's Day Parade, as the 12th entourage were waiting to set off, the band marched past, with Bill drumming and chewing gum in a manner that would make Sir Alex Ferguson's mastications appear almost refined. He was captain of an excellent Grammar School football eleven, and would later find local fame as the lead singer of the wonderful Chequers, a rock band that played at the Lotus Ballroom, Forest Gate, in the early 1960s. I liked him immensely – a Jack-the Lad sort of precursor to Harry Redknapp.

The Bushman's Thong events were administered at District level, rather than by an individual troop. As a result, we came under the watchful eyes of Scouters from other localities. My clearest recollection is of Jimmy Green and Charlie Sharp orchestrating affairs. Jimmy, as I have already said, erred on the side of serious, whereas Charlie was a somewhat gentler specimen. Thin, balding, and bespectacled, he could only have been in his early thirties. His spindly legs – despite the winter, we were often dressed in shorts – gave him an almost ornithic appearance, helped (or otherwise) by a thin pointed nose. His hobby, as well as his business, was photography, and he ran a shop in High Street North, somewhere up by Shelley Avenue. By all accounts, he was pretty good at it.

Although many of the serious aspects of that course are now very distant memories, the tree climbing exercise is etched into my memory. Each boy was required to climb a tree to a height of thirty feet (nine meters, give or take an inch, centimetre, or what have you). Heights were never my strong suit and if I were to have any chance of success, there was going to be some gritting of teeth and closing of eyes! I'd looked forward to it not one bit and the night for which the escapade was planned was far from ideal. In the middle of January with the freezing cold making everything both slippery and hazardous, there we all were, lined up alongside a massive oak. Just to prove it could be done, one of the older boys was assisted up onto a lower branch and, from there, made his way effortlessly to the point agreed as being thirty feet above ground. With no less effort, he nonchalantly made the reverse trip, hopping back onto *terra firma*, and announcing, "That's the way to do it." Quotes from "Punch and Judy" I did not need.

The line of boys snaked slowly forward and, one by one, lads were hoisted onto the branch to begin the ascent. I began to understand a little of what it must have been like to be lined up before a firing squad. This was, I knew, the very last thing on God's earth that I wanted to do. In fact, one false step and it *could* have been the very last thing that I did on God's earth! But what can you do when all your mates had taken on the challenge and, in most cases, got up and down with minimum fuss, resulting in a tick on their card under the section marked "Tree climbing." But now I am next in line, and there is no backing out. What am I going to do or say? Do I cry and go home to Mum? Or do I take my little courage in both hands and shin up the thing? Oh, well. Here we go.

The first part was not as difficult as I had been expecting. There were sufficient branches to hold onto, and my rubber slippers enabled me to get a reasonable grip on the cold, slippery, wood. Before you could say, "Derby for England," I had reached the point where I could justifiably say that I had climbed a tree to a height of thirty feet. However, what goes up must come down, as the saying goes, and I hadn't taken into full and proper consideration just how hard it might be to do the return journey. Going up, the silvery moon had provided a silhouette of branches, making it easy to see the next logical step. But coming down was an entirely different matter and, from the off, I was in trouble. In the dark, there was no way that I could see the safest place for me to put my feet. In such circumstances, there is but one thing to do…..PANIC! So I did.

"I can't get down. I can't get down."

Just in case there was any lack of understanding at base camp, sheer panic spiced my message and I abandoned the old "pure in thought word, and deed" principle.

"I can't get down! I bloody well can't get down!"

The statement heralded a tortuous descent, what with all the conflicting instructions being called out to me.

"Go to the left – no, to the right."

"Put your left foot on the branch just below the one that you've just moved from."

Torches were shone in my direction and I had a taste of how a German paratrooper, caught in the branches, must have felt. When, ultimately, I reached the ground safely, I resolved that I would never try such a fool thing again. And, by the grace of God, I never have. Despite this embarrassment, I truly loved those weekends at the Mallinson. It so happened that neither Keith nor myself managed to achieve the Bushman's Thong standard, but did it really matter? We had had a wonderful time, made even more friends, and continued to build a wonderful friendship, grounded in laughter.

By the time that I reached fifteen, or thereabouts, to my modest astonishment, it was deemed that I might very well make a leader of some sort, or another. Akela Pat Stevens, having married and left the area, had been replaced by Bob Penfold, a lovely guy, just a couple of years older than me. He had the presence required for the role and asked me if I would like to help him with the Wolf Cub pack. In this environment, I learned something about myself, namely that, for whatever reason, a lot of kids liked my company. I'd never worked on it, neither had I been particularly conscious of it. No, I think it could only have been nothing more than that I was developing into a bloke who genuinely liked young people, and wanted them to have the same fun growing up as had been afforded to me. I've always wanted that for kids.

The pack had maintained its numbers over the years by adhering to the same principles and tests that had faced me some five years earlier. There were some magnificent characters in that little group that I recall with much fondness. As I write, I am looking at a group photograph of twenty-five Cubs, with Bob and myself as bookends for the back row. In the front, little Freddie Hannaford was what you might have described as a loveable urchin. A perpetual smiler was Freddie, and there wasn't a single boy who didn't like him. It might have been because he was one of the smallest of our number but, if that was the case, it could only have been part of the story. He was just such an honest, straight-as-they-come kid, that if you were ever annoyed with him, the first question you asked yourself was, "What am I doing wrong?" Bless you, Freddie, wherever you are.

Just along from Freddie, is young Wakefield. For the life and shame of me, I can't recall his Christian name, but maybe that doesn't matter, as he was always referred to as "Wakefield." This was a comedian in the making and whatever prank he played, it was always done with a deadpan expression. He was no fool, though, for on his cap there are not one but two stars. Closer examination of the photograph confirms him as the only boy able to claim that distinction.

Next to me, almost shoulder to shoulder is a lad I shall never forget. Whenever Bob and I took the boys into the playground for football, I ashamedly confess that there was no easing off for me. By this time, my love for football was on a continous upward curve and, as in many other areas of my life, always played to win. Quite why it was, I don't know, but there was this lad who always seemed to be on the opposite side to me. He was reasonably easy to beat – after all, I was nearly sixteen, and he was no more than eight or nine. Yet no sooner than I had beaten him, the next player to confront me was – yes, you've guessed it – my eight-year old nemisis. No matter how many times I thought I had him beaten, back he came, and I have to own up that I never truly had the better of him. John McDowell – for it was he - went on to make around 300 appearances for West Ham's first team, not least significant a place in the victorious eleven that lifted the F A Cup at Wembley, in 1975. I'm so proud of that picture. It represents the closest I ever got to being photographed in a West Ham team line-up!

Having been initially attracted to uniformed organisations through marching bands, the highlight of my year was always the St. Georges Day Parade. It was a grand occasion when Scouts, Cubs, Guides, and Brownies from all over the area congregated to march on the great Methodist Central Hall, alongside the Town Hall. From all points of the compass they came, marching from their mother churches to meet one of the two bands that led the Parade. Those of us of 12th East Ham persuasion met up with the Girl Guides at Chester Road Church, smart as whistles, before marching down Chester Road, along Shrewsbury Road to Plashet Grove, to join the gathering Scout and Guide throng outside the Presbyterian Church, at the top of East Avenue. The 17th East Ham was based there, and it was their band (featuring Bill Hunt) that we followed. As we marched to take our place in the Parade, we passed the drummers going through their warm up. It put an extra spring in my stride, knowing that, in just a few minutes, the whole bally lot of us would be swaggering to the beat and bugles down High Street North to the Town Hall. Parents and idle bystanders lined the way, and applauded as we all marched past. I still hankered after the opportunity to play in a band, but I guess it was never to be.

Of course, we were there on serious business too, and the Superintendent Minister of the Church, the Reverend George Pollard, annually took us through the formalities of hymn singing, readings, and prayers. He must have given a sermon but, for the life of me, I can't remember a word uttered and, with all due respect, it was probably nowhere near as good as anything that I heard at "Scouts Own." My recollection of the Reverend Pollard is that he had a bit of a twang to his voice that put me in mind of dear old Father Butterfield, of Rutland Road fame. I'm probably doing him an injustice, for I do believe that he reached a couple of positions of real significance in Methodism. But throughout most of the service, my mind was focussed on being out in the sunshine again with that band bashing and blowing eight bells out of the drums and bugles, parading around the Town Hall, in front of what was always a substantial crowd.

Save for those couple of years in primary school, education and recreational activities had remained on a strictly segregated basis, and it was Scouting that gave me my first proper introductions to the fair sex. Let me fantasise for a moment or two. The Guide uniform, comprising blue blouses and navy skirts were a perfect blend, along with such scarves and badges as were appropriate. I can never recall seeing a girl who didn't look twice as good when dressed in this smart, oh, so right uniform. One of my trainspotting fraternity had an elder sister, Pat, who used to go to the Full Gospel Hall. She also belonged to a Guide company and I first noticed her at one of the Parades. She looked so attractive, and I was constantly badgering my mate about her, what she was interested in, and whether or not she might like me. In my own little way, I guess I was besotted, so much so that, at age thirteen, I plucked up courage to write and ask if she would come out with me. Pat was just under three years older than me - would this indicate an early preference for the older woman, I ask myself? Anyhow, bless her, she agreed and for a string of Sunday mornings, the pair of us spent time walking through Wanstead Park, each as embarrassed as the other. Bless her, Pat put up with me until I came to realise and accept that I was more irritation than flirtation, and the little *affaire de couer* fizzled out.

With Scouts and Guides continuing to come into at least monthly contact with each other through church parades, it became increasingly easier to start conversations and make friends. Those relationships started to become increasingly important and, given the choice of a Queen's Scout badge, or talking to a pretty girl, I would have taken the girl every time. Shortly after Pat, I swooned for Betty, Doc's daughter, and looked for any old excuse to go round to see my Scoutmaster, although I am pretty sure that he saw through my little game. For sure, Betty did. She was a good four months older than me and, in those days, such things mattered. If a boy was younger than the object of his desire, he may as well throw in the towel before the show got on the road. Well, I did my level best and even Doc suggested to his daughter that it would be a good idea if she allowed me to take her to a football match. Gosh, talk about how to show a girl a good time. Betty would have none of it, and that was that.

Margaret was a very attractive brunette whose grandmother lived in Walpole Road, next door to Derek.Each Saturday morning, she would travel the few miles from her home to do her grandmother's shopping. At the time, I was striving for my Grade IV piano certificate whilst, at the same time, scratching around as to how I might impress Margaret when she came down the street. Suddenly, it hit me. In the summer of 1958, there was this massive hit record by the Four Preps – an American college quartet – called "Big Man." All about a bloke with too much faith in his hold on his girl, suddenly discovering that any one can be given the old "heave-ho!" The introduction was a fabulous classical piano riff, all thump and arpeggios, before the boys got into their vocal stride. Everyone loved it and, at one of the Guide/Scout get-togethers, Margaret told me it was her favourite record. So what's a boy to do? I'll tell you exactly what he does. He goes straight down to the Green Street music shop, buys a copy of the sheet music, and practices until he's got it note perfect. And that's just what I did. Every Saturday morning, around at 10'o'clock, I would be looking out of the bay window of No.7, waiting for Margaret to appear. As soon as she turned the corner, I rushed to the keyboard, and "big-manned" for all I was worth. What a plonker!

A few weeks later, at Church Parade, she came over to where I was involved in a teenage huddle.

"Steve, why is it that, every time I go past your house on a Saturday morning, you're always playing, "Big Man?"

Err. Ummm. I could hardly tell the truth and look silly in everyone's eyes. So I simply stopped playing the piece, period. Even though that put a stop to the little business, Margaret remained a friend in our ever-expanding circle. On my fifteenth birthday,

Mum allowed me to invite some friends around for the evening. The net result was a jolly gang of us made up of Keith, Ken Hinds, Jack Penfold, Margaret and her younger brother David, Ian Fulcher, Ann (who lived next door to Jack), Lesley, and Daryl (from Lincoln Road), all meeting together for lemonade, biscuits, chatter, and music. I have re-established contact with some of that happy breed and, many years later, Ann recalled how I spent the evening constantly playing some Buddy Holly record or another, although she couldn't remember which one. Let me help you, Ann – it was "Peggy Sue."

As I moved beyond my 15th birthday, Scouting began to take on a slightly different purpose in my life. Friendships cultivated on Tuesday nights, at Gilwell, and at Church Parades continued, with Christmas parties and concerts added to the mix. At the 1957 Christmas party, John Kinch impressed the lot of us with his amazing ability to dance – and I'm not talking slow, slow, quick, quick, slow, - although he could do that as well. John was the first bloke that I ever saw jiving with real intent and class, and everyone envied him. Girls lined up to partner him and if the rest of us had only taken the opportunity to learn a few steps, we might have stood a better chance of holding some female hands, rather than staying in our corner, grinning wallflowers all. Scouting, for me, was moving on from camping, knots, campfires, and the like. It became the vehicle that brought me into contact with girls and my little social life began to take on a very different and much rosier hue.

Now denuded of the violin and kitted up with a guitar, music and our little skiffle group were making a minor star of me. I still enjoyed my running and managed to win the Scouts Mile at the District Sports Day. Yet there comes a time for all Scouts and Guides to make a decision. Either you fade gracefully from the scene, or you take out a warrant and become a leader. In my case, I followed the former route, and I shall tell you a little more about that in the coming pages.

Full time work was little more than a year away for me, and moving on from Scouts in no way devalued my opinion of the organisation. It had provided me with much social and spiritual nourishment, and an ever-widening group of friends. They, in turn, opened other doors for me and if ever a fifteen-year old was truly happy with his lot, then I was that fifteen-year old.

I find it worthwhile hearing what Arthur Stevens Jr, Skip's son, has to say about matters, some fifty years on.

At the 12th, I had a great time. Quite apart from the badgework – astronomers, plumbers, etc., - I loved knots, splicing, producing a fancy lanyard, turkshead woggles, etc. I also produced a newsletter by means of hectographic jelly and ink. It would print about fifty copies. At camp, I used to rig up crystal sets and tent-to-tent telephones, using ex-Army moving coil headphones. No batteries were required for any of these things.

There were years when we had many camping weekends at Gilwell Park, walking the ten miles from East Ham with a trek cart. I recall seeing from our campsite on The Quick (a sloping field which looked towards the King George V reservoir), all the many celebration fires lit around Chingford on the occasion of VJ-Day 1946 at the end of the war. At those camps, we also took a powerful lamp (ex-Army) a good half a mile away from the site and sent messages back using Morse. During the day, we would use semaphore flags. Somehow, we conjured up both challenging and exciting things, often out of very little. I was thrilled with my first success at baking cakes in a biscuit-tin oven.

Mind you, we had good discipline. Once, my dad and I ran a camp for fifty boys for two weeks on a field belonging to Mr. Coleman, the butcher on Bread and Cheese Hill, Benfleet. We used to get all the gear and us up in a large covered truck. No camp beds (except my dad's), no primus stoves, no other adult help. Bet no one would manage that today!

Probably not.

I have watched with interest and some little involvement at how the Scout and Guide movements have developed. In my opinion, it has adapted quite splendidly and, in a changing world, continues to embrace and include even more young people, all striving toward the best standards of friendship and harmony. Long may that continue and, with a man of the quality of Bear Grylls as Chief Scout, you would hardly bet against it.

DYB, DYB, DYB!

CHAPTER ELEVEN

ONLY SIXTEEN – AN EPILOGUE

"You know, Steve. I think I'd like to be sixteen forever."
Keith it was, who made that observation. It has lived with me ever since.

The first sixteen years of my life had been to die for. I'd had the best of schooling, meaningful spiritual education, heard magnificent music, made fabulous friends, been influenced by perfect role-model teachers, and West Ham United had flavoured the whole jolly cake. If that were not enough to be going on with, I had parents who loved me beyond reason, alongside relatives who were always watching out for me. I would never have wished to be raised anywhere other than Upton Park, no, not for a king's ransom. As if that were not enough, a new dimension was added to my life when I realised that blokes who went out with girls were not really "cissies." Rather, I envied the most successful ones and wanted desperately to join their number. It is my joy and pleasure to record that Keith, Tony, and I jolly well did!

"You know, Steve. I think I'd like to be sixteen forever."
But it had all started so gently.

It happened during my pre-school days, when I was still in the daily tender care of Mum. Not necessarily my favourite way of passing time, but when she went shopping, I had to go along with her. In Green Street, just off the corner of Crescent Road, stood Caters, a grocery and general provision store, where we used to go to buy cheese.

The good Lord alone knows why, but I was totally entranced by the simple method by which a slab of cheese was cut for the customers. A substantial block of cheese would be placed on a board that had a wire secured to one side, and a handle on the other end. The assistant would rest the wire across the cheese and, by pulling it taut and downward, lop off a piece sufficient to meet the customer's requirements. Don't ask me why this process fascinated me – it just did.

What I can tell you, however, is that I was far more fascinated by the pretty young girl who used to conduct this operation. Her name was Millie, and she always smiled and said something nice to me when I was in the shop. Being about four at the time, I can't recall having any particular designs on Millie, but that didn't stop a nice warm feeling in my heart whenever I saw her. A slab of cheese and a length of wire can turn a young man's head, you know.

Mum and I were walking back home through Crescent Road when, for the first of many times in my life, I wore my heart on my sleeve.

"Mum, you know that Millie? She's a real sweetie-pie, isn't she?"

Short pause to check that she's heard me right before Mum roared out laughing.

"Where on earth did you hear someone say that?" she asked me.

Well, I didn't have a clue. It was just something I felt, but didn't understand. All the way home, Mum chuckled and, from then on, every visitor, relative, or sundry hobbledehoy who passed the gate, heard the story. And it got worse.

On our next visit to Caters, I was a little reluctant to go into the shop. Oh, grief! What if Mum told Millie what I had said? Please, Mum, no. Over at the cheese section of the store, Millie was waiting, cheese, board, and wire at the ready. Whilst she was in mid cut, Mum looked down at me.

"Tell Millie what you called her the other day, Stephen."

Oh, Lord! I want to die, crawl under somewhere, never to be seen again. The embarrassment welled up within me and I'm sure I must have turned a shade of scarlet. I was hot and cold all at the same time. Mum, how could you?

"Sweetie Pie, he called you, Millie. Isn't that lovely?"
Well, Millie was obviously impressed. She was probably only in her late teens or early twenties, and for a little boy to say something as sweet as that, well, it wouldn't happen too often. Bigger boys might say it, but a little four-year old?
She smiled.
"That's really sweet of you, Stephen," she said to the ever decreasing me.
I couldn't wait to get out of the rotten place.

On close analysis of that very early encounter with womankind, it is scarcely any wonder that my early teenage years would find me extremely shy in female company. I resolved that, if ever another "sweetie pie" came along, I would keep my trap firmly shut. Shortly after my romantic nature had been held up for public scrutiny, Millie disappeared off the face of planet Derby. Perhaps I had scared her away. But you can't keep a good man down and, blow me if other "sweetie pies" didn't come into my life at regular intervals.

Two of the Guides – Lesley and Daryl – lived in Lincoln Road, and Keith and I started to visit their home often – with their parents always present, it has to be said. As the pair of us continued on our road to puberty, the girls introduced us to their stunningly beautiful fourteen-year old neighbour, Jean. Talk about smitten. Jean's dark hair, pencil-slim figure, beautiful face, radiated an elegance that would knock any bloke sideways. The five of us became very good friends.

Encouraged by her father, Jean had become a very competent ballroom dancer by age fourteen. One Sunday, her parents thought it would be a jolly good idea if they took Keith and me to a competition that Jean had entered, at the Streatham Ballroom, South London. Frankly, I would have gone anywhere that Jean asked me to, but I was hardly ready for what greeted us. All these "mummy's darlings" – not you, Jean! - going through their paces whilst the audience yelled and hooted in such a fashion as to make a Millwall riot appear like a line of devout and orderly

Catholics waiting for a blessing from the Pontiff! This was, most certainly, not for me.

However, remembering the impact that John Kinch's dancing demonstrations at the Scout parties had made, Keith and I reasoned that if we were to stand any chance with Jean, I would have to come to terms with the old, "slow, slow, quick, quick, slow." After all, if you couldn't dance, how were you going to make it with the opposite sex? You go up to some pretty girl, smile and ask her if you could have the pleasure of the next dance.

"Certainly, as long as you can find a partner."

Apart from the refusal, the last thing you wanted was an acceptance, only to find out is that neither of you had a clue how to put one foot in front of the other, much less in time with music. So, it was off to the Magenta Ballroom, on Romford Road, with the pair of us.

Friday night was music night at the Magenta. I had hoped that Jean might come along to give us a bit of moral support – but no. It was going to be a case of every man for himself. Entering the dance hall, the first thing I noticed was how the boys were lined up against one wall, and the girls congregated directly opposite. For most teenage boys, the full range of their dancing capabilities was stretched by "Knees up Mother Brown" or, if they were really classy, "The Gay Gordons," a Scottish-flavoured little item akin to "The Lambeth Walk." At least you managed to get your arms around your partner in this one. So we were, it has to be said, a little nervy about the whole set-up, although our unease was offset somewhat by the sight of some really pretty potential partners.

Dutifully doing our stuff, we paid full attention to the dance master, following him through the steps of the waltz. What a plonker I felt, stepping around the room solo, counting "one, two, three," before being allowed to take a lady of my choice and do the thing for real. The girls had to endure pretty much the same process. However, I wasn't one to give up too quickly, and I persevered for about four weeks, during which time I came to an early realisation that Fred Astaire I was not. With a struggle, Keith and I just about managed a waltz, whereas the quickstep was a shade too quick for either of us and, after about three or four months, we gave the whole thing up as a bad job. In reality, I don't think Jean expected very much more from us, but I was to remain in her debt for a very long time, as she introduced me to my very first real girlfriend.

Janet was one of Jean's very best friends and lived just a few doors down from Lesley. She often walked past when we were in one of our little post school huddles, and always greeted us. From the start, I thought she was really nice. She had a lovely smile and her eyes sparkled with fun. Black hair and a cuddly figure, she was the sort of girl that you couldn't help smiling back at. Well, at least, I couldn't. Grammar School girls wore a predominantly green uniform, whereas those from Plashet Secondary Modern, situated directly opposite the Grammar, favoured blue. Janet was from Plashet and a good job, too, as I thought blue suited her far more than green ever would have done. Word on the street was that Janet's dad was an enthusiastic member of the St. John Ambulance Brigade and that his daughter was similarly committed.

One afternoon, early in October 1958, Jean let me in on a secret such as had never found its way down to my eardrums in my life up to this point.

"Steve, you know my friend Janet? Well, she thinks that you are really nice."

Oh, gosh! What does a sensitive fifteen-year old do in such circumstances? No girl had ever given me the slightest indication that I might be, well, "nice." Shall I giggle? Blush? Oh, come on, Derby. Stop messin' about.

"So, Jean….do you think that if I asked her out, she might say "yes."

She smiled.

"I'm almost certain that she would. Why don't you call and ask her?"

I've just realised how long ago all of this took place. Nowadays, youngsters go around with electronic communication packages jammed to their earholes. You can scarcely get their attention as they text all and sundry about God alone knows what. But in 1958, if you had a telephone in your house, you could count yourself amongst the elite. Neither Janet nor I were in that illustrious company, so I decided on a knock at her door, and open confrontation. The very next Monday, in the darkness of early evening, I cycled over to Lincoln Road and knocked at her door. Through the frosted glass, I could make out someone coming along the passageway, but it wasn't Janet. It was her mum! I managed to mix courtesy with terror as she opened the door.

"Hello. Can I help you?"

"I'm so sorry to trouble you, but is Janet in?" I asked......whimpered, rather.

Janet was hovering just behind her mum, and I wondered if Jean had tipped her off about my impending visit. I'll bet she did. Well, I won't go into the details, but I have to say that Janet's "Yes" gave me one of the biggest thrills of my near sixteen years of life. The *Duchess of Atholl* could have steamed up Lincoln Road, whistle blowing for all it was worth with "fourteen coaches on," and I wouldn't have noticed. It heralded the beginning of four months of a lovely friendship.

Janet had a gentle sense of humour, and her parents were a dream. So caring and funny, they made me feel very much at home. When Janet came to my house, for the umpteenth time it was proved to me that I had parents of exceptional quality. They accepted her totally as though she was their own daughter and, after all, this was no more than a little teenage romance. And I want to say emphatically that the pair of us never stepped over a single line of convention. Hugs and kisses, yes. Anything else was strictly off of the menu. I don't think the pair of us cared – we just had too much fun being in each other's company. When the relationship came to an end – as most teenage relationships do - I experienced my very first, real heartbreak.

By the end of the first week in February 1959, I had a sense that things were not quite the same as they had been and, perhaps, Janet was not as happy as she had been earlier. Could there be someone else? I would have to face reality at some time or another and, when I built up the courage to ask if all was well or not, she gently told me the truth. In fact, I gave her the bullet to fire on one cold night, outside the same front door where, just four months earlier, I had been so elated.

"Janet, can I ask if you still want to go out with me?"

A short pause before she looked up at me - eyes full of integrity - and simply said the dreaded word.

"No."

We parted on the very best of terms and, as I rode back home, I mused on how, just a few days earlier, Buddy Holly had been killed. The loss of both Janet and Buddy made it a bloody rotten week and it took me some time to get over both events.

Today, we live in a sex-saturated environment, entirely at odds with the time in which I grew up, and I truly can't believe that we are any the better for it. Looking back, there is always the temptation for those of my generation to assume that nothing untoward was going on in our days of innocence. I doubt if that was reality. Del would fill me in with details of his escapades – some of which astonished me. Whether or not they were true, isn't for me to judge, much less record. In those days, there was more than a vestige of respectability about relationships. Marriage was, in the eyes of most, "until death do us part" – better or worse, richer or poorer, in sickness and in health. Having been grounded in this thinking, I find it hard to accept that it has become unexceptional for unmarried couples to co-habit, and unfaithful married partners to produce offspring outside of wedlock. This, and more, has become part of life's rich tapestry, disconnected as we are from that old restrictive regime. Family trees are becoming harder to trace, and kids will have, do have, brothers and sisters all over the shop. And are we all so much better for it? I think not! I grew up with the concept of marrying one woman, for life, under the terms that the marriage vows set. It provided such a clear mind set for me that, as soon as I realised that girls did more than dance backwards and put both legs in the same trouser leg, I never courted a girl without it crossing my mind that she might be the one that I married. As a result, despite girls being very much a part of my friendships from age fourteen onwards, I was never constantly switching from one to another. The girls I "went out with," for even the shortest time were few, and I bow to each and every one of them. If you ever read this, girls, I remember you all, and not one of you was less than wonderful. There! Now I've said it.

"You know, Steve. I think I'd like to be sixteen forever."

Most Saturday or Sunday evenings, I would cycle to Keith's, at No. 375 Sherrard Road, when we would share teenage thoughts, dreams, and fantasies to our hearts' content. His parents were a fabulous couple.

Harry Hollington had served in the Navy during wartime with some distinction. Ivy, Keith's mum, was a soul of immense good nature and one of the few who had the measure of Keith's laid-back humour. The pair of them produced a classic one winter's evening.

Mr. and Mrs. Hollington had decided to do a bit of ceiling repair in their front lounge, whilst Keith and I stayed in the back dining room, lounging about and listening to music. About half way through the evening, a shriek came from the decorating department, followed by the unmistakable sound of Mrs. Hollington, laughing fit to bust. A clearly exasperated Mr. Hollington supplied his own observation.

"Oh, Gawd, Ivy. What 'ave you done?"

Laughter continued to reign supreme. Keith never moved a muscle, but simply continued to lay back in his armchair, non-plussed. As for me, I was a bit concerned.

"What do you think has happened in there, Keith?" I asked.

He shook his head, and shrugged his shoulders.

"Probably the mum has put her foot in a bucket of whitewash."

Keith often referred to Mrs. Hollington as "the mum," yet never in a disrespectful way.

Anyhow, all things come to him who waits and, accompanying the laughter, we heard the sound of footsteps coming down the hall. The door opened and there stood Mrs. Hollington, still laughing, with her left foot covered in whitewash! What could I do but join her in the laughter. Keith's prediction had been spot on.

"Don't walk it all down the hall, Ivy. Blimey, what a bleedin' mess it all is."

As for Keith, clairvoyant extraordinaire, he just sat there knowingly, making no other contribution other than prolonging his listening pleasure.

And listening pleasure we most certainly had. In a very short space of time, the Lonnie Donegan, Vipers skiffle fare had come a very long way – a very long way indeed. The pair of us became totally besotted with the records of that era as 1958 and 1959 produced a veritable tsunami of magnificent music that has lived on to this day. Buddy Holly, the Everly Brothers, and Elvis Presley were well established, of course, but we could never have done without Fats Domino, Sam Cooke, Ricky Nelson, Jerry Lee Lewis, Chuck Berry, Connie Francis, the Platters, Ray Charles, Little Richard – the list is endless, and there were still another couple of months to go before the Drifters and Ben E. King came onto the scene! There was more to the records than being just a disc, providing (as they did) balm for the soul when you had no chance of making progress with the lady of your dreams. Bobby Darin's "Dream Lover" helped out in that situation. At the other end of the scale, if you'd had the emotional carpet whipped from under your feet by your heart's desire, Ricky Nelson's "Poor Little Fool" was about as good as it got. It would not be overstating the case to say that that music was the soundtrack of our teenage lives.

Keith had a reel-to-reel tape recorder and regularly taped radio shows for us to listen to together. The technology of those days was a million miles from what is available to youngsters today. Our evening listening provided us with a musical education, as we heard and learned about other styles and artists. Keith tuned in to traditional jazz, the clarinet of the great George Lewis, and the blues of Big Bill Broonzy. As for me, although I was still a pop and rock merchant, band line-ups became my specialist subject in which, ultimately, I like to think, I became an expert. For sure, the foundation stones of my love for music were being very firmly laid down for what has resulted in my very catholic – some might say slightly eccentric - taste of today.

One night, Keith greeted me in a state of high dudgeon.

"Come and listen to this. It's fantastic!"

One of Keith's relatives had given him a scratchy old 78 shellac, "Ain't it grand to be bloomin' well dead?" by Leslie Saronie, recorded in 1933. It was about a bloke who dreamed about his own funeral and the less than dignified attitude of all and sundry that had bothered to attend his bowing out. We creased to hear Leslie moaning about the children laughing, the neighbours being delighted, and – worst of all - the missus bloomin' well laughing! On and on it went, the pair of us laughing more every time we played the thing.

"You know, Steve. I think I'd like to be sixteen forever."

In October 1957, Mum and Dad had been wooed by this new-fangled notion of owning their own home. They had taken a shine to No. 10 Hollington Road, just off High Street South, beyond Central Park, on the way to Woolwich. Having raised the requisite finance, they invested it in purchasing the property lock, stock and barrel for the grand sum of £1,200. £1,200? Can you believe that? My life had such stability about it that I thought things would never be the same and, inevitably, they weren't. By the time that the summer of 1959 rolled around, I like to think that I had evolved into a little gentleman – of sorts. Playing in the street was long past and Scouting had all but fallen off the agenda. Trainspotting was no more than a pleasant memory, although I never could resist waiting by a bridge if I heard a whistle. I might not have noted the numbers anymore, but the magic was still there. *No.35023 Holland-Afrika Line; No.35024 East Asiatic Company; 35025 Brocklebank Line.....*

If I am honest – and I think I am - I was more than a little disappointed to have only obtained four "Ordinary Level" passes, the coconuts knocked off their stand being English Language, English Literature, French, and History. I was lined up to start at National Provincial Bank, 22 London Road, Barking, at the end of September 1959, so I enrolled at the local college and, under my own steam, added Mathematics to the list. I mean to say, you can't work in a bank not knowing how many beans make five, can you? Can you? I would go on to gain a degree in banking, hold down a few pretty responsible jobs and, now, people pay me good money to give them the benefit of my advice on people management. I wonder how many would have forecast those achievements, modest as they might appear, back in Shaftesbury Road days?

In August 1959, Keith and I took a week's holiday at Atherstone Bay Holiday Camp, on the Isle of Wight. The pair of us went out as virgins and, one week later, returned home in precisely the same pristine condition. But that is not the point I wish to make. That holiday was very much an affirmation that we were big boys now, young men, if you will. Within myself, I felt well placed for whatever was to come my way. My wonderful parents had set me a sterling example and I had accumulated cousins and friends – blokes and girls - to die for. Miss Churchill and Mr. Jones, at Shaftesbury, and Eric Cryer at the Grammar had set me up very nicely on the academic front. Spiritually, Dan Crick was probably unaware of the massive impact that he had had on my life even if, at that stage, I was taking a sabbatical from church. West Ham, against all the logic and conviction of their followers, were playing in the top league, and doing quite nicely, thank you very much. General consensus was that I was a far from bad goalkeeper and, at age fifteen, played a number of reserve games for Uncle Sid's soccer team – Burnham United - with men several years my senior. Music and guitars were becoming synonymous with my name. Yeah, being sixteen was wonderful and things could hardly get much better.

And yet......they did. One August evening, in the middle of a miles too long summer holiday, Keith and myself were wasting time with Tony, round at his house. Suddenly, from out of left field, Tony made a proposal.

"Here, Stevie, Keith. Why don't we join that youth club at the Methodist Church, in High Street South? There'll be some terrific girls there. It'll be wonderful."

So we did.........and there were.........and it was!

By the close of the year, the three of us had become part of a new and happy breed. I never regretted that decision for, over the next three years, amazing things would happen to me in the company of some of the very best people I would ever meet. I wouldn't have missed any of it – or them - for a pension.

CHAPTER TWELVE

FRIENDS REUNITED

Fifty years have passed since Keith made that wish – to which I subscribed so fully – about being sixteen forever. Since that time, much of what I hoped for has been achieved in my life, and then some. A very happy marriage to Ann has produced two terrific children who, in turn, have provided us with four splendid grandchildren. Working life, by and large, has been pretty good to me, and commitment to my Christian faith has proved a bedrock, standing me in very good stead throughout a number of scrapes over the years.

In 1990, a re-union of past members of High Street South Methodist Church Youth Club brought back into my life many of the people that I had journeyed with. Thank God, after our thirty year sabbatical, a host of us elected to stay in touch. Over the ensuing years, other names have come into the frame, detective work done, and more friends added to the list. I have always believed that, back in the late 50s and early 60s, we must have done something right.

The brown envelope delivered to my home in December 2001, had my name and address printed on it boldly – and badly - too far to the left hand side. It looked as though it had been produced by one of those John Bull printing sets of the 1950s. By the time that you had done all the typesetting, you might as well have written the blessed thing freehand anyway. The postmark "Romford Mail Centre" provided no clue as to who might have sent it, and the envelope bears witness to the fact that I opened it carelessly. Instead of a neat cut across the top, it is torn across the face.

I took out the single sheet content and there, before my very eyes, was a photograph (that I instantly recognised) of the Boy Scouts of the 12th East Ham, at their 1954 summer camp at Thundersley, in what was then the heart of the Essex countryside.

Effortlessly, I put a name to them all. On the back row, Ollie Chester, John "The Hat" Barrett, George Tyler, Tony Warren, "Skipper" Arthur Stevens, Eddie Harris, and John Kinch. Crouched in the front row were John Cole, along with the "Walpole Holy Trinity" of Dickie Culver, Derek, and me. Typically, Derek has his arm in plaster, orthopaedic damage often being part and parcel of his way of life. How young we all look. Ollie and George were heroes of mine when I first joined the Scouts and, at the time, seemed years older than me. Now I saw them for what they were - little lads, probably not much older than fourteen.

On the back of the photograph, a short message;-

I WONDER HOW MANY OF US ARE STILL ALIVE? CAMPING AUGUST 1954 THUNDERSLEY ESSEX "HAPPY DAYS"

I scrutinised the envelope to find some clue as to the sender, for there was no accompanying letter. This omission would have been a rotten trick were it not for the fact that I would have put money on whose handiwork this was, for I was sure that there was only one person who would have sent this to me. Somewhere out there, Del Fletcher was still working his magic, stirring his cauldron, chanting his spells....but where? What was his address? What was his telephone number?

When Ann and I married in 1965, we rented the upstairs flat at No. 14 Walpole. Derek and his wife, Edna, took the downstairs accommodation. When our first child was on the way, we moved to a larger home, as the opportunity for more space just couldn't be passed up. Shortly after that, something horrible happened - Derek and Edna parted. What on earth went wrong, I couldn't begin to guess. Edna was lovely and I wondered if, had we had stayed a little longer at the flat, Ann and I might have been able to have had some influence with them. Maybe. Maybe not. What I do know is that, from that point, Derek and I drifted and, for over thirty years, I had no knowledge of his whereabouts.

It was somewhere around September 2002. I had recently set up my own business and the little venture often found me working late in my office. One particular evening, somewhere around 8'o'clock, the telephone rang. The likelihood was that this was just another one of those callers offering to save me five pounds a year if I would but switch electricity/gas suppliers. Or perhaps I'd won an overseas holiday for two. On the other hand, I could be wrong and there might be some potential business up for grabs, so I slipped into my standard telephone-answering mode.

"Good evening. Steve Derby here. How can I help you?"

There was a pause. Damn! It **is** a nuisance call. I'll put the blessed receiver down. But before I could do so, a voice.

"'Ullo. Is that Stephen Derby?"

I'd owned up to that much already, but courtesy is always the best policy, and this could be a really big lead. Best not blow it by being lippy.

"Yes, this is Steve Derby. What can I do for you?"

A deep East End voice replied.

"Do you know who this is?"

God, the voice was so familiar - one of those awful moments when you dreaded saying you didn't know who was speaking in case it was someone you'd been talking to only hours, or days, beforehand. But, for the life of me, a name wouldn't come.

"I'm sorry. I'm sure that I know your voice but I can't pin it down."

Remaining incognito, my caller persevered with his game.

"D'ya wanna clue?"

"Go on, then."

An intake of breath at the other end of the line before the caller burst into song, roughly in tune...only roughly, mind.

> *"Ging gang goooley-goooley-gooley-gooley watcha,*
> *Ging gang goo, ging gang goo."*

It was that piece of nonsense that we'd all learned at Gilwell. I'd sung it around campfires in Gilwell Park, Wimborne, and....Thundersley. Oh, Lord. Thundersley! Instantly, my suspicions were confirmed and I knew, beyond doubt, who it was at the other end of the line.

"Are you the guy who sent me that photograph of the 12th East Ham at Thundersley?"

"That's right."

"You're Derek Fletcher, aren't you?"

"'Course I bleedin' am!"

I'd had the privilege and joy of meeting with so many friends from years past. Each one of those reunions proved deeply moving for a whole range of different reasons. But throughout those years of rediscovery and reunification, Derek remained the missing piece of my puzzle. But now, here he was, and the picture could be completed. He was living on Canvey Island, and hadn't been back to Walpole Road for years. For the better part of half an hour, we reminisced about our old haunts and the people that haunted them. We swapped tales of work and family and, before we finished our conversation, both of us knew that we needed to walk those streets again - together. There was the better part of thirty-five years worth of history waiting for us to catch up on. We checked our diaries and agreed on a date and time.

"'Ere, why don't we meet on the wall outside No.11, where Terry and Ricky used to live?" he suggested.

"That sounds absolutely brilliant, Del. But what about work? Isn't that going to be a problem for you?"

"Nah....I'll go sick!"

It is Monday, mid-morning, mid-week, and mid-February at the station in Upton Park, East London. Early morning rush hour has long passed. A couple of hours earlier, the platform serving west bound trains would have been teeming with City staff, male and female, young and old, and all stations in between. The newsagent would have taken a fair few pounds, selling papers and periodicals reflecting the varied range of political bias and taste still found in this neck of the woods. But by the time that the sleek District Line train that has brought me here hums and glides into Upton Park station for its intermediate stop *en route* from Ealing to Upminster, an air of calm and tranquillity has been restored.

The automatic door slides open and half a dozen of us alight and make for the stairs leading to the ticket barrier. At the barrier, I feed my Oyster card into some piece of gadgetry. Ticket collectors have long since left the stage at Upton Park to be replaced by impersonal yet efficient technology. Just a cursory glance at an *A-Z Street Map* suggests that very little has changed in Upton Park. Yet, just one step from the concourse into the hustle, bustle and untidiness that is modern-day Green Street, and the truth is there for me to see - it has truly been a case of all change for Upton Park.

Yes, you have read this before but, first time around, I never let you in on why I was back in Upton Park. But now you know, and the secret is out. I'd had my initial walk about, but now, here I am, outside Terry and Ricky's, waiting for the arrival of the oldest friend that I have. Ever since that telephone conversation, I had contemplated just what Derek might look like now. I'd taken a long hard look at myself in the mirror before leaving home, and what greeted me was hardly to my personal satisfaction. I had become noticeably thicker set since Derek last saw me, carrying at least a stone more than was good for me. Despite my battles over the years with a thinning and receding hairline, I had reached the point at which giving up the fight was the only option. I had never been a champion in the looks department, and retained that standing. Derek, on the other hand, was always good-looking and I imagined a slim, dark, smart, mature, etc., etc., sort of a guy, casually leaning against a flash sports car waiting for me to turn up. Soon, all will be revealed.

All the parking spaces in Walpole Road are occupied. It is unthinkable that you now have to pay to park your vehicle in a street where, once, there was free space for all. Congestion demands that Walpole and those roads that run parallel are all "one way" and there is positively no room whatsoever for playing in the street. A red truck coming from the St. Stephens Road end ambles past and the driver looks out at me suspiciously. His search for a parking spot frustrated, he turns into Plashet Grove, doubtlessly hoping for better luck. I continue my patient wait. Little more than five minutes pass, when a round-ish faced guy, with thinning gray hair walks from the Grove toward where I am standing. He is wearing jeans and a jacket designed to keep out the cold – much the same informal garb as I am dressed in. I recognise him as the driver who had passed in the truck just a little earlier. He comes closer and pauses in front of me – not threatening – but, nevertheless, checking me out. I do much the same. I can't quite be sure, so I point at him quizzically.

"Derek?" I mouthed.

He nodded.

"Stephen?"

I confirmed.

There, outside the wall of their triumphs of over fifty years ago, two middle-aged men hugged each other – in broad daylight. Not everyone in this world is put together in that way and Del admitted that that was why he had not included his address with the photograph of the Scouts at Thundersley. What if I proved to be one of those who preferred to remain *incognito* and let old times remain just that? In this case, he couldn't have been more wrong.

"So, how did you find me, Del?"

"Your cousin, Val – Eileen's girl. We both work in Basildon Hospital – I do security work. Anyhow, there I was in the canteen – minding me own business – when this lady comes up to me, and asks if I'm Derek Fletcher and whether I'd once lived in Walpole Road. I thought the old under-covers had caught up with me again! Something about her voice rang some bells, and I realised who it was I was talking to. She told me how you'd moved to Somerset, and gave me your address and telephone number. Said you'd been trying to find me for years."

"Yeah – finding you again before we both snuffed it was pretty important to me. There's **never** been a time when the name "Derek Fletcher" didn't mean something to me."

He visibly weakened and I am sure that the emotion of that moment got to him. Perhaps no one had ever said anything like that to him throughout his entire life, and I reached out and rested my hand on his shoulder. He regained his composure.

"S'alright, Del. Come on, let's have a look round the old manor."

I never understood why those link roads between Plashet Grove and St. Stephens Road all began with "W." Washington, Waterloo, Walpole, Whitfield, Whittaker, Wyndham, and Wortley. There had to be an answer but, to this day, it has evaded me. Answers on a postcard, please. And while you are at it, how come not all of those roads – save for Whittaker - were able to boast a community like the one that existed in Walpole? Wortley struggled to raise just Peter Tourelle and Paul Hardy, both of whom became Scouting colleagues. Granted, Derek's Uncle Frank and Aunt Glad lived there with their daughter Irene – a right little *agent provocateur*, if ever there was one. But if a young community existed, it certainly escaped my attention.

Washington had been a desert when it came to under-tens, only rescued from being totally nondescript by the presence of Mr. Titmus, the cobbler, who plied his trade from an upstairs, terraced accommodation. I loved it when Mum took our shoes to be "soled and heeled." The smell of the leather was almost hypnotic, and I became totally absorbed by the cobbler's skill with the knife and tacks. But, apart from "the sole man," Washington Road was definitely a "no go" area for kids. As for Waterloo, well, its only purpose, as far as I could see, was to form part of our running track. When athletics caught our fancy in the wake of Roger Bannister's first sub-four-minute mile, we worked out that "the block" - comprising Walpole, St.Stephens, Waterloo, and Plashet Grove - was exactly a quarter of a mile round. Or should that be square? No matter. I'd run that circuit so many times and when the pair of us strolled around it, I savoured again that never to be forgotten moment when I proved that I was the best runner down Walpole, smashing previous record-holder Georgie Brewerton to pulp in a "four-laps around the block" dash. But kids and playmates in Waterloo were there none.

Wyndham, I thought, boasted only Terry Hart and Jimmy Gilbey, two lads a year older than me, - again, future Scouting friends. For the life of me, I couldn't recall any other young people living there during my infancy although, perhaps, all was not quite what it seemed for, here, I struck lucky. Jacky and her family had lived in Wyndham during the immediate post-war years, and she shed some interesting light on what went on behind closed doors.

"When we first moved to Wyndham - no idea of the year, but my sister was born there and her birth year was 1949 - there did not appear to be many children in the street. However, over the years, one family moved in at the top of the street and their little boy was very ill (never did know what was wrong) and we would both play with him in his house until they moved away. Then another family moved in. They were all ginger-haired so Mum and Dad nicknamed them - wait for it - "Ginger" and they were allowed to play outside and eat bread and butter in the street. I used to envy them and asked if I could play out too, also with a thick chunk of bread and butter. I was told in no uncertain terms that, "nice little girls did not play in the street and certainly did not eat their tea outside!" I'm sure it was a gender thing and that, had we been boys, we would have had much more fun."

Whitfield *did* have a strong kids' community, despite the drawback of having houses on one side of the road only. The day nursery that truncated Whittaker Road and separated Whitfield from Wyndham, naturally restricted the potential for more houses and families, and despite our similarities, there was no real social integration between the Walpole and Whitfield gangs. We both just minded our own businesses and got on with life as we found it on our respective doorsteps.

"So, where do we start then, Stephen?"

Where, indeed? We were both set on reminiscing about the people we had known in Walpole who didn't, perhaps, have the profile of some of the high-flyers that I have recalled already. There were schools, churches, parks, and other little corners of the area to revisit. Perhaps it was the spell of the "Merchant Navies" still at work – *No.35026 Lamport and Holt Line; No. 35027 Port Line* – that led to my suggestion that we go to the place that had given me so much delight in my childhood.

"Let's go over to the bally-ole, Del,"

The bally-ole was the local name for what had been the coal yard alongside the bridge where I took my first train spotting steps. It is no more than a few minutes walk to Plashet Grove and then on to Grangewood Street, where the road bridge crosses the railway line. Prefabricated accommodation once rife along Park Road just after the war, has long since disappeared. Primarily asbestos constructions, they were intended to be a short term housing strategy until such times as peace allowed a proper building programme to be planned and activated. It took another five years, at least, after the cessation of hostilities before they were replaced by something more substantial and permanent. The railings at the side of the bridge through which I watched the trains have been replaced by higher and more robust versions, although a clear view up the line remains.

Derek and I crossed the bridge to where the former coal yard and sidings are now designated as Priory Park. Of course, the Electron Works and railway sidings have disappeared – we expected that. More housing has claimed the land it once occupied, and I can live with it. A friend had told me that, a few years back, he had visited the area to find that it had been allowed to fall into decline with the grass becoming worn and patchy. Between what could have been very attractive paving, grass and weeds were pushing up through the brickwork. So it is good on this day to record that someone has taken responsibility for the area and I would have been quite content to have sat down for an hour and reminisced. But Del and I have work to be done.

We turned back toward Plashet Grove, and left into Park Road, pausing at the bend, which once cradled the diminutive Elim Gospel Hall. The signal box that once stood alongside the line is no longer, having given best to a more modern, and less visible, means of control. Opposite the Gospel Hall, the wooden footbridge that took you across the line and set you down in Kings Road, has been

370

replaced by a concrete and steel construction, lacking the character of its predecessor. Unenamoured, we continue on to Green Street, the main artery of Upton Park where once, major national stores dominated proceedings. Marks and Spencer, John Lewis, British Home Stores, and Woolworths once held substantial sway here. How sad it is to have seen Woolworths go into liquidation. Forget the managerial and marketing howlers, it was like losing a relative. I was particular fond of Lewis's, the scene of Derek's *contretemps* with Gort all those years ago.

"Del, do you remember Christmas time, when Lewis's used to give you rides to see Father Christmas?"

He did.

You know those "virtual reality rides?" Some contraption big enough to get a dozen or so people in, with a screen in front of the seats. The door is closed, you're belted in, and on the screen, a film taken from the front of, say, a scenic railway, is projected. The contraption rocks and rolls, thereby creating the sensation that you are in the car itself, climbing up and plunging down the rails.

Well, Lewis's must have been a few steps ahead of the technology game in the late 1940s. In their store, they had created a sizeable compartment and made it up to look like the interior of a boat. Portholes at the side through which you looked out on paintings of sea, islands, and palm trees. Once you had paid your entrance fee and sat down on one of the dozen or so seats, the whole thing started to gently shake, at which point - wonder of wonders - you thought you were actually moving. The trees and islands started to pass by your window and, up until the age of ten or so, there wasn't a kid not taken in by the illusion. After that age, you realised that the islands, trees, and sea, were painted on a continuous band of canvas that was simply being circulated past the portholes. Clever, though.

But the illusion didn't finish there. At the back of the "boat" was the entrance door. Once our little bit of oscillation was done, up we all got to exit the self same door. Imagine our surprise to find that, when it was opened, instead of seeing a queue of kids waiting

371

for their turn, there was a passage lit up by lights and tinsel, and a passage that would lead us to dear old Santa. So how did we get there? The "boat" must have moved. But, of course, it hadn't. It was nothing more than a simple idea whereby there were two doors, one for incoming traffic, the other for outgoing. But it fooled loads of us for a very long time.

There is little to excite either of us in Green Street nowadays. As I had discovered earlier, the majors have gone and commerce is handled in small shops, seemingly over-stocked, given the limited space available to them. Once, there was room to swing a cat in almost any one of the stores – even the smaller ones. We remembered the newspaper vendor who used to ply his trade outside Upton Park station.

The guy had a voice like a nasal foghorn, yet you couldn't understand a blind word that he said.

"Sar, Noos'n'Sannard" were just about translatable as "Star, News, and Standard."

One night, my Aunt Joan came into our house, positively steaming. Joan was a lot of fun and the last of my mum's sisters to get married. I can't recall where she was working at the time, but she had clearly had to come past the station, where "Jimmy Brown the Newsboy" had been proclaiming and selling his wares. As Joan walked by him – imagine an attractive girl in her twenties – he yelled in her ear.

"Old Joe's feet's cold!"

What? Joan was furious that he had got so close that he almost had his nose in her ear when making this pronouncement. When she got home, she clearly hadn't got over the experience. What with my dad being named "Joe," it wasn't unreasonable for her to think that something was wrong with him. But that wasn't the case at all.

"You see, Del, I can tell you exactly when that happened. 5th March 1953."

"Blimey, Steve. Your memory's good. How did you know that?"

"Joseph Stalin. That was the day he died, you see. Hence – Old Joe's feet's cold."

Mind you, it offered naught for Aunt Joan's comfort and she never forgave the poor bloke for yelling in her ear.

We doubted if there were any characters quite like that around today. On Saturday nights, around 6'o'clock, blokes trudged around the streets selling late editions of newspapers containing not just the football results, but reasonably detailed accounts of what had happened during the matches. Nowadays, we have to wait until the following day before we are presented with match reports that say precious little about the game and too much about the latest scandal that this or that player might or might not be involved with.

Outside the Duke of Edinburgh, we remembered the horse trough that was once situated there. Like me, Derek couldn't recall anyone ever having been thrown in the thing. Yet we both agreed that Alan Scarlett, Billy Collins, and, of course, Ricky would have been prime contenders for a bath, were it to have happened. Perhaps we just weren't as naughty as we thought! Further along Green Street, we hoped to find the Carlton cinema. Its frontage is now the site of a green grocery business, and we wondered if the auditorium itself was still intact. So, round the back via Shaftesbury Road for a closer look to see what we could see. A bit of a shock awaited us for, there it was.....GONE! A building that, by and large, had resisted the might of the Blitz had not been able to survive the power of the DVD. The Odeon had survived by catering for the new Upton Park population, providing Bollywood material whereas the Granada had bowed to the pressures of Bingo, and suchlike. Both had survived. But the poor old Carlton had missed both of those boats and paid the ultimate price of oblivion.

Turning back to Plashet Grove, we opted to stick closer to the territory that we had known best, and seek out the little businesses and concerns that once populated the Grove like a rash. Some of them I had long forgotten, but Del pulled them out of his memory hat like rabbits. He pointed out where once Bowyers, the radio and record shop had traded. I needed to keep pace.

"And what about that place just along, Del. I used to have my haircut there. It was basically a tobacconist but, in the adjoining room, Mr. English did a bit of hair-cutting - you could scarcely call him a barber. I once took a copy of "Football Monthly" and showed him a picture of Peter Taylor, the Middlesborough goalie. I asked him to tart my hair up like Pete's, but after hacking it around for all he was worth, I finished up looking no more like Peter Taylor than I did Liz Taylor. Cost me a shilling, that did."

On our right, once stood Setchell's, a quality bakers where you could dosh out on bread, cakes, and all sorts. For some reason I never came to understand, Mum used to favour Dillaways, in Green Street - something to do with price, I guess. Anyhow, the shop is now the site of an exotic restaurant which, at least, keeps it in the food family.

Next to the old bakery once stood one of the bastions of Upton Park commerce – Frank Pratt's timber business. The Pratt family had long association with West Ham United and Reg Pratt, a director of both concerns, had made a not inconsiderable contribution to the progress of the club. I wondered what he would have made of the shenanigans of the past twenty years, or so. We'll never know, and it's probably just as well. With this sort of history, you will understand that I almost had apoplexy to discover that the site had been closed and was up for sale. Surely not. Not after all these years. Thankfully, a chat with a local puts our minds back at ease – the company had relocated to Barking. We were glad about that, even though it meant that one of the landmarks of Plashet Grove is no more. The world continued to turn.

Graingers, the cycle shop, separated Pratts from my favourite shop on the block. In our infancy, it was the local sweet shop, run by two elderly ladies whose names I either struggle to recall or never really knew in the first place. In addition to confectionary, they ran a profitable line in tobacco and cigarettes. Always keen to ensure that the tobacco companies stayed in business, Dad invested quite heavily as a mark of his commitment. Yet, in the early 1950s, I almost cured him of his habit.

The age of distributing quality cigarette cards with each purchase was disappearing into the distance, if it hadn't done so already. Somewhere around 1950, TURF – for that was the brand name of the product – decided to print pictures of steam locomotives on the drawer of the cigarette box. This train mad kid just had to have 'em, so good old Dad – at heart, a "roll your own" man – converted to a packet of TURF each week until I had collected the entire set of fifty. Bless him, the wretched things were well named, and I was glad to let him off the hook once I had completed my collection.

Early in the 1950s, proprietorship of the shop passed to Mr. and Mrs. Lingwood. The Lingwoods were a very friendly couple (nowhere near as dour as their predecessors), and their son, Paul, became a popular member of the Walpole fraternity. Some of their success must have been down to the advent of the greatest ice lollipop ever known to man – the magnificent GloJoy. It couldn't be licked! Well, it could, of course – that was its *raison d'etre*. But you know what I mean. For the sum of just three pence – less than two new pence at today's exchange rate – you had the choice from what seemed an endless list of flavours. Orange, banana, chocolate, lemon, lime, raspberry, strawberry, and spearmint, would you believe? Orange was my particular tipple, but we all had our favourites.

We recalled the time when the proprietors of Gricks, the eel people, paid for a mural of one of the company vans to be daubed high up on the wall on the corner of Crescent Road. It was a superb piece of work, although as to its marketing value, I had my doubts. What I can testify to is the rotten smell that emanated from the yard. The place ponged and, amongst one or two other reasons, probably accounts for the fact that I can hardly look a jellied eel in the eye, much less eat one. Now all trace of the yard has disappeared under the development of a block of four-storey flats.

Derek had his eye on the other corner of Crescent Road.

"Here, Steve. Do you remember what used to be here?"

I most certainly did. A reasonably smart property company has set up an office on the spot once occupied by a quality stonemason, specialising in headstones. I wondered if my memory was playing tricks in thinking that the premises had once been the operation centre of Godfreys, the funeral directors and stonemasons. Perhaps there had been a bit of diversification somewhere along the line.

"Yeah, I remember. You sent Ricky in there once to ask if they'd got any dead bodies!"

Derek feigned mock horror.

"Oh, yes. So I did. Silly bugger did it an' all."

Opposite, on the corner of Walpole and Plashet Grove, E.W Moore, the supplier of wallpaper, paints, and general home improvements are no more. Yet the news is good, for they continue to trade from smarter and larger premises on the corner of Waterloo Road. Along the same block, A.W.Phillips continue to purvey an excellent array of tools. Clearly, they have both been well managed, and are making profits. Somehow, that feels very reassuring.

The block row of terraced buildings that once linked Crescent Road to Park Road used to play host to three very special shops, each for different reasons. In the wonderful Disney animation "101 Dalmatians," there is a suggestion that dogs grow to look like their owners. I think that I could make out a good case for saying that businesses reflected the personality of their proprietors. Take for example, the fish and chip shop. Every community in the East End required one, and Upton Park was extremely well served in this department by Mr. and Mrs. Lennie Baggs. Mr. Baggs was a friendly, hard-working soul and, armed with our pocket money, we would roll in and order, "A penn'orth of chips, please Mr.Baggs." If we were able to swank in with an order for two penn'orth of chips, well, we felt like kings. Either order would be served up generously, overflowing with salt and vinegar, and wrapped in a reasonably recent edition of the "Daily Mirror." The *bonhomie* of Mr. Baggs was almost like an added ingredient.

"Did you know that Mr. Baggs was a Canadian?" Derek asked.

I didn't and was temporarily amazed at how a Canadian had fitted in so well with the community that I was about to describe him as "typically East End." Ah, well. I continue to live and learn.

A few doors along, the Post Office was once run by two female clerks. One of the tellers was a thin bespectacled soul, a little like Dr. Evadne Hinge, of "Hinge and Brackett" fame. Constantly stamping one document after another, I am sure that she must have gone home on "automatic pilot," stamping everything and everyone who got in her way. It seemed such a mundane task but my recollection of her has lasted for almost sixty years. Perhaps that alone qualifies her for her fifteen minutes of fame. Recollection tells me that she was a "miss," but perhaps I do her an injustice.

But it was the shop next to the Post Office that aroused the strangest curiosity amongst us kids. There was something dark and mystical about the place where Mr. Sonn made his living as a jeweller and watch repairer. He must have been around forty and had a somewhat swarthy complexion. Rather than ply his intricate trade out of the public gaze, quite logically he set up his working area in the window looking out onto Plashet Grove, where the light was more accessible. There he would be, with a magnifying eyeglass the size of a thimble, held in place against his eye by screwing up his cheek. Kids would press their snotty noses against his window, which must have been tremendously off-putting for a man undertaking such delicate work. But Mr. Sonn carried on unabashed. When the terrace was knocked down for development, he took another shop at the Green Street end of Crescent Road and, from then on, hid himself away from the great prying public.

It could have been nothing more than idle gossip but tales began to circulate that he had caught something of a cold in connection with some rather dubious literature found in his possession. Were that true, it is ironic that, nowadays, you can buy far worse under a cloak of respectability, from W.H.Smiths, described as adult artistic literature. As I grew into more mature years, I felt that, perhaps, we had given him a hard time. He never did me any harm.

Mind you, Derek had a take on the affair.

"I happen to know that the stories about those magazines were true," he announced.

"How'd you know that, Del?"

"My Grandad sold them to him!"

I could scarcely imagine dear old Mr. Norman, prolific reader that he was, ever getting tangled up in the sort of stuff we are talking about here. As always, Del laughed and left me not knowing whether he had told me the truth or was just winding me up.

The Grove sweeps sharply to the left, where Porters, specialising in hardware, wood, tools, mangles, and paraffin had once stood proud. The shop always appeared very well stocked – almost to overflowing. Beyond that, separated from Porters by the place where my school mate Eddie Collard used to live, was Pitmans, a diminutive competitor to Mr. and Mrs. Lingwood. The middle-aged proprietors set themselves a class apart by opening for a few brief hours on a Sunday morning, whilst every other shop remained closed for, in those days, Sundays were, most definitely, different. Perhaps being close to the Full Gospel Hall should have encouraged a more ecclesiastical outlook on Sunday opening, but the point clearly eluded Mr. and Mrs. Pitman. They were noteworthy for being prime purveyors of Tizer, the fizzy drink to end them all. It may be still on the market today, but in name only. The flavour of the original version has never been – never will be - bettered. Mum and Dad made their one concession to Sunday shopping when they allowed me to go round to Pitmans and buy a bottle of Tizer, swapping last week's empty container for a "penny back on the bottle." It was a common practice in those days.

We crossed Whitfield Road to pay homage to the Gospel Hall.

"Jesus, who loved me and gave himself for me."

Derek had remembered that text, emblazoned, as it was, across the stage in the dowstairs hall where we receive our Sunday school education. I took out my 1956 photograph of the scholars standing on the steps leading up to the church itself. Between us, we identified something like fifteen of our then colleagues – not bad from a cast of around eighty. All the stories tumbled out about John Barrett, Terry and Ricky, Uncle Arthur, and speaking in tongues. I might have been the one who followed more ecclesiastical leanings, but Derek was no less grateful for what the church had given to him and his life.

Beyond the truncated Whittaker Road and past Wyndham, we reach the corner of Wortley Road, where there had once been a newsagent and tobacconist shop. Mr. and Mrs. Root ran it until they sold out, in 1955, to Mr. and Mrs Hammond who were, in my view, first class at what they did. This was in the days when the paperboy would rise early from his warm bed to collect the already sorted papers and periodicals, and poke them through the letterboxes in the area allocated to him. I persuaded Dad that it would be a jolly fine idea if we arranged to add "Trains Illustrated" to our order, a not unreasonable request given that the periodical cost only just over a shilling (5p). No sooner the order than the deed and the following day, Mr. Hammond made a personal visit to our door, all smiles, clutching the latest edition for my edification. His enthusiasm must have worked for, all through my early teens, the name Hammonds was frequently extolled. When train-spotting days were done, Mr. Hammond was only too pleased to replace my "Trains Illustrated" order with one for "Charles Buchan's Football Monthly."

Further along the Grove on the opposite side of the street, Fred Parker and his son Fred Jnr. had converted their front living room into a gentleman's haircutting shop. As with Mr. English, you would have insulted it had you described it as a salon. A couple of chairs faced the obligatory mirror in which you could see what a God forsaken mess Harry senior (in particular) was making of the job. About a dozen chairs were set around the room, with copies of the "Daily Mirror" liberally chucked here and there to tempt men and boys in for a short back and sides, and general chit-chat about horse racing. Harry senior was never without a roll-your-own fag stuck to his bottom lip and if you weren't very careful, you could finish up with a hair-do liberally spiced with ash – it looked like dandruff. It was almost like being offered an additional service – "And will you be taking fag ash with your haircut today, Stephen?" My eventual transfer to Mr. English for hair cutting requirements was a step up only in not having this option available.

At the crossroads with Katherine Road, we were shocked to see that both the Green Man and the Harmonic Hall had been demolished. Dad would have been in tears. The place where he courted Mum and one of his favourite drinking holes swept from the map, without a by your leave. It is striking to see how many old familiar sites have been developed to provide more housing, and this is yet another example of the policy.

"Do you remember "Savages," who used to be up here on the left?" asked Derek. "Sort of a garden nursery, it was, with greenhouses. And over there, opposite, there was a doctor. Now, what was his name?"

"Dr. Sher," I told him. "He was always our doctor. A bit rotund, thinning, and very dark – I think Jewish. He was softly spoken with an accent that I am sure was Scottish, and a bedside manner second to none. I always had confidence in the guy throughout the time that he was our GP. He had a thing about the Navy, and Dad took full advantage when Dr. Sher asked, "And what will the boy be doing when he goes to work.""

"Well, Doctor, he told me that he would like to join the Navy."

The good doctor nearly had apoplexy! So did I, for I had said nothing of the kind.

"What? Don't let him do that! Whatever you do, don't let him do that."

Dad grinned as he clearly knew something of Dr. Sher's feelings about the Navy, and his comment had been no more than a bit of gentle nerve-touching. I never got to the bottom of it all, but I do know for certain that Dr. Sher was a fine doctor.

Passmore Edwards Library alongside Plashet Park is no longer fit for that particular purpose, despite the legend "Passmore Edwards Public Library" carved in white stone above the entrance. Both Derek and I are much taken with the condition of the building.

It continues to look as good as it did in our childhood – better probably - as we have, perhaps, over the years developed a little more appreciation of class architecture. Today, the building is a register office for births, marriages, and deaths. At least there's some dignity in that. What a travesty if it had been pulled down, or redeveloped beyond recognition, so put this one down as a place where it hasn't quite been all change for Upton Park.

The big Baptist church that once played host to the Boys Brigade band all those years ago, still stands proud opposite Shrewsbury Road, and open for business. A couple of hundred yards further on would take us to the schools where so many of the girlfriends of my youth had been educated. Today, the school is part and parcel of Plashet School, dating back to 1932 when the East Ham Grammar School for Girls first opened on the south site. In the 1950s, Plashet County Secondary Modern School for Girls was built opposite and the two schools were amalgamated to become Plashet School, in 1972. Plashet Unity Bridge reaches over Plashet Grove, so that students have a safer way to get to and from the sites without getting into accidents or missing school. As if. Still, you can't knock the place and even if the old division between secondary modern and grammar school means nothing to any of the current 1,350 scholars, Plashet's record of being one of the twelve outstanding schools in the country - according to OFSTED – can't be sniffed at.

I reminded Derek of one of the earliest memories I had of the old grammar school.

"You know, Del, I remember that, when the grammar school girls came out for their physical education sessions, they would have their blouses tucked into green knickers. No skirts, mind you. Just green knickers. Most of them looked fantastic!"

I don't think he believed me.

"You'll get yerself locked up, talking like that."

"But, it's true, Del. I asked Norma. She told me all about it."

Steve Derby

"I wasn't sure that we had to tuck our blouses in and just rang Mary - a PE fiend and her favourite lesson. She said, like me, that she didn't recall doing that, and, anyway, they wouldn't stay tucked in for long. But yes, they were bottle green and we had to have a little pocket in them for our hankie during PE lessons. We felt really silly and quite embarrassed, walking along the road to Plashet Park in our green knickers, with our sticks over our shoulder, to play a game of hockey. I think after a couple of years we were allowed to wear little skirts or shorts - much better."

So much for education.

We turned into Shrewsbury Road where, on our left, the East Ham Memorial Hospital now has notices outside identifying it as "East Ham Care Centre." Just to add to the confusion, across the entrance to the main building, a stone carving announces that you are entering "East Ham Memorial Hospital." I'm tempted to ask the blessed place to make its mind up. But the area and buildings look well tended and, if the service within is of the same quality of what the passer-by sees, then all could be well – very well indeed. My only foray into the place was for a dislocated thumb, in 1962. The Indian doctor who tended me was absolutely brilliant and ensured that my piano playing career would last – for a couple more weeks, at least!

Chester Road is another hundred yards or so further on, and we make for where the Congregational Church stands strong, just before the junction with Katherine Road. It is no longer a place of worship although, in my book, it has become one of the next best things, for this is Grangewood School with an ethic to be applauded. It is a Christian-based school that opens its arms to those of other faiths. We are just hoping that the same warm greeting will be offered to a couple of middle-aged blokes exploring their roots. Security is, naturally, very tight and, through the intercom, we explain who we are, and can we come and have a look around, please? A very short wait before the Head Teacher comes to the door, greets us, and takes us to her office. As best as our joint memories served us, we shared our recollections of the structure and layout, so she knew that we were genuine.

The large upstairs hall, where once we congregated before church parades, has been tastefully divided into classrooms. The basement where the 12th East Ham tents had been stored is now a far tidier affair than in our young days. Everything about the school felt right and the scholars that we passed were a total credit to what is clearly a very popular establishment. But it was the church that I wanted to see most of all. In my mind's eye, I recalled a predominantly blue and white colour scheme, with wooden steps leading up to the dais, at the top of which had been a communion table and preaching desk. Behind them had been the choir stalls.

Our guide took us to the place where I had once carried the flags at church parade, opened the door and – well, blow me down – it was as though time had stood still. The pews had long been removed, but the colour scheme is virtually identical. Instead of communion table and lectern, the tools of the teaching trade are set out on the dais in superb order. The background wooden lattice, forming square patterns against a blue backdrop remains, as do the choir stalls. I sat in one of the chairs and conjured up memories and images of that choir. There they all were; Margaret and David Armstrong, Ian Fulcher, Janet Pearce (gorgeous red hair and the voice of an angel), Anne Barker and, to the astonishment of all, Dave Ruddock, who got me my only caning. I was so glad that, even after making all reasonable adjustments for its new purpose, the room still looked and felt like a church. This had truly been a good and worthwhile home-coming.

We thanked our host before setting off along the couple of hundred yards of Katherine Road to Shaftesbury Road, to see how our Primary and Junior school had fared. The building that housed the Trebor sweet factory still stands under the shadow of the redundant chimney, although the once familiar aroma of sweetmeats is no longer. The factory has been converted to up-market private apartments and, much as I would like to have seen the survival of the business, I have to admit that the transformation has been achieved splendidly. There are miniature trees surrounding the place, and it is clearly kept in top condition as, no doubt, is the rental/purchase price. Still, I'd sooner see the building put to this use, rather than for it to be razed to the ground.

The senior playground of the school is easily recognisable as the place where I once used to take a football round John McDowell time and time again, and the site of my massive rounders hit. Where once was the shed provided for cover on rainy days, there is now a wooden structure somewhat akin to a miniature stand. Closer to the surrounding wall is a large wooden play ark, available for kids to clamber over – I would have like that. Gardens have been created between the school itself and Shaftesbury Road and, all in all, it looks a well-cared for establishment.

To our astonishment, the area once taken up by the infants' playground now has a substantial annexe built on it. Independently, it is an attractive enough addition, although, to my eye, it doesn't sit well with the Victorian construction that forms the main body of the school. Some time in the future, we'll have to make an appointment to visit the school. On the corner of Ashley Road, "Len's" and Ted's" have long been converted back to private dwelling houses and we wend our way back to Walpole Road, via Dorset, Katherine, and St. Stephens Roads.

High on the wall of the end terrace property that was once the home of Trevor Sealey and his family, there is a gap where once was affixed an iron street name. We grinned, knowing full well that I had bought the item, had it fully reconditioned, and that it was sitting in my office, down in Somerset. So much had been recalled and enjoyed during our reunion tour that recollecting other tales might seem like squeezing the pips out of an already well-crushed orange. But it wasn't that way at all, and off we went again. Del first.

"What about the rag and bone man? Pushing his cart up and down the streets, yelling, "Ole rag er lumber."

The translation was, of course, "Old rags and lumber." The rag and bone man was one of many tradespeople for whom you needed a degree in linguistics if you were to understand a word. Now it's my turn.

"Do you remember the United Dairies milk cart coming down Walpole Road? Horse drawn, it was. As soon as it turned the corner from St. Stephens, we'd all rush up to get a ride, while the milkman made his deliveries. Him and his horse coming down the street, dropping dung all over the place."

"What – the horse, or the milkman?"

"Dads used to come out into the street, like shots from a gun, armed with buckets and spades to collect up the manure. My mum used to go spare when Dad trolled it in through the house."

"It's good for the roses, Lil," was his defence, and off he went to swamp the poor plants with steaming yellowy-brown stuff. In fairness, we always had a fine show of roses.

As we wandered through Walpole, we recalled others who had been on the periphery of our little gang. Derek remembered an incident involving a young girl who I shall call Carol Clough – not her real name.

"You know, Stephen, I once chased young Carol Clough with my penknife. I told her that I was going to cut the elastic out of her knickers for my catapult. She ran a mile."

As well she might!

Now this struck something of an unpleasant chord with me. Mrs. Clough had, apparently – and quite rightly – raised the matter with the school, and Derek was looking for either an alibi or witness. I met his need on both counts and was duly called up to Mr. Level's office.

"Now, Derby," Mr. Level commenced. "Fletcher here tells me that you walked home with him last Tuesday. I want you to tell me the truth – did he meet Carol Clough and threaten her with a knife? The truth, mind you."

There was no way that I would ever lie to Mr. Level and, thank goodness, there was no reason for me to do so. I recalled Tuesday well because, on that particular day – and that day only - instead of walking home via Green Street, I had taken the Katherine Road route, with Derek. We never saw Carol and there had certainly been no incident involving either threat or knife. I gave Mr. Level my evidence.

"No, sir. We definitely didn't see Carol, and Derek never had a knife with him."

That truth, the whole truth, and nothing but the truth, ensured that Derek was pronounced innocent by Mr. Level. The word of Steve Derby was something to have in your favour back then. Quite how it all went down in the Clough household, I couldn't say, but the matter seemed to die the death and was never mentioned in Walpole Road again – until this moment.

"Here, Del. You got me to tell Mr. Level that you never had a knife or threatened Carol. Now you're telling me that you did. I lied for you, you rotter."

"No, you didn't. You said that, on the Tuesday, I hadn't had a knife, or said what Carol accused me of. That was the absolute truth. Mind you, had he said that it had all happened on Wednesday, well, that would have been a very different matter!"

We sauntered on to the wall outside No. 11, leaned against it, and looked up and down the street where we had both been brought up.

"Here, Stephen. Why don't you go and knock at Mrs. Finch's door, and we'll run away?"

Lord, I was more terrified of doing that now than I had been all those years earlier. Even though Mrs. Finch would have departed this world many years earlier, I declined his kind offer.

"I don't know what you'd be worried about. She's probably still locked in the chicken coop at the end of the garden, where Alan and Michael left her."

Poor old Mrs. Finch. So often she had been the butt of some prank or another instigated by Derek. Even when the pair of us had married and were living with our respective wives in No. 14, she couldn't rid herself of him.

Someone or other down Walpole had made Mrs. Finch the offer of a rather large, yet comfortable, padded armchair. It was a

386

deal too good to turn down, but presented what appeared to be an insurmountable problem. You see, the passageway to Mrs. Finch's lounge was narrow, and made more so by the staircase to the upstairs flat, halfway down the hall. Even the most un-educated eye could see that negotiating the chair through the gap was going to call for a rather special expertise. Enter Messrs. Derby and Fletcher.

"Yerse, Mrs. Finch. I think that between us, Stephen and meself can do the job. As long as we take it easy."

I genuinely doubted Derek's confidence. The gap looked far too small, but if it was going to give Mrs. Finch a little luxury in the winter of her years, who was I to deprive her of it? The pair of us bent to hoist the chair up and over the wall, and toward the door of No.10. Some gentle manoeuvring got us into the passageway, and I started to believe that we might yet achieve what I had perceived to be the impossible. Inch by inch, we progressed toward the bend in the hall where the stairs restricted the space available to us.

Our strategy served us well enough for the first yard or so. The chair pressed against the banisters, and I feared that they might give way and we would be left with a bill for the repair. But, no. They might have buckled and bent just a little, but we were going to make it. Until, that is, Del suggested that we push the chair up a little higher

"If we can work it up to the ceiling," he said, "it'll be easier for us to drop it down into the lobby before the door."

I was convinced not at all and, sure enough, once we had the wretched thing at optimum height, it stuck there, unwilling to move. We pushed, we pulled, we cussed, we prayed, but nothing would persuade the chair to move the few, vital few inches that would enable us to get it to the door of Mrs. Finch's lounge. There was not much that she could do but, bless her, she certainly made both her feelings and opinion of the pair of us abundantly clear.

"Oh, my Gawd! What **have** you two silly sods done? We'll never move it now. Silly sods. Silly, silly sods. Oh, my Gawd!"

You could see her point, and there was little mileage in trying to assure the good soul that all would yet be well for, quite frankly, I couldn't see how it was going to be.
"What are we going to do, Del?" I whispered, out of Mrs. Finch's earshot.
"I dunno. We'll just have to sound as though we know what we are doing and persevere trying to get to the lounge without ripping off every inch of the wallpaper."
I couldn't see a better plan, but thought Mrs. Finch needed some sort of reassurance. Del agreed.
"Right, Mrs. Finch. No need to worry. We've got a plan and if it doesn't work, Stephen and me are going to push the chair right up to the ceiling.....and you'll be able to walk underneath it!"
As it was, we did manage to loosen the chair and get it into the lounge. Lord knows how. My lasting memory is of Mrs. Finch, flopped back in the chair, relief etched all over her face, and providing the Almighty with a little more respect than earlier, exclaiming, "Fank Gawd! Oh, fank Gawd!"
Derek summarised our effort.
."There," he said. "Fitted by experts."

Along the road from the direction of Plashet Grove, an elderly lady was struggling along with her shopping. Twice she stopped to take a firmer grasp on her wares and the only decent thing to do was offer help. Ignoring the fact that we might have been a pair of Jehovah's Witnesses, she was grateful for our offer.
"Where do you have to go?" Del asked.
"Oh, not far. Just a couple of doors up here, on the right."
I have always been ready to talk with anyone and everyone. It can be a blessing and a curse, but you have to play the cards you have been dealt in life. I asked her if she had lived very long in Walpole Road.
"Goodness, yes. At least sixty years."
"And do you remember," asked Del, joining in where I had left off, "a little boy who lived with his mum over at No.12?"
She did.

"Are you talking about Derek Fletcher? Lived there with his mum, Lil, and his grandparents. When he got married, I think he moved into No.14. Yes, I remember him. Always up to some nonsense or other – but a decent lad at heart."

"And what about at No. 7? Do you remember anyone who used to live there?"

Our friend had to think a bit about this.

"I think there was a couple who had a little boy. Yes, that was it. The wife's mother lived at No.5, and her sister was at No. 3. They were a nice family, but I can't remember their name."

I chipped in. "Was it "Derby?""

"Yes, that was it. Derby. I think the boy moved back here when he got married. He and his wife lived at…….."

Suddenly, the penny dropped, and she realised that she was talking to the very same Derek and the little boy from No. 7. Older, fatter, and balder we might have been, but the essence remained. Mrs. Crick – for it was she - had been a fixture in the street even when Del and I were knee-high to grasshoppers. And here we all were, recalling names like Collins, Brewerton, Wright, Round, Longhurst, and all with affection.

Mrs. Crick is a lovely lady, and we were set to spend as much time as we could with her, reminiscing about all sorts. And we jolly well would have done just that, had it not been for some movement two doors away, outside No.7. A smartly dressed, middle-aged man – perhaps Iranian, perhaps Pakistani - had come out from the house and began loading up his motor car before driving off somewhere. I rested my hand on Derek's shoulder.

"Mrs. Crick, Del, - I hope you don't mind but I must go and have a word with that man who has come out of No.7."

There are moments in all our lives, I believe, when we are affirmed by a spirit that tells us that everything has been put in place for our well-being and benefit. This is one such moment for me for if God was looking down on all this, then, surely, this was His way of letting me know. With me, I have some of the text that I have written about this place and its surrounding area, and I am hoping that it will serve as a passport to prove my authenticity. As I approach him, the stranger nods to me in respect and smiles a, "Good afternoon." I respond accordingly before beginning a conversation that, I am sure, took him by surprise. I start tentatively.

"I hope you won't mind me troubling you but, fifty years ago, I used to live in this house with my parents. I'm writing a book about growing up in Upton Park and all the things that I remember going on in this little street. Look, - here are some of the pages."

He took them from me, scanned down a few, and smiled. In that moment, I am sure that he knew exactly what was coming. I explained how my grandparents had lived next door, and one of my aunts in the house next door to them. As I gave him a detailed description of all that I remembered about the house of my childhood, his smile became broader, fascinated (I hope) by my photographic memory of so much. I nodded to where Derek and Mrs. Crick were still engrossed.

"That man up there, he is my oldest friend. We have known each other almost since birth. We've only just met up again. And the lady he is talking to......"

"You mean, Mrs. Crick?"

"Yes. She lived here when we were little boys. And, do you know, she remembered us both."

I was so excited and, probably, beginning to become a bit of a pain. After all, my new friend – and already I felt that he was a friend – was, just a few minutes ago, preparing to drive away to some destination or another, and here I am, delaying the process. But this was a once in a lifetime opportunity.

"Could you tell me, is there still a folding door that separates the front......"

Whilst I was in mid-flow, a peaceful hand was raised in front of me, and I stuttered to a halt. With my enthusiasm once more out of control, I feel truly embarrassed. But am I greeted with frustration? I am not. Instead, a warm smile, accompanied by the most gentle and genuine of invitations.

"Would you like to come in and see the house?"

My jaw must have dropped, my eyes must have popped. Oh, dear Lord. I am going back to where it all began.

"Oh, yes, please. Yes, I would – very much indeed. Thank you."

My friend escorted me across the threshold into the long passage, at the end of which was the staircase that gave access to the upstairs quarters. On the left, we passed the door to what had once been our front room – you remember, the one where I always found my Christmas presents, listened to my rock'n'roll 78s, played the "Big Man" piano riff when Margaret Armstrong came strolling by, and had my first birthday party when I was allowed to invite girls. The structure had changed little over the years. When we entered the room that had served as our lounge, do you know, I almost expected to find Grandad Clark sat in his armchair alongside the spot where once there had been a fireplace. Central heating had long since laid that structure to rest.

Of course, some changes had taken place, not least the acquisition of an indoor toilet and bathroom. No more creeping out to the smallest room - cold, dark, and unforgiving - if you wanted to do a bit of reading. In those days, when the cold rain was falling, it was only the call of nature that got you out to the place, and the desperate need for warmth and comfort that brought you back. The little garden so expertly nurtured by my dad is, as a result of the development, drastically reduced in size. On our way back to the passage, we passed the door that led to the coal cellar. In my day, it had looked like the descent into Hades but, over the years, the new owners have made it a good deal tidier. Of course, now that the aforementioned black stuff is no longer king, the smell of coal dust that hung around this part of the house has disappeared entirely.

We took the stairs to the upper floor. On the first landing, what was once the living room for the Polyblanks is serving pretty much the same purpose for an elderly relative. As we walk past, she looks at me – quite reasonably – with a suspicious eye. There is no stop for a formal introduction.

"Grandmother," my host whispers to me. It is enough. His expression and delivery of that one word tell me all I need to know about grandmother.

On the upper floor itself, there are just two bedrooms – one for my friend and his wife and, to the right, what I am told is, "my little boy's room." I hesitate, for this re-union had not been on my agenda at all. I had travelled to Upton Park with the sole intent of re-uniting with Derek, so that the pair of us could see how our old stamping ground had changed. Never once was it my intent to actually visit No.7 Walpole Road, other than to view it from the outside. Yet, here I am, standing at the door of the little room where, for almost fifteen years, I grew up, wrote my earliest love letters, cried my first emotional tears, prayed my first prayers, and realised that I had the best mum and dad in the world. Here it was that Dad had given me rollickings, and Mum had followed on to apply the balm of comfort and healing. What am I going to find on the other side of this door?

There is a lump in my throat, and the customary tears are not far away, for this is a truly emotional moment; a reunification of friends neither planned nor anticipated. My friend asks if I am alright. I'm sure he understands as I press my lips together and nod. Before I walk through the door into this holiest of holies, he rests his hand on my arm.

"Come along, now," he says quietly and empathetically. "You are only coming home."

I duly "come home."

Immediately, I know this room, its layout, and, most importantly, its spirit. The cupboard, on whose door I once pinned photographs of West Ham's first team of 1957 remains. The bed is pressed against the wall, with storage for shirts, socks, pants, and all sorts alongside. Some books are neatly placed on the floor alongside a computer. Now that *is* a change. No computers when I was a lad, let me tell you. I am moved to find that this little room remains so very much as it was back in the '50s. Perhaps it was a bit presumptuous but, without invitation, I sat down on the bed, and lost myself in thought.

I had a big thing about snakes when I was a toddler and remembered how, before going off to sleep, I would check under the bed, just in case there was some mighty python lurking there, ready to devour me once I had dropped my guard and fallen off to sleep. I never found anything other than an enamel po. During winter months, Mum always took up a hot water bottle and placed it between the bed sheets, with my pillow on top. This made sure that I not only had a warm patch to lie on, but also a warm pillow on which to rest my head. It was really cosy. But the lump caused by the pillow under the sheets got my imagination going again, and I feared that the wretched snake had somehow crawled into my bed itself! Of course, all this was tosh, and nothing more than the work of a little boy's fears and fantasies.

This bed – or, rather, its predecessor – had once served as an imaginary locomotive for me to "drive" anywhere - from Fenchurch Street to Shoeburyness, or Euston to Glasgow. Mum and Dad had left me a wooden stick about a yard long, so that, if I needed them during the night, all I had to do was bang on the floor with the thing. Didn't need it too often, and my imagination converted it to an imaginary regulator. Leaning on the edge of the bed, I would look around like the engine driver that I wasn't. In my mind's eye, crowds of on-lookers watched me enviously as I prepared to move my steed from the "station," doing a more than passable vocal imitation of *City of Glasgow* taking up the slack, in readiness to do battle with Camden bank.

As I grew older, I would creep around the room, imitating Eric Cryer in front of a classroom, holding forth on some historical epoch or another. Strange how, as time unfolded, teaching, training, and development became the meat and drink of my working and social life. So, if it all started with the wonderful Eric, then it was certainly nurtured here in this tiny room. Later still, the bed morphed into a motor car in which I was able to take any young lady of my choice out for a spin. The Everlys had it bang on when they pointed out that, "All I have to do is Dream." You would never believe the number of gorgeous girls that my imagination and dreams allowed me to escort. Not one of them ever turned me down. All this, and more, flowed through my mind as I sat on the edge of that bed, and acknowledged that, underneath it all, I had been a funny little bloke.

Apart from the computer, there is something else that attracts my eye. On the wall at the foot of the bed, is a display reciting the five tenets of Islam; a profession of faith, the need for prayer, the giving of alms, fasting, and a pilgrimage to Mecca. I might not be able to make Mecca, but I could live easily with the other four Islamic objectives. I remembered the photograph of Christ that once rested by the side of my pillow, alongside the text, "God is Able." How strange that, back in the 1950s, this room was occupied by a young boy with superb parents, and an affinity for God, whilst today, it is occupied by.....a young boy with superb parents, and an affinity for God. What goes around comes around, I guess.

All through my journey of memories and emotions, my friend had kept his respectful distance, clearly sensitive enough to realise what was going on within me. I didn't know his name, and I might not have been able to pronounce it if I had. But one thing for certain - this was a good man and, in just fifteen minutes, he has given me a gift that I would treasure for the rest of my life. I stood up from the bed, and we moved toward each other.

"Thank you. Thank you so much. You don't know how deeply I appreciate you letting me see this house again."

"Oh, but I think that I do."

"I don't know what I should say to you. Should it be, "God bless you," or, "May the peace of the Prophet rest upon you and your family?" Just what do I say?"

The pair of us shook hands. He placed his other hand on my shoulder, smiled, and said words that I shall never forget.

"Either will do, my friend. Either will do."

In that room, in Upton Park, a Muslim and a Christian enjoyed a meeting of hearts and minds. I don't think I could have asked for a more perfect end to my re-unions.

By the time that I rejoined Derek outside No.11, he had finished speaking with Mrs. Crick and she had moved on. He could see that I had been deeply – and profitably – moved by my mini tour of No. 7, and I told him about all that had happened - particularly that wonderful ending.

"You didn't blub, did you, Stephen?" he asked.

Emotion was still running high and my response reflected it. "Oh, get out of it, Del. You know me better than that. Of course I did."

This was not the end of our reunion – it was the beginning. Over the years, Derek and I have taken care to ensure that we remain in touch. Like I said, there has never been a time when the name Derek Fletcher didn't mean something to me – it always will. There was still so much that we needed to catch up on – good, bad, and ugly - and it is source of joy to be able to say that we continue to do just that.

And it gets better. Over the years, I have found so many of the characters mentioned in my recollections who have been willing to "swap notes" with me about those halcyon days. It may well have been a case of all change for Upton Park itself, but what Upton Park and its community did to, and for, the majority of us back in the 1940s and 1950s, surely we can all assume that someone up there liked the whole lot of us.

No.35028 Clan Line ; No.35029, Ellerman Lines ; No.35030 Elder Dempster Lines - and that's the lot!